**Keep this book. You will
need it and use it throughout
your career.**

About the American Hotel & Motel Association (AH&MA)

Founded in 1910, AH&MA is the trade association representing the lodging industry in the United States. AH&MA is a federation of state lodging associations throughout the United States with 11,000 lodging properties worldwide as members. The association offers its members assistance with governmental affairs representation, communications, marketing, hospitality operations, training and education, technology issues, and more. For information, call 202-289-3100.

LODGING, the management magazine of AH&MA, is a "living textbook" for hospitality students that provides timely features, industry news, and vital lodging information. For information on subscriptions and student rates, call 202-289-3113.

About the Educational Institute of AH&MA (EI)

An affiliate of AH&MA, the Educational Institute is the world's largest source of quality training and educational materials for the lodging industry. EI develops textbooks and courses that are used in more than 1,200 colleges and universities worldwide, and also offers courses to individuals through its Distance Learning program. Hotels worldwide rely on EI for training resources that focus on every aspect of lodging operations. Industry-tested videos, CD-ROMs, seminars, and skills guides prepare employees at every skill level. EI also offers professional certification for the industry's top performers. For information about EI's products and services, call 800-349-0299 or 407-999-8100.

About the American Hotel Foundation (AHF)

An affiliate of AH&MA, the American Hotel Foundation provides financial support that enhances the stability, prosperity, and growth of the lodging industry through educational and research programs. AHF has awarded hundreds of thousands of dollars in scholarship funds for students pursuing higher education in hospitality management. AHF has also funded research projects on topics important to the industry, including occupational safety and health, turnover and diversity, and best practices in the U.S. lodging industry. For information, call 202-289-3100.

ACCOUNTING for CLUB OPERATIONS

Educational Institute Books

2/00

ACCOUNTING for CLUB OPERATIONS

Raymond S. Schmidgall, Ph.D., CPA
James W. Damitio, Ph.D., CMA

Contributing Author:
Michael L. Kasavana, Ph.D.

EDUCATIONAL INSTITUTE
American Hotel & Motel Association

Sponsored by

Hospitality
Financial and
Technology
Professionals

Disclaimer

This publication is designed to provide accurate and authoritative information in regard to the subject matter covered. It is sold with the understanding that the publisher is not engaged in rendering legal, accounting, or other professional service. If legal advice or other expert assistance is required, the services of a competent professional person should be sought.

>   *—From the Declaration of Principles jointly adopted by the American Bar Association and a Committee of Publishers and Associations*

The authors, Raymond S. Schmidgall and James W. Damitio, are solely responsible for the contents of this publication. All views expressed herein are solely those of the authors and do not necessarily reflect the views of the Educational Institute of the American Hotel & Motel Association (the Institute) or the American Hotel & Motel Association (AH&MA).

Nothing contained in this publication shall constitute a standard, an endorsement, or a recommendation of the Institute or AH&MA. The Institute and AH&MA disclaim any liability with respect to the use of any information, procedure, or product, or reliance thereon by any member of the hospitality industry.

Editors: Robert Bittner
Tim Eaton
Jim Purvis
Jennifer Smith

Cover photo: the Hartford Golf Club in West Hartford, Connecticut. We thank the club's controller, Wendy K. Zurstadt, CPA, CHAE, CHTP, and its general manager, Kevin P. Vitale, CCM, for their permission to use this photo.

Hospitality Financial and Technology Professionals

A few words from the sponsor of *Accounting for Club Operations*

Hospitality Financial and Technology Professionals is the international society for financial and technology professionals in the hospitality industry. Serving the industry since 1953, HFTP provides outstanding educational programs, networking opportunities, and information resources to hospitality professionals around the world. HFTP also awards the Certified Hospitality Accountant Executive (CHAE) and Certified Hospitality Technology Professional (CHTP) designations.

The goal of HFTP is to be recognized by the global business community as the authoritative information source on finance and technology for the hospitality industry. We are reaching that goal through the following.

Invaluable Resources

- *www.hftp.org.* The HFTP web site provides members with convenient access to industry checklists, forms, and tips; streaming video and audio educational sessions; CHAE and CHTP reviews; online meeting registration; publication archives; Job Mart; membership directory and ability for members to update their profiles; and resources for chapter leaders.

- *The Bottomline.* Produced eight times a year, HFTP's professional journal provides members with industry news covering everything from taxes and technology to HR and accounting issues.

- *Infoline.* HFTP's bimonthly newsletter notifies members of association activities on both the local and international levels, providing well-deserved recognition to chapters and individual members for their contributions to the hospitality industry.

- *Industry Partnerships.* We pride ourselves on enhancing the image of financial and technology professionals through increased visibility, support, and networking in the hospitality industry. HFTP represents members at industry meetings and associations, and has collaborated with other organizations to conduct industry research in the areas of hospitality salaries, technology, capital, and e-business.

Education and Technology

- *HITEC (Hospitality Industry Technology Exposition and Conference): www. hitec.org.* Internationally known, this conference offers industry professionals the largest, most comprehensive coverage of hospitality technology of its kind in the world. HITEC offers live demonstrations of the latest in hospitality technology, equipment, products and services, first-rate educational programs, and networking.

- *Annual Convention & Tradeshow.* More than 600 members attend the Annual Convention & Tradeshow each year to participate in information-sharing, educational sessions, and fun-filled entertainment.

- *Professional Development Seminars.* Each year, a series of specialized educational opportunities are offered to various segments of the hospitality industry, including the Club Controllers Conference, Hotel Controllers Conference, and Casino Controllers Conference.

- *Online Master's Program.* HFTP has collaborated with the University of Nevada Las Vegas to provide an online master's degree in hospitality administration (finance or technology concentration). HFTP members are eligible for tuition discounts.

Professional Opportunities

- *Certification.* The Certified Hospitality Accountant Executive (CHAE) designation is recognized worldwide as a symbol of achievement and competence. The Certified Hospitality Technology Professional (CHTP) designation— co-sponsored with the Educational Institute—symbolizes a high level of competency and professionalism in hospitality technology. Individuals who earn these designations are respected by employers and colleagues for their high level of commitment and dedication.

- *Networking.* The Colleague Advisory Network connects members who have expressed experience on particular subjects with members who have questions in that area. In addition, local chapters around the world provide members with leadership opportunities, discussion forums, and social activities.

For more information, contact HFTP at 11709 Boulder Lane, Ste. 110, Austin, TX 78726, membership@hftp.org, 800-646-4387, fax: 512-249-1533, or visit www.hftp.org and www.hitec.org.

Contents

Preface

Accounting for Club Operations presents accounting concepts and explains how they apply to specific operations within the club industry. This book is written primarily for financial executives and managers in the club industry. In addition, hospitality students at both the two-year and four-year college levels will find it instructional. Readers of this book should already be familiar with basic accounting concepts and procedures and perhaps will have taken an introductory course in basic accounting.

Each chapter begins with an outline and a list of the competencies that the chapter addresses. At the end of each chapter, there are a number of review questions and problems designed to test the reader's understanding of the concepts covered within the chapter. In addition, each chapter has a glossary of key terms used within the chapter. Terms that are boldfaced in the chapter text are defined at the end of the chapter.

The text consists of 15 chapters. It begins with an introduction of club accounting. In addition to some basic information regarding the club industry, a brief overview of the mechanics of accounting is provided.

Chapters 2 through 4 cover the three basic financial statements—the Statement of Financial Position, the Statement of Activities, and the Statement of Cash Flows. This coverage of these statements is based on the statements presented in the *Uniform System of Financial Reporting for Clubs*. In addition to the Statement of Activities, several supporting schedules from the uniform system are also presented.

Chapter 5 focuses on ratio analysis as a means of interpreting information reported on financial statements. For each ratio presented, its purpose, the sources of data needed to calculate it, the formula by which it is calculated, and the interpretation of the results are discussed.

Chapter 6 covers understanding and applying cost concepts. Various types of costs and how managers can identify the relevant costs in particular decision-making situations are presented. The cost-volume-profit analysis coverage commonly found in hospitality accounting texts is applied to the specifics of a club, including the unique aspects of initiation fees and dues. Finally, this chapter includes a discussion of pricing from a cost perspective.

Chapter 7 discussed how budgets are prepared and used for control operations. The chapter includes the results of recent surveys of club budgeting practices conducted by the authors.

Chapter 8 covers the management of cash, accounts receivable, and inventory. Both the cash receipts and disbursement and adjusted net income approaches to cash budgeting are presented.

Chapter 9 presents basic requirements of internal accounting control for various accounting functions including cash receipts, cash disbursements, accounts receivable, accounts payable, purchasing and receiving, inventories, and property and equipment.

Chapter 10 examines capital budgeting. The capital models presented and illustrated include accounting rate of return, payback, net present value, and internal rate of return.

Chapter 11 focuses on the accounting for property, equipment, and other assets. The initial recording of these assets, the depreciation of tangible assets, and accounting for the disposal of assets are discussed in detail.

Chapter 12 covers accounting for payroll and related liabilities. The largest expense of a social club is payroll. Various controls over payroll are presented as well as the necessary forms to facilitate reporting. Tax requirements related to payroll are also discussed.

Chapter 13 covers technology applications in the club environment. The focus is on the use of technology rather than the equipment. The authors are grateful to Michael L. Kasavana, the NAMA Professor at Michigan State University, for writing this chapter.

Chapter 14 covers leasing accounting. The rules promulgated by the Financial Accounting Standards Board regarding leases are discussed and the accounting for both operating and capital leases is presented. In addition, this chapter covers the process of determining whether to lease or purchase.

Chapter 15 covers taxes. The focus is primarily on not-for-profit clubs and covers areas of emphasis to *avoid* income tax liability. The authors are grateful to Kevin Reilly, U. S. National Director of Taxation and Managing Director of the Washington, DC office of PKF Worldwide, for co-authoring this chapter.

We are also grateful for the industry support we received in writing this book. First, Hospitality Financial and Technology Professionals underwrote the cost of the production of this book. Second, a club accounting task force consisting of several members of the HFTP associated with the club industry provided invaluable comments. The task force provided many suggestions that have greatly enhanced this publication. The members of the club accounting task force were:

Frank Anthony Agnello, Jr., CMA, CHAE, Controller, The Wyndgate
Thomas Blaney, CPA, Condon O'Meara McGinty & Donnelly
Randall A. Gudanowski, CCM, Manager, Rumson Country Club
Peter A. Lans, Senior Manager, Pannell Kerr Forster
Robert M. Salmore, CHAE, CPA, Partner, McGladrey & Pullen
Katherine Cavanaugh, CHAE, Controller, Royal Oaks Country Club
Virgilijus A. Kaulius, CT, Controller, Hollyburn Country Club
Andrew G. Moderski, CHAE, Controller, Harvard Club of Boston
Virginia E. Clarizia, CHAE, Administrative Manager, Tedesco Country Club
Mitchell R. Less, CHAE, CPA, Partner in charge of Assurance Services, Grant
   Thornton

Patricia M. Dinger, CHAE, Assistant Manager Finance & Administration,
    The University Club of Washington, DC
Jeannie Kohler Porter, CPA, Controller, LaJolla Beach & Tennis Club
Wendy K. Zurstadt, CHAE, CPA, Controller, Hartford Golf Club
Rosemary Panno, Controller, Indian Trail Club
Mary Risi Watkins, General Manager, Hunter's Run Golf & Racquet Club

Finally, we thank our families and especially our wives, Diane Damitio and
Barbara Schmidgall, for their patience and support during this major undertaking.

Raymond S. Schmidgall,	James W. Damitio
Hilton Hotels Professor	Professor
The School of Hospitality Business	Department of Accounting
Michigan State University	Central Michigan University
East Lansing, Michigan	Mt. Pleasant, Michigan

Raymond S. Schmidgall   James W. Damitio

About the Authors

Raymond S. Schmidgall is a professor in the School of Hospitality Business at Michigan State University. He holds a B.B.A. in accounting from Evangel College and an M.B.A. and a Ph.D. in accounting from Michigan State University. He is also a Certified Public Accountant. He has published articles in *Lodging, Club Management, The Bottom Line, The Consultant, Restaurant Business,* and the *Cornell Hotel and Restaurant Administration Quarterly.* Dr. Schmidgall has also written or co-written five accounting textbooks oriented to the hospitality industry, including basic texts on financial management, financial accounting, and managerial accounting. He conducts workshops and seminars for the Club Managers Association of America, American Hotel & Motel Association, National Restaurant Association, Hospitality Financial and Technology Professionals, Golf Course Superintendents Association of America, and Meeting Planners International. Dr. Schmidgall is Secretary of the Association of Hospitality Financial Management Educators, a member of the AH&MA's financial management committee, a member of International CHRIE's finance committee, a member of HFTP's communications and CHAE committees, serves on the editorial board of CHRIE's *Journal of Hospitality and Tourism Research,* and is a member of several professional accounting associations.

James W. Damitio is a professor in both the Department of Accounting and the Department of Marketing and Hospitality Services Administration at Central Michigan University, where he is also Director of the Perry Schools of Banking and Director of the Entreprenership Program. He received a B.S. in accounting from Central Michigan University and an M.B.A. in finance and a Ph.D. in curriculum and instruction for business from Michigan State University. He is a Certified Management Accountant and a member of the editorial review board of the Association of Hospitality Financial Management Educators. He is also a member of Hospitality Financial and Technology Professionals and the Institute of Management Accountants. He is a contributing author of a financial management text and has published numerous articles in the area of hospitality accounting in *Internal Auditing, Lodging, The Bottom Line,* the *Journal of Hospitality and Tourism Research,* the *Cornell Hotel and Restaurant Administration Quarterly, Florida International Review,* and the *Journal of Hospitality Management.* Dr. Damitio worked for Ernst & Young CPAs and was self-employed in retailing for 14 years.

Chapter 1 Outline

Overview of the Club Industry
    Ownership of Clubs
    The Origins of Private Clubs
    Club Operating Statistics
    Short Distribution Chain and Time
        Span
    A Labor-Intensive Industry
    Major Investment in Property and
        Equipment
The Accounting Function in the Club
    Industry
Principles of Accounting
    Cost
    Business Entity
    Continuity of the Business Unit
    Unit of Measurement
    Objective Evidence
    Full Disclosure
    Consistency
    Matching
    Conservatism
    Materiality
    Cash Versus Accrual Accounting
Branches of Accounting
Review of Accounting Mechanics
    Debit and Credit
The Accounting Cycle
Ethics and Club Accounting

Competencies

1. Describe the characteristics of the club industry and identify the major function of club accounting. (pp. 3–15)

2. Apply generally accepted accounting principles to club situations. (pp. 15–19)

3. Distinguish between cash basis and accrual basis accounting. (pp. 19–20)

4. Describe the six branches of accounting. (pp. 20–21)

5. Explain the fundamental accounting equation and identify normal account balances for various types of accounts. (pp. 21–22)

6. Demonstrate the nine steps of the accounting cycle. (pp. 23–27)

1

Introduction to Club Accounting

CLUB MANAGERS NEED more knowledge today than ever before, and they will need even more tomorrow. Much of this needed information can be found in accounting data and systems. To manage effectively, club managers must be able to interpret and use accounting information. This introductory chapter will provide answers to many questions, including the following:

- What is the size of the club industry?
- What are the different types of clubs?
- What is the scope of the accounting function in clubs?
- What are the major principles of accounting?
- What are the various branches of accounting?
- What are the basic mechanics of accounting?

This chapter will present an overview of the club industry and then focus on the accounting function within the industry. We will briefly review the principles, branches, and mechanics of accounting and discuss the accounting cycle.

Overview of the Club Industry

The club industry consists of several different types of operations providing both products and services to its members. It includes country clubs, city clubs, yacht clubs, military clubs, racquet clubs, athletic clubs, and university clubs, just to mention a few. The purpose of a private club is to serve its members. It is a place where people with a common bond congregate for social and recreational purposes. Private clubs, by definition, are not open to the public. Generally, an individual applicant must be accepted by the membership of the club before he or she may join. Generally, each member must pay an initiation fee and periodic dues (typically monthly). Many clubs have a minimum spending requirement. For example, the University Club of Michigan State University has a minimum monthly food and beverage spending requirement of $10. The average annual minimum is $1,000 for clubs in New Jersey.[1]

Private clubs are built for many reasons. U.S. clubs were often started by small groups of individuals who bought land or buildings to begin clubs for purely social reasons. Many modern-day private clubs are built by developers as a way to help them sell homes; the club and its golf course are the centerpiece of a housing development, and individuals who buy the homes surrounding the club either are automatically members of the club or have the option to become members.

Part of the appeal of private clubs is their unique environment. Private clubs tend to have the best of furnishings and impressive, well-kept grounds. The goal of most private clubs is to provide a level of service that is rarely found in public facilities. A member's club is a place where the member is called by name and is treated as someone special; a club is the member's home-away-from-home.

All of a club's facilities face competition from public facilities. Competitors of a club's food and beverage outlets are independent gourmet restaurants, family dining chain restaurants, and even fast-food restaurants (if a club has a fast-food type of food and beverage outlet). Public golf courses compete with a club's golf facilities. Public health clubs, including many large chain operations, compete with the fitness facilities of private clubs. Luxury resorts and hotels pamper their guests with extraordinary service and compete with private clubs for a club member's discretionary dollars. All of these competitive pressures make it essential that private clubs be led by professional managers who can provide quality club products and the extraordinary level of service members want, at a cost members perceive as giving their club membership high value.

There are over 11,000 private clubs in the United States and 8,500 are "total facility" clubs that feature food and beverages, athletic facilities, as well as other activities. According to a recent survey of Club Managers Association of America (CMAA) members:[2]

- 71 percent of CMAA members' clubs are golf and country clubs; approximately 20 percent are city clubs.

- Annual gross revenue is more than $7 billion for all clubs.

- Club dues revenues total $2.2 billion.

- Food and beverage revenues equal $2.5 billion.

- The average club income is $2.7 million.

- Clubs employ more than 256,000 people.

- Club payrolls equal $2.6 billion.

- Clubs annually raise close to $90 million for charity.

- Clubs recently gave a total of $10 million in student scholarships.

- 33 percent of clubs sponsor student internship programs.

Clubs managed by CMAA members pump $2.9 billion into state economies around the United States. More than $2.2 billion is spent in the local communities surrounding the club. The average club pays more than $95,000 a year in property taxes, up from $87,000 reported in 1991. Clubs account for $246 million in tax revenues across the country. Clubs generate another $392 million in state sales taxes.

Ownership of Clubs

Private clubs are owned in one of two ways: they are either member-owned clubs, called equity clubs, or non-member-owned clubs, called non-equity clubs. Non-equity clubs may be owned by real-estate developers, corporations, or other owners.

Equity clubs are owned by their members and governed by a board of directors elected by the members. In effect, the members are not just "customers," but also shareholders (they own equity in the club). Each member has a vote when it comes to electing board members or deciding major club issues (unless the member has purchased a type of membership that does not include voting rights). The managers of equity clubs work directly for the members, since the members own the club. Equity clubs are usually established as nonprofit corporations that are exempt from federal income taxes and some state and local taxes. Most private clubs are equity clubs.

Non-equity clubs represent another form of ownership; the assets of the club are owned by an individual or a corporation, not the club's members, and the members' control over the club is much more limited. Members do not often participate in major policy decisions, as they do in equity clubs. Non-equity clubs typically are not tax-exempt, but rather are usually for-profit organizations. Most non-equity clubs are corporate clubs or developer-owned clubs.

The Origins of Private Clubs

Although English social clubs and the golf club of St. Andrews in Scotland are the direct forerunners of city clubs and country clubs in the United States, the origins of clubs extend back to ancient times.[3] For example, the Roman baths can be viewed as clubs, in the sense that the baths were establishments run by managers in which selected groups of people met with their peers for recreational and social purposes. In some respects, the merchant and craft guilds of medieval Europe resembled clubs.

Clubs have been an integral part of the social fabric of upper-class English society for centuries. The origins of English city clubs lie in the coffeehouses that sprang up in the mid-seventeenth century with the importation of coffee. The first coffeehouses were formed at three major English universities: Oxford, All Souls, and Cambridge. The Oxford coffeehouse was the first to be called a club.

Early London city clubs featured extensive libraries and cultivated a quiet, relaxed atmosphere where members could read the *Times* or hold quiet conversations. Venerable London clubs such as White's and the Marlborough Club are still open today, having survived economic depressions, political upheavals, radical social changes, and two world wars.

The Royal and Ancient Golf Club of St. Andrews, established in Edinburgh in 1754, is world renowned for its contributions to the game of golf; the club's committees have formulated and periodically updated the rules of golf during the more than 200 years of the club's existence. This club is considered the first country club.

The first U.S. city clubs were established in the Colonies during the eighteenth century. These were loosely formed men-only social clubs that met in lodges or taverns, where the men drank rum and other alcoholic beverages and discussed the news of the day.

A wave of city-club building occurred in the mid-nineteenth century. The Somerset Club in Boston was founded in 1842; the San Francisco Commercial Club and Honolulu's Pacific Club were founded in 1851. The Pacific-Union Club in San Francisco dates from 1852, Delaware's Wilmington Club from 1859. The Olympic Club in San Francisco, the Union Leagues in Philadelphia and New York City, and the Rochester Club in Rochester, New York, were all organized during the Civil War. Then, as now, U.S. city clubs were organized primarily to provide a place for individuals with similar interests to dine and socialize together.

The Country Club in Brookline, Massachusetts, founded in 1882 with antecedents to 1860, is generally considered the oldest U.S. country club. Until the 1940s, country clubs were reserved for the most affluent members of U.S. society; applicants were carefully screened by powerful membership committees, and merely submitting one's name for membership sometimes required tremendous influence. However, during World War II, hundreds of thousands of ordinary servicemen were exposed to the game of golf on military bases, and after the war they generated a demand for public golf courses and affordable clubs with golf facilities. This led to the vast country club construction programs of the sixties, seventies, and eighties. Today, country club membership is within the reach of many more Americans than in the past.

Club Operating Statistics

Club operating statistics are produced by several consulting companies servicing the club industry. PKF Worldwide produces *Clubs in Town and Country*, which reflects average operating results for both country and city clubs in the United States. Other consulting firms produce reports for regions of the United States. For example, Condon O'Meara McGinty & Donnelly LLP provides an annual operating report for clubs on the Northeastern part of the United States. The discussion in this section is based primarily on PKF Worldwide's 2000 annual report.

Over the 20-year period of 1980–1999, total *country* club revenues rose from $1,635 per member to $6,907 per member, a 322 percent increase. The percentage breakdown of revenues for 1980 and 1999 are as follows:

	1980	1999
Membership dues	47.8%	44.8%
Food and beverage sales	37.9	33.1
All other sales and income	14.3	22.1
Total	100.0%	100.0%

These figures suggest an increasing reliance on other sales and income, such as greens fees, pro shop sales, and investment income, and a decreasing reliance on food and beverage sales.

Over the same 20-year period, total costs and expenses of country clubs have increased from $1,478 per member in 1980 to $6,316 per member in 1999, leaving $157 and $591 per member in 1980 and 1999, respectively, for debt service, capital improvements, etc. The percentage breakdown operating expenses for 1980 and 1999 are as follows:

	1980	1999
Payroll and related costs	47.8%	46.0%
All other sales and income	52.2	54.0
Total	100.0%	100.0%

A major activity at most country clubs is golf. The cost per hole to maintain a golf course in the United States has risen dramatically, from around $10,000 in 1979 to nearly $55,000 in 1999. The total expenses differ by geographic region, however. According to PKF Worldwide, the average annual maintenance costs per hole in 1999 were $50,845 in the East region, $40,823 in the Central region, and $68,525 in the West. Golf course maintenance costs for U.S. courses collectively can be divided among the major categories as follows: payroll = 58 percent, payroll taxes and benefits = 11 percent, course supplies and contracts = 14 percent, repairs = 6 percent, and all other expenses = 11 percent.

Exhibit 1 reveals the sources and uses of the 1999 country club income dollar. Exhibit 2 presents a five-year summary of country club initiation fees.

Over the 20-year period of 1980–1999, total *city* club revenues rose from $995 per member to $3,470 per member, a 249 percent increase. The percentage break-down of revenues for 1980 and 1999 are as follows:

	1980	1999
Membership dues	38.6%	37.7%
Food and beverage sales	48.0	47.4
All other sales and income	13.4	14.9
Total	100.0%	100.0%

This breakdown suggests the revenue sources are staying relatively consistent. Over the same 20-year period, total annual operating costs increased from $939 per member in 1980 to $3,082 per member in 1999. The breakdown between payroll and related costs and all other operating expenses is as follows:

	1980	1999
Payroll and related costs	47.6%	47.2%
All other sales and income	52.4	52.8
Total	100.0%	100.0%

Exhibit 3 reveals the source and use of the 1999 city club income dollar.

Exhibit 1   The Country Club Income Dollar

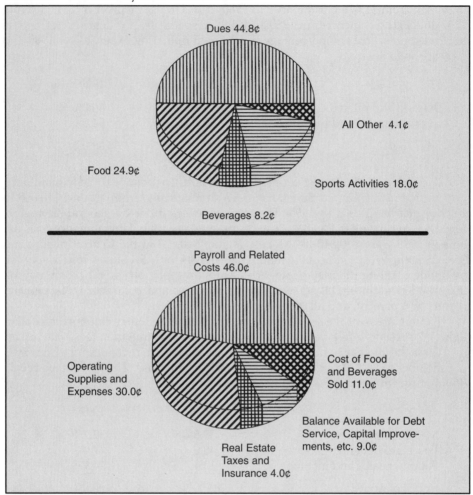

Source: *Clubs in Town & Country* (New York: PKF Worldwide, 2000), p. 9.

Exhibit 2   Five-Year Summary of Country Club Initiation Fees

Year	Amount	% Increase
1995	$19,665	—
1996	20,711	5.3
1997	21,990	6.2
1998	25,930	17.9
1999	28,879	11.4

Source: Condon O'Meara McGinty & Donnelly LLP.

Exhibit 3 The City Club Income Dollar

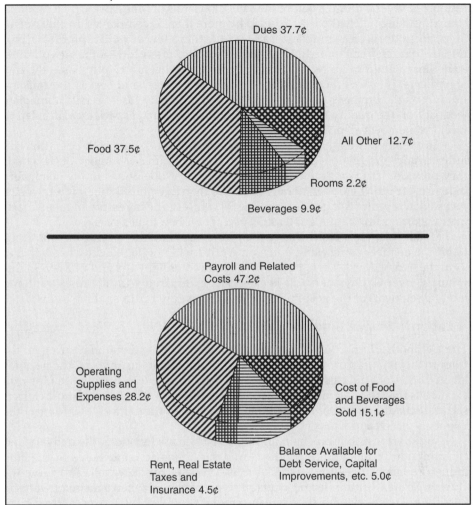

Source: *Clubs in Town & Country* (New York: PKF Worldwide, 2000), p. 19.

Clearly, the above statistics reveal the heavy reliance by clubs on membership dues and initiation fees. These revenue sources are non-existent in other segments of the hospitality industry.

Short Distribution Chain and Time Span

In a club operation, there is a relatively fast conversion of raw materials into a finished product and of the product into cash. Like manufacturing operations, club operations must offer products and services that meet the members' expectations. However, the distribution chain and time span is considerably shorter for club "products" than for most consumer goods.

For example, a new automobile purchased from a dealer may have been assembled several months before the sale, thousands of miles away, by a different company using finished parts supplied by more than 50 companies. In club operations, inventory is often purchased and sold within a few days. The product is produced, sold, and consumed at the same location, often in less than two hours, sometimes within minutes. The food service "manufacturer" purchases the raw ingredients, prepares them to suit the members' tastes, and serves the finished product on the premises. The club operator will in many cases receive immediate feedback on the quality of the food and service product, especially if it failed to meet the members' expectations.

As a result of this short distribution chain and time span, club operations do little advance production. Thus, they maintain a minimal inventory of the goods they provide. This is reflected in the fact that major operations in the hospitality industry, including clubs, generally have less than five percent of their total assets invested in inventory of goods for resale. In contrast, the inventory of many major manufacturing firms equals at least 30 percent of their total assets.

Members of most clubs charge their purchases and are given generous terms to pay. A member purchasing lunch on April 1 will not be billed by his/her club until the end of April. Then, payment is required only by the end of May. In this example, over 60 days of credit is extended. Compared with the restaurant and lodging segments of the hospitality industry, these are relatively long terms.

A Labor-Intensive Industry

There is another important difference between the club and manufacturing industries. In the manufacturing sector, automatic equipment has reduced the need for labor. This is not the case in the club industry. As we have already seen, payroll expense is the major element of the total costs of a club. The focus at most clubs is service. Scheduling personnel for busy times is important if a club is to meet the members' needs and wants.

The short distribution chain and time span characteristic of the delivery and consumption of hospitality products and services also contributes to the club industry's labor intensity. Personnel must prepare, produce, sell, and serve the club's offerings. Labor must be available to prepare food when a member wants it. Quality member-oriented service can only be provided by a large and efficient staff. Controlling labor costs while satisfying the needs and wants of members is crucial to the success of any club operation.

Major Investment in Property and Equipment

In addition to being labor-intensive, club properties are, for the most part, property and equipment intensive. Clubs provide space for members to relax, rest, entertain, and conduct business. The clubhouse is carried as a fixed asset, and its cost is written off (depreciated) over time. The cost of the clubhouse and golf course are the same whether or not they are used. The cost of the clubhouse and golf course represents a major investment by clubs. Exhibit 4 shows the average annual capital expenditure by country clubs in the annual survey by Condon *et al.* The average country club in their survey spends nearly three-quarters of a million dollars in

Exhibit 4   Five-Year Summary of Country Club Capital Expenditures

Year	Amount
1994	$424,013
1995	534,932
1996	629,718
1997	699,593
1998	740,902

Source: Condon O'Meara McGinty & Donnelly LLP.

capital expansion and/or improvements. The fixed assets of clubs make up between 70 and 90 percent of their total assets. In contrast, the fixed assets of many manufacturing companies approximate only 30 percent of their total assets.

This overview of the club industry has described many of the different types of clubs and indicated the impressive dimensions of the industry. As we have seen, the club industry is greatly affected by the short distribution chain and quick consumption of its offerings, by the need for a large, efficient work force, and by large investment in property and equipment. These characteristics of club operations give shape to the challenges that the accounting function must face within the industry.

The Accounting Function in the Club Industry

The accounting function in club properties is performed by a group of specialists ranging from bookkeepers to executives with such titles as Chief Financial Officer and Controller. Chief financial executives of clubs are responsible for all accounting functions such as receivables, payables, payroll, and, in some cases, storage and security. In many clubs, the chief financial executives are responsible for the information system and the human resource functions. Exhibit 5 summarizes the results of a survey of over 200 club financial executives and shows a wide range of reported responsibilities.

This survey also gathered data on the size of accounting staffs, which may vary widely with the size and diversity of the club's operations—from a part-time accountant in a small club to more than 10 people in a large club. The survey found that 49 percent of club financial executives supervise fewer than five people. One-third of the respondents supervised between five and ten people, while only 17.7 percent supervised more than ten.

Exhibit 6 is a sample organization chart for a country club that shows the controller reporting to the general manager; however, since the controller is the "eyes and ears" of the board, the controller ideally should have a dual reporting role, either to the club treasurer or president.

The accounting function within a club is information-oriented—that is, its major role is providing information to users. For external users such as financial institutions, accounting usually communicates through financial statements.

Exhibit 5   Responsibilities of Club Financial Executives

Area	Percentage of respondents
General accounting	99.0%
Computer system—accounting	98.5
Accounts payable	98.5
Accounts receivable	98.0
Payroll	97.5
Cash management	91.5
Computer system—club operations	80.9
Human resources	79.9
Tax returns	78.4
Club security	75.9
Investments	68.8
Food controls	49.7
Beverage controls	48.2
Risk management	43.7
Purchasing	43.2
Cashiers	35.2
Receiving	26.6
Storage	26.1
Income auditors	24.1
Internal auditors	23.6
Night auditors	12.1

Internally, accounting provides a wide variety of financial reports, including operating statements. The operating statements are formatted to reflect revenues and related expenses by areas of responsibility. In addition to the statement of activities of the property as a whole, departmental statements are prepared for each department generating revenues and incurring expenses, such as food and beverage and the golf course.

Regardless of the size of an operation's accounting department, the diversity of its responsibilities, or the number and types of reports produced, the accounting staff is responsible for providing *service.* The accounting staff must work closely with operating management and other service departments in order for the club to meets its objectives.

Exhibits 7–9 reveal results from the recent survey of over 200 club financial executives. Exhibit 7 reflects the technical skills and knowledge required of club financial executives. Every single respondent indicated a need for computer skills and knowledge. More than 90 percent of the respondents said cash management, internal controls, financial reporting, and cash budgeting knowledge and skills were also required. Each of these areas is financial in nature and would seem to be under the domain of a club's chief financial executive. Only Financial Accounting

Exhibit 6   Sample Organization Chart for a Country Club

```
                              Members
                                 |
                          Board of Directors
                                 |
                         Executive Committee
                                 |
                          General Manager
                                 |
  ┌──────────┬──────────────┬──────────────┬──────────────┬──────────────┬──────────────┐
Controller*  Golf Course   Golf Pro     Clubhouse     Executive      Tennis       Aquatics
             Superintendent              Manager        Chef          Pro          Director
  │            │              │            │              │              │             │
Accountant   Crew         Assistant        │          Kitchen         Staff       Swimming
                          Professional      │           Staff                      Instructor
                              │             │                                         │
                      ┌───────┴───────┐     │                                      Lifeguard
                  Golf Shop      Golf Car    │
                  Salesperson    Mechanic    │
                                             │
        ┌──────────────┬──────────────┬──────────────┬──────────────┬──────────────┐
   Locker Room    Maintenance    Executive     Dining Room      Head         Security
    Manager       Supervisor    Housekeeper      Manager      Bartender     Supervisor
```

*Also may report to Club President or Treasurer.

Exhibit 7   Technical Skills and Knowledge of Club Financial Executives

Area	Percentage of respondents
Computers	100.0%
Cash management	98.0
Internal controls	96.5
Financial reporting	96.0
Cash budgeting	94.5
HR management	87.5
Taxes	82.5
Non-profit accounting	68.5
Auditing	67.0
Statistics	61.0
Loan details	52.5
Risk management	50.0
FASB pronouncements	31.0

Exhibit 8   Authority of Club Financial Executives

Area	Percentage of respondents
Approve purchases	92.8%
Sign checks	72.2
Invest funds	59.8
Enter into contracts	57.2
Extend credit	44.8
Borrow funds	34.5
Set or change prices	26.8

Standards Board (FASB) pronouncements received less than a 50 percent response. Many FASB pronouncements have minor impact on the club's financial reporting, and this may well account for the relatively low response for this skill.

Exhibit 8 reveals the authority of club financial executives. Over 90 percent of the respondents indicated that they approve purchases, 72 percent sign checks, 60 percent invest funds, and 57 percent have the authority to enter into contracts for their clubs. The least common area of authority was to set or change prices. This is no real surprise, as the authority to set or change prices is normally vested in the club's operating management team.

Exhibit 9 reveals both the percentage of clubs having specific committees and the percentage of the respondents who were members of those committees. The summary indicates that over 75 percent of the club financial executives were members of their finance/budget committees (which existed in 89 percent of the

Exhibit 9   Committee Responsibilities and Participation of Club Financial Executives

Committee	Club has committee	Financial executive is on committee
Finance/budget	89.0%	75.5%
Pension/fringe benefit	26.5	17.9
Long-range planning	72.0	15.8
Executive	74.0	15.2
Risk management	16.5	12.0
Safety	27.5	12.0
Membership	89.5	11.4
Compensation	21.5	9.2
House	85.0	9.2
Golf	77.0	3.8
Tennis	63.5	3.3
Entertainment	65.5	2.7
Training	4.0	1.1

NOTE: Fifty-eight respondents indicate they also serve on at least one other committee than the committees listed above.

respondents' clubs). In other words, when this committee exists, the surveyed financial executives are members nearly 85 percent of the time (75.5 ÷ 89). The next most frequent committee memberships were pension/fringe benefits, long-range planning, and executive. Just over a quarter of the respondents' clubs had a pension/fringe benefit committee. When a club has this committee, the respondent was a member 67.6 percent of the time. As researchers, we were surprised by the relatively low participation on the long-range planning and executive committees. These are extremely important committees of a club, and we believe that the club financial executive could offer unique input that is quite valuable to the overall club operations. Perhaps as club financial executives continue to grow as professionals, the percentages will increase.

Principles of Accounting

In order to understand accounting methods, you must understand basic accounting principles. These **generally accepted accounting principles** (often referred to by the acronym *GAAP*) provide a uniform basis for preparing financial statements. Although not "etched in stone," accounting principles have become accepted over time through common usage and also through the work of such major accounting bodies as the American Institute of Certified Public Accountants, the American Accounting Association, and the FASB.

Students of club accounting may often wonder why an accounting transaction is recorded in a particular way at a particular time or why some asset value is not changed at some point. Generally, the reasons relate to accounting principles. The following sections briefly discuss several generally accepted accounting principles.

Cost

The **cost principle** states that when a transaction is recorded, it is the transaction price or cost that establishes the accounting value for the product or service purchased. For example, if a club buys a dishwasher, the agreed-upon price between the club and the supplier determines the amount to be recorded. If the agreed-upon price is $5,000, then the dishwasher is initially valued at $5,000 in the club's accounting records. The supplier may have acquired the dishwasher from the manufacturer for $4,000 and the club may receive an offer of $5,500 for it the day it is purchased; however, it is the actual cost that established the amount to be recorded. If amounts other than cost (such as estimates or appraisals) were used to record transactions, then accounting records would lose their usefulness. When cost is the basis for recording a transaction, the buyer and seller determine the amount to be recorded. This amount is generally an objective and fair measure of the value of the goods or services purchased.

When the value of current assets is clearly less than the cost recorded on the books, this decline in value must be recognized. Thus, the *conservatism principle* (discussed later) overrides the cost principle. On the other hand, property and equipment (frequently called fixed assets) are normally carried at cost less the depreciated amounts and are not reduced to market value as long as management plans to retain them for their useful life. This treatment of property and equipment is based on the *going-concern principle* (also discussed later).

Business Entity

Accounting and financial statements are based on the concepts that (1) each business is a **business entity** that maintains its own set of accounts and (2) these accounts are separate from the other financial interests of the owners. For example, if a club manager decides to take some food home from the club for personal use, the cost of the food should be properly charged by the club to the manager's account. Recording business activity separately from the manager's or owner's personal affairs allows a reasonable determination of the property's profitability. Not only does separate recording provide excellent information for managing the business, it is also necessary for properly filing tax returns, especially for non-tax- exempt clubs.

Continuity of the Business Unit

According to the **continuity of the business unit principle**, in preparing the accounting records and reports, it is assumed that the club will continue indefinitely and that liquidation is not in prospect—in other words, the business is a **going concern**. This assumption is based on the concept that the real value of the club is its ability to provide services, rather than the value its assets would bring in liquidation. According to this concept, the market value of the property and equipment need not appear on the financial statements, and prepaid expenses are considered assets. If there is a reasonable chance the club may be unable to continue operations in the near future, allowance for this future event should be reflected in the financial statements. This may be best accomplished by reducing asset values to their market values.

Unit of Measurement

The financial statements are based on transactions expressed in monetary terms. The monetary unit is assumed to represent a stable unit of value so that transactions from past periods and the current period can be included on the same statement.

In the late 1970s and early 1980s, annual inflation (as measured by the Consumer Price Index) exceeded 10 percent. The FASB responded by requiring public companies to show current replacement cost of their property and equipment in footnotes to their financial statements. For some businesses, the current values of property and equipment exceeded twice the amount of the fixed assets carried on the books. Since inflation has been relatively low for the past several years, the FASB has rescinded this reporting requirement.

Objective Evidence

Accounting transactions and the resulting accounting records should be based as much as possible on **objective evidence**. Generally, this evidence is an invoice and/or a canceled check. However, estimates must be assumed in the absence of such objective evidence. For example, suppose that the corporate owner of a residential club contributes equipment, purchased several years ago for personal use, to the club. The owner may believe the equipment is worth $2,000, while the original catalog shows the cost several years ago of $2,500 and an appraiser appraises the equipment at $1,000. In this example, the most objective estimate of its value today would be the appraiser's estimate of $1,000.

Full Disclosure

The financial statements must provide information on all the facts pertinent to the interpretation of the financial statements. This **full disclosure** is accomplished either by reporting the information in the body of the financial statements or in footnotes to the financial statements. Footnote disclosures might include the accounting methods used, changes in accounting methods, contingent liabilities, events occurring after the financial statement date, and unusual and nonrecurring items. An example of each type of disclosure is presented in Exhibit 10.

Consistency

Several accounting methods are often available for reporting a specific kind of activity. Management chooses the method most appropriate under the circumstances. For example, there are several ways to determine inventory values, and there are several methods of depreciating fixed assets. The **consistency principle** requires that, once an accounting method has been adopted, it should be followed from period to period unless a change is warranted and disclosed. The

Exhibit 10   Types of Disclosure

Type of Disclosure	Example
Accounting methods used	Straight-line method of depreciation
Change in the accounting methods	A change from depreciating a fixed asset using the straight-line method to using the double declining balance method
Contingent liability	A lawsuit against the club for alleged failure to provide adequate security for a member who suffered personal injury
Events occurring after the financial statement date	A fire destroys significant assets of the club one week after the end of the year
Unusual and nonrecurring items	A club in Michigan suffers significant losses due to an earthquake

consistency principle allows a user of financial information to make reasonable comparisons between periods. Without consistent accounting, trends indicated by supposedly comparable financial statements might be misleading. When it becomes necessary to change to another method, the change must be disclosed and the dollar effect on earnings and/or the statement of financial position must be reported.

Matching

The **matching principle** refers to relating expenses to revenues. For example, suppose that a club purchases a computerized golf reservations system that will benefit the club for several years. The cost is therefore recorded as a fixed asset and the cost of the system is written off over the system's life. The result is a partial write-off of the fixed asset each year against the revenues generated in part by using the system. This process is referred to as *matching* and is the basis for adjusting entries at the end of each accounting period. The matching principle is used when transactions are recorded on an accrual rather than cash basis. The accrual basis and cash basis of accounting are discussed later in this chapter.

Conservatism

The **conservatism principle** calls for recognizing expenses as soon as possible, but delaying the recognition of revenues until they are ensured. The practical result is to be conservative (low) in recognizing an increase in net assets for the current year. It is not proper to deliberately understate an increase in net assets; however, many accountants wish to be cautious in recognizing revenues and "generous" in recognizing expenses.

A good example of this is the accounting treatment of lawsuits. If a club is a plaintiff in a lawsuit and its legal counsel indicates the case will be won and estimates the amount of settlement, the amount is not recorded as revenue until a judgment is rendered and collection is reasonably assured. On the other hand, if the same club is a defendant in a lawsuit and its legal counsel indicated the club will lose the lawsuit and most likely will pay a stated amount, this "expense" is recognized immediately.

Conservatism is apparent in the valuation of temporary investments at the lower of cost or current market value and the recognition of nonrefundable deposits for future banquets as a liability until the banquet is catered.

Materiality

According to the **materiality principle**, events or information must be accounted for if they "make a difference" to the user of the financial information. An item is material in comparison to a standard. Some accountants have attempted to establish materiality by rules of thumb; for example, an item may be recognized if it exceeds a certain percentage of total assets or total income. However, this approach fails to address an item's relative importance over time. In addition, several immaterial items may be material when viewed collectively.

The materiality principle is often applied to property and equipment. Tangible items with useful lives beyond one year are commonly recorded as property and equipment. However, when such items cost less than a certain amount (specified by the board of directors of the purchasing organization), they are expensed because the cost is considered immaterial. An example would be a wastebasket. A $39 wastebasket might have a useful life of ten years, but if the club's board has set a $100 limit for recording expenditures as equipment, the cost of the wastebasket would be immaterial and the wastebasket would be expensed.

When a club provides footnotes to supplement its financial statements, only material or potentially material items are presented.

Cash Versus Accrual Accounting

The cash and accrual bases of accounting are two methods of determining when to record a transaction.

Cash basis accounting recognizes an accounting transaction at the point of cash inflow or outflow. For example, cash received in 20X2 for food sold in 20X1 would be treated as 20X2 revenues. Likewise, expenses incurred in 20X1 for which cash was disbursed in 20X2 would be treated as 20X2 expenses. Because of these improper assignments of revenues and expenses, cash basis accounting is generally not a fair reflection of business operations. Cash basis accounting usually violates the generally accepted accounting principles discussed earlier. However, using this method is acceptable if the results do not differ *materially* from those that accrual basis accounting would produce. This method may be used only by very small operations. Most likely, every club should use accrual basis accounting.

The more commonly used **accrual basis accounting** recognizes revenues when earned (regardless of when cash is received) and expenses when incurred (regardless of when cash is disbursed). For example, suppose that a club with overnight rooms sells a room for the period of December 30, 20X1, through January 2, 20X2, and the club member pays the bill of $240 ($60 per night for four nights) during February 20X2. Under accrual basis accounting, two days of rooms revenue are recorded in December and two days of rooms revenue are recorded in January, even though the payment was received from the member in February.

Expenses must be recognized periodically (because of the matching principle) even when no transaction has occurred. Examples of nontransaction expense recognition include depreciation of property and equipment, reduction of prepaid insurance, accrual of payroll, and provisions of an allowance for uncollectible receivables. For example, insurance coverage may be purchased 12 months in advance. Accrual basis accounting would recognize insurance expense over the 12-month period rather than when the cash is disbursed. The vehicle for this recognition is *adjusting entries*, which are briefly discussed later in this chapter.

Branches of Accounting

Accountants classify accounting activities in a variety of ways. However, most agree that there are distinct (though overlapping) branches. These branches are financial accounting, cost accounting, managerial accounting, tax accounting, auditing, and accounting information systems.

Financial accounting refers to accounting for revenues, expenses, assets, and liabilities. It involves the basic accounting processes of recording, classifying, and summarizing transactions. This area is often limited to the accounting necessary to prepare and distribute financial reports. Financial accounting is historical in nature; that is, it deals with past events. Managerial accounting, on the other hand, deals with proposed events.

Cost accounting is the branch of accounting dealing with the recording, classification, allocation, and reporting of current and prospective costs. Cost accountants determine costs by departments, functions, responsibilities, and products and services. The chief purpose of cost accounting is to help operations personnel control operations.

Managerial accounting is the branch of accounting designed to provide information to various management levels for the purpose of enhancing controls. Management accountants prepare performance reports, including comparisons to the budget. One major purpose of these reports is to provide in-depth information as a basis for management decisions. Although managerial accounting may vary among segments of the hospitality industry and certainly among different establishments, many management accountants use various statistical techniques.

Tax accounting is the branch of accounting relating to the preparation and filing of tax forms with governmental agencies. Tax planning to minimize tax payments is a significant part of the tax accountant's work. Tax accounting usually focuses on income tax at the federal, state, and local levels, but may also include sales, excise, payroll, and property taxes. Many clubs contract the services of tax accountants employed by certified public accounting firms.

Auditing is the branch of accounting involved with reviewing and evaluating documents, records, and control systems. Auditing may be either external or internal. It is most often associated with the independent, external audit called a

financial audit. The external auditor reviews the financial statements of the club, its underlying internal control system, and its accounting records (journals, vouchers, invoices, checks, bank statements, and so forth) in order to render an opinion of the financial statements. The auditor usually then provides recommendations for strengthening the operation's internal controls. Financial audits may only be conducted by certified public accounting firms.

Over the past several years, hospitality operations (such as hotels and restaurant chains) have increasingly employed internal auditors, whose primary purpose is to review and evaluate internal control systems. Many large hospitality firms have a full staff of internal auditors who conduct audits at individual properties to help management maintain the internal control system. Very few clubs have full-time internal auditors, though internal audit functions will be performed by accounting staff on a part-time basis.

The final branch of accounting is accounting information systems. Accounting information systems personnel review the information systems of hospitality organizations. Information systems include not only the accounting system but other elements of a club's information system, such as reservations. Because virtually all clubs are now computerized, many accounting systems experts are also electronic data processing specialists.

Review of Accounting Mechanics

Introductory accounting textbooks use several chapters to cover the mechanics of accounting, from the fundamental accounting equation to the preparation of the financial statements. Let us briefly review these topics.[4]

The **fundamental accounting equation** is simply *assets equal liabilities plus members' equity*. In not-for-profit organizations, it is restated as *assets equal liabilities plus net assets*. The equation is a balance to be tested and proven, not a formula to be calculated. This equality is reflected in the statement of financial position prepared at the end of each accounting period. **Assets**, simply defined, are things the club owns, including cash, inventory, accounts receivable, land, buildings, and equipment. **Liabilities**, simply stated, are obligations to outside parties and include accounts payable, notes payable, income tax payable, long-term debt payable, and accrued payroll. **Members' equity** (or **net assets**) is the residual claims members have on assets. In other words, assets less liabilities equals members' equity. After each business transaction is recorded, the total assets must equal the total of liabilities and members' equity (net assets).

There are two major sub-classifications of members' equity (net assets)—**permanent accounts** and **temporary accounts**. An **account** is simply a device for showing increases and/or decreases in an individual asset, liability, or members' equity item. For example, a club operation would have an account for cash in its bank account called "cash in bank." Permanent members' equity accounts are not closed at the end of an accounting period. Temporary members' equity accounts are closed out at the end of each fiscal year and include all revenue and expense accounts. Revenues increase members' equity, while expenses decrease members' equity.

The fundamental accounting equation can now be expanded as follows:

Assets (A)   =   Liabilities (L)
+   Permanent Members' Equity Accounts (PMEA)
+   Temporary Members' Equity Accounts (TMEA)

Revenues (R) and expenses (E) can be substituted for the TMEA, producing the following equation:

$$A = L + PMEA + R - E$$

Debit and Credit

The left side of any account is called the **debit** side and the right side is the **credit** side. To *debit an account* means to record an amount on the left side, while to *credit an account* means to record an amount on the right side. The difference between the total debits and total credits of an account is called the **balance**. The normal balance of an account is the kind of balance, either debit or credit, which the account generally shows. The major classes of accounts have normal balances as follows:

Type of Account	Normal Balance
Asset	Debit
Liability	Credit
Members' Equity:	
Permanent	Credit
Revenue	Credit
Expense	Debit

Each transaction is recorded with equal dollar amounts of debits and credits in **ledger** accounts. This equality of debits and credits in ledger accounts is tested by preparing a **trial balance**, which will be discussed later.

Debits (dr) and credits (cr) increase (+) and decrease (−) the various classes of accounts as follows:

Assets				Liabilities				Members' Equity	
+	−	=		−	+	+		−	+
dr	cr			dr	cr			dr	cr

Revenues		Expenses	
−	+	+	−
dr	cr	dr	cr

Exhibit 11 Documents and Transactions

	Documents	
Type of Transaction	**Prepared by Firm**	**Prepared Outside of Club**
Sales of products and services	Member guest check	—
Cash receipts	Cash register tape	Checks
Purchases of products and services	Purchase order	Suppliers' invoices
Payroll	Time cards Payroll checks	—
Cash disbursements	Check	—

The Accounting Cycle

In every accounting period (generally one year), an **accounting cycle** begins, starting with recording transactions and ending with a post-closing trial balance. Each step in the cycle will be defined and discussed briefly.

There are five common transactions in a club operation:

1. Sales of products and services

2. Cash receipts

3. Purchases of products and services

4. Payroll

5. Cash disbursements

With each transaction, documents are prepared and/or received from which bookkeepers record the transaction. Exhibit 11 lists a few key documents for each type of transaction.

Step 1 in the accounting cycle is recording the transactions in journals. **Journals** are simply books used for initially recording individual transactions. There is generally a separate journal (generically called a **specialized journal**) for each type of transaction. In addition, each establishment maintains a **general journal** for recording entries not recorded in specialized journals. The process of recording requires that each transaction be analyzed and that a minimum of two accounts be affected. For example, a cash sales transaction results in increases to the cash account and the sales account.

Step 2 in the accounting cycle is transferring the amounts from the journals to the ledger accounts. This process, called **posting,** tracks individual accounts. For example, assume that cash at the beginning of the period is $1,000, cash receipts for the month total $50,000 (per the cash receipts journal), and cash disbursements equal $45,000 (per the cash disbursements journal). The cash account after these postings would show the following:

CASH

Date	P/R	Debit	Credit	Balance
Bal.		1,000		1,000
EOM	CR	50,000		51,000
EOM	CD		45,000	6,000

Normally, the columns of each specialized journal are totaled and these totals are posted to the proper accounts at the end of the month (EOM). Amounts recorded in the general journal, however, are posted individually. The example shows posting references (P/R) of CR for the cash receipts journal and CD for the cash disbursements journal. The beginning cash balance of $1,000 increased to $6,000 by the end of the month because $50,000 was received and $45,000 disbursed.

Step 3 in the accounting cycle is preparing a trial balance. The trial balance is simply a listing of all account balances, with debit balance accounts and credit balance accounts in separate columns. The totals of each column should be equal and prove the equality of debits and credits. Exhibit 12 presents the hypothetical and very small Mason Club's trial balance for the month ended December 31, 20X1. Notice that the debit and credit columns both total $488,000.

Step 4 in the accounting cycle is preparing **adjusting entries**. Adjusting entries are required to adjust accounts to reflect the proper account balances. The adjusting entries are recorded in the general journal at the end of the accounting period. The major categories of adjusting entries, along with examples, are shown in Exhibit 13.

Step 5 is posting the adjusting entries. All adjusting entries are posted individually from the general journal. All adjustments are different, so there are no common accounts affected by the adjustments (in contrast to the entries recorded in specialized journals).

Step 6 in the accounting cycle is preparing an adjusted trial balance. After the adjusting entries are posted to the accounts, an adjusted trial balance is prepared to once again test the equality of debit and credit accounts. This process may be facilitated by using a worksheet (see Exhibit 14).

Step 7 is the preparation of the financial statements. Using a worksheet approach, the accountant simply extends all figures from the adjusted trial balance to the proper columns on the statements of activities and financial position. Exhibit 14 reveals that the difference between the debit and credit columns under the "statement of activities" results in an increase in net assets. For the Mason Club, revenues of $150,000 exceeded expenses of $105,350, resulting in an increase in net assets of $44,650. The increase in net assets of $44,650 added to the total credits of $353,150 (statement of financial position columns) equals total debits of $397,800 (statement of financial position).

The accountant then prepares a formal statement of activities and statement of financial position in accordance with generally accepted accounting principles (especially the full disclosure principle). This process may include footnotes to the

Exhibit 12 Mason Club Trial Balance

Mason Club
Trial Balance
December 31, 20X1

	Debits	Credits
Cash	$ 5,000	
Marketable Securities	10,000	
Accounts Receivable	8,000	
Food Inventory	2,500	
Prepaid Insurance	4,500	
Furniture	40,000	
Accumulated Depreciation, Furniture		$ 20,000
Equipment	10,000	
Accumulated Depreciation, Equipment		5,000
Building	300,000	
Accumulated Depreciation, Building		100,000
Land	20,000	
Accounts Payable		5,000
Notes Payable		5,000
Mortgage Payable		100,000
Members' Equity		103,000
Food Revenue		150,000
Salaries	15,000	
Wages	22,500	
Payroll Taxes	3,000	
Operating Supplies Expense	2,000	
Office Supplies	1,000	
Utilities	5,000	
Promotion	500	
Repairs and Maintenance	9,000	
Cost of Food Sold	22,000	
Interest Expense	8,000	
Total	$ 488,000	$488,000

statements and additional financial statements, such as the statement of cash flows.

In step 8, after preparation of the financial statements, the revenue and expense accounts are closed. These temporary members' equity accounts are closed into the appropriate members' equity account. The closing entries either increase the appropriate members' equity account (if the club operation earned a profit) or decrease the appropriate members' equity account (if a loss was suffered). The closing entries result in zero balances in all revenue and expense accounts. The closing entries are recorded in the general journal and posted to the proper accounts.

Exhibit 13   Major Categories of Adjusting Entries

Category	Examples	Accounts	
		Debited	Credited
1. Prepaid expense	a. Reduction of prepaid insurance	Insurance Expense	Prepaid Insurance
	b. Reduction of prepaid rent	Rent Expense	Prepaid Rent
2. Accrued expense	a. Accrual of payroll	Payroll Expense	Accrued Payroll
	b. Accrual of interest expense on a note payable	Interest Expense	Interest Payable
3. Unearned revenue	Reduction of unearned rent	Unearned Rent	Rental Revenue
4. Accrued revenue	Accrual of interest earned on note receivable	Interest Receivable	Interest Income
5. Estimated items	Depreciation expense	Depreciation Expense	Accumulated Depreciation, Property and Equipment
6. Inventory adjustment	Recording of ending inventory from physical inventory. (Note: other account balances such as Purchases are also transferred to the Cost of Goods Sold account.)	Inventory end of month	Cost of Goods Sold

Step 9, the final step in the accounting cycle, is the preparation of a post-closing trial balance. This balance is prepared to prove once again the equality of debits and credits.

Ethics and Club Accounting

In recent years, considerable attention has been devoted to ethics, both in classrooms and boardrooms. Many major corporations have a code of ethics, and their managers are required to sign a statement saying that they will abide by the firm's code of ethics. Failure to follow the code often results in termination. Studies of the codes of ethics in America's largest corporations reveal the following common elements: (1) privacy of communication, (2) conflict of interests, (3) political contributions in the United States, (4) company records, (5) gifts, favors, entertainment, trips, and outings, (6) use of company assets, (7) anti-trust laws, (8) relations with competitors, (9) relations with suppliers, and (10) relations with customers.[5]

In the book *Ethics in Hospitality Management* by Stephen S. J. Hall, the role of ethics in accounting is discussed. The topic is divided into two sections: (1) the impact of ethics on accounting and (2) the marriage of theory and practice. The first section includes several ethical conflicts commonly encountered by hospitality accountants. For example:

Exhibit 14 Mason Club Worksheet

Mason Club
Worksheet
For the month ended December 31, 20X1

Account Title	Trial Balance Debit	Trial Balance Credit	Adjustments Debit	Adjustments Credit	Adjusted Trial Balance Debit	Adjusted Trial Balance Credit	Statement of Activities Debit	Statement of Activities Credit	Statement of Financial Position Debit	Statement of Financial Position Credit
Cash	5000				5000				5000	
Marketable Securities	10000				10000				10000	
Accounts Receivable	8000				8000				8000	
Food Inventory	2500			700 (b)	1800				1800	
Prepaid Insurance	4500			1500 (a)	3000				3000	
Furniture	40000				40000				40000	
Accumulated Depreciation, Furniture		20000		4000 (c)		24000				24000
Equipment	10000				10000				10000	
Accumulated Depreciation, Equipment		5000		1000 (d)		6000				6000
Building	300000				300000				300000	
Accumulated Depreciation, Building		100000		10000 (e)		110000				110000
Land	20000				20000				20000	
Accounts Payable		5000				5000				5000
Notes Payable		5000				5000				5000
Mortgage Payable		100000				100000				100000
Members' Equity		103000				103000				103000
Food Revenue		150000				150000		150000		
Salaries	15000				15000		15000			
Wages	22500		150 (f)		22650		22650			
Payroll Taxes	3000				3000		3000			
Operating Expense	2000				2000		2000			
Office Supplies	1000				1000		1000			
Utilities	5000				5000		5000			
Promotion	500				500		500			
Repairs & Maintenance	9000				9000		9000			
Cost of Food Sold	22000		700 (b)		22700		22700			
Interest Expense	8000				8000		8000			
Insurance Expense		(a)	1500		1500		1500			
Depreciation Expense, Furniture		(c)	4000		4000		4000			
Depreciation Expense, Equipment		(d)	1000		1000		1000			
Depreciation Expense, Building		(e)	10000		10000		10000			
Accrued Wages				150 (f)		150				150
	488000	488000	17350	17350	503150	503150	105350	150000	397800	353150
Increase in Net Assets							44650			44650
							150000	150000	397800	397800

> A management company president, whose incentive compensation is based on a percentage of income before fixed charges, directs that all repair and maintenance items costing more than $500 be capitalized as capital improvements.

Clearly, this practice will result in greater management fees for the management company when revenue expenditures (expenditures that should be expensed) are accounted for as capital expenditures.

The second section under ethics in accounting states that it is unwise to separate ethical theories and practices. Theories of ethical behavior that are applied to situations at home and church should also be practiced in business. In accounting, "creativity" is allowed in certain situations if it is clearly explained. For example, different accounting methods can be used for various purposes, such as using an accelerated depreciation method for tax purposes and the straight-line method of depreciation for book purposes. However, this same "creativity" in accounting can lead to unethical practices if it does not reflect reality or is intended to deceive.

When faced with an ethical dilemma, the following questions can be used to make an appropriate decision:

1. Is the decision legal?

2. Is the decision fair?

3. Does the decision hurt anyone?

4. Have I been honest with those affected?

5. Can I live with my decision?

6. Am I willing to publicize my decision?

7. What if everyone did what I did?

If a decision can pass this seven-step test, it will most likely be considered ethical.

Summary

The major objectives of this chapter have been to provide a brief overview of the club industry and a review of basic accounting procedures and concepts. Businesses in the club industry, although different in several respects from firms in many other industries, maintain their accounts according to the same basic principles. A club executive should therefore be well versed in general accounting and the special accounting considerations of a club operation.

Clubs may experience large fluctuations in demand and often maintain very perishable products. Although a manufacturing firm's inventory may have a shelf life of several years, a club's inventory will perish after a few days and an unsold overnight room can never be recovered. Clubs do not maintain extensive inventories, so labor must be readily available to prepare and serve food and other products.

In order to reflect accurately the operations of these businesses and to ensure consistent recording between periods and properties, club accountants follow generally accepted accounting principles. The cost principle stipulates that items be recorded at the amount for which they are purchased. The continuity of the business unit principle assumes that the organization is a going concern that is not threatened by having to liquidate immediately. The property must be treated as an entity separate from its owners according to the business entity principle. Other requirements are that accountants use objective evidence whenever possible and fully disclose financial items of significance to the users of the financial statements. If these principles are adhered to, the resultant statements will more accurately report the club's operations and financial position.

This chapter also provided a brief overview of basic accounting mechanics. Assets are items owned by the club and have debit balances; liabilities are amounts the club owes and have credit balances. The difference between assets and liabilities is members' equity—the amount of residual claims members have on assets.

Endnotes

1. Based on July 25, 2000, correspondence from Randy Godonowski, Controller, Rumson Country Club in Rumson, New Jersey.

2. These data are drawn from CMAA's web site: www.cmaa.org.

3. The discussion in this section draws on information in Ted E. White and Larry C. Gerstner, *Club Operations and Management*, 2d ed. (New York: Van Nostrand Reinhold, 1991), pp. 5–9; *Club Management Operations*, 4th ed. (Dubuque, Iowa: Kendall/Hunt, 1989), p. 2; and Rocco M. Angelo and Andrew N. Vladimir, *Hospitality Today: An Introduction*, 2d ed. (East Lansing, Mich: Educational Institute of the American Hotel & Motel Association, 1994), p. 207.

4. This text assumes that the reader has read an introductory accounting text or has access to one. *Hospitality Industry Financial Accounting*, 2d ed. by Raymond S. Schmidgall and James W. Damitio (East Lansing, Mich.: Educational Institute of the American Hotel & Motel Association, 1999) contains several chapters that provide detailed coverage of the concepts in this section. Another appropriate text is Raymond Cote's *Understanding Hospitality Accounting I*, 4th ed. (East Lansing, Mich.: Educational Institute of the American Hotel & Motel Association, 1997).

5. W. F. Edmonson, *A Code of Ethics: Do Corporate Executives and Employees Need It?* (Fulton, Miss.: Itawamba Community College Press, 1990).

Key Terms

account—A record containing information regarding a particular type of business transaction.

accounting cycle—Sequence of principal accounting procedures of a fiscal period; analyzing transactions, journal entry, posting to ledger, trial balance, adjustments, preparation of periodic financial statements, account closing, post-closing trial balance.

accrual basis accounting—System of reporting revenues and expenses in the period in which they are considered to have been earned or incurred, regardless of the actual time of collection or payment.

adjusting entries—Entries required at the end of an accounting period to record internal transactions.

assets—Resources available for use by the clubs; that is, anything owned by the business that has monetary value.

balance—The difference between the total debits and total credits of an account.

business entity—The generally accepted accounting principle that requires that a club maintain its own set of accounts that are separate from other financial interests of its members (owners).

cash basis accounting—Reporting of revenues and expenses at the time they are collected or paid.

conservatism principle—The generally accepted accounting principle that requires accounting procedures that recognize expenses as soon as possible, but delay the recognition of revenues until they are ensured. For example, nonrefundable deposits for future services should be recognized as a liability until the service is actually performed.

consistency principle—The generally accepted accounting principle that requires that once an accounting method has been adopted, it should be followed from period to period in the future unless a change in accounting methods is warranted and disclosed.

continuity of the business unit principle—The generally accepted accounting principle that requires the assumption in preparing the accounting records and reports that the business will continue indefinitely and that liquidation is not in prospect—in other words, that the business is a going concern. Also called the going concern principle.

cost principle—The generally accepted accounting principle that requires recording the value of transactions for accounting purposes at the actual transaction price (cost).

credit—Decrease in an asset or increase in a liability or capital, entered on the right side of an account; such amounts are said to be credited to the account.

debit—Increase in an asset or decrease in a liability or capital, entered on the left side of an account; such amounts are said to be debited or charged to the account.

equity clubs—Private clubs owned by their members and governed by boards of directors elected by the members.

financial audit—An independent external audit.

full disclosure—The generally accepted accounting principle that requires that financial statements must provide information on all the significant facts that have a bearing on their interpretation. Types of disclosures include the accounting methods used, changes in the accounting methods, contingent liabilities, events occurring subsequent to the financial statement date, and unusual and nonrecurring items.

fundamental accounting equation—Assets equal liabilities plus members' equity. This equation is a balance to be tested and proven, not a formula to be calculated.

general journal—Record of all accounting transactions.

generally accepted accounting principles—Accounting principles that have become accepted over time through common usage and also through the work of major accounting bodies. They provide a uniform basis for preparing financial statements.

going concern—The generally accepted accounting principle that requires the preparation of accounting records and reports under the assumption that the club will continue indefinitely and that liquidation is not in prospect; also referred to as continuity of the business unit.

journals—Accounting records of business transactions.

ledger—A group of related accounts that constitute a complete unit.

liabilities—Obligations of a business; largely indebtedness related to the expenses incurred in the process of generating income.

matching principle—The generally accepted accounting principle that requires recording expenses in the same period as the revenues to which they relate.

materiality principle—The generally accepted accounting principle that requires that events be recognized and recorded by accounting procedures if they make a difference as determined by some relative standard of comparison. For example, materiality may be established by a rule of thumb which states that an item is recognized if it exceeds x percent of total assets or income.

members' equity—Financial interest of the members of a club; assets minus liabilities.

net assets—For not-for-profit organizations, net assets is the difference between assets and liabilities.

non-equity clubs—Clubs owned by an individual or a corporation, not the members.

objective evidence—The preferred basis of accounting transactions and the resulting accounting records.

permanent accounts—A classification of members' equity accounts that are not closed at the end of an accounting period.

posting—Transferring data entered in a journal to the appropriate account.

specialized journal—A journal used to accelerate the recording of specific kinds of accounting transactions.

temporary accounts—A classification of members' equity accounts that are closed out at the end of each fiscal year; for example, all revenue and expense accounts.

trial balance—Listing and totaling of all the general ledger accounts on a worksheet.

unit of measurement principle—The accounting principle that the monetary values stated in financial statements should represent a stable unit of value so that meaningful comparisons of current and past periods are possible.

Review Questions

1. What are some differences between club operations and manufacturing firms?

2. What is the major use of the general journal?

3. Approximately what percentage of total revenues is labor cost in the club industry?

4. What is the matching principle?

5. How does inflation affect the unit of measurement principle?

6. How do revenues for clubs differ from revenues of firms in other segments of the hospitality industry?

7. What is posting?

8. What are the five types of accounts that are included in the general ledger of all clubs?

9. What is the concept of materiality?

10. What are the six branches of accounting and the major responsibilities of each?

Problems

Problem 1

What is the normal balance of each account listed below?

1. Cash		10.	Mortgage payable
2. Members' equity		11.	Equipment
3. Accounts payable		12.	Food sales
4. Food inventory		13.	Payroll taxes expense
5. Cost of food sold		14.	Accounts receivable

Problem 2

The Williamston Club experienced several cash transactions on July 1, 20X1, as follows:

1. Received cash on account for $3,000.

2. Received cash from sales of July 1, 20X1, for $100.

3. Paid payroll taxes on $450.

4. Purchased a new range costing $6,000 by paying $1,000 and signing a note payable for $5,000 with the supplier.

5. Paid a food supplier $2,000 on account.

Required:

Determine the balance of the cash account at the end of the day. The cash balance at the beginning of the day was $2,000.

Problem 3

Fill in the blanks below with the accounting principle that best applies.

Cost principle	Continuity of the business unit
Business entity	Consistency
Conservatism	Matching
Full disclosure	Unit of measurement
Materiality	Objective evidence

1. A club records accrued wages at the end of the fiscal year because of the _____ principle.

2. A club reduces its inventory values to reflect the market value of its food stocks, which are lower than the original cost, because of the _____ principle.

3. A club does *not* reduce the value of its glassware to liquidation value because of the _____ principle.

4. The cost of ten replacement wastebaskets is expensed rather than recorded as equipment due to the _____ principle.

5. The method of depreciation used is reflected in the financial report because of the _____ principle.

6. When one method of inventory valuation is used at the end of 20X1 and another method is used at the end of 20X2, this violate the _____ principle.

7. A boat dock is recorded at $22,500 (the amount paid) rather than the original contract price of $25,000 because of the _____ principle.

Chapter 2 Outline

Purposes of the Statement of Financial
  Position
Limitations of the Statement of Financial
  Position
Content of the Statement of Financial
  Position
    Current Accounts
    Noncurrent Receivables
    Designated Funds
    Property and Equipment
    Other Assets
    Long-Term Liabilities
    Net Assets
    Footnotes
Statement of Financial Position Analysis
    Horizontal Analysis
    Vertical Analysis
    Base-Year Comparisons

Competencies

1. Explain the purposes and limitations
   of a statement of financial position for
   clubs. (pp. 35–37)

2. Describe the content of a club's
   statement of financial position—assets,
   liabilities, net assets (members' equity),
   and footnotes. (pp. 37–46)

3. Explain how a club's statement of
   financial position can be analyzed
   using horizontal and vertical analysis
   as well as base-year comparisons.
   (pp. 46–50)

2

The Statement of Financial Position

THE STATEMENT OF FINANCIAL POSITION (also called the balance sheet) is a major financial statement prepared for the end of each accounting period. It reflects a balance between a club's assets and claims to its assets (called liabilities) and net assets (members' equity) or owners' equity (for investor-owned clubs). Since the vast majority of clubs are organized as nonprofit, member-owned clubs, "net assets" will be used throughout the chapter to refer to the equity of members in a club's assets. The statement of financial position contains answers to many questions that club managers, members, and creditors may have, such as:

- How much cash was on hand at the end of the period?
- What was the total debt of the club?
- What was the mix of internal and external financing at the end of the period?
- How much was owed to the club by members?
- What amount of taxes was owed to the various governmental tax agencies?
- What was the club's ability to pay its current debt?
- What was the financial strength of the club?
- How much interest do members or owners have in the club's assets?

This chapter addresses the purposes and limitations of the statement of financial position. We will also pay special attention to the format and content of the suggested statement of financial position from the *Uniform System of Financial Reporting for Clubs (USFRC)*.[1] In addition, we will discuss the kinds and purposes of footnotes attached to the statement of financial position. Finally, we will consider techniques for analyzing the financial information contained in a statement of financial position.

Purposes of the Statement of Financial Position

Other major financial statements—the statement of activities and the statement of cash flows—pertain to a period of time. The statement of financial position reflects the financial position of the club's operation—its assets, liabilities, and net assets—on a given date. It is the financial statement that reflects, or tests and proves, the fundamental accounting equation (assets equal liabilities plus net assets).

Club managers, although generally more interested in the statement of activities and related department operations statements, will find a statement of financial position useful for conveying financial information to creditors and members. In addition, management must determine if the statement of financial position reflects to the best extent possible the financial position of the club's operation. For example, many long-term loans specify a required **current ratio** (which is current assets divided by current liabilities). Failure to meet the requirement may result in all long-term debt being reclassified as current and thus due immediately. Since few clubs could raise large sums of cash quickly, bankruptcy could result. Therefore, management must carefully review the statement of financial position to determine that the operation is in compliance. For example, assume that at December 31, 20X1 (year-end), a club has $500,000 of current assets and $260,000 of current liabilities. Further assume that the current ratio requirement in a bank's loan agreement with the club is 2 to 1. At this point, this club's current ratio is 1.9 to 1, determined by dividing $500,000 by $260,000. The required current ratio can be attained simply by taking the appropriate action. In this case, the payment of $20,000 of current liabilities with $20,000 cash results in current assets of $480,000 and current liabilities of $240,000, resulting in a current ratio of 2 to 1.

A club's creditors are interested in the club's ability to pay its current and future obligations. The ability to pay its current obligations is shown, in part, by a comparison of current assets and current liabilities. The ability to pay its future obligations depends, in part, on the relative amounts of long-term financing by club members and creditors. Everything else being the same, the greater the financing from members, the higher the probability that long-term creditors will be paid and the lower the risk that these creditors take in "investing" in the club.

In addition, the statement of financial position reveals a club's liquidity. **Liquidity** measures a club's ability to convert assets to cash. Even when a club's past earnings have been substantial, this does not in itself guarantee that the club will be able to meet its obligations as they become due. The club should have sufficient liquidity to pay its bills.

Analysis of several statements of financial position at the end of several periods will yield trend information that is more valuable than figures at the end of a single period. In addition, comparison of statement of financial position information with projected statement of financial position numbers (when available) will reveal management's ability to meet various financial goals.

Limitations of the Statement of Financial Position

As useful as the statement of financial position is, club members, long-term creditors, and especially managers generally consider it less useful than the statement of activities. Since the statement of financial position is based on the cost principle, it often does not reflect current values of some assets, such as property and equipment. For club operations whose assets are appreciating rather than depreciating, this difference may be significant.

Another limitation of statements of financial position is that they fail to reflect many elements of value to the club. Most important to clubs and other sectors of the hospitality industry are people. Nowhere in the statement of financial position is there a reflection of the human resource investment. Millions of dollars are spent by the thousands of clubs in the club industry in recruiting and training an efficient and highly motivated work force, yet this essential ingredient for successful club operations is not shown as an asset. Other valuable elements not directly shown on the statement of financial position include such things as goodwill, superior location, loyal members, and so on. Understandably, it may be difficult to assign an objective value to these elements. Nevertheless, not only are they critical to a club's success, they are also of significant value. An exception to this is purchased goodwill, which is shown on the statement of financial position. This goodwill results when a purchaser of a club is unable to assign the entire purchase price of an acquisition to the operation's individual assets. The excess of the purchase price over the dollars assigned to the individual assets is labeled "goodwill." For example, if a club costs $3 million, $2 million of that price may be assigned to the building, $500,000 may be assigned to the land, and $300,000 may be assigned to furniture, fixtures, and equipment. The $200,000 difference between the club's cost and the amounts assigned to specific assets is assigned to goodwill. Self-generated goodwill is not shown on the statement of financial position.

Statements of financial position are limited by their static nature; that is, they reflect the financial position for only a moment. They become less useful as they become outdated. Thus, the user of the statement of financial position must be aware that the financial position reflected at year-end may be quite different one month later. For example, a club with $500,000 cash may seem financially strong at year-end, but if it invests most of this cash in equipment two weeks later, its financial flexibility and liquidity are greatly reduced. This situation would generally be known to a user of financial documents only if a statement of financial position and/or other financial statements were available for a date after this investment had occurred.

Finally, the statement of financial position, like much of accounting, is based on judgments; that is, it is *not* exact. Certainly, assets equal liabilities plus members' (or owner's) equity. However, several statement of financial position items are based on estimates. The amounts shown as accounts receivable (net) reflect the estimated amounts to be collected. The amounts shown as inventory reflect the lower of the cost or market value (that is, the lower of original cost and current replacement cost) of the items expected to be sold, and the amount shown as property and equipment reflects the cost less estimated depreciation. In these cases, accountants use estimates to arrive at values. To the degree that these estimates are in error, the statement of financial position items will be wrong.

Content of the Statement of Financial Position

The statement of financial position consists of assets, liabilities, and net assets (sometimes called members' equity on *internal* statements). Simply stated, assets are things owned by the club, liabilities are claims of outsiders to club assets, and net assets are claims of club members (or the club's owner) to assets. Thus, assets must equal (balance) liabilities and net assets. Assets include various accounts

Exhibit 1   Major Elements of the Statement of Financial Position

Assets	Liabilities and Net Assets
Current Assets	Current Liabilities
Noncurrent Assets:	Long-Term Liabilities
Noncurrent Receivables	Net Assets
Designated Funds	
Property and Equipment	
Other Assets	

such as cash, inventory for resale, buildings, and accounts receivable. Liabilities include accounts such as accounts payable, wages payable, and mortgage payable. Net assets include membership certificates (capital stock), designated equity, and undesignated equity. These major elements are generally divided into various classes, as shown in Exhibit 1. While statements of financial position may be organized differently, most clubs follow the order shown in Exhibit 1.

Current Accounts

Under both assets and liabilities is a "current" classification. **Current assets** normally refer to items to be converted to cash or used in club operations within one year or in a normal operating cycle. **Current liabilities** are obligations that are expected to be satisfied either by using current assets or by creating other current liabilities within one year or a normal operating cycle.

Exhibit 2 reflects a normal operating cycle that shows (1) the purchase of inventory for resale and labor to produce goods and services, (2) the sale of goods and services (cash sales, credit sales), and (3) the collection of accounts receivable from the credit sales of goods and services.

A normal operating cycle may be as short as a few weeks for some clubs; for others, however, it may extend over several months. By comparison, quick-service restaurants may have an operating cycle as short as a few days. It is common in the hospitality industry to classify assets as current/noncurrent on the basis of one year rather than on the basis of the normal operating cycle.

Current Assets. Current assets, listed in the order of liquidity, generally consist of cash and cash equivalents, investments, receivables, inventories, prepaid expenses, and other current assets.

Cash and cash equivalents consist of cash in house banks, cash in checking and savings accounts, and certificates of deposit. The exception is cash restricted for the retiring of long-term debt, which should be shown under designated funds. Cash is shown in the statement of financial position at its face value.

Investments are shown as current assets when they are available for conversion to cash. Investments should be carried on the statement of financial position at fair market value (FMV) if FMV is readily determinable. If FMV is not readily determinable, then such investments should be carried at cost.

Exhibit 2   Normal Operating Cycle

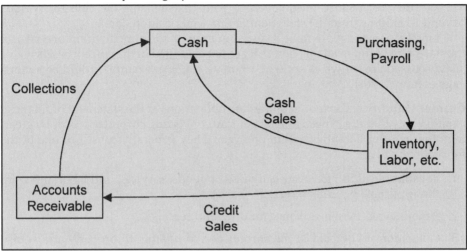

The current asset category of receivables consists of accounts receivable, notes and deferred initiation fees receivable, and other receivables. Accounts receivable consist of the total amount due on the members' open accounts for dues, assessments, and member charges. Notes and deferred initiation fees expected to be collected within one year are reflected in this account. Notes receivable from members and employees should be shown separately. Notes and deferred initiation fees that are not due within one year should be included under noncurrent receivables. Receivables other than those mentioned above are reported as "other." Receivables should be stated at the amount estimated to be collectible. An allowance for "doubtful" accounts—the amount of receivables estimated to be uncollectable—should be subtracted from receivables to provide a net receivables amount.

Inventories of a club consist primarily of merchandise held for resale. If the amount of inventory is significant and the difference between cost and market value is significant, then the inventory should be stated on the balance sheet at the lower of cost or market.

Prepaid expenses represent purchased goods and services to be used by the club within one year. For example, assume that a fire insurance premium of $6,000 affords insurance protection for one year after the transaction. At the date of the expenditure, the $6,000 is classified as prepaid insurance and, thereafter, is amortized by a monthly reduction of $500 ($\frac{1}{12}$ of $6,000), which is shown on the statement of activities as insurance expense. Other prepaid expenses include prepaid rent, prepaid property taxes, prepaid interest, and prepaid maintenance and service contracts.

Prepaid expenses that will benefit the club beyond one year from the statement of financial position date should be classified as "other assets." For example, assume that a three-year fire insurance policy costs $18,000. The entry to record the cash disbursement would be to debit prepaid insurance for $6,000 (the cost of coverage for the next 12 months) and to debit "deferred charges—insurance" for $12,000 (the cost of insurance coverage paid that benefits the club for periods beyond 12 months from the statement of financial position date).

Finally, items that are to be realized in cash or consumed within one year of the statement of financial position that are not classified in the current assets we've just discussed are shown as "other current assets." An example would be a mortgage escrow deposit.

Current Liabilities. Current liabilities are obligations at the statement of financial position date that are expected to be paid by converting current assets or by creating other current liabilities within one year. They generally consist of one of the four following types:

1. Payables resulting from the purchase of goods, services, and labor and from the applicable payroll taxes.

2. Amounts received in advance for dues and rentals.

3. Obligations to be paid in the current period relating to property and equipment purchases or to the reclassification of long-term debt as current.

4. Income taxes payable.

According to the *USFRC*, the major classifications of current liabilities are notes payable, accounts payable, taxes payable and accrued, accrued expenses, current portion of long-term debt, and unearned income. Notes payable include short-term notes that are due within 12 months from the statement of financial position date. Accounts payable include amounts due to creditors for merchandise, services, equipment, or other purchases. Accrued expenses are expenses incurred before the statement of financial position date that are not due until after the statement of financial position date. Current portion of long-term debt includes the principal payments of long-term debt, such as notes and similar liabilities, sinking fund obligations, and the principal portion of capitalized leases due within 12 months.

Obligations to be paid with **restricted cash** (that is, cash that has been deposited in separate accounts, often for the purpose of retiring long-term debt or as a reserve for capital improvements) should be classified as long-term, not current, obligations.

Current liabilities are often compared with current assets. The difference between the two is commonly called **working capital.** The current ratio results from dividing current assets by current liabilities. Many clubs operate successfully with a current ratio approximating 2 to 1, compared with a reasonable current ratio for other segments of the hospitality industry of 1 to 1. The major reason for this difference lies with the relatively low turnover of receivables by clubs as compared with restaurants and lodging operations.

Noncurrent Receivables

Noncurrent receivables include both accounts and notes receivable that are *not* expected to be collected within one year from the statement of financial position date. If any collectibility is uncertain regarding noncurrent receivables, an allowance for doubtful noncurrent receivables should be used (similar to the allowance account for current receivables) and subtracted from total noncurrent receivables to provide net noncurrent receivables.

Designated Funds

Designated funds include both cash and investments that have been designated by the club's board for special purposes. For example, cash may be set aside to pay off long-term debt or for a reserve for capital improvement. Since this cash is not available to pay current bills as they become due, it should be reported on the statement of financial position in the "designated funds" classification. Two particular designated funds often used by clubs are capital improvements and endowment funds. If both of these designated funds are used, they should be shown separately on the statement of financial position. See Exhibit 3 for an example of this presentation.

Property and Equipment

Property and equipment consists of land; buildings; leasehold and leasehold improvements; construction in progress; and furniture, fixtures, and equipment. Property and equipment under capital leases should also be shown in this section of the statement of financial position. With the exception of land, the cost of all property and equipment is written off to expense (depreciation expense) over time due to the matching principle. Depreciation methods used should be disclosed in a footnote to the statement of financial position. On the statement of financial position, property and equipment are shown at cost and are reduced by the related accumulated depreciation and amortization.

Other Assets

Other assets consist of all noncurrent assets not included in the aforementioned categories. Other assets include deferred charges and security deposits. Deferred charges typically are related to financing activities and represent the direct costs of obtaining financing, such as loan fees and bond issuance costs. Such costs are usually amortized over the life of the related financing. The method and period of amortization should be disclosed in notes to the financial statements. Security and similar types of deposits are funds deposited to secure occupancy or utility services (such as telephone, water, electricity, and gas).

Long-Term Liabilities

Long-term liabilities are obligations at the statement of financial position date that are expected to be paid beyond the next 12 months or, if paid in the current year, will be paid from designated funds. Common long-term liabilities consist of notes payable, mortgages payable, bonds payable, capitalized lease obligations, deferred income taxes, and refundable deposits. Any long-term debt to be paid with current assets within the next year is reclassified as current liabilities. Still, long-term debt is often reported on the balance sheet in total, with the amount due within 12 months subtracted as "Less Current Maturities."

Exhibit 3   Sample Statement of Financial Position, Showing Capital Improvement and Endowment Funds

XYZ CLUB
STATEMENT OF FINANCIAL POSITION

October 31, 2000

Assets		Liabilities and Net Assets	
Operating fund		**Operating fund**	
Cash and cash equivalents	$ 102,000	Accounts payable	$ 50,000
Investments	50,000	Taxes payable	20,000
Accounts receivable	200,000	Accrued expenses	30,000
Inventories, at cost	20,000	Unearned income	50,000
Prepaid expenses	50,000	Total operating fund liabilities	150,000
Property & equipment, at cost—net of accumulated depreciation	2,000,000		
Total operating fund assets	2,422,000	**Capital improvement fund**	
		Notes payable	50,000
		Accounts payable	25,000
Assets restricted for capital improvements		Total capital improvement fund liabilities	75,000
Cash and cash equivalents	50,000		
Investments	100,000	Total liabilities	225,000
Total capital improvement fund assets	150,000	**Net assets**	
		Operating fund	2,272,000
Assets restricted for endowments		Capital improvement fund	75,000
Cash and cash equivalents	101,000	Endowment fund	601,000
Investments	500,000	Total net assets	2,948,000
Total endowment fund assets	601,000		
Total assets	$ 3,173,000	Total liabilities and net assets	$ 3,173,000

Adapted from Condon O'Meara McGinty and Donnelly, LLP, *Financial Accounting Standards Board Procurement: What They Mean to Your Club.*

Lease obligations reported as long-term liabilities generally cover several years, while short-term leases are usually expensed when paid. Deferred income taxes pertain to clubs that are subject to income taxes. They result from timing differences in reporting for financial and income tax purposes—that is, the accounting treatment of an item for financial reporting purposes results in a different amount of expense (or revenue) than that used for tax purposes. Generally, the most significant timing difference for clubs relates to depreciation. Clubs that are subject to income taxes generally use the straight-line method for financial report-ing purposes and an accelerated method for income tax purposes. For example, suppose a club subject to income taxes decides to depreciate equipment on a straight-line basis at \$15,000 a year for reporting purposes, and depreciate the same asset \$25,000 for the year using an accelerated depreciation method for tax purposes. If the club's marginal tax rate is 25 percent, then the difference in depreciation expense of \$10,000 (\$25,000 − \$15,000) times 25 percent results in \$2,500 cash saved and must be reported as a noncurrent liability. The book entry to record this savings is as follows:

Income Tax Expense	\$2,500	
Deferred Income Taxes		\$2,500

Refundable deposits are deposits by members that are refundable upon ter-mination of membership in the club.

Net Assets

According to the *USFRC,* the **net assets** section of the statement of financial posi-tion reflects the members' interests in the club's assets. Exhibit 4 (which shows the *USFRC'*s prescribed formats of the assets, liabilities, and net assets sections of the statement of financial position) shows this section as "Members' equity (net assets)." Although either term is appropriate for internal documents, FASB State-ment No. 117 ("Financial Statements of Not-for-Profit Organizations"), which U.S. clubs must follow, specifies that "net assets" be used in the external financial docu-ments of nonprofit clubs. The detail of the net assets section in Exhibit 4 includes membership certificates, designated members' equity, and undesignated mem-bers' equity. Membership certificates include refundable deposits by members for which they receive a certificate entitling them to vote for the governing board of the club. Designated members' equity includes amounts designated by the club's board for restricted purposes; examples include capital improvement assessments and other nonoperating assessments to augment the capital of the club. Undesig-nated members' equity includes equity generated from normal operations of the club which has not been restricted.

Footnotes

The statement of financial position, although packed with financial information, is not complete without the other financial statements (statement of activities and statement of cash flows) and footnotes. Footnotes will be discussed in this section.

The full disclosure principle requires that financial information be sufficient to inform the financial information's users—creditors, club members, and others. This can only be accomplished by providing footnote disclosure in addition to the financial statements. Thus, footnotes are an integral part of a club's financial state-ments. They should contain additional information not presented in the body of the financial statements. They should not contradict or soften the disclosure of the

Exhibit 4   Sample Statement of Financial Position

	Assets		
		Date	
		20X2	20X1
Current assets		$	$
Cash and cash equivalents			
Investments			
Receivables			
Accounts receivable–members			
Notes and deferred initiation fees receivable			
Other		_____	_____
Total			
Less allowance for doubtful accounts		_____	_____
		_____	_____
Inventories			
Food			
Beverages			
Other			
Prepaid expenses			
Insurance			
Licenses and taxes			
Real estate taxes			
Other			
Other current assets		_____	_____
Total current assets		_____	_____
Noncurrent receivables, net of current portion		_____	_____
Designated funds			
Cash			
Investments		_____	_____
		_____	_____
Property and equipment			
Land			
Buildings			
Leasehold and leasehold improvements			
Construction in progress			
Furniture, fixtures, and equipment		_____	_____
Total			
Less accumulated depreciation and amortization		_____	_____
		_____	_____
Other assets			
Deferred charges			
Security deposits			
Other		_____	_____
Total assets		$_____	$_____

Exhibit 4   *(continued)*

Liabilities and Members' Equity (Net Assets)

	Date	
	20X2	20X1
Current liabilities	$	$
Notes payable		
Accounts payable		
Taxes payable and accrued		
Accrued expenses		
Salaries and wages		
Interest		
Other		
Current portion of long-term debt		
Unearned income		
Other current liabilities	_____	_____
Total current liabilities	_____	_____
Long-term debt net of current portion		
Notes payable		
Mortgage or other long-term debt	_____	_____
Total long-term debt	_____	_____
Other noncurrent liabilities		
Deferred income taxes		
Refundable member deposits	_____	_____
Total liabilities	_____	_____
Members' equity (net assets)		
Membership certificates (or capital stock)	_____	_____
Designated equity		
Undesignated equity	_____	_____
Total members' equity	_____	_____
Total liabilities and members' equity	$_____	$_____

---

financial statements, but rather provide needed explanations. The financial statements of clubs generally include, but are not limited to, the following footnotes:

- Brief description of the club (to include services to members and type of ownership)
- Pension and/or deferred compensation plans
- Lease agreements
- Long-term debt agreements
- Contingent liabilities

- Pending lawsuits

- Tax status

- Changes in accounting methods

- Extraordinary items of income or expense

- Long-term contracts

- Definition of cash and cash equivalents

- Description of designated funds

- Concentration of credit risk

- Description of operating funds

- Use of significant estimates in preparing financial statements

Any such relevant information may affect how a financial statement's users interpret that statement. The statement would be incomplete and potentially misleading without all relevant footnotes.

Statement of Financial Position Analysis

The information shown on the statement of financial position is most useful when it is properly analyzed. The analysis of a statement of financial position may include the following:

1. Horizontal analysis (**comparative statements**)

2. Vertical analysis (**common-size statements**)

3. Base-year comparisons

4. Ratio analysis

   In the remainder of this chapter, the first three techniques will be discussed. The fourth technique, ratio analysis, is a complex subject requiring a chapter-length treatment and will not be covered in this chapter.

Horizontal Analysis

Horizontal analysis compares two statements of financial position: the current statement of financial position and the statement of financial position for the end of the previous period. In this analysis, the two statements of financial position are often referred to as **comparative statements of financial** position. This represents the simplest approach to analysis and is essential to the fair reporting of financial information. Often included for management's analysis are the two sets of figures with the changes from one period to the next expressed both in absolute and relative terms.

   Absolute changes show the change in dollars between two periods. For example, assume that cash was $50,000 at the end of year 20X1 and $70,000 at the end of year 20X2. The absolute change is the difference of $20,000.

The relative change (also called the percentage change) is found by dividing the absolute change by the amount for the previous period. The relative change, using the cash example just discussed, is 40 percent ($20,000 ÷ $50,000). The $20,000 absolute change may not seem significant by itself, but viewed as a relative change, it is a 40 percent increase over the previous year.

Examine the comparative statement of financial position for the fictional Mason Country Club found in Exhibit 5. Comparative analysis shows that cash increased by $5,000 in absolute terms and 25 percent in relative terms, while accounts receivable increased by $30,000 and 5.8 percent. Are these increases substantial? A club manager might desire answers to several questions, including (1) Are the amounts of the increases justified? and (2) What measures are being taken to ensure the collection of the accounts receivable? Significant changes in all accounts should be investigated.

Vertical Analysis

Another approach to analyzing a statement of financial position is to reduce category entries to percentages. This **vertical analysis**, often referred to as common-size statement analysis, is accomplished by having total assets equal 100 percent and individual asset categories equal percentages of the total. Likewise, total liabilities and net assets equal 100 percent and individual categories equal percentages of the total.

Common-size statements of financial position permit a comparison of amounts relative to a base within each period. For example, assume that cash at the end of year 20X1 is $50,000 and total assets are $5,000,000. At the end of year 20X2, assume that cash is $70,000 and total assets are $7,000,000. Horizontal analysis shows a $20,000/40 percent increase. But cash at the end of each year is one percent of the total assets ($50,000 ÷ $5,000,000 = $70,000 ÷ $7,000,000). What may first appear to be excessive cash at the end of year 20X2 ($20,000) may not be excessive, since cash is one percent of total assets in both cases. However, only a detailed investigation would resolve whether cash equal to one percent of total assets is required in each case.

Examine the Mason Country Club's common-size statement of financial position (Exhibit 6). Notice that cash of $20,000 at the end of 20X1 is 0.5 percent of total assets, while cash of $25,000 at the end of 20X2 is 0.6 percent of total assets. Management should investigate significant changes to determine if they are reasonable. If the changes are found to be unreasonable, management should attempt to remedy the situation.

Common-size statement comparisons are not limited strictly to internal use. Comparisons may also be made against the financial statements of other clubs, when available, and against industry averages. Common-size figures are helpful in comparing club operations that differ materially in size. For example, assume that a large club operation has current assets of $500,000, while a much smaller club's current assets are $50,000, and that both figures are for the same period. If total assets equal $5,000,000 for the large club and $500,000 for the small club, then both operations have current assets equaling 10 percent of total assets. These

Exhibit 5   Horizontal Analysis: Comparative Statement of Financial Position, Mason Country Club

| | | | Change from 20X1 to 20X2 | |
| | **December 31** | | | |
	20X2	**20X1**	**Amount**	**%**
Assets				
Current assets				
Cash	$ 25,000	$ 20,000	$ 5,000	25.0%
Accounts receivable	550,000	520,000	30,000	5.8
Inventories	35,000	30,000	5,000	16.7
Prepaid expenses	12,000	11,000	1,000	9.1
Total current assets	622,000	581,000	41,000	7.1
Property and equipment				
Land	800,000	800,000	0	0.0
Buildings	3,000,000	3,000,000	0	0.0
Furniture, fixtures, and equipment	1,200,000	1,150,000	50,000	4.3
Total	5,000,000	4,950,000	50,000	1.0
Less accumulated depreciation	1,200,000	1,100,000	100,000	9.1
Net property and equipment	3,800,000	3,850,000	(50,000)	(1.3)
Other assets	3,000	3,000	0	0.0
Total assets	$4,425,000	$4,434,000	($ 9,000)	−0.2%
Liabilities and Net Assets				
Current liabilities				
Accounts payable	$ 325,000	$ 300,000	$ 25,000	8.3%
Taxes payable	75,000	70,000	5,000	7.1
Current portion of long-term debt	100,000	100,000	0	0.0
Total current liabilities	500,000	470,000	30,000	6.4
Long-term debt				
Notes payable	300,000	350,000	(50,000)	(14.3)
Mortgage payable	2,000,000	2,200,000	(200,000)	(9.1)
Total long-term debt	2,300,000	2,550,000	(250,000)	(9.8)
Net assets				
Membership certificates	1,000,000	1,000,000	0	0
Designated equity	200,000	200,000	0	0
Undesignated equity	425,000	214,000	211,000	98.6
Total net assets	1,625,000	1,414,000	211,000	14.9
Total liabilities and net assets	$4,425,000	4,434,000	($ 9,000)	−0.2%

Exhibit 6   Vertical Analysis: Common-Size Statement of Financial Position, Mason Country Club

		Assets			
		December 31		**Common–Size**	
		20X2	**20X1**	**20X2**	**20X1**
Current assets					
Cash	$	25,000	$ 20,000	0.6%	0.5%
Accounts receivable		550,000	520,000	12.4	11.7
Inventories		35,000	30,000	0.8	0.7
Prepaid expenses		12,000	11,000	0.3	0.2
Total current assets		622,000	581,000	14.1	13.1
Property and equipment					
Land		800,000	800,000	18.1	18.0
Buildings		3,000,000	3,000,000	67.8	67.7
Furniture, fixtures, and equipment		1,200,000	1,150,000	27.1	25.9
Total		5,000,000	4,950,000	113.0	111.6
Less accumulated depreciation		1,200,000	1,100,000	27.1	24.8
Net property and equipment		3,800,000	3,850,000	85.9	86.8
Other assets		3,000	3,000	0.1	0.1
Total assets		$4,425,000	$4,434,000	100.0%	100.0%

		Liabilities and Net Assets			
Current liabilities					
Accounts payable	$	325,000	$ 300,000	7.3%	6.8%
Taxes payable		75,000	70,000	1.7	1.6
Current portion of long-term debt		100,000	100,000	2.3	2.3
Total current liabilities		500,000	470,000	11.3	10.6
Long-term debt					
Notes payable		300,000	350,000	6.8	7.9
Mortgage payable		2,000,000	2,200,000	45.2	49.6
Total long-term debt		2,300,000	2,550,000	52.0	57.5
Net assets					
Membership certificates		1,000,000	1,000,000	22.6	22.6
Designated equity		200,000	200,000	4.5	4.5
Undesignated equity		425,000	214,000	9.6	4.8
Total net assets		1,625,000	1,414,000	36.7	31.9
Total liabilities and net assets		$4,425,000	$4,434,000	100.0%	100.0%

Exhibit 7   Example of Base-Year Comparisons

	Current Assets Mason Country Club		
	20X2	**20X1**	**20X0**
Current assets			
Cash	138.9%	111.1%	100.0%
Accounts receivable	110.0%	104.0%	100.0%
Inventories	109.4%	93.8%	100.0%
Prepaid expenses	120.0%	110.0%	100.0%
Total current assets	111.1%	103.8%	100.0%

percentages provide a more meaningful comparison than the dollar amount of the current assets when comparing the financial statements of these two clubs.

Base-Year Comparisons

A third approach to analyzing statements of financial position is **base-year comparisons.** This approach allows a meaningful comparison of the statements of financial position for several periods. A base period is selected as a starting point, and all subsequent periods are compared with the base. Exhibit 7 illustrates the base-year comparisons of the fictional Mason Country Club's current assets for the years 20X0–20X2.

The base-year comparisons of the Mason Country Club use 20X0 as the base. Total current assets for 20X2 are 111.1 percent of the total current assets for 20X0. The user of this analysis is quickly able to determine the changes of current assets over a period of time. For example, cash increased by 38.9 percent from the end of 20X0 to the end of 20X2, while accounts receivable increased by only 10 percent.

Summary

Although the statement of financial position may not play the vital role in management decision making that other financial statements play, it is still an important tool. By examining it, club managers, members, and creditors may determine the financial position of the club at a given point in time. It is used to help determine a club's ability to pay its debts and purchase property and equipment.

The statement of financial position is divided into three major categories: assets, liabilities, and net assets. Assets are the items owned by the club, while liabilities and net assets represent claims to the club's assets. Liabilities are amounts owed to creditors. Net assets (members' equity) represent the residual interest in assets for club members. Both assets and liabilities are divided into current and noncurrent sections. Current assets are cash and other assets that will be converted to cash or used in the property's operations within the next year. Current liabilities represent present obligations that will be paid within one year. The major categories of noncurrent assets include noncurrent receivables, designated funds, property and equipment, and other assets. Long-term liabilities are present obligations expected to be paid beyond the next 12 months from the date of the statement of financial position.

Net assets generally include membership certificates, designated member equity, and undesignated member equity.

As assets are the items owned by the club, and liabilities and net assets are claims to the assets, the relationship involving the three is stated as follows: Assets = Liabilities + Net Assets.

In order to gain more information from the statement of financial position, it is frequently compared to the statement of financial position prepared at the end of the previous period. One tool used is horizontal analysis, which calculates absolute and relative differences between the current period's data and the data from the prior period. Significant differences are generally analyzed. Another type of analysis is vertical analysis, which states all accounts as percentages of either total assets or total liabilities and net assets. Differences between the end results of two periods can then be examined. Alternatively, the statement of financial position figures for a particular club may be compared with data from other clubs or with averages for the club industry as a whole. These comparisons can highlight differences and help management identify areas of concern. A third type of analysis is called base-year comparisons. This approach expresses changes over two or more years as percentages of a base year.

Endnotes

1. *Uniform System of Financial Reporting for Clubs* (Washington, D.C.: Club Managers Association of America, Inc., 1996).

Key Terms

base-year comparison—An analytical tool that allows a meaningful comparison of financial statements for several periods by using a base period as a starting point (set at 100 percent) and comparing all subsequent periods with the base.

common-size statement of financial position—A statement of financial position used in vertical analysis, whose financial entries for two or more periods have been reduced to percentages to facilitate comparisons.

common-size statements—Financial statements used in vertical analysis whose information has been reduced to percentages to facilitate comparisons.

comparative statement of financial position—Statements of financial position from two or more successive periods used in horizontal analysis.

comparative statements—The horizontal analysis of financial statements from the current and previous periods in terms of both absolute and relative variances for each line item.

current assets—Resources of cash and items that will be converted to cash or used in generating income within a year through normal business operations.

current liabilities—Obligations that are due within a year.

current ratio—Ratio of total current assets to total current liabilities expressed as a coverage of so many times; calculated by dividing current assets by current liabilities.

horizontal analysis—Comparing financial statements for two or more accounting periods in terms of both absolute and relative variances for each line item.

liquidity—The ability of a club to meet its short-term (current) obligations by maintaining sufficient cash and/or investments easily convertible to cash.

long-term liabilities—Obligations at the statement of financial position date that are expected to be paid beyond the next 12 months, or, if paid in the next year, they will be paid from restricted funds; also called noncurrent liabilities.

net assets—The financial interest of club members (or the club's owner) in the club, calculated by subtracting club liabilities from club assets.

noncurrent receivables—Accounts and notes receivable that are not expected to be collected within one year from the statement of financial position date.

restricted cash—Cash that has been deposited in separate accounts, often for the purpose of retiring long-term debt.

statement of financial position—A statement of the financial position of a club at a given date, giving the account balances for assets, liabilities, and members' (or owner's) equity.

vertical analysis—Analyzing individual financial statements by reducing financial information to percentages of a whole; for example, statement of financial position assets are expressed as percentages of total assets, and so forth.

working capital—Current assets minus current liabilities.

 # Review Questions

1. How do creditors use the statement of financial position?

2. What are some of the limitations of the statement of financial position?

3. What are assets, liabilities, and net assets? What is the relationship among the three?

4. What is meant by the phrase "the lower of cost or market"? When is it used?

5. What are deferred income taxes? Where are they recorded on the statement of financial position?

 # Problems

Problem 1

Using major classifications from the *USFRC* statement of financial position (see Exhibit 4), classify the following accounts:

Food inventory
Front office computer
Utility deposits
State income taxes payable
Mortgage payable (long-term)

Prepaid insurance
Leased equipment under capital leases
Petty cash
Fairway mower

Designated equity
Banquet deposits
Land
Accrued payroll
Cash—First National Bank

Problem 2

Listed below are asset, liability, and net assets accounts for the Brynica Club as of December 31, 20X1.

Membership certificates	$344,600
Inventories	23,241
Land	111,158
Accumulated depreciation	190,038
Designated equity	115,501
Notes payable (current)	42,611
Undesignated equity	327,137
Cash	8,803
Taxes payable	21,246
Accounts receivable	128,179
Accrued salaries	78,293
Investments (current)	2,934
Prepaid expenses	13,499
Notes receivable (noncurrent)	22,420
Building	1,682,093
Equipment	496,493
Long-term debt (noncurrent)	1,262,930
Accounts payable	58,690
Allowance for doubtful accounts	16,316
Advance deposits – banquets	14,203
Current maturities on long-term debt	25,824
Security deposits	8,569

Required:

Prepare the current assets section of the statement of financial position for the Brynica Club in accordance with the *USFRC* (see Exhibit 4).

Problem 3

Cody Murphy, the manager of the Foxtail Club, a small dinner club, has asked for your help in understanding the statement of financial position for 20X1 and 20X2. He is able to present you with the condensed statement of financial position as follows:

The Foxtail Club
Condensed Statement of Financial Position

December 31, 20X1 and 20X2

	20X1	20X2
Cash	$ 10,000	$ 12,000
Accounts Receivable	26,500	18,500
Investments	10,000	20,000
Equipment	200,000	325,000
Accumulated Depreciation	(20,000)	(64,000)
Total Assets	$ 226,500	$ 311,500
Current Liabilities:		
Accounts Payable	$ 18,000	$ 21,000
Mortgage Payable (current)	5,000	22,000
Dividends Payable	5,000	8,000
Noncurrent Liabilities:		
Mortgage Payable	75,000	110,000
Notes Payable	20,000	0
Membership Certificate	50,000	70,000
Undesignated Equity	53,500	80,500
Total Liabilities and Net Assets	$ 226,500	$ 311,500

Required:

Answer the following questions.

1. What amount of existing debt must be paid during 20X3?

2. What is the total of current assets at the end of 20X2?

3. What is the amount of net working capital at the end of 20X2?

4. How has the change in accounts receivable during 20X2 affected cash at the end of 20X2?

5. What is the net book value of the Foxtail Club's equipment at the end of 20X2?

6. What amount of investments were purchased during 20X2? (Assume no investments were sold during 20X2 and investments are reported at their original cost.)

7. What amount of the mortgage was paid during 20X2?

Chapter 3 Outline

Major Elements of the Statement of
    Activities
Relationship with the Statement of
    Financial Position
Management's Use of Financial Information
Uniform Systems of Accounts
Approach to Club Industry Statements of
    Activities
        Statements for City and Country Clubs
        Departmental Statements
Club Industry Operating Statistics
Analysis of Statements of Activities

Competencies

1. Describe revenues, expenses, gains, and losses as presented on the statement of activities. (p. 58)

2. Describe the contents of a statement of activities as recommended by the *Uniform System of Financial Reporting for Clubs (USFRC)*. (pp. 58–71)

3. Identify the differences between departmental statements of activities prepared for profit centers and those prepared for service centers in a club facility. (pp. 71–72)

4. Discuss information found in and details of club industry operating statistics. (p. 72)

5. Interpret statements of activities using horizontal and vertical analysis as well as base–year comparisons. (pp. 72–78)

3

The Statement of Activities

THE STATEMENT OF ACTIVITIES, also called the statement of earnings, the profit and loss (P&L) statement, the statement of operations, the income statement, and various other titles, reports the success of the club's operations for a period of time. This statement may be prepared on a weekly or monthly basis for management's use and quarterly or annually for members and creditors.

Users of financial statements examine a club's **statements of activities** for answers to many questions, such as:

- How profitable was the club during the period?

- What were the total sales for the period?

- How much was paid for labor?

- What is the relationship between sales and cost of sales?

- How much have sales increased over last year?

- What is the utilities expense for the year and how does it compare with the expense of a year ago?

- How much was spent to maintain the golf course?

- How does the bottom line compare with total sales for the period?

These and many more questions can be answered by reviewing the statements of activities that cover several periods of time. Statements of activities, including statements by individual departments called departmental statements, are generally considered to be the most useful financial statements for management's review of operations. Creditors, especially long-term creditors, find that the statement of activities yields significant information for determining creditworthiness. However, when analyzing the operating results of any entity, a statement of activities should be considered in conjunction with other financial statements as well as with the footnotes to those financial statements.

In this chapter, we will address the major elements of the statement of activities and consider its relationship with the statement of financial position (also called the balance sheet). The uniform system of accounts and the general approach to statements of activities in the club industry will also be discussed. We will provide an in-depth discussion of the contents of the statement of activities, consider the uses of departmental statements and industry operating statistics, and discuss guidelines and techniques for analyzing statements of activities.

Major Elements of the Statement of Activities ——————

The statement of activities reflects the revenues, expenses, gains, and losses for a period of time. **Revenues** represent the inflow of assets, reduction of liabilities, or a combination of both resulting from the sale of goods and services. For a club, revenues generally include but are not limited to dues, food sales, beverage sales, greens fees, room rentals, and interest from investments.

Expenses are defined as the outflow of assets, increase in liabilities, or a combination of both in the production and rendering of goods and services. Expenses generally include cost of goods sold (for example, food and beverages), payroll and related expenses, utilities, insurance, depreciation, and taxes, to list a few.

Gains are defined as increases in assets, reductions in liabilities, or a combination of both resulting from a club's incidental transactions and from all other transactions and events affecting the operation during the period, except those that count as revenues or investments by members. For example, there may be a gain on the sale of equipment. Equipment is used by the club to provide goods and services and, when sold, only the excess proceeds over its net book value (purchase price less accumulated depreciation) are recognized as gain.

Finally, **losses** are defined as decreases in assets, increases in liabilities, or a combination of both resulting from a club's incidental transactions and from other transactions and events affecting the operation during a period, except those that count as expenses. In the equipment example above, if the proceeds were less than the net book value, a loss would occur and would be recorded as "loss on sale of equipment." Another example would be a loss from an act of nature, such as a tornado or hurricane. The loss reported is the reduction of assets less the insurance proceeds received.

In the statement of activities for clubs, revenues are reported separately from gains, and expenses are distinguished from losses. These distinctions are important in determining management's success in operating the club. Management is held accountable primarily for operations (revenues and expenses) and only secondarily (if at all) for gains and losses. Generally, gains and losses are shown near the bottom of the statement of activities.

Relationship with the Statement of Financial Position ——————

The statement of activities covers a period of time, while the statement of financial position is prepared as of the last day of the accounting period. Thus, the statement of activities reflects operations of the club for the period between the dates of two statements of financial position. The result of operations is added to the proper equity account and shown on the statement of financial position at the end of the accounting period.

Management's Use of Financial Information ——————

Although the amount of operating information shown in the statement of activities and accompanying footnotes may be adequate for external users to evaluate the club's operations, management requires considerably more information.

Management also needs this information more frequently than outsiders. In general, the more frequent the need to make decisions, the more frequent the need for financial information. Management's information needs are met, in part, by detailed monthly statements of activities that reflect budget numbers and report performance for the most recent period, the same period a year ago, and year-to-date numbers for both the current and past year.

If any difference between the year-to-date numbers and the originally budgeted numbers is expected, the statements of activities of some clubs also show the latest forecast of results (reforecasting). Management is then able to compare actual results against the most recent forecasts.

Management's need for financial information on a monthly basis may be met, to a large degree, by using a statement of activities and the accompanying departmental statements that are in the format presented in the *Uniform System of Financial Reporting for Clubs (USFRC)*. In addition to the monthly statement of activities, a more frequent major report prepared for management is the daily sales report.

Ultimately, however, club managers require even more information than is provided by daily reports and monthly statements. Exhibit 1 lists various management reports and the frequency, content, comparisons, intended readers, and purpose of each report. Even this list does not include all reports required by the various levels of management in a club. For example, two major financial statements, the statement of financial responsibilities and the statement of cash flows, are absent from the list.

Uniform Systems of Accounts

Uniform systems of accounts are standardized accounting systems prepared by various segments of the hospitality industry.[1] The uniform system for country and city clubs is the *USFRC*. A uniform system of accounts provides a turnkey system for new entrants into an industry by offering detailed information about accounts, classifications, formats, and the different kinds, contents, and uses of financial statements and reports. For example, the *USFRC* contains not only the basic financial statements, but also 16 supplementary departmental operating statements.

A uniform system of accounts also allows for a more reasonable comparison of the operational results of similar operations. When various establishments follow a uniform system of accounts, the differences in accounting among these operations are minimized, thus ensuring comparability.

Standardized accounting systems of country clubs began as early as 1915; however, it was not until 1918 that the Chicago District Golf Association published *Standardized Accounting System for Country Clubs*. In 1932, two officers of the Club Managers Association of America prepared a draft of the suggested classification of accounts for country clubs. A decade later a similar publication was produced for city clubs. In 1954, the *Uniform System of Accounts for Clubs* was released; this publication covered both city and country clubs for the first time. The most recent revision of the uniform system, the *USFRC*, presents model formats of financial statements for both country and city clubs.

Exhibit 1   Management Reports

Report	Frequency	Content	Comparisons	Who Gets It	Purpose
Daily Sales Report	Daily, on a cumulative basis for the month, the year to date.	Food sales by meal period and other revenue by outlet.	To operating plan for prior year results.	Top management	Basis for evaluating the current sales of club.
Summary Report— Flash	Monthly at end of month (prior to monthly financial statement).	Known elements of revenue and direct costs; estimated departmental indirect costs.	To operating plan; to prior year results.	Top management and supervisory personnel responsible for function reported.	Provides immediate information on financial results for rooms, food and beverages, and other.
Cash Flow Analysis	Monthly (and on a revolving 12-month basis).	Receipts and disbursements by time periods.	With cash flow plan for month and for year to date.	Top management.	Predicts availability of cash for operating needs. Provides information on interim financing requirements.
Labor Productivity Analysis	Daily, weekly, monthly.	Dollar cost; manpower hours expended; hours as related to sales and services (covers, rooms occupied, etc.).	To committed hours in the operating plan (standards for amount of work to prior year statistics).	Top management and supervisory personnel.	Labor cost control through informed staffing and scheduling. Helps refine forecasting.
Departmental Analysis	Monthly (early in following month).	Details on main categories of income; same on expense.	To operating plan (month and year to date) and to prior year.	Top management and supervisors by function (e.g., rooms, each food and beverage outlet, other profit centers).	Knowing where business stands, and immediate corrective actions.
Room Rate Analysis	Daily, monthly, year to date.	Actual rates compared to rack rates by rate category or type of room.	To operating plan and to prior year results.	Top management and supervisors of sales.	If goal is not being achieved, analysis of strengths and weaknesses is prompted.
Long-Range Planning	Annually.	5-year projections of revenue and expenses. Operating plan expressed in financial terms.	Prior years.	Top management.	Involves staff in success or failure of enterprise. Injects more realism into plans for property and service modifications.
Exception Reporting	Concurrent with monthly reports and financial statements.	Summary listing of line item variances from predetermined norm.	With operating budgets.	Top management and supervisors responsible for function reported.	Immediate focusing on problem before more detailed statement analysis can be made.
Member History Analysis	At least semi-annually; quarterly or monthly is recommended.	Historical records of corporate business, travel agencies, group bookings.	With previous reports.	Top management and sales.	Gives direction to marketing efforts.
Future Bookings Report	Monthly.	Analysis of reservations and bookings.	With several prior years.	Top management, sales and marketing, department management.	Provides information on changing guest profile. Exposes strong and weak points of facility. Guides (1) sales planning and (2) expansion plans.

  This uniform system of accounts can be adapted for use by large and small clubs. The *USFRC* contains many more accounts and classifications than may be used by a single club. Therefore, each club simply selects the schedules and accounts that are required for its use and ignores the others.

  The *USFRC* is designed to be used at the club level rather than the corporate level of a chain of clubs. The format of the statement of activities is based on **responsibility accounting**. That is, the presentation is organized to focus attention on departmental results such as the food and golf departments. The statements of activities prepared at the corporate level, where more than one club is owned by a club corporation, would probably be considerably different and would include sale of clubs, corporate overhead expenses, and so on, not necessarily shown on an individual club's statement of activities.

Approach to Club Industry Statements of Activities ————————

In many industries, the basic statement of activities format consists of the following:

	Revenues
Less:	Cost of goods sold
Equals:	Gross profit
Less:	Overhead expenses
Equals:	Net income

For wholesale and retail firms, the cost of goods sold is the cost of goods purchased for resale, while for manufacturers it is a combination of labor, raw materials, and overhead expenses incurred in the manufacturing process. The expenses subtracted from gross profit to equal net income consist of all other expenses such as administration and selling expenses, depreciation, and income taxes.

By contrast, the statement of activities format in the *USFRC* approach consists of the following:

	Revenues
Less:	Direct operating expenses
Equals:	Departmental operating income
Less:	Overhead expenses
Equals:	Increase (decrease) in net assets

Direct operating expenses include not only the cost of goods sold, but also the direct labor expense (including payroll and related expenses) and other direct expenses. Direct labor expense is the expense of personnel working in the profit centers, such as the food department and the golf department. Other direct expenses include supplies used by these revenue-producing departments. Therefore, everything else being the same, gross profit would exceed departmental operating income, since direct operating expenses include direct labor and other direct expenses in addition to cost of goods sold.

The statements of activities based on the *USFRC* provide separate reporting by profit center—that is, sales and direct expenses are shown separately for the food department, the beverage department, and so forth. In addition, the overhead expenses are divided among undistributed operating expenses and fixed expenses. The undistributed operating expenses are further detailed on the statement of activities by major service centers such as administrative and general and energy costs. The detail provided by both profit centers and service centers reflects reporting by areas of responsibility. Thus, the *USFRC* statement of activities is useful to managers in the club industry because it is designed to provide the information necessary to evaluate the performance of managers of the club facility by area of responsibility.

Statements for City and Country Clubs

The *USFRC* contains statement of activities formats for both city and country clubs. Further, the *USFRC* also contains statements of activities formatted for providing financial information both to members and to management. The statements formatted for management reflect departmental operations, and they are accompanied by several supporting schedules. Those formatted for members do not reflect departmental operations nor are departmental schedules provided. According to the *USFRC*, the format of these statements is simple and more readily understood by members. Exhibit 2 is the recommended statement for members of city clubs.

Exhibit 3 is the statement of activities in departmental form for a city club. There are four sections, as follows:

- membership income

- clubhouse operating income

- undistributed operating expenses

- fixed expenses and provision for income taxes

The bottom line reflects the results of operations.

Exhibit 4 is the statement of activities in departmental form for a country club. The detailed discussion of a club's statement of activities that follows will focus on this formatted statement of activities. The statement of activities per the *USFRC* (see Exhibit 4) is divided into five major sections: membership income, cost of sports activities, clubhouse operating income, undistributed operating expenses, and the final section, which includes fixed expenses and income tax.

Membership income includes membership dues, initiation fees, and unused food and beverage minimums. Initiation fees are included in membership income when used for normal operations. If initiation fees are designated for capital improvements or the other nonoperating purposes, they should be included under the other support section of the statement of activities that would follow the bottom line, results of operations, shown on Exhibit 4. In all cases, the initiation fees must be shown on the statement of activities. There are a variety of ways clubs account for food and beverage minimums. If the amounts are significant, the *USFRC* recommends such income be reported as membership income. If food and beverage minimums are treated as food and beverage revenues, it should be reported as other income after cost of sales on the food and beverage departmental schedules.

The second section reflects the cost of sports activities. For each sports activity, there is a detailed schedule. The detailed schedule for the golf operations of a country club is shown in Exhibit 5. This schedule reflects income from all activities related to golf, as well as the related expenses. The amount on the bottom line of this schedule, departmental net income (loss), is shown on the statement of

Exhibit 2   Statement of Activities for City Clubs

City Club
Statement of Activities

Period Ended

Income	$
Membership dues	
Initiation fees	
Overnight rooms revenue	
Unused food and beverage minimum	
Food revenue	
Beverage revenue	
Other operating departments	
Other income	
Total income	_____
Operating expenses	
Rooms	
Food	
Beverage	
Other operating departments	
Clubhouse	
Entertainment	
Administrative and general	
Energy costs	_____
Total expenses	_____
Income before capital expenses	_____
Fixed expenses	
Real estate taxes and other municipal charges	
Insurance	
Interest	
Depreciation and amortization	
Total capital expenses	_____
Income (loss) before income taxes	_____
Provision for income taxes	_____
Results of operations	_____
Other support	
Initiation fees	
Capital assessments	
Proceeds from sale of membership certificates	_____
Disbursement for redemption of membership certificates	
Increase (decrease) in members' equity	$ _____
See notes to financial statements	

activities. The reader of the statement of activities would turn to schedule 1-C for the detailed amounts.

A special schedule for golf course maintenance is shown in Exhibit 6. This schedule includes the detailed expenses to maintain the golf course. The two major

Exhibit 3   Statement of Activities (in Departmental Form) for a City Club

Blank City Club
Statement of Activities
(In Departmental Form)

	Schedule	Period Ended
Membership income		$ $
Membership dues		
Initiation fees		
Unused food and beverage minimum		
Total membership income		___ ___
Clubhouse operating income (loss)		
Overnight rooms	2-A	
Beverage	1-B	
Minor operated departments	1-B	
Rentals and miscellaneous income	2-E	___ ___
Total clubhouse operating income (loss)		___ ___
Deduct undistributed operating expenses		
Clubhouse	3-C	
Administrative and general	3-B	
Energy costs		
Total undistributed operating expenses		___ ___
Clubhouse net (loss)		___ ___
Income before fixed expenses		___ ___
Fixed expenses	4-D	
Real estate taxes		
Insurance		
Interest		
Depreciation and amortization		
Total fixed expenses		
Provision for income taxes	4-D	___ ___
Results of operations		___ ___

categories are payroll and related expenses and other expenses. The total golf course maintenance expense is subtracted from golf operations income to equal net golf profit or expense on the statement of activities.

Other items listed in the sports activities section of the statement of activities are racquet sports, swimming pool, and health and fitness. In addition, a separate line should be used to report any other significant sports activity. Total membership income less the net cost of sports activities equals dues available for clubhouse operation and fixed charges available per the statement of activities.

The section titled clubhouse operating income (loss) includes food, beverage, overnight rooms, minor departments, and rentals and miscellaneous income. The detailed schedule for the food department is shown in Exhibit 7. The bottom line of

Exhibit 4　Statement of Activities (in Departmental Form) for a Country Club

Blank Country Club
Statement of Activities
(In Departmental Form)

	Schedule	Period Ended
Membership income	$	$
Membership dues		
Initiation fees		
Unused food and beverage minimum		
Total membership income		
Cost of sports activities		
Golf operations income (loss)	1-C	
Less golf course maintenance	3-A	
Net golf profit (expense)		
Racquet sports	2-B	
Swimming pool	2-C	
Health and fitness	2-D	
Other sports		
Net cost of sports activities		
Dues available for clubhouse operation and fixed charges		
Clubhouse operating income (loss)		
Food	1-A	
Beverage	1-B	
Overnight rooms	2-A	
Minor departments		
Rentals and miscellaneous income	2-E	
Total clubhouse operating income (loss)		
Undistributed operating expenses		
Clubhouse	3-C	
Locker rooms		
Administrative and general	3-B	
Energy costs	4-A	
Total undistributed operating expenses		
Net cost and expenses and clubhouse operations		
Income before fixed expenses		
Fixed expenses	4-D	
Real estate taxes		
Insurance		
Interest		
Depreciation and amortization		
Total fixed expenses		
Income (loss) before income taxes		
Provision for income taxes	4-D	
Results of operations	$	$

Exhibit 5   Detailed Schedule for Golf Operations of a Country Club

Country Club
Golf Operations
(Owned by Club)

Pro-shop sales
Cost of merchandise sold
                Gross profit on sales $ _____
Other income
    Greens fees
    Guest fees
    Trail fees
    Club storage
    Club repair
    Range fees
    Cart rentals
    Service of member owned carts
    Lessons
                Total gross profit and other income   _____
Departmental expenses
    Payroll and related expenses
        Salaries and wages
        Payroll taxes and employee benefits
        Employees' meal
                Total payroll and related expenses   _____
Operating expenses
    Tournament expense
    Cart rentals
    Driving range
    Gasoline and lubricants
    Equipment rental
    Operating supplies
    Other operating expenses
    Repairs and maintenance
                Total other expenses   _____
                Total expenses   _____
Departmental net income (loss) $ _____

this schedule, departmental net income (loss), is shown on the statement of activities for the food department. The reader of the statement of activities must look to the departmental schedule to see the details of the food sales, cost of sales, other income, payroll and related expenses, and other expenses. The details of this supporting schedule will be discussed in greater detail in a later section of this chapter. Similar schedules are provided for other clubhouse profit centers—that is, departments generating sales and incurring expenses, including the beverage and overnight rooms department.

Exhibit 6   Special Schedule for Golf Course Maintenance

> ### Golf Course Maintenance
>
> Departmental expenses $
>   Payroll and related expenses
>   Salaries and wages
>   Payroll taxes and employee benefits
>   Employees' meals   _____
>   Total payroll and related expenses   _____
>
> Other expenses
>   Grounds and greens supplies
>   Fertilizer and topsoil
>   Insecticides
>   Gasoline and lubricants
>   Sand and cinders
>   Seeds, flowers, plants, and shrubs
>   Other supplies
>   Equipment rental
>   Other operating expenses
>   Repairs
>   Course buildings
>   Fences and bridges
>   Mowers, tractors, and trucks
>   Roads and paths
>   Water and drainage systems
>   Uniforms
>   Water and electricity   _____
>   Total other expenses $ _____
> Total golf course maintenance expenses $ _____

The rentals and miscellaneous income includes various other revenues as shown in Exhibit 8. Additional lines should be added for any other significant sources of miscellaneous income.

The fourth section of the statement of activities is undistributed operating expenses. In general, this group of expenses represents operating overhead expenses. These expenses are incurred for the overall operation of the club but are not distributed to profit centers in the clubhouse since they do not generate revenue. The four undistributed operating expenses are clubhouses, locker rooms, administrative and general, and energy costs. The clubhouse expenses include expenses for club rooms in general and various other services to members that are not shown in any other department. Examples include expenses related to the club's lobby area and library. The cost of maintaining the locker rooms is also shown as an undistributed operating expense. The various energy costs are listed

Exhibit 7   Detailed Schedule for Food Department

City or Country Club
Food

Food sales (list revenue by location)	$ _____
Cost of food sold	
Cost of food consumed	
Less credit for employees' meals	
Cost of food sold	_____
Gross profit on food sale	_____
Other income	
Unused minimum	
Service charge	
Dining room rental	
Total other income	_____
Total gross profit and other income	_____
Departmental expenses	
Payroll and related expenses	
Salaries and wages	
Payroll taxes and employee benefits	
Employees' meals	
Total payroll and related expenses	_____
Other expenses	
China, glassware, and silver	
Contract cleaning	
Equipment rental	
Kitchen fuel	
Laundry and dry cleaning	
Licenses and permits	
Linens	
Music and entertainment	
Operating supplies	
Other operating expenses	
Printing and stationery	
Refuse removal	
Repairs and maintenance	
Uniforms	
Total other expenses	_____
Total departmental expenses	_____
Departmental net income (loss)	$ _____

on the energy costs schedule. The administrative and general schedule is shown in Exhibit 9. This schedule includes payroll and related costs to administer the club.

Exhibit 8   Rentals and Miscellaneous Income Schedule

Rentals and Miscellaneous Income

Rentals	$
Stores	
Offices	
Other	_____
Total rentals	_____
Concessions	
Cigar and newsstand	
Guest laundry	
Hair stylists	
Transportation	
Valet	
Total concessions	_____
Commissions	
Concierge services	
Florist	
Parking or garage	
Photography	
Taxicab	
Telefax	
Sundry	
Total commissions	_____
Cash discounts earned	
Dividends	
Interest income	
Miscellaneous	
Salvage	
Vending machines	_____
Total rentals and other income	$ _____

In addition, this schedule reflects the many operating overhead expenses of a club as shown in the second section of this schedule titled "other expenses."

The income before fixed expenses on the statement of activities is determined by adding "dues available for clubhouse operation and fixed charges" and "total clubhouse operating income" and then subtracting "total undistributed operating expenses."

The final major section of the statement of activities is the fixed expenses. These expenses are also referred to as **capacity costs**, as they relate to the physical plant or the capacity to provide goods and services to members. Fixed expenses include real estate taxes, insurance, interest, and depreciation and amortization. Real estate taxes include real estate taxes, personal property taxes, business and occupation taxes, and other taxes (but not income and payroll taxes). Insurance

Exhibit 9   Administrative and General Schedule

	Schedule 3–B
Administrative and General	
Departmental expenses	
Payroll and related expenses	$
Salaries and wages	
Payroll taxes and employee benifits	
Employee's meals	
Total payroll and related expenses	_____
Other expenses	
Club publications	
Credit and collection expenses	
Data processing expense	
Directors and committees	
Donations	
Dues and subscriptions	
Equipment rental	
Insurances	
Internal communicating systems	
Loss and damage	
Management expenses	
Postage	
Printing and stationery	
Professional fees	
Provision for doubtful accounts	
Secretary's office	
Trade associations and conferences	
Travel expense	
Entertainment expense	
Uniforms	
Miscellaneous	_____
Total other expenses	$ _____
Total administrative and general	$ _____

expense is the cost of insuring the facilities, including contents, for damage caused by fire or other catastrophes.

Interest expense is the cost of borrowing money and is based on the amounts borrowed, the interest rate, and the length of time for which the funds are borrowed. Generally, loans are approved by the club's board of directors, as most relate to the physical plant. Thus, interest expense is considered to be a fixed expense.

Depreciation of property and equipment and amortization of other assets are shown on the fixed expenses. The depreciation methods and useful lives of fixed assets are normally disclosed in footnotes. If the club's property is leased, the rent expense should be shown as a fixed expense. Other rentals that should be shown in this section of the statement of activities include the cost of other major items which, if not rented, would be capitalized as fixed assets.

Finally, for clubs that must pay income taxes, the income taxes are subtracted from income before income taxes to determine results of operations.

Departmental Statements

Departmental statements, supplementary to the statement of activities and referred to as **schedules**, provide management with detailed information. The classifications listed in the statement of activities (Exhibits 3 and 4) suggest several schedules and the *USFRC* provides additional schedules for greater detail. Several of these schedules have already been mentioned and illustrated (Exhibits 5–9).

Exhibit 7 illustrates a profit center schedule using the food department. The food department schedule reflects both revenues (sales) and direct expenses. The sales and other income shown on this schedule includes food sales, which should be reported by location according to the *USFRC*, such as dining room, banquets, etc., and other income, which includes unused food minimums, service charges, and dining room rental.

The expenses are subdivided on the food department schedule between "payroll and related expenses" and "other expenses." Under payroll and related expenses, salaries and wages, payroll taxes and employee benefits, and employees' meals, are shown. Employee benefits include both payroll taxes and benefits, such as the cost of health insurance and pensions paid by the club operation and similar benefits. The cost of employee meals is the actual or, in many clubs, the estimated cost of food consumed by employees. The cost of meals is recorded in the appropriate account by department. Failure to account for employee meals properly results in a misstatement of cost of food sold.

Other expenses include direct expenses of the food department. According to the *USFRC*, 14 expense categories are shown under other expenses of the food department. All other food department expenses should be classified in these 14 categories if the *USFRC* is to be followed. When a classification is not used, it should simply be left off of the food department schedule.

In contrast to the profit center schedules prepared for the revenue-producing departments of a club, a service center schedule reports only expenses by area of responsibility. Although these activity areas do not generate revenues, they do provide service to the profit centers and, in some cases, to other service centers. Exhibit 9 illustrates a service center departmental schedule for administrative and general. This schedule contains two major sections—payroll and related expenses and other expenses. The three categories under payroll and related expenses are the same as for the food department. Twenty-one items are listed under other expenses on this schedule.

The number and nature of the supporting schedules reported in a club facility depend on the size and organization of the establishment. A smaller club generally provides fewer services to its members; thus, fewer schedules would be used. Other types of clubs, such as yacht clubs, would tailor schedules to their operations. The key is to use the schedules that communicate relevant financial information to the various management levels of the club.

Club Industry Operating Statistics

Several accounting and consulting firms provide statistical reports covering operating results for the club industry. These reports generally provide median figures for the clubs. The figures provided in these reports should not be viewed as standards but as industry averages.

Statistics are produced for the club industry for the United States by PKF Worldwide. Other firms produce similar statistics for geographical areas of the United States. For example, Condon O'Meara McGinty & Donnelly LLP produces an annual statistical report for clubs in the tri-state area of Connecticut, New York, and New Jersey.

The PKF statistical report for 1998 contains operating details for many areas of clubs including, but not limited to, the following:

- trends in club membership

- 20-year trend of income and expense

- results of operations by geographic divisions and size classification

- restaurant operations by geographic divisions and size classification

- annual operating costs by geographic divisions and size classifications

- golf course expenses by geographic divisions

Several of these reports are presented separately for both country and city clubs.

Exhibits 10 and 11 illustrate these reports. Exhibit 10 contains the results of operations of country clubs by geographic divisions and by size classifications. The results of operations are shown for all clubs and then by four geographic divisions and four size classifications. Also, a blank column is provided for the user to place figures for comparative purposes. A quick review of this exhibit reveals major differences based on geographical location and size of the country club.

A second report from this PKF publication reveals the 20-year trend of income and expense of city clubs as shown in Exhibit 11. It is interesting to note the continuous increase year after year in total revenue per member and the increases and decreases in "available for debt service, capital improvements, etc." year by year.

Statistical reports are most interesting to study each year; however, the reader must remember these reports reflect averages of respondents to their surveys. The figures provided in the reports must be considered as averages and not as benchmarks or standards. Though comparisons will often be made by members of a club's management team and/or the board of directors, the statistical averages are simply that: *averages.*

Analysis of Statements of Activities

The analysis of statements of activities enhances the user's knowledge of a club's operations. This can be accomplished by horizontal analysis, vertical analysis,

Exhibit 10   Annual Operating Costs per Regular Member

	Your Figures	All Country Clubs	Geographic Divisions			Sized (Membership)			
			East	Central	West	Under 400	400 to 550	551 to 700	Over 700
Costs and expenses	$								
Clubroom expenses		$395	$277	$420	$458	$298	$378	$290	$459
Administrative and general		1,095	728	1,136	1,299	1,511	1,201	1,000	1,050
Heat, light, and power		185	125	161	227	201	256	185	152
Repairs and maintenance		186	106	110	254	154	200	162	192
Sports activities — net cost		1,312	707	1,118	1,721	1,871	1,734	1,075	1,173
Other operating expenses		176	88	154	234	235	196	216	144
Total		3,349	2,031	3,099	4,193	4,270	3,965	2,928	3,170
Deduct									
Nonresident and other dues		521	191	441	737	511	423	470	589
Food and beverage net income (loss)		(202)	(38)	(109)	(325)	(276)	(316)	(215)	(138)
All other income		338	133	231	488	274	421	220	359
Total deductions		657	286	563	900	509	528	475	810
Net cost of operations		2,692	1,745	2,536	3,293	3,761	3,437	2,453	2,360
Real estate taxes and insurance		372	254	342	451	476	441	389	324
Net operating cost per regular member		3,064	1,999	2,878	3,744	4,237	3,878	2,842	2,684
Average dues per regular member		3,064	2,089	3,119	3,615	3,718	3,786	2,875	2,752
Balance of dues per regular member available for debt service, capital improvements, etc.	$0	$0	$90	$241	($129)	($519)	($92)	$33	$68

Source: *Trends in the Club Industry—USA Edition 1999* (San Francisco: PKF Consulting, 1999).

Exhibit 11 Income per Member

Year	Source of income per member				Disposition of income per member			Available for debt service capital improvements, etc.
	Membership dues	Food and beverage sales	All other sales and income	Total revenue	Payroll and related cost	All other operating expenses	Total costs and expenses	
1978	363	440	122	925	417	455	872	53
1979	384	478	133	995	447	492	939	56
1980	405	522	150	1,077	483	534	1,017	60
1981	426	592	175	1,193	530	602	1,132	61
1982	465	662	206	1,333	584	677	1,261	72
1983	514	738	223	1,475	647	753	1,400	75
1984	570	767	233	1,570	710	788	1,498	72
1985	604	775	245	1,624	755	825	1,580	44
1986	656	810	270	1,736	819	857	1,676	60
1987	699	840	284	1,823	865	890	1,755	68
1988	741	849	291	1,881	907	926	1,833	48
1989	787	852	304	1,943	952	938	1,890	53
1990	796	895	329	2,020	998	952	1,950	70
1991	892	1,135	243	2,270	1,026	1,174	2,200	70
1992	916	1,137	247	2,300	1,057	1,180	2,237	63
1993	1,000	1,123	389	2,512	1,336	1,104	2,440	72
1994	1,054	1,165	350	2,569	1,263	1,256	2,519	50
1995	1,032	1,187	402	2,621	1,317	1,207	2,524	97
1996	996	1,253	395	2,644	1,249	1,261	2,510	134
1997	1,146	1,384	482	3,012	1,305	1,554	2,859	153

Source: *Trends in the Club Industry—USA Edition 1999* (San Francisco: PKF Consulting, 1999).

Exhibit 12   Comparative Food Department Schedules

Bulldog Club
Comparative Food Department Schedules

	20X1	20X2	Difference $	%
Food sales	$1,100,000	$1,200,000	$100,000	9.09%
Cost of food sold:				
Cost of food consumed	420,000	440,000	20,000	4.76%
Less: Employees' meals	20,000	22,000	2,000	10.00%
Cost of food sold	400,000	418,000	18,000	4.50%
Gross profit on food sales	700,000	782,000	82,000	11.71%
Other income:				
Service charge	100,000	105,000	5,000	5.00%
Dining room rental	50,000	45,000	(5,000)	−10.00%
Total other income	150,000	150,000	0	0.00%
Total gross profit and other income	850,000	932,000	82,000	9.65%
Departmental expenses				
Payroll and related expenses				
Salaries and wages	500,000	550,000	50,000	10.00%
Payroll taxes and empl. benefits	80,000	90,000	10,000	12.50%
Employees' meals	15,000	18,000	3,000	20.00%
Total payroll and related expenses	595,000	658,000	63,000	10.59%
Other expenses				
China, glassware, silver	22,000	24,000	2,000	9.09%
Laundry and dry cleaning	20,000	22,000	2,000	10.00%
Linens	15,000	16,000	1,000	6.67%
Operating supplies	10,000	11,000	1,000	10.00%
Other operating expenses	8,000	9,000	1,000	12.50%
Refuse removal	4,000	4,500	500	12.50%
Repairs and maintenance	5,000	5,500	500	10.00%
Uniforms	2,000	2,200	200	10.00%
Total other expenses	86,000	94,200	8,200	9.53%
Total departmental expenses	681,000	752,200	71,200	10.46%
Departmental net income	$169,000	$179,800	$10,800	6.39%

base-year comparisons, and ratio analysis. Since much less financial information is available to members and creditors than is available to management, their analytical approaches will generally differ.

Horizontal analysis compares statements of activities for two accounting periods in terms of both absolute and relative variances for each line item. The user should investigate any significant differences. Another common comparative analysis approach is to compare the most recent period's operating results with the budget by determining absolute and relative variances.

Exhibit 12 illustrates the horizontal analysis of food department results of the Bulldog Club for years 20X1 and 20X2. In this comparative analysis, 20X1 is considered the base. Because the revenues for 20X2 exceed revenues for 20X1, the dollar difference is shown as positive. If 20X2 revenues had been less than 20X1 revenues, the difference would have been shown as negative. Actual 20X2 expenses increased compared to 20X1, resulting in a positive difference. This should be expected, since as revenues increase, expenses should also increase. If actual 20X2 expenses had decreased compared to 20X1, the differences would have been shown as negative. The percentage differences in this statement are determined by dividing the dollar difference by the base (that is, the 20X1 numbers).

Another approach in analyzing statements of activities is vertical analysis. The product of this analysis is also referred to as common-size statements. These statements result from reducing all amounts to percentages using total sales as a common denominator. Exhibit 13 illustrates two **common-size statements of activities** for the Bulldog Club.

Vertical analysis allows for more reasonable comparisons of two or more periods when the activity for the two periods was at different levels. For example, assume the following:

	20X1	20X2
Food sales	$500,000	$750,000
Cost of food sales	150,000	225,000

A $75,000 increase in cost of sales may at first appear to be excessive. However, vertical analysis reveals the following:

	20X1	20X2
Food sales	100%	100%
Cost of food sales	30%	30%

In this example, vertical analysis suggests that, despite the absolute increase in cost of sales from 20X1 to 20X2, the cost of food sales has remained constant at 30 percent of sales for both years. The relatively large dollar increase from 20X1 to 20X2 can be attributed to the higher level of activity during the 20X2 period rather than to unreasonable increases in the cost of sales.

Vertical analysis allows more meaningful comparisons among clubs that differ substantially in size. This common-size analysis also allows comparisons to industry averages, as discussed previously. However, a note of caution is offered at this point. Industry averages include clubs of all sizes from vastly different locations operating in entirely different markets. The industry averages reflect neither any particular operation nor an average operation, and they certainly do not depict an ideal operation.

A third approach to analyzing statements of activities is base-year comparisons. This approach allows a meaningful comparison of statements of activities for several periods. A base period is selected as a starting point and its figures are assigned a value of 100 percent. All subsequent periods are compared with the base on a percentage basis. Exhibit 14 illustrates the base-year comparison of the Bulldog Club for 20X0–20X2 (with 20X0 as the base). Note that some percentages increase quite dramatically.

A fourth approach to analyzing statements of activities is ratio analysis (which is beyond our scope in this chapter). Ratio analysis gives mathematical expression to a relationship between two figures and is computed by dividing one figure by the other figure. Financial ratios are compared with standards in order to evaluate

Exhibit 13   Common-Size Food Department Schedules

Bulldog Club
Common-Size Food Department Schedules

	20X1	20X2	Percentages 20X1	Percentages 20X2
Total Sales and Income	$ 1,250,000	$ 1,350,000	100.00%	100.00%
Food sales	$ 1,100,000	$ 1,200,000	88.00%	88.89%
Cost of food sold:				
Cost of food consumed	420,000	440,000	33.60%	32.59%
Less: Employees' meals	20,000	22,000	1.60%	1.63%
Cost of food sold	400,000	418,000	32.00%	30.96%
Gross profit on food sales	700,000	782,000	56.00%	57.93%
Other income:				
Service charge	100,000	105,000	8.00%	7.78%
Dining room rental	50,000	45,000	4.00%	3.33%
Total other income	150,000	150,000	12.00%	11.11%
Total gross profit and other income	850,000	932,000	68.00%	69.04%
Departmental expenses				
Payroll and related expenses				
Salaries and wages	500,000	550,000	40.00%	40.74%
Payroll taxes and empl. benefits	80,000	90,000	6.40%	6.67%
Employees' meals	15,000	18,000	1.20%	1.33%
Total payroll and related expenses	595,000	658,000	47.60%	48.74%
Other expenses				
China, glassware, silver	22,000	24,000	1.76%	1.78%
Laundry and dry cleaning	20,000	22,000	1.60%	1.63%
Linens	15,000	16,000	1.20%	1.19%
Operating supplies	10,000	11,000	0.80%	0.81%
Other operating expenses	8,000	9,000	0.64%	0.67%
Refuse removal	4,000	4,500	0.32%	0.33%
Repairs and maintenance	5,000	5,500	0.40%	0.41%
Uniforms	2,000	2,200	0.16%	0.16%
Total other expenses	86,000	94,200	6.88%	6.98%
Total departmental expenses	681,000	752,200	54.48%	55.72%
Departmental net income	$ 169,000	$ 179,800	13.52%	13.32%

the financial condition of a club operation. Since vertical analysis is a subset of ratio analysis, there is considerable overlap between these two approaches.

Summary

The statement of activities, complete with all departmental statements, is generally considered the most useful financial statement for management. It highlights the important financial aspects of a club's operations over a period of time. The statement of activities shows four major elements: revenues, expenses, gains, and losses. Revenues (increases in assets or decreases in liability accounts) and expenses (decreases in assets or increases in liability accounts) are directly related

Exhibit 14   Base-Year Comparison—Food Department

	20X0	20X1	20X2
	Bulldog Club **Base-Year Comparisons** **Food Department**		
Food Sales	100.0%	110.0%	120.0%
Cost of food sold:			
Cost of food consumed	100.0%	107.7%	112.8%
Less: Employees' meals	100.0%	111.1%	122.2%
Cost of food sold	100.0%	107.5%	112.4%
Gross profit on food sales	100.0%	111.5%	124.5%
Other income:			
Service charge	100.0%	105.3%	110.5%
Dining room rental	100.0%	111.1%	100.0%
Total other income	100.0%	107.1%	107.1%
Total gross profit and other income	100.0%	110.7%	121.4%
Departmental expenses			
Payroll and related expenses			
Salaries and wages	100.0%	106.4%	117.0%
Payroll taxes and employee benefits	100.0%	106.7%	120.0%
Employees' meals	100.0%	115.4%	138.5%
Total payroll and related expenses	100.0%	106.6%	117.9%
Other expenses			
China, glassware, silver	100.0%	115.8%	126.3%
Laundry and dry cleaning	100.0%	105.3%	115.8%
Linens	100.0%	107.1%	114.3%
Operating supplies	100.0%	111.1%	122.2%
Other operating expenses	100.0%	106.7%	120.0%
Refuse removal	100.0%	105.3%	118.4%
Repairs and maintenance	100.0%	111.1%	122.2%
Uniforms	100.0%	111.1%	122.2%
Total other expenses	100.0%	109.4%	119.8%
Total departmental expenses	100.0%	107.0%	118.2%
Departmental net income	100.0%	128.6%	136.8%

to operations, while gains and losses result from transactions incidental to the club's major operations.

In order to standardize statements of activities within the club industry, the original *Uniform System of Accounts for Clubs* was written in the 1950s. Since then, there have been changes and revisions, the most recent being the *Uniform System of Financial Reporting for Clubs* published in 1996. By using an accounting system based on a uniform system of accounts, the management of a new club has a turn-key accounting system for a complete and systematic accounting of the club's operations.

In order to enhance the usefulness of the statement of activities, the format set up by the *USFRC* for country clubs includes statements of departmental income showing the membership income, the cost of sports activities, and the clubhouse operating departments. These operating departments show revenues produced by each profit center and subtract from each the corresponding direct operating expenses. Included in the direct operating expenses are not only the cost of goods sold but also the direct payroll and other direct expenses.

Next, undistributed operating expenses, which consist of four cost categories—administrative and general expenses, clubhouse, locker rooms, and energy costs—must be subtracted to determine "income before fixed expenses." This is followed by fixed expenses, which include rent, property taxes, insurance, interest, depreciation, and amortization. Next, income taxes, if applicable, are subtracted to determine the results of operations.

As a supplement to the statement of activities, several departmental schedules should be presented. These offer management additional insight into the operation of each department. The number of schedules necessary depends on the complexity of the club; the more centers of activity operated, the more supplemental statements should be presented. These departmental statements can be very useful for management. First, they can be used to compare the club's operations with industry averages, prior performance, and, most important, budgeted standards or goals. Also, the relative profitability of various departments can be compared.

Managers can use four major methods to analyze the statement of activities and the related schedules. The first method is horizontal analysis, which considers both the relative and absolute changes in the statement of activities between two periods and/or between the budgeted and actual figures. Any major variances exceeding levels predefined by management can be further investigated to determine their causes. The next type of analysis is vertical analysis, which reduces all items to a percentage of sales. These percentages, often referred to as common-size statements, can then be used to compare the results of the club's operations with those of other clubs or with industry standards. Again, any significant differences should be studied. The third method is base-year comparisons, in which two or more years are compared on a percentage basis with the base year set at 100 percent. The final method, ratio analysis, gives mathematical expression to a relationship between two figures and is computed by dividing one figure by the other figure. Financial ratios are compared with standards in order to evaluate the financial condition of a club.

Endnotes

1. Uniform systems of accounts are available as follows:

    Uniform System of Financial Reporting for Clubs (Washington, D.C.: Club Managers Association of America, 1996).

    Uniform System of Accounts for the Health, Racquet, and Sportsclub Industry (Lansing, Mich.: Educational Institute of the American Hotel & Motel Association, 1998).

    Uniform System of Accounts for the Lodging Industry, 9th rev. ed. (East Lansing, Mich.: Educational Institute of the American Hotel & Motel Association, 1996).

Uniform System of Accounts for Restaurants (Washington, D.C.: National Restaurant Association, 1996).

Key Terms

capacity costs—Fixed charges relating to the physical plant or the capacity to provide goods and services to members.

common-size statements of activities—Statements of activities used in vertical analysis whose information has been reduced to percentages to facilitate comparisons.

departmental statements (schedules)—Supplements to the statement of activities that provide management with detailed financial information for each profit center and service center.

expenses—Costs incurred in providing the goods and services offered.

gain—An increase in assets, a reduction in liabilities, or a combination of both resulting from incidental transactions and from all other transactions and events affecting the operation during the period, except those that count as revenues or investments by members.

loss—A decrease in assets, an increase in liabilities, or a combination of both resulting from incidental transactions and from other transactions and events affecting the operation during a period, except those that count as expenses.

responsibility accounting—The organization of accounting information (as on a statement of activities) that focuses attention on departmental results.

revenues—The inflow of assets, reduction of liabilities, or a combination of both resulting from the sale of goods and services.

schedules—See departmental statements.

statement of activities—A report on the profitability of operations, including sales and expenses incurred in generating the revenues for the period of time covered by the statement.

uniform systems of accounts—Standardized accounting systems prepared by various segments of the hospitality industry offering detailed information about accounts, classifications, formats, the different kinds, contents, and uses of financial statements and reports, and other useful information.

Review Questions

1. What are the major differences between the statement of activities and the statement of financial position?

2. Why are members interested in the statement of activities?

3. What are the major differences between a revenue and a gain?

4. What are three examples of direct operating expenses for the food department?

5. How is the cost of food sold determined?

6. What are the advantages of a uniform system of accounts?

7. What detailed expenses are included in the administrative and general and energy costs of the statement of activities?

8. Why are supplemental statements valuable to management?

9. What techniques are useful in analyzing statements of activities?

 **Problems** ──

Problem 1

The Lafayette Country Club sold two pieces of equipment during 20X2. Relevant information is as follows:

1. Sale of range
   Selling price = $500
   Original cost = $3,000
   Accumulated depreciation = $2,700

2. Sale of van
   Selling price = $3,500
   Original cost = $20,000
   Accumulated depreciation = $15,000

Required:

Determine the gain or loss on the sale of each piece of equipment.

Problem 2

Marita Lo, the general manager of the MaLo Club, has requested your assistance in determining some monthly expenses. She provides you with the following information.

	Food	Beverages
Beginning inventory 1/1	$ 8,000	$ 3,000
Ending inventory 1/31	10,000	3,500
Purchases	40,000	20,000
Employee meals	500	———
Food transfers to beverage department	300	———

Required:

Determine the following:

1. Cost of food used

2. Cost of food sold

3. Cost of beverages sold

Problem 3

Selected accounts and their year-end balances of the food department for the Wilson Club are as follows:

Food sales	$1,345,000	
China and glassware	18,500	
Laundry	19,200	
Linen	16,300	
Salaries	520,000	
Operating supplies	12,000	
Food inventory 1/1/X1	22,000	
Food purchases	400,000	
Service charges	150,000	
Payroll taxes	45,000	
Employees' meals	60,000	*
Employees' meals	30,000	**
Employee benefits	80,000	***
Other operating expenses	10,000	
Uniforms	2,000	
Repairs and maintenance	7,000	
Refuse removal	5,000	

Required:

Prepare the food department schedule for 20X1. The food inventory on December 31, 20X1 was $24,000.

*For all club employees.
**For only the food department staff.
***This amount does *not* include employee meals.

Chapter 4 Outline

The Purpose of the Statement of Cash
Flows
    The SCF in Relation to Other
        Financial Statements
Classification of Cash Flows
Conversion of Accrual Income to Net Cash
Flows from Operations
    Direct and Indirect Methods
Preparing the SCF
    Step 1: Determine Net Cash Flows
        from Operating Activities
    Step 2: Determine Net Cash Flows
        from Investing Activities
    Step 3: Determine Net Cash Flows
        from Financing Activities
    Step 4: Present Cash Flows by Activity
Analysis of Statements of Cash Flows

Competencies

1. Explain the purpose of the statement
   of cash flows and describe how it is
   used by club managers. (pp. 85–87)

2. Identify cash flows as reported on the
   statement of cash flows in terms of
   operating activities, investing
   activities, and financing activities.
   (pp. 87–89)

3. Explain the direct and indirect
   methods of converting net income to
   net cash flow from operations.
   (pp. 89–92)

4. Describe the four steps involved in
   preparing a statement of cash flows.
   (pp. 92–100)

5. Identify issues involved in the analysis
   of statements of cash flows.
   (pp. 100–101)

4

The Statement of Cash Flows

Traditionally, the principal financial statements used by club operators have been the statement of activities and the statement of financial position. The statement of activities reflects the results of operations for the accounting period. The statement of financial position shows the financial position of the business at the end of the accounting period; that is, the assets and liabilities and net assets of the club. Although these statements provide extensive financial information, they do not provide answers to such questions as:

- How much cash was provided by operations?

- What amount of property and equipment was purchased during the year?

- How much long-term debt was borrowed during the year?

- What amount of funds was raised through the sale of membership certificates?

- How much was invested in long-term investments during the year?

The **statement of cash flows (SCF)** is designed to answer these questions and many more. The Financial Accounting Standards Board (FASB), which is the current accounting rule-making body, has mandated that the SCF be included with the other financial statements issued by profit-oriented business to external users; with the issuance of Statement No. 117, the FASB now also requires not-for-profit organizations to issue a statement of cash flows.

Our discussion will address the definition of cash, the relationship of the SCF to other financial statements, the purposes and uses of the SCF, a classification of cash flows, alternative formats that may be used for the SCF, and a four-step approach for preparing the SCF.

The Purpose of the Statement of Cash Flows

The statement of cash flows shows the effects on cash of a club's operating, investing, and financing activities for the accounting period. It explains the change in cash for the accounting period; that is, if cash increases by $5,000 from January 1, 20X1 (the beginning of the accounting period), to December 31, 20X1 (the end of the accounting period), the SCF will reflect the increase in the sum of cash from the club's various activities.

For purposes of this statement, cash is defined to include both cash and cash equivalents. **Cash equivalents** are short-term, highly liquid investments such as U.S. Treasury bills and money market accounts. Clubs use cash equivalents for investing funds temporarily not needed for operating purposes. Generally, these short-term investments are made for 90 days or less. Since cash and cash equivalents are considered the same, transfers between cash and cash equivalents are not considered cash receipts or cash disbursements for SCF purposes.

The SCF provides relevant information regarding the cash receipts and disbursements of a club to help users (investors, creditors, members, managers, officers, and others) to:

1. Assess the club's ability to generate positive future net cash flows. Although users of financial statements are less interested in the past than in the future, many users, especially external users, must rely on historical financial information to assess an operation's future abilities. Thus, the financial creditor interested in future cash payments will review the SCF to determine past sources and uses of cash to evaluate the club's ability to make its mortgage and/or loan payments.

2. Assess the club's ability to meet its obligations. Users of financial statements want to determine the club's ability to pay its bills as they come due. If a club has little likelihood of being able to pay its bills, then suppliers will most likely not be interested in selling the club their goods and services.

3. Assess the difference between the club's increase in net assets, as shown on the statement of activities, and cash receipts and disbursements. The SCF allows a user to quickly determine the major net sources of cash and how much relates to the club's operations. Creditors and other users generally prefer clubs that are able to generate cash from operations (that is, from their primary purpose for operating), as opposed to those generating cash solely from financing and investing activities (that is, activities that are incidental to the primary purpose).

4. Assess the effect of both cash and noncash investing and financing during the accounting period. Investing activities relate to the acquisition and disposition of noncurrent assets, such as property and equipment. Financing activities relate to the borrowing and payment of long-term debt and the sale and purchase of membership certificates. Noncash activities include such transactions as the acquisition of a piece of equipment in exchange for long-term debt.

The three major user groups of the SCF are management (internal), members, and creditors (external). Management may use the SCF to (1) assess the club's liquidity, (2) assess its financial flexibility, and (3) plan investing and financing needs. Members and creditors will most likely use the SCF to assess the club's ability to pay its bills as they come due and its need for additional financing, including borrowing debt.

The SCF in Relation to Other Financial Statements

The relationship of the SCF to other financial statements is shown in Exhibit 1. The statement of activities reflects results of operations and reconciles the members' equity accounts of two successive statements of financial position. The change in net assets on the statement of activities is transferred to the members' equity when

Exhibit 1   Relationship of SCF to Other Financial Statements

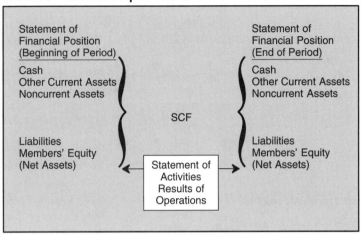

the temporary accounts (revenues and expenses) are closed at the end of the accounting period. In addition, the change in net assets is shown on the SCF when the SCF is prepared using the indirect approach (discussed later in this chapter). Finally, the SCF indirectly reconciles most accounts other than cash on the statement of financial position by showing the sources and uses of cash.

Classification of Cash Flows

The SCF classifies cash receipts and disbursements as operating, investing, and financing activities. Both **cash inflows** and **cash outflows** are included within each category. Exhibit 2 presents classifications of cash flows under the various activities, which are further described below:

- **Operating Activities:** This category includes cash transactions related to revenues and expenses. Revenues (on an accrual basis) include membership dues; sales of food, beverages, and other goods and services to club members; as well as interest and dividend income. Collected revenues are cash inflows. Expenses (an accrual basis) are for operational cash expenditures, including payments for salaries, wages, taxes, supplies, and so forth. Interest expense is also included as an operation's cash outflow. The payment of expenses uses cash, resulting in cash outflows.

- **Investing Activities:** These activities relate primarily to cash flows from the acquisition and disposal of all noncurrent assets, especially property, equipment, and investments. Also included are cash flows from the purchase and disposal of marketable securities (short-term investments other than cash equivalents).

- **Financing Activities:** These activities relate to cash flows from the issuance and retirement of debt and the issuance and repurchase of membership certification. Cash inflows include cash received from issues of stock and both

Exhibit 2   Classification of Cash Flows

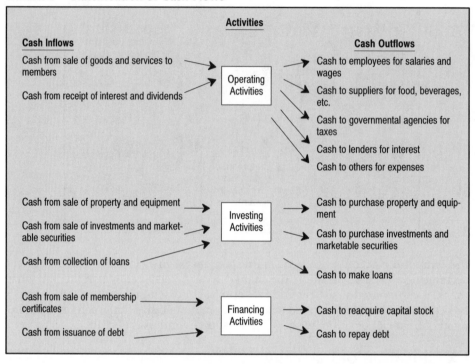

short-term and long-term borrowing. Cash outflows include repayments of loans (although the interest expense portion of the debt payment is an operating activity) and payments to members for any repurchase of stocks. Payments of accounts payable, taxes payable, and the various accrued expenses—such as wages payable—are not payments of loans under financing activities, but are classified as cash outflows under operating activities.

Finally, clubs engage in noncash investing and financing activities, such as the exchange of long-term debt for equipment. Since this represents only an exchange, no cash transaction has occurred. These noncash activities, therefore, are not included on the SCF in any of the three categories described above. However, since a major purpose of the SCF is to reflect all financing and investing activities, and since these activities will affect future cash flows, they must be disclosed on a separate schedule of noncash transactions to the SCF. Thus, the user of financial information is provided with a complete presentation of investing and financing activities, both cash and noncash.

The basic format of the SCF is shown in Exhibit 3. Generally, cash flows from operating activities are shown first. The indirect or direct approaches (to be discussed later) may be used to show cash flows from operating activities. Cash flows from investing and financing activities follow. Individual cash outflows and inflows are shown in each section. For example, long-term debt may increase by $100,000 due to the payment of $50,000 and subsequent borrowing of $150,000.

Exhibit 3   Basic Format of the SCF

Cash Flows from Operating Activities	$XX
(direct or indirect approaches may be used)	
Cash Flows from Investing Activities	XX
(list cash inflows and outflows)	
Cash Flows from Financing Activities	
(list cash inflows and outflows)	XX
Net Increase (Decrease) in Cash	XX
Cash at the beginning of the period	XX
Cash at the end of the period	$XX
Schedule of Noncash Investing and Financing Transactions	
List individual transactions $XX	

Each cash flow should be shown gross rather than netting the two flows. Finally, as stated above, a supplementary schedule of noncash investing and financing activities to the SCF must be included.

Conversion of Accrual Income to Net Cash Flows from Operations

A major purpose of the SCF is to show net cash flows from operations. The statement of activities is prepared on an **accrual basis**; that is, revenues are recorded when earned, not when cash is received from members, and expenses are recorded when incurred, not necessarily when cash is disbursed. Consequently, there may be little correlation between the results of operations (change in net assets) and cash flow. Consider the hypothetical Wales Club, which had $2,000,000 revenues for 20X1. Its accounts receivable (AR) from members totaled $100,000 at the beginning of the year and $110,000 at the end of the year, for an increase of $10,000. The cash received from sales during 20X1 is determined as follows:

$$\text{Cash receipts from sales} = \frac{\text{Revenue} - \text{increase in AR}}{or \quad + \quad \text{decrease in AR}}$$

$$= \$2,000,000 - \$10,000$$

$$= \$1,990,000$$

Thus, even though the Wales Club had revenues of $2,000,000, as reported on its income statement, it would show cash receipts from sales on its SCF as $1,990,000.

Direct and Indirect Methods

There are two methods for converting the increase in net assets as shown on the statement of activities to net cash flow from operations: direct and indirect. The **direct method** shows cash receipts from revenues and cash disbursements for expenses. This method requires that each item on the statement of activities be converted from an accrual basis to a cash basis, as were the revenues of the Wales Club above. Another example of this conversion process for the Wales Club is payroll expense. Assume that the Wales Club reported $1,000,000 as payroll expense for 20X1, and its statement of financial position's accrued payroll (AP) account showed $50,000 at the beginning of the year and $60,000 at the end of the year, for an increase of $10,000. Its cash disbursements for payroll for 20X1 is determined as follows:

$$
\begin{aligned}
\text{Cash Disbursement for Payroll Expense} \quad &= \quad \text{Payroll Expense} \quad \begin{matrix} - \\ or \quad + \end{matrix} \quad \begin{matrix} \text{increase in Accrued Payroll} \\ \text{decrease in Accrued Payroll} \end{matrix} \\
&= \quad \$1,000,000 - \$10,000 \\
&= \quad \underline{\underline{\$990,000}}
\end{aligned}
$$

So, even though payroll expense for the year totaled $1,000,000, as shown on the statement of activities, only $990,000 was disbursed during the year.

Some expenses shown on the statement of activities do not involve any direct cash disbursement and are simply ignored when using the direct method. For example, depreciation expense is only an adjustment to help match expenses to revenues; it does not involve any cash. The same approach is taken for amortization expense and gains and losses on the sale of property and equipment. The basic formats of cash flows from the operating activities section of the SCF for both the direct and indirect methods are shown in Exhibit 4.

The FASB prefers the direct approach. However, most clubs use the indirect method because the information needed to prepare it is more readily available than that needed for using the direct method. For that reason, the major focus in this chapter will be the indirect method.

The **indirect method** for determining net cash flows from operations starts with the change in net assets from the statement of activities. The increase/decrease in net assets is then adjusted for noncash items included on the statement of activities. Depreciation is the most common noncash expense deducted to determine the change in net assets. Therefore, since depreciation is subtracted to compute the change in net assets on the statement of activities, it is added back to the change in net assets to compute net cash flows from operating activities. Other items on the statement of activities that must be added or subtracted include amortization expense and gains and losses on the sale of noncurrent assets and marketable securities.

To illustrate the add back of a loss on the sale of investments, assume that the Wales Club sold a parcel of undeveloped land (an investment) in 20X1 for $200,000 that originally cost $250,000. The journal entry to record the sale was as follows:

Cash	$200,000	
Loss on sale of investments	50,000	
Investment in land		$250,000

Exhibit 4   Basic Formats of the Net Cash Flow from Operating Activities Sections

Operating Activities		
Direct Method		
Cash Flows from Operating Activities:		
Cash receipts from revenues		$ XXX
Interest and dividends received		XXX
Total		XXX
Cash Disbursements for:		
Payroll	$ XXX	
Purchases of inventory	XXX	
Other expenses	XXX	
Interest expense	XXX	
Income taxes	XXX	XXX
Net Cash Flows from Operating Activities		$ XXX
Indirect Method		
Cash Flows from Operating Activities:		
Increase (Decrease) in Net Assets		$ XXX
Adjustments to reconcile increase (decrease) in net assets to net cash flows from operating activities:		
Depreciation expense	$ XXX	
Gain on sale of property	(XXX)	
Loss on sale of investments	XXX	
Increase in accounts receivable	(XXX)	
Decrease in inventories	XXX	
.		
.		
.		
Increase in accrued payroll	XXX	XXX
Net Cash Flows from Operating Activities		$ XXX

The $200,000 of cash inflow will be shown as an investing activity on the SCF; however, the loss on sale of investments of $50,000 was included on the statement of activities in determining the change in net assets. Since it was subtracted in determining the Wales Club's change in net assets and it did not use cash, it must be added back to the change in net assets to determine the net cash flows from operating activities for the SCF.

In addition, in order to determine the net cash flows from operating activities using the indirect method, the Wales Club's change in net assets must be adjusted for revenues that were recorded but which members did not pay for during 20X1. This adjustment is accomplished by subtracting the $10,000 increase in accounts receivable from the increase in net assets on the SCF (as discussed previously).

There are several similar adjustments that must be made using the indirect method, which will be discussed later in this chapter.

Regardless of the method used, the result will show the same amount of net cash provided (or used) by operating activities. The FASB requires that clubs using the indirect method report the amount of interest expense and taxes paid in separate disclosures either directly on the SCF or in footnotes to the financial statements.

Preparing the SCF

The principal sources of information needed for preparing the SCF are the statement of activities, the statement of members' equity, and two successive statements of financial position from the beginning and end of the accounting period. In addition, details of transactions affecting any change in noncurrent statement of financial position accounts must be reviewed. For example, if a comparison of two successive statements of financial position shows the building account has increased by $5,000,000, the account must be analyzed to determine the reason(s) for the change. Simply reflecting the net change of $5,000,000 on the SCF is generally not acceptable.

To prepare the SCF:

1. Determine net cash flows from operating activities.

2. Determine net cash flows from investing activities.

3. Determine net cash flows from financing activities.

4. Present cash flows by activity on the SCF.

Exhibits 5 and 6 show a statement of financial position and a condensed statement of activities and statement of members' equity for the Sample Club, respectively. These will be used to illustrate this four-step approach. The preparation of the SCF is illustrated using the indirect method for showing net cash flows from operating activities.

Step 1: Determine Net Cash Flows from Operating Activities

To determine the net cash flow from operating activities using the indirect method, we focus first on the statement of activities by starting with the increase in net assets of $500,000. Next, we need to adjust the increase in net assets for items on the statement of activities that did not provide or use cash. In particular, consider depreciation expense and the gain on the sale of the investment. Since depreciation was subtracted on the statement of activities to determine the increase in net assets, it must be added to increase in net assets on the SCF to determine net cash flow from operating activities. Since the gain on the sale of investments is not a cash flow (the proceeds from the sale of investments of $150,000 are an investing activity on the SCF and will be discussed later), the gain of $100,000 must be subtracted from the increase in net assets on the SCF. Thus, the net cash flows from operating activities are determined as follows:

Exhibit 5   Statement of Financial Position

Sample Club
Statement of Financial Position
December 31, 20X1 and 20X2

Assets		20X1	20X2
Current Assets:			
Cash		$ 5,000	$ 10,000
Accounts Receivable		30,000	26,000
Inventory		10,000	12,000
	Total	45,000	48,000
Investments		50,000	300,000
Property and Equipment:			
Land		200,000	200,000
Building		10,000,000	10,000,000
Equipment		1,000,000	1,252,000
Less: Accum. Depreciation		(5,000,000)	(5,500,000)
	Total	6,200,000	5,952,000
Total Assets		$ 6,295,000	$ 6,300,000
Liabilities and Members' Equity (Net Assets)			
Current Liabilities:			
Accounts Payable		$ 16,000	$ 16,500
Accrued Payroll		4,000	4,500
Payroll Taxes Payable		7,000	11,000
	Total	27,000	32,000
Long-Term Debt		4,500,000	3,750,000
Members' Equity (Net Assets):			
Membership Certificates		1,000,000	1,250,000
Undesignated Equity		768,000	1,268,000
	Total	1,768,000	2,518,000
Total Liabilities and			
Members' Equity (Net Assets)		$ 6,295,000	$ 6,300,000

Net Cash Flows from Operating Activities:		
Increase in Net Assets		$500,000
Adjustments to Reconcile Increase in		
Net Assets to Net Cash Flows from		
Operating Activities:		
Depreciation expense	$500,000	
Gain on sale of investments	(100,000)	400,000
Partial Net Cash Flows from		
Operating Activities		$900,000

The second type of adjustment includes changes in current accounts from the statement of financial position. The cash account is not considered, since we are

Exhibit 6   Statement of Activities and Statement of Undesignated Equity

Sample Club
Condensed Statement of Activities and Statement of
Undesignated Equity
For the year ended December 31, 20X2

Revenues	$7,000,000
Cost of Goods Sold	1,000,000
Labor Expenses	2,000,000
Payroll Taxes	700,000
Other Expenses	2,400,000
Depreciation Expenses	500,000
Gain on the Sale of Investments	100,000
Increase in Net Assets	500,000
Undesignated Equity—12/31/X1	768,000
Undesignated Equity—12/31/X2	$1,268,000

Other Information:

1. No property and equipment were disposed of during 20X2.
2. Investment and equipment purchases during 20X2 were made with cash. No funds were borrowed.
3. Investments costing $50,000 were sold for $150,000, resulting in a $100,000 gain on the sale of investments during 20X2.
4. Interest expense paid during the year totaled $400,000.

essentially looking at all other statement of financial position accounts to determine what caused the change in cash for purposes of the SCF. The change in the remaining five current accounts is as follows:

Account	Balances—December 31 20X1	20X2	Change in Account Balance
Current Assets:			
Accounts Receivable	$30,000	$26,000	$4,000 (dec.)
Inventory	$10,000	$12,000	$2,000 (inc.)
Current Liabilities:			
Accounts Payable	$16,000	$16,500	$ 500 (inc.)
Accrued Payroll	$ 4,000	$ 4,500	$ 500 (inc.)
Payroll Taxes Payable	$ 7,000	$11,000	$4,000 (inc.)

A brief explanation follows for each of the above current accounts, including how the change affects net cash flow from operating activities.

Accounts receivable relate directly to revenues, which were $7,000,000 for the Sample Club for 20X2. Revenues result in cash inflows when the members pay their bills. However, under accrual accounting, the revenues are recorded when services are provided. Most of the revenues during 20X2 resulted in cash as the members paid their accounts, but at year end the accounts receivable account balance was $26,000. Analysis of the account will reveal how much cash resulted from sales:

Accounts Receivable

12/31/X1 Balance	30,000	Cash received	7,004,000
Revenues	7,000,000		
12/31/X2 Balance	26,000		

Alternatively, the cash receipts from club members could be determined as follows:

$$\text{Cash Receipts from Members} = \text{AR Beginning Balance} + \text{Revenues} - \text{AR Ending Balance}$$

$$= \$30,000 + \$7,000,000 - \$26,000$$

$$= \$7,004,000$$

In preparing the SCF, we need to show a decrease in accounts receivable of $4,000, which is added to the increase in net assets as an increase in cash to determine net cash flows from operating activities.

The change in the balances of the inventory account is an increase of $2,000. Inventory relates to the purchases and cost of goods sold (food and beverages) accounts. Remember, the cost of goods sold is the cost of food and beverage inventory sold, not the cash disbursed for purchases. Therefore, we need to determine the purchases for the year as follows:

	Ending inventory	$ 12,000
+	Cost of goods sold	1,000,000
=	Goods available for sale	1,012,000
−	Beginning inventory	10,000
	Purchases	$1,002,000

The $2,000 increase in inventory causes the accrual-basis cost of goods sold to be $2,000 less than purchases. By assuming that the balance in the purchases account represents the cash amount paid for purchases, we must show a decrease in cash flows from operating activities of $2,000.

However, not all purchases were made for cash. The $500 increase in accounts payable represents the difference between purchases on account and cash paid to suppliers during 20X2. An increase in accounts payable means the amount of cash paid was less than the amount of purchases. Thus, the $500 increase in accounts payable must be added back to the accrual-basis change in net assets to determine net cash flows from operating activities. An analysis of the accounts payable account shows:

Accounts Payable

		1/1/X2 Balance	6,000
		Purchases	1,002,000
Payments to suppliers	1,001,500		
		12/31/X2 Balance	6,500

The increase in the accrued payroll account of $500 represents the difference between the accrual basis labor costs of $2,000,000 and the cash payments to personnel of $1,999,500. This determination is apparent in the analysis of the accrued payroll account:

Accrued Payroll

		12/31/X1 Balance	4,000
Payments for payroll	1,999,500	Labor expense	2,000,000
		12/31/X2 Balance	4,500

Since the payroll payments were $500 less than the payroll expense, the $500 increase in accrued payroll is added back to the accrual-basis increase in net assets to determine net cash flows from operations.

Finally, the increase of $4,000 in payroll taxes payable represents the difference between the accrual-basis payroll taxes expense of $700,000, shown on the condensed statement of activities of the Sample Club (Exhibit 6), and the $696,000 paid, as determined by the analysis of the payroll taxes payable account as follows:

Payroll Taxes Payable

		12/31/X1 Balance	7,000
Payroll taxes paid	696,000	Payroll taxes	700,000
		12/31/X2 Balance	11,000

In reality, the $7,000 of payroll taxes due at the end of 20X1 was paid along with $689,000 of payroll taxes due for 20X2. The remaining $11,000 of taxes for 20X2 will be paid in early 20X3. However, since payroll taxes expenses for 20X2 exceed payroll taxes paid during 20X2 by $4,000, the $4,000 must be added to the accrual-basis increase in net assets to determine the net cash flows from operations.

The Sample Club's net cash flows from operating activities would appear on the SCF as:

Net Cash Flows from Operating Activities:		
Increase in Net Assets		$500,000
Adjustments to Reconcile Increase in Net Assets		
Income to Net Cash Flows from		
Operating Activities:		
Depreciation expense	$500,000	
Gain on sale of investments	(100,000)	
Decrease in accounts receivable	4,000	
Increase in inventory	(2,000)	
Increase in accounts payable	500	
Increase in accrued payroll	500	
Increase in payroll taxes payable	4,000	407,000
Net Cash Flows from Operating Activities		$907,000

When determining net cash flows provided by operating activities, follow these general rules for noting changes in current accounts:

- A decrease in a current asset is added to the increase in net assets.

- An increase in a current asset is deducted from the increase in net assets.

- A decrease in a current liability is deducted from the increase in net assets.

- An increase in a current liability is added to the increase in net assets.

Step 2: Determine Net Cash Flows from Investing Activities

The next step focuses on investing activities—specifically, noncurrent assets of the Sample Club. The investment account increased by $250,000. Further analysis indicates:

Investments

12/31/X1 Balance	50,000	Sale of investments	50,000
Purchase of investments	300,000		
12/31/X2 Balance	300,000		

The analysis reveals both a sale of $50,000 of investments and a purchase of investments of $300,000. Thus, cash of $300,000 was used to purchase investments, which is a use of cash in the investing activities section of the SCF. However, further analysis of the sale of investments shows the journal entry to record this transaction as follows:

Cash	$150,000	
Investments		$ 50,000
Gains on sale of investments		100,000

The entry clearly shows a cash inflow of $150,000. Thus, this source of cash should be shown as an investing activity. Notice that the cost of investments sold ($50,000) and the gain on the sale of investments ($100,000) has no impact on net cash flow from investing activities.

There were no changes in the land and building accounts, as no purchases or sales were made during 20X2. Therefore, cash was not affected.

According to note #1 under "Other Information" (Exhibit 6), no equipment was disposed of during 20X2. Thus, the $252,000 difference noted in Exhibit 5 must be due to purchases of equipment. The $252,000 equipment is shown as a use of cash in determining net cash flows from investing activities.

The Sample Club's final noncurrent account is accumulated depreciation, which increased by $500,000, the exact amount of depreciation expense for the year. Because depreciation does not affect cash, under the indirect method the $500,000 is added back to the accrual-basis change in net assets as discussed under Step One. The change in no way affects investing activities of the Sample Club.

Now that the noncurrent asset accounts of the Sample Club have been analyzed, the investing activities section of the SCF would reflect the following:

Net Cash Flows from Investing Activities:	
Proceeds from sale of investments	$ 150,000
Purchase of investments	(300,000)
Purchase of equipment	(252,000)
Net cash flows from investing activities	$(402,000)

Step 3: Determine Net Cash Flows from Financing Activities

To determine the net cash flows from financing activities, we must consider noncurrent liabilities and net assets (members' equity) accounts. First, the change in the long-term debt account is a decrease of $750,000. The analysis of the long-term debt is as follows:

Long-Term Debt (LTD)

		12/31/X1 Balance	4,500,000
Payment of LTD	750,000		
		12/31/X2 Balance	3,750,000

The above analysis is based on note #2 (Exhibit 6), which indicates no funds were borrowed; therefore, the $750,000 reduction in LTD had to be due to payment of LTD. The $750,000 payment is a cash outflow from financing activities.

The sale of membership certificates has resulted in an increase for 20X2 of $250,000. This is shown as a source of cash from financing activities. The statement of undesignated equity at the bottom of the condensed statement of activities reflects the detailed changes in this account:

Undesignated Equity

	12/31/X1 Balance	768,000
	Results of Operations	500,000
	12/31/X2 Balance	1,268,000

The Sample Club's SCF financing activity section would show the following:

Net Cash Flows from Financing Activities:	
Payment of long-term debt	$(750,000)
Sale of membership certificates	250,000
Net cash flows from financing activities	$(500,000)

Step 4: Present Cash Flows by Activity

We now are ready to prepare the SCF based on the analysis of the preceding steps. The SCF for the Sample Club is shown in Exhibit 7. The three activities show cash flows as follows:

Exhibit 7   SCF for the Sample Club

Sample Club
Statement of Cash Flows
For the year ended December 31, 20X2

Net Cash Flow from Operating Activities:		
Increase in net assets		$ 500,000
Adjustments to reconcile increase in net assets to		
net cash flows from operating activities:		
Depreciation	$ 500,000	
Gain on sale of investments	(100,000)	
Decrease in accounts receivable	4,000	
Increase in inventory	(2,000)	
Increase in accounts payable	500	
Increase in accrued payroll	500	
Increase in payroll taxes payable	4,000	407,000
Net cash flows from operating activities		907,000
Net Cash Flow from Investing Activities:		
Sale of investments	$ 150,000	
Purchase of investments	(300,000)	
Purchase of equipment	(252,000)	
Net cash flows from investing activities		(402,000)
Net Cash Flow from Financing Activities:		
Payment of long-term debt	$ (750,000)	
Sale of membership certificates	250,000	
Net cash flows from financing activities		(500,000)
Net increase in cash during 20X2		5,000
Cash at the beginning of 20X2		5,000
Cash at the end of 20X2		$ 10,000
Supplementary Disclosure of Cash Flow Information:		
Cash paid during the year for:		
Interest	$ 400,000	

Operating activities provided cash	$907,000
Investing activities used cash	(402,000)
Financing activities used cash	(500,000)
Total	$ 5,000

The result is a bottom line of $5,000 cash inflow. The Sample Club's operating activities provided cash inflows large enough to cover the outflows for investing and financing.

In the preparation of the SCF, the net increase in cash of the Sample Club per the SCF is added to the Sample Club's cash at the beginning of 20X2 to equal the cash at the end of 20X2. The $5,000 net increase in cash per the SCF equals the

$5,000 increase in cash per the Sample Club's successive statement of financial position (Exhibit 5). This does not *prove* that the SCF is prepared correctly; however, if the $5,000 increase per the SCF had *not* been equal to the change per the successive statements of financial position, we would know that we had improperly prepared the SCF. We would then need to locate our mistake and make the correction. Thus, this is at least a partial check of the SCF's accuracy.

Finally, notice the supplementary schedule to the SCF, which shows the supplementary disclosure of the amount of interest paid during 20X2.

Analysis of Statements of Cash Flows

Unlike the statement of financial position and statement of activities, the SCF is generally not analyzed by itself. Rather, figures from the SCF are compared with specific statement of financial position and statement of activities numbers. For example, the operating cash flows to total liabilities ratio is determined by dividing operating cash flows from the SCF by average total liabilities from the statement of financial position.

There are several reasons for the comparatively minimal analysis of the SCF. First, management tends to focus on operations (which are shown on the statement of activities). Though cash is critical to business, the club's board and general manager often handle the cash activities. Second, the SCF is relatively new, being required by the FASB only since 1988 for profit-oriented entities and only since 1995 for not-for-profit entities. As we continue to issue this statement, more analysis will no doubt be conducted on the cash flow numbers.

Though a common-size SCF could possibly be prepared, it might be useless. What figure would be the base figure of 100 percent? Net revenues and total assets from the statement of activities and statement of financial position, respectively, serve that purpose. Since the SCF is divided into three distinct, independent sections, no similar base figure appears reasonable. A comparative SCF could also be prepared. However, the results reflecting details of some sections would be relatively useless. For example, how would the change in accounts receivable be shown? Assume that in 20X1 accounts receivable increased by $10,000 and that during 20X2 accounts receivable decreased by $15,000. On the SCF, the increase is shown as a negative figure, while the decrease is shown as a positive figure. The change over the two periods is $25,000, yet the change in accounts receivable balance over the two periods is a decrease of $5,000.

Useful analysis over time on a comparative basis would examine the changes in the net cash flows from each activity. For example:

	20X1	20X2	Difference $	Difference %
Net cash flows from:				
Operations	$300,000	$350,000	$ 50,000	16.67%
Investing	(400,000)	(300,000)	100,000	25.00%
Financing	150,000	100,000	(50,000)	(33.33%)
Change in cash	$ 50,000	$150,000	$100,000	200.00%

This analysis clearly reflects the changes in cash from the major activities. The user does not get lost in meaningless detail.

Summary

The SCF is an FASB-mandated financial statement that must be issued with other financial statements released to external users. It reflects the inflow and outflow of cash for a period of time. It helps the user understand the correlation between accrual accounting and cash accounting.

The SCF must show operating, investing, and financing activities. Operating activities reflect cash flows as they relate to revenues and expenses. Investing activities relate to changes in marketable securities and noncurrent asset accounts. The purchase and sale of property and equipment are commonly included in these activities. Financing activities relate to changes, current maturaties of long-term debt, long-term debt, and equity accounts. The sale of membership certificates and payment of long-term debt are two examples of financing activities. The net sum of the three activities shown on the SCF must equal the change in the cash amount shown on the two successive statements of financial position.

There are two basic approaches to preparing the SCF: direct and indirect. The difference between the two is reflected only in the operating activities section of the SCF. The indirect approach starts with the increase in net assets and includes various adjustments made to determine the increase in net assets that did not affect cash. Other adjustments for the indirect approach are the changes in current accounts related to operations. The direct approach shows the direct sources of cash, such as cash receipts from sales, and direct uses of cash, such as disbursements for payroll. Most clubs use the indirect approach because it is easier to prepare.

Key Terms

accrual basis—A system of accounting in which revenues and expenses are reported in the period in which they are considered to have been earned or incurred, regardless of the actual time of collection or payment.

cash equivalents—Short-term, highly liquid investments such as U.S. Treasury bills and money market accounts.

cash inflows—Cash received by a club during an accounting period.

cash outflows—Cash disbursed by a club during an accounting period.

direct method—One of two methods for converting the increase (decrease) in net assets to net cash flow from operations. This method shows cash receipts from revenues and cash disbursements for expenses and requires that each item on the statement of activities be converted from an accrual basis to a cash basis.

indirect method—One of two methods for converting the increase (decrease) in net assets to net cash flow from operations. This method starts with the increase in net assets and then adjusts for noncash items included on the statement of activities.

statement of cash flows (SCF)—Explains the change in cash for the accounting period by showing the effects on cash of a club's operating, investing, and financing activities for the accounting period.

Review Questions

1. What is the major purpose of the SCF?
2. How do different users of the SCF use this statement?
3. What are the three major classifications of cash flows in the SCF?
4. What are the two alternative approaches to preparing the SCF?
5. How do the two methods of preparing the SCF differ?
6. What supplementary information must be provided when the indirect approach is used in preparing the SCF?
7. How are changes in the various current statement of financial position accounts shown on an SCF prepared using the indirect approach?
8. Where is the $10,000 loss on the sale of an investment shown on the SCF prepared using the indirect approach?
9. How does the sum of the cash flows from the three major classifications on the SCF relate to the change in statement of financial position accounts from two successive statements of financial position?
10. How is the exchange of long-term debt for equipment shown on the SCF?

Problems

Problem 1

The Nittany Lion Club has engaged in various activities listed below:

1. Sold food on account
2. Received interest income
3. Purchased underdeveloped land
4. Opened a payroll checking account
5. Purchased food on account
6. Paid income taxes
7. Reclassified long-term debt as current debt
8. Collected cash on a noncurrent note receivable
9. Recorded depreciation
10. Sold equipment at a loss

11. Sold membership certificates

12. Paid a food supplier

13. Paid interest on long-term debt

Required:

Identify each activity for SCF purposes as (1) an operating activity, (2) an investing activity, (3) a financing activity, (4) a noncash transaction, or (5) none of the above.

Problem 2

The Pennsy Club has engaged in various activities described in each situation below:

1. During 20X2, the Pennsy Club's total payroll expense was $805,000. The payroll payable account at the beginning and end of 20X2 equaled $6,000 and $8,000, respectively. What were the total cash disbursements for payroll during 20X2?

2. The insurance expense for 20X2 was $15,000. Prepaid insurance was $3,000 at the beginning of 20X2 and $5,000 at the end of 20X2. The prepaid insurance account is debited when insurance premiums are paid, and insurance expense is recorded as time passes. What was the amount of total insurance premiums paid during 20X2?

3. The utility expense was $30,000 during 20X2. The accrued utility expense was $3,000 and $4,000 at the beginning and end of the year, respectively. What was the total amount paid to the utility company during 20X2?

4. During 20X2, all equipment purchased was obtained by using excess cash. The equipment account had a beginning balance of $200,000 and an ending balance of $250,000. During 20X2, equipment that cost $20,000 was sold for $5,000. A loss of $2,000 was recorded on this sale. How much was expended during the year for equipment?

5. The balance of marketable securities was $20,000 and $25,000 at the beginning and end of 20X2, respectively. Marketable securities were sold during 20X2 for $8,000, and a gain on the sale of $3,000 was recorded. How much was expended during 20X2 for marketable securities?

Problem 3

You have been hired by the Illini Club to assist with the preparation of financial statements. Your next task is to prepare the SCF. The following are copies of the condensed statement of financial position and the statement of activities of the Illini Club.

Illini Club
Condensed Statement of Financial Position
December 31, 20X1 and 20X2

	20X1	20X2
Cash	$ 30,000	$ 40,000
Accounts Receivable	190,000	225,000
Inventory	30,000	35,000
Property and Equipment (net)	1,400,000	1,500,000
Other Assets	200,000	100,000
Total Assets	$1,850,000	$1,900,000

Accounts Payable	$ 140,000	$ 185,000
Wages Payable	10,000	15,000
Current Maturities-LTD	50,000	50,000
Long-Term Debt	1,000,000	950,000
Total Liabilities	1,200,000	1,200,000
Net Assets	650,000	700,000
Total Liabilities and Net Assets	$1,850,000	$1,900,000

Illini Club
Condensed Statement of Activities
For the year ended December 31, 20X2

Revenue	$1,600,000
Cost of Goods Sold	200,000
Contribution Margin	1,400,000
Operating Expenses	950,000
Depreciation Expense	300,000
Increase in Net Assets	$ 150,000

Additional information:

1. Equipment was purchased for $400,000.

2. Long-term debt of $50,000 was reclassified as current at the end of 20X2.

3. Other assets costing $100,000 were sold during 20X2 for $100,000.

4. There was a purchase of membership certificates from members of $100,000.

Required:

Prepare the SCF for the Illini Club using the indirect method.

Chapter 5 Outline

Standards for Evaluating Ratios
Purposes of Ratio Analysis
What Ratios Express
Classes of Ratios
    Liquidity Ratios
    Solvency Ratios
    Activity Ratios
    Profitability Ratios
    Operating Ratios
Limitations of Ratio Analysis

Competencies

1. Explain what ratio analysis is, identify standards against which the results of ratio analysis can be compared, describe the function and purposes of ratio analysis, and identify what ratios express. (pp. 107–110)

2. Identify common classes of ratios, calculate common liquidity and solvency ratios, and describe how club board members, creditors, and managers view them. (pp. 110–121)

3. Calculate common activity, profitability, and operating ratios and describe how club board members, creditors, and managers view them. (pp. 121–131)

4. Explain the limitations of ratio analysis. (pp. 131–133)

5

Ratio Analysis

Financial statements produced by clubs contain a lot of financial information. A thorough analysis of this information requires more than simply reading the reported facts. Users of financial statements need to be able to interpret the reported facts to discover aspects of the club's financial situation that could otherwise go unnoticed. This is accomplished through **ratio analysis**, which is the comparison of related facts and figures, most of which appear on the financial statements. A ratio gives mathematical expression to a relationship between two figures and is computed by dividing one figure by the other figure. By bringing the two figures into relation with each other, ratios generate new information. In this way, ratio analysis goes beyond the figures reported in a financial statement and makes them more meaningful, informative, and useful. In particular, ratio analysis generates indicators for evaluating different aspects of a club's financial situation.

Ratio analysis can provide users of financial statements with answers to such questions as:

- Is there sufficient cash to meet the club's obligations for a given time period?

- Are the bottom-line results of the club reasonable?

- Is the level of the club's debt acceptable in comparison with the net assets (members' equity)?

- Is the inventory usage adequate?

- Are accounts receivable reasonable in light of total revenues?

- Is the club able to service its debt?

In this chapter, we will first explain the different kinds of standards against which ratios are compared in order to evaluate the financial condition of a club. We will discuss the variety of functions or purposes that ratio analysis serves in interpreting financial statements and the ways in which different ratios are expressed in order to make sense of the information they provide. The bulk of the chapter is devoted to a detailed discussion of the ratios most commonly used in the club industry. The chapter concludes with a section on the limitations of ratio analysis.

Standards for Evaluating Ratios

Ratio analysis is used to evaluate the favorableness or unfavorableness of various financial conditions. However, the computed ratios alone do not say anything about what is good or bad, acceptable or unacceptable, reasonable or unreasonable. By themselves, ratios are neutral and simply express numerical relationships between figures. A ratio can compare any two figures, but for the result to be meaningful, the figures must be related. Furthermore, in order to be useful as indicators or measurements of the success or well-being of a club, the computed ratios must be compared against some standard. Only then will the ratios become meaningful and provide users of financial statements with a basis for evaluating a club's financial condition.

There are three common standards that are used to evaluate the ratios computed for a given club for a given period: ratios from a past period, club industry averages, and budgeted ratios. Many ratios can be compared with corresponding ratios calculated for the prior period in order to discover any significant changes. For example, the food cost percentage (discussed later in this chapter) for the current year may be compared with the food cost percentage of the prior year in order to determine whether the club is succeeding in controlling these costs compared to the prior year.

Industry averages provide another useful standard against which to compare ratios. Club managers may want to compare the food cost percentage for their own operation with industry averages in order to evaluate their abilities to compete with other clubs. Published sources of average club industry ratios are readily available.

While ratios can be compared against results of a prior period and against industry averages, ratios are best compared against planned ratio goals. For example, in order to more effectively control the cost of labor, management may project a goal for the current year's labor cost percentage (also discussed in this chapter) that is slightly lower than the previous year's percentage. The expectation of a lower labor cost percentage may reflect management's efforts to improve scheduling procedures and other factors related to the cost of labor. By comparing the actual labor cost percentage with the planned goal, management is able to assess the success of its efforts to control labor cost.

Different evaluations may result from comparing ratios against these different standards. For example, a food cost of 40 percent for the current period may compare favorably with the prior year's ratio of 42 percent and with an industry average of 41 percent, but may be judged unfavorably when compared with the operation's planned goal of 38 percent. Therefore, care must be taken when evaluating the results of operations using ratio analysis. It is necessary to keep in mind not only which standards are being used to evaluate the ratios, but the purpose of the ratio analysis as well.

Purposes of Ratio Analysis

Club managers, creditors, and board members often have different purposes in using ratio analysis to evaluate the information reported in financial statements.

Ratios help managers monitor operating performance and evaluate their success in meeting a variety of goals. By tracking a limited number of ratios, club managers are able to maintain a fairly accurate perception of the effectiveness and efficiency of their operations. In a club's food service operation, most managers compute food cost percentage and labor cost percentage in order to monitor the two largest expenses of their operations. For clubs with a rooms operation, occupancy percentage is one of the key ratios that managers use on a daily basis. Management often uses ratios to express operational goals. For example, management may establish ratio goals as follows:

- Maintain a 1.5 to 1 current ratio.
- Do not exceed a debt-equity ratio of 1 to 1.
- Maintain a profit margin of five percent.
- Maintain property and equipment turnover of 1.2 times.

These ratios, and many more, will be fully explained later in this chapter. The point here is to notice that ratios are particularly useful to managers as indicators of how well goals are being achieved. When actual results fall short of goals, ratios help indicate where the problem or problems may be. In the food cost percentage example presented earlier, in which an actual ratio of 40 percent compared unfavorably against the planned 38 percent, additional research is required to determine the cause(s) of the two percent variation. This two percent difference may be due to cost differences, sales mix differences, or a combination of the two. Only additional analysis will determine the actual cause(s). Ratio analysis can contribute significant information to such an investigation.

A club's creditors use ratio analysis to evaluate the solvency of the club and to assess the riskiness of future loans. For example, the relationship of current assets to current liabilities, referred to as the *current ratio*, may indicate a club's ability to pay its upcoming bills. In addition, lenders sometimes use ratios to express requirements for club operations as part of the conditions set forth for certain financial arrangements. For example, as a condition of a loan, a lender may require a club to maintain a current ratio of 2 to 1.

Boards of directors, as representatives of the club's membership, are also interested in ratios. Though the overall financial objectives of clubs differ, most members of a club's board (as well as club members at large) desire a financially strong club and will view ratios as a tool to measure the financial health of their clubs. The perspective discussed for members throughout this chapter will be of the board member who represents the club's membership.

Ratios are used to communicate financial performance. Different ratios communicate different results. Individually, ratios reveal only part of the overall financial condition of a club. Collectively, however, ratios are able to communicate a great deal of information that may not be immediately apparent from simply reading the figures reported in financial statements.

What Ratios Express ——————————————————————

In order to understand the information communicated by the different kinds of ratios used in ratio analysis, it is necessary to understand the various ways in which ratios express financial information. Different ratios are read in different ways. For example, many ratios are expressed as *percentages.* An illustration is the food cost percentage, which expresses the cost of food sold in terms of a percentage of total food sales. If total food sales for a given year are $430,000, while the cost of food sold is $135,000, then the result of dividing the cost of food sold by the total food sales is .314. Because the food cost percentage is a ratio expressed as a percentage, this figure is multiplied by 100 to yield a 31.4 percent food cost. Another example of a ratio expressed as a percentage is paid occupancy percentage, calculated by dividing rooms sold by rooms available for sale. If a club has 50 rooms available for sale and sells only 25 of them, then 25 divided by 50 yields .5, which is then multiplied by 100 to be expressed as a percentage (50 percent).

Other ratios are expressed on a *per unit* basis. For example, the average dinner check is a ratio expressed as a certain sum per meal served. It is calculated by dividing the total dinner sales by the number of members served during the dinner period. Thus, on a given day, if 100 members were served dinner and the total revenue during the dinner period amounted to $2,000, then the average dinner check would be $20 per meal ($2,000/100).

The proper way to express some ratios is as a *turnover* of so many times. **Seat turnover** is one such ratio, determined by dividing the number of members served during a given period by the number of seats in the food service area being studied. If a club's main dining room has a seating capacity of 100 seats, then the main dining room's seat turnover for a dinner period in which the club serves 100 members in the main dining room is one (100/100). This means that, during that dinner period, the club's main dining room used its entire seating capacity one time.

Finally, some ratios are expressed as a *coverage* of so many times. The denominator of such a ratio is always set at 1. The current ratio, determined by dividing current assets by current liabilities, is one of the ratios expressed as a coverage of so many times. For example, if a club reported current assets of $200,000 and current liabilities of $100,000 for a given period, then the operation's current ratio at the statement of financial position date would be 2 to 1 ($200,000/$100,000). This means that the club possessed sufficient current assets to cover its current liabilities two times. Put another way, for every $1 of current liabilities, the operation had $2 of current assets.

The proper way to express the various ratios used in ratio analysis depends entirely on the particular ratio and the nature of the relationship it expresses between the two facts it relates. The ways in which different ratios are expressed are a function of how we use the information that they provide. As we discuss the ratios commonly used in the club industry, you should be careful to note how each is expressed.

Classes of Ratios

Ratios are generally classified by the type of information that they provide. Five common ratio groupings are as follows:

1. Liquidity
2. Solvency

3. Activity

4. Profitability

5. Operating

Liquidity ratios reveal the ability of a club to meet its short-term obligations. **Solvency ratios**, on the other hand, measure the extent to which the club has been financed by debt and is able to meet its long-term obligations. **Activity ratios** reflect management's ability to use the club's assets, while several **profitability ratios** show management's overall effectiveness as measured by returns on sales and investments. Finally, **operating ratios** assist in the analysis of a club's operations.

The classification of certain ratios may vary. For example, some texts classify the inventory turnover ratio as a liquidity ratio, but this text and some others consider it to be an activity ratio. Also, profit margin could be classified as an operating ratio, but it is generally included with the profitability ratios.

Knowing the meaning of a ratio and how it is used is always more important than knowing its classification. We will now turn to an in-depth discussion of individual ratios. For each ratio discussed, we will consider its purpose, the formula by which it is calculated, and the sources of data needed for the ratio's calculation. Exhibits 1 through 3, financial statements of the hypothetical Grand Club, will be used throughout our discussion of individual ratios.

Liquidity Ratios

The ability of a club to meet its current obligations is important in evaluating its financial position. For example, can the Grand Club meet its current debt of $614,500 at the end of 20X2 as it becomes due? Several liquidity ratios can be computed that suggest answers to this question.

Current Ratio. The commonest liquidity ratio is the **current ratio**, which is the ratio of total current assets to total current liabilities and is expressed as a coverage of so many times. Using figures from Exhibit 1, the 20X2 current ratio for the Grand Club can be calculated as follows:

$$\text{Current Ratio} = \frac{\text{Current Assets}}{\text{Current Liabilities}}$$

$$= \frac{\$1,140,000}{\$614,500}$$

$$= \underline{\underline{1.86}} \text{ times}$$

This result shows that for every $1 of current liabilities, the Grand Club has $1.86 of current assets. Thus, there is a cushion of $.86 for every dollar of current debt. Considerable shrinkage of receivables could occur before the Grand Club would be unable to pay its current obligations. By comparison, the 20X1 current ratio for the Grand Club was 1.36. An increase in the current ratio from 1.36 to 1.86 within one year is considerable and would no doubt please creditors. However, would a

Exhibit 1   Statement of Financial Position

Statement of Financial Position Grand Club December 31, 20X0, 20X1, 20X2			
ASSETS	**20X0**	**20X1**	**20X2**
Current Assets:			
Cash	$ 20,000	$ 21,000	$ 24,000
Investments	10,000	31,000	297,000
Accounts Receivable (net)	700,000	690,000	740,000
Inventories	64,000	67,000	65,000
Prepaid Expenses	13,000	12,000	14,000
Total Current Assets	$ 807,000	$ 821,000	$ 1,140,000
Property and Equipment:			
Land	268,500	268,500	268,500
Buildings	1,810,000	1,850,000	1,880,000
Furniture, Fixtures, & Equipment	670,000	690,000	708,000
Total Cost	2,748,500	2,808,500	2,856,600
Less: Accumulated Depreciation	205,500	264,500	318,200
Total Property and Equipment, net	2,543,000	2,544,000	2,538,300
Total Assets	$ 3,350,000	$ 3,365,000	$ 3,678,300
LIABILITIES AND NET ASSETS			
Current Liabilities:			
Accounts Payable	$ 391,000	$ 353,500	$ 371,000
Taxes Payable and Accrued	60,000	32,000	34,000
Accrued Expenses	70,000	94,500	85,000
Current Portion of Long-Term Debt	125,000	121,500	124,500
Total Current Liabilities	646,000	601,500	614,500
Long-Term Debt:			
Mortgage Payable	1,565,000	1,443,500	1,419,500
Total Liabilities	2,211,000	2,045,000	2,034,000
Members' Equity:			
Members' Certificates	965,000	965,000	965,000
Undesignated Equity	174,000	355,000	679,300
Total Net Assets	1,139,000	1,320,000	1,644,300
Total Liabilities and Net Assets	$ 3,350,000	$ 3,365,000	$ 3,678,300

current ratio of 1.86 please the club's board? The board normally prefers a current ratio that indicates the club's bills can be paid on a timely basis. Yet they most likely are not as conservative as creditors.

Management is caught in the middle, trying to satisfy the club's board members and its lenders while, at the same time, maintaining adequate working capital and sufficient liquidity to ensure the smooth operation of the club. Management can take actions that will affect the current ratio. In the case of the Grand Club, a current ratio of 2.0 could be achieved by selling $89,000 worth of marketable investments on the last day of 20X2 and paying current creditors.[1] Other possible

Exhibit 2   Statement of Activities

Statement of Activities Grand Club For the years ended December 31, 20X1 and 20X2		
	20X1	**20X2**
Income		
Membership dues	$ 1,150,000	$ 1,200,000
Initiation fees	100,000	110,000
Food revenue	2,200,000	2,400,000
Beverage revenue	700,000	750,000
Golf operations	400,000	450,000
Other income	250,000	300,000
Total income	4,800,000	5,210,000
Operating expenses		
Food	1,980,000	2,100,000
Beverage	560,000	615,000
Golf operations	850,000	900,000
Clubhouse	110,000	120,000
Entertainment	180,000	185,000
Administrative and general	480,000	500,000
Energy costs	40,000	42,000
Total operating expenses	4,200,000	4,462,000
Income before fixed expenses	600,000	748,000
Fixed expenses		
Real estate taxes	140,000	155,000
Rent expense	40,000	45,000
Insurance	60,000	70,000
Interest	120,000	100,000
Depreciation	59,000	53,700
Total fixed expenses	419,000	423,700
Increase in net assets	$ 181,000	$ 324,300

actions to increase a current ratio include obtaining long-term loans and converting noncurrent assets to cash.

An extremely high current ratio may mean that accounts receivable are too high because of liberal credit policies and/or slow collections, or it may indicate that inventory is excessive. Since ratios are indicators only, management must follow through by analyzing possible contributing factors.

Acid-Test Ratio. A more stringent test of liquidity is the **acid-test ratio**. The acid-test ratio measures liquidity by considering only "quick assets"—cash and near-cash assets. Inventories and prepaid expenses are not considered. In many industries, inventories are significant and their conversion to cash may take several months. The extremes appear evident in the hospitality industry. In some

Exhibit 3   Statement of Cash Flows

Statement of Cash Flows		
Grand Club		
For the years ended December 31, 20X1 and 20X2		
	20X1	**20X2**
Cash flows from operating activities:		
Increase in net assets	$ 181,000	$ 324,300
Adjustments to reconcile increase in members' equity to net cash provided by operating activities:		
Depreciation	59,000	53,700
(Increase) decrease in assets:		
Accounts receivable	10,000	(50,000)
Inventories	(3,000)	2,000
Prepaid expenses	1,000	(2,000)
Increase (decrease) in liabilities:		
Accounts payable	(37,500)	17,500
Taxes payable and accrued	(28,000)	2,000
Accrued expenses	24,500	(9,500)
Net cash provided by operations	207,000	338,000
Cash flows from investing activities:		
Expenditures for property and equipment	(60,000)	(48,000)
Purchases of investments	(21,000)	(266,000)
Net cash used by investing activities	(81,000)	(314,000)
Cash flows from financing activities:		
Proceeds from long-term debt	-0-	100,500
Repayment of debt	(125,000)	(121,500)
Net cash used by financing activities	(125,000)	(21,000)
Increase in cash	1,000	3,000
Cash, beginning of year	20,000	21,000
Cash, end of year	$ 21,000	$ 24,000

hospitality operations, especially quick-service restaurants, food inventory may be entirely replenished twice a week. On the other hand, the stock of certain alcoholic beverages at some food service operations, including clubs, may be replaced only once in three months.

The difference between the current ratio and the acid-test ratio is a function of the amount of inventory relative to current assets. In some operations, the difference between the current ratio and the acid-test ratio will be minor, while in others it will be significant. Using relevant figures from Exhibit 1, the 20X2 acid-test ratio for the Grand Club is computed as follows:

$$\text{Acid-Test Ratio} \quad = \quad \frac{\text{Cash, Investments, and Accounts Receivable}}{\text{Current Liabilities}}$$

$$= \quad \frac{\$1,061,000}{\$614,500}$$

$$= \quad \underline{\underline{1.73 \text{ times}}}$$

The 20X2 acid-test ratio reveals quick assets of $1.73 for every $1 of current liabilities. This is an increase of .49 times over the 20X1 acid-test ratio of 1.24. The viewpoints of club board members, creditors, and managers toward the acid-test ratio parallel those held toward the current ratio. That is, board members of a club can live with a lower ratio than creditors, and club managers must keep both groups—the board members and creditors—happy.

Operating Cash Flows to Current Liabilities Ratio. A fairly new ratio made possible by the statement of cash flows is **operating cash flows to current liabilities**. The operating cash flows are taken from the statement of cash flows for a period, while current liabilities come from the statements of financial position at the start and end of that period. This measure of liquidity compares the cash flow from the club's operating activities to its obligations at the statement of financial position date that must be paid within 12 months. Using the relevant figures from Exhibits 1 and 3, the 20X2 operating cash flows to current liabilities ratio is computed as follows:

$$\text{Operating Cash Flows to Current Liabilities Ratio} \quad = \quad \frac{\text{Operating Cash Flows}}{\text{Average Current Liabilities}}$$

$$= \quad \frac{\$338,000}{\$608,000}$$

$$= \quad \underline{\underline{55.6\%}}$$

The 20X2 ratio of 55.6 percent shows that $.556 of cash flow from operations was provided by the Grand Club during 20X2 for each $1 of average current debt at the end of 20X1 and 20X2. The prior year's ratio was 33.2 percent. This is a fairly dramatic change and reveals greater liquidity at the end of 20X2 than 20X1 for the Grand Club.

All users of ratios would prefer to see a high operating cash flow to current liabilities, as this suggests club operations are providing sufficient cash to pay the club's current liabilities.

Accounts Receivable Turnover. In clubs, accounts receivable is generally the largest current asset. Therefore, in an examination of a club's liquidity, the "quality" of its accounts receivable must be considered.

In the normal operating cycle, sales are made on account and then accounts receivable are converted to cash. The **accounts receivable turnover** measures the speed of the conversion. The faster the accounts receivable are turned over, the more credibility the current and acid-test ratios have in financial analysis.

This ratio is determined by dividing total revenues by average accounts receivable. A refinement of this ratio uses only charge sales in the numerator; however, quite often charge sales figures are unavailable to outsiders (creditors). Most clubs have very little cash sales; therefore, all sales will be considered charge sales for this discussion. Regardless of whether total revenues or charge sales are used as the numerator, the calculation should be consistent from period to period. The average accounts receivable is the result of dividing the sum of the beginning-of-the-period and end-of-the-period accounts receivable by two. When a club operation has seasonal sales fluctuations, a preferred approach (when computing the *annual* accounts receivable turnover) is to sum the accounts receivable at the end of each month and divide by 12 to determine the average accounts receivable.

Using relevant figures from Exhibits 1 and 2, the accounts receivable turnover for the Grand Club in 20X2 is determined as follows:

$$\text{Accounts Receivable Turnover} = \frac{\text{Total Revenues}}{\text{Average Accounts Receivable}}$$

$$= \frac{\$5,210,000}{\$715,000^*}$$

$$= \underline{\underline{7.3 \text{ times}}}$$

$$^*\text{Average Accounts Receivable} = \frac{\text{Balances at Beginning and End of Year}}{2}$$

$$= \frac{\$690,000 + \$740,000}{2}$$

$$= \underline{\underline{\$715,000}}$$

This accounts receivable turnover indicates that average receivables turned over (were collected) 7.3 times in 20X2. This is higher than the Grand Club's 20X1 accounts receivable turnover of 6.9 times. Management should compare these results to their turnover targets and generally investigate any significant differences. An investigation may reveal problems, or management may discover that changes in the club's credit policies and/or collection procedures significantly contributed to the difference.

Although the accounts receivable turnover measures the overall rapidity of collections, it fails to address individual accounts. This matter is resolved by preparing an aging of accounts receivable schedule that reflects the status of each account. In an aging schedule, each account is broken down to the period when the charges originated. Like credit sales, this information is generally available only to management.

Creditors prefer a high accounts receivable turnover, as this reflects a lower investment in nonproductive accounts receivable. However, they understand how a tight credit policy and an overly aggressive collections effort may result in lower sales. Nonetheless, everything else being the same, a high accounts receivable turnover indicates that accounts receivable are being managed well. Long-term creditors also see a high accounts receivable turnover as a positive reflection of management.

Club managers want to maximize club sales. Offering credit not only is the club industry's traditional sales approach, it also helps maximize sales. Club managers realize that offering credit to maximize sales may result in more accounts receivable and in selling to some club members who will be slow to pay. So one result of management's decision to offer credit is a lower accounts receivable turnover. While club managers may see a lower accounts receivable turnover as an unavoidable consequence of encouraging higher sales, they should not lose sight of the fact that they also must maintain the club's cash flow—that is, they must effectively collect on the credit sales.

Average Collection Period. A variation of the accounts receivable turnover is the **average collection period**, which is calculated by dividing the accounts receivable turnover into 365 (the number of days in a year). This conversion simply translates the turnover into a more understandable result. For the Grand Club, the average collection period for 20X2 is as follows:

$$\text{Average Collection Period} = \frac{365}{\text{Accounts Receivable Turnover}}$$

$$= \frac{365}{7.3}$$

$$= \underline{\underline{50 \text{ days}}}$$

The average collection period of 50 days means that on an average of every 50 days throughout 20X2, the Grand Club was collecting all its accounts receivable. The 50 days is a three-day decrease over the 20X1 average collection period of 53 days.

What should be the average collection period? Generally, the time allowed for average payments should not exceed the terms of sale by more than 7 to 10 days. Therefore, if the terms of sale are $n/30$ (entire amount is due 30 days from the billing date), the maximum allowable average collection period is 37 to 40 days. In the club business, member purchases are often not billed until the following month; therefore, the average collection period is expected to be considerably longer in clubs than in other hospitality industry segments.

The average collection period preferred by club board members, creditors, and managers is similar to their preferences for the accounts receivable turnover, because the average collection period is only a variation of the accounts receivable turnover.

Solvency Ratios

Solvency ratios measure the degree of debt financing by a club and are partial indicators of the club's ability to meet its long-term debt obligations. These ratios reveal the equity cushion that is available to absorb any operating losses. Primary users of these ratios are outsiders, especially lenders, who generally prefer less risk rather than more risk. High solvency ratios generally suggest that a club has the ability to weather financial storms.

This class of ratios includes two major groups—those based on statement of financial position information and those based on statement of activities information.

Solvency Ratio. A club is solvent when its assets exceed its liabilities. Therefore, the **solvency ratio** is simply total assets divided by total liabilities. Using figures from Exhibit 1, the solvency ratio in 20X2 for the Grand Club is determined as follows:

$$\text{Solvency Ratio} \; = \; \frac{\text{Total Assets}}{\text{Total Liabilities}}$$

$$= \; \frac{\$3,678,300}{\$2,034,000}$$

$$= \; \underline{1.81} \text{ times}$$

At the end of 20X2, the Grand Club has $1.81 of assets for each $1 of liabilities, or a cushion of $.81. The Grand Club's assets could be discounted substantially ($.81 ÷ $1.81 = 44.8 percent) and creditors could still be fully paid. The Grand Club's solvency ratio at the end of 20X1 was 1.64 times. The 20X2 ratio would be considered more favorable from the perspective of creditors.

The greater the financial leverage (use of debt to finance the assets) used by a club, the lower its solvency ratio. Board members prefer to use some leverage in order to minimize their investment. Creditors, on the other hand, prefer a high solvency ratio, as it provides a greater cushion should the club experience losses in operations. Managers must satisfy both board members and creditors. Thus, they desire to finance assets so as to minimize members' investments, while not unduly jeopardizing the club's ability to pay creditors.

Debt-Equity Ratio. The **debt-equity ratio**, one of the commonest solvency ratios, compares the club's debt to its net assets (members' equity). This ratio indicates the establishment's ability to withstand adversity and meet its long-term debt obligations. Figures from Exhibit 1 can be used to calculate the Grand Club's debt-equity ratio for 20X2:

$$\text{Debt-Equity Ratio} \; = \; \frac{\text{Total Liabilities}}{\text{Total Net Assets}}$$

$$= \; \frac{\$2,034,000}{\$1,644,300}$$

$$= \; \underline{1.24 \text{ to } 1}$$

The Grand Club's debt-equity ratio at the end of 20X2 indicates that for each $1 of members' net worth, the Grand Club owed creditors $1.24. The debt-equity ratio for 20X1 for the Grand Club was 1.55 to 1. Thus, relative to its net assets, the Grand Club reduced its 20X2 debt.

Board members view this ratio similarly to the way they view the solvency ratio. That is, they desire to minimize their investment by using leverage. The greater the leverage, the higher the debt-equity ratio. Creditors generally would favor a lower debt-equity ratio because their risk is reduced as net assets increase relative to debt. Club managers, as with the solvency ratio, seek a middle position between creditors and board members.

Long-Term Debt to Total Capitalization Ratio. Still another solvency ratio is the calculation of long-term debt as a percentage of the sum of long-term debt and net assets, commonly called total capitalization. Figures from Exhibit 1 can be used to calculate the 20X2 **long-term debt to total capitalization ratio** for the Grand Club:

$$\text{Long-Term Debt to Total Capitalization Ratio} = \frac{\text{Long-Term Debt}}{\text{Long-Term Debt and Net Assets}}$$

$$= \frac{\$1,419,500}{\$3,063,800}$$

$$= 46.33\%$$

Long-term debt of the Grand Club at the end of 20X2 is 46.33 percent of its total capitalization. This can be compared to 52.23 percent at the end of 20X1. Creditors prefer a lower percentage because it indicates a reduced risk on their part; club members, on the other hand, prefer a higher percentage because of their desire to minimize their investments.

Number of Times Interest Earned Ratio. The **number of times interest earned ratio** is based on financial figures from the statement of activities and expresses the number of times interest expense can be covered. The greater the number of times interest is earned, the greater the safety afforded to a club's creditors. Since interest is subtracted to determine the bottom line of the statement of activities, it is added to "increase in net assets" to form the numerator of the ratio, while interest expense is the denominator. Figures from Exhibit 2 can be used to calculate the 20X2 number of times interest earned ratio for the Grand Club:

$$\text{Number of Times Interest Earned Ratio} = \frac{\text{Increase in Net Assets and Interest Expense}}{\text{Interest Expense}}$$

$$= \frac{\$424,300}{\$100,000}$$

$$= 4.24 \text{ times}$$

The result of 4.24 times shows that the Grand Club could cover its interest expense by more than four times. The number of times interest earned ratio in 20X1 for the Grand Club was 2.51 times. This two-year trend suggests a much improved position from a creditor's viewpoint. In general, a number of times interest earned ratio of greater than 4 reflects a sufficient amount of earnings for a club to cover the interest expense of its existing debt.

All interested parties (a club's board members, creditors, and managers) prefer a relatively high ratio. Board members are generally less concerned about this ratio than creditors, as long as interest obligations are paid on a timely basis and leverage is working to their advantage. Creditors and especially lenders also prefer a relatively high ratio, because this indicates that the club is able to meet its interest payments. To the lender, the higher this ratio, the better. Management also prefers a high ratio. However, since an extremely high ratio suggests leverage is probably not being optimized for the members, management may prefer a lower ratio than do lenders.

The number of times interest earned ratio fails to consider fixed obligations other than interest expense. Many clubs have long-term leases that require periodic payments similar to interest. This limitation of the number of times interest earned ratio is overcome by the fixed charge coverage ratio.

Fixed Charge Coverage Ratio. The **fixed charge coverage ratio** is a variation of the number of times interest earned ratio that considers operating leases as well as interest expense. Clubs that have obtained the use of property and equipment through operating leases may find the fixed charge coverage ratio to be more useful than the number of times interest earned ratio. This ratio is calculated the same as the number of times interest earned ratio, except that lease expense (rent expense) is added to both the numerator and denominator of the equation. Using figures from Exhibit 2, the Grand Club's fixed charge coverage ratio for 20X2 can be calculated as follows:

$$\text{Fixed Charge Coverage Ratio} = \frac{\text{Increase in Net Assets} + \text{Interest Expense} + \text{Rent Expense}}{\text{Interest Expense} + \text{Rent Expense}}$$

$$= \frac{\$469,300}{\$145,000}$$

$$= \underline{\underline{3.24 \text{ times}}}$$

The result indicates that earnings prior to rent expense and interest expense cover rent and interest expense 3.24 times. The Grand Club's fixed charge coverage ratio for 20X1 was 2.13 times. The change of 1.11 times reflects a major increase in the Grand Club's ability to cover its fixed expenses of interest and lease expense. The viewpoints of a club's board members, creditors, and managers regarding the fixed charge coverage ratio are similar to the views they hold regarding changes in the number of times interest earned ratio.

Operating Cash Flows to Total Liabilities Ratio. The final solvency ratio presented in this chapter uses figures from the Grand Club's statement of financial position and statement of cash flows (Exhibits 1 and 3) by comparing operating cash flows to average total liabilities. Both the debt-equity and long-term debt to total capitalization ratios are based on static numbers from the statement of financial position. The **operating cash flows to total liabilities ratio** overcomes the deficiency of using debt at a point in time by considering cash flow for a period of time.

Figures from Exhibits 1 and 3 are used to calculate the 20X2 operating cash flows to total liabilities ratio for the Grand Club as follows:

$$\text{Operating Cash Flow to Total Liabilities Ratio} = \frac{\text{Operating Cash Flows (Net Cash)}}{\text{Average Total Liabilities}}$$

$$= \frac{\$338,000}{\$2,039,500*}$$

$$= \underline{\underline{16.6\%}}$$

$$*\text{Average Total Liabilities} = \frac{\text{Total Liabilities at the Beginning and End of Year}}{2}$$

$$= \frac{\$2,045,000 + \$2,034,000}{2}$$

$$= \underline{\underline{\$1,739,500}}$$

The 20X1 operating cash flows to total liabilities ratio was 9.7 percent; thus, the Grand Club's ability to meet its total obligations with operating cash flows has improved from 20X1 to 20X2.

All users of financial information prefer this ratio to be relatively high; that is, the cash flow from club operations should be high relative to total liabilities, given that the amount of debt used is optimal.

Activity Ratios

Activity ratios measure management's effectiveness in using its resources. Management is entrusted with inventory and property and equipment (and other resources) to provide services for club members. Since the property and equipment of most clubs constitute a large percentage of the club's total assets, it is essential to use these resources effectively. Although inventory is generally not a significant portion of total assets, management must adequately control it in order to minimize the cost of sales.

Inventory Turnover. The **inventory turnover** shows how quickly the inventory is being used. Generally speaking, the quicker the inventory turnover the better, because inventory can be expensive to maintain and, in some cases (food, for example), long storage periods can compromise quality. Maintenance costs include

Exhibit 4   Condensed Food Department Statement

Condensed Food Department Statement Grand Club For the year ended December 31, 20X2	
Food sales	$ 2,400,000
Cost of food sold	
Cost of food consumed	990,000
Less credit for employees' meals	30,000
Cost of food sold	960,000
Gross profit on food sales	1,440,000
Departmental expenses:	
Payroll and related expenses	1,000,000
Other expenses	140,000
Total	1,140,000
Departmental income	$ 300,000

Notes: (1) Food inventory at the end of 20X0–20X2, was $50,000, $52,000 and $54,000, respectively.

(2) Total covers served during 20X2 equaled 200,000.

storage space, freezers, insurance, personnel expense (including the time required to complete a physical inventory each month, or more frequently), recordkeeping, and, of course, the opportunity cost of the funds tied up in inventory. Inventories held by clubs are also highly susceptible to theft and must be carefully controlled: the larger the inventory, the more difficult to keep track of all the inventoried items, and, thus, the greater the temptation.

Inventory turnovers should generally be calculated separately for food supplies and for beverages. Some club food service operations will calculate several beverage turnovers based on the types of beverages available.

Exhibit 4 is a condensed food department statement of the Grand Club for 20X2. Figures from this statement will be used to illustrate the food turnover ratios. The 20X2 food inventory turnover for the Grand Club is calculated as follows:

$$\text{Food Inventory Turnover} = \frac{\text{Cost of Food Consumed}}{\text{Average Food Inventory}}$$

$$= \frac{\$990,000}{\$53,000}$$

$$= \underline{\underline{18.7 \text{ times}}}$$

The food inventory turned over 18.7 times during 20X2, or approximately 1.5 times per month. The speed of food inventory turnover generally depends on the type of food service operation.

Although a high food inventory turnover is desired because it means that the club is able to operate with a relatively small investment in inventory, too high a turnover may indicate possible stockout problems. Failure to provide desired food items to club members may result not only in immediately disappointed members, but also in negative goodwill if this problem persists. Too low an inventory turnover suggests that food is overstocked, and, in addition to the costs to maintain inventory previously mentioned, the cost of spoilage may become a problem.

All interested parties (club board members, creditors, and managers) prefer relatively high inventory turnovers to low ones, as long as stockouts are avoided. Ideally, as the last inventory item is sold, the shelves are being restocked.

Property and Equipment Turnover. The **property and equipment turnover** (sometimes called the fixed asset turnover) is determined by dividing average total net book value of property and equipment (cost less accumulated depreciation) into total revenue for the period. A more precise measurement would be to use only revenues related to property and equipment usage in the numerator. However, revenue by source is not available to some users of financial statements so total revenue (income) is generally used.

This ratio measures management's effectiveness in using property and equipment. A high turnover suggests the club is using its property and equipment effectively to generate revenues, while a low turnover suggests the club is not making effective use of its property and equipment and should consider disposing of part of them.

A limitation of this ratio is that it places a premium on using older (depreciated) property and equipment, since their book value is low. Further, this ratio is affected by the depreciation method employed by the club. For example, a club using an accelerated method of depreciation will show a higher turnover than a club using the straight-line depreciation method, all other factors being the same.

Using figures from Exhibits 1 and 2, the Grand Club's property and equipment turnover ratio for 20X2 is determined as follows:

$$\text{Property and Equipment Turnover} = \frac{\text{Total Income}}{\text{Average Net Book Value of Property and Equipment}}$$

$$= \frac{\$5,210,000}{\$2,541,150^*}$$

$$= 2.05 \text{ times}$$

$$^*\text{Average Net Book Value of P\&E} = \frac{\text{Beginning and Ending P\&E}}{2}$$

$$= \frac{\$2,544,000 + \$2,538,300}{2}$$

$$= \$2,541,150$$

The turnover of 2.05 reveals that income was 2.05 times the average total net book value of property and equipment. For 20X1, the Grand Club's property and equipment turnover was 1.89 times. The change of .16 times is viewed as a positive trend.

All interested parties (club board members, creditors, and managers) prefer a high property and equipment turnover. Club managers, however, should resist retaining old and possibly inefficient property and equipment, even though they result in a high property and equipment turnover.

Asset Turnover. Another ratio to measure the efficiency of management's use of club assets is the **asset turnover**. It is calculated by dividing total income by average total assets. The two previous ratios presented, food inventory turnover and especially property and equipment turnover, concern a large percentage of the total assets. The asset turnover examines the use of total assets in relation to total income. Limitations of the property and equipment ratio are also inherent in this ratio to the extent that property and equipment make up total assets.

Using figures from Exhibits 1 and 2, the Grand Club's 20X2 asset turnover ratio is calculated as follows:

$$\text{Asset Turnover Ratio} = \frac{\text{Total Income}}{\text{Average Total Assets}}$$

$$= \frac{\$5,210,000}{\$3,521,650^*}$$

$$= 1.48 \text{ times}$$

$$^*\text{Average Total Assets} = \frac{\$3,365,000 + \$3,678,300}{2}$$

$$= \$3,521,650$$

The asset turnover indicates that each $1 of assets generated $1.48 of income in 20X2. The asset turnover ratio for 20X1 was 1.43. Thus, there was a slight change of $.05 for the two years.

As with the property and equipment turnover, all concerned parties (club board members, creditors, and managers) prefer this ratio to be high, because a high ratio means effective use of assets by management, unless management is hanging on to old (depreciated) assets, as discussed previously.

Both the property and equipment turnover ratio and the asset turnover ratio are relatively low for most hospitality segments, especially clubs and lodging. The relatively low ratios are due to the hospitality industry's high dependence on fixed assets and its inability to quickly increase output to meet maximum demand.

Paid Occupancy Percentage. For clubs with a rooms operation, an additional measure of management performance is occupancy. In particular, the paid occupancy percentage is a major indicator of management's success in selling the club's rooms. Paid occupancy percentage refers to the percentage of rooms sold in relation to rooms available for sale in the club. In restaurant operations, a comparable ratio is seat turnover, and it is calculated by dividing the number of people served by the number of seats available. Seat turnover is commonly calculated by meal period. In most restaurants, different seat turnovers are experienced for different dining periods. The paid occupancy percentage for lodging facilities and the seat turnovers for food service facilities are key measures of facility utilization for clubs that have guestrooms and food service outlets.

To illustrate the paid occupancy percentage, assume a club has 40 guestrooms. Further, assume that all are available for sale each night of the year and that 9,400 are sold during a given year. The paid occupancy percentage for the year would be determined as follows:

$$\text{Paid Occupancy Percentage} \quad = \quad \frac{\text{Rooms Sold}}{\text{Rooms Available}}$$

$$= \quad \frac{9,400}{14,600}$$

$$= \quad 64.4\%$$

To use this figure to gauge how well the club is doing in this area, managers should compare it to the budgeted paid occupancy percentage, percentages from previous years, or to club industry averages.

Profitability Ratios

Profitability ratios reflect the results of all areas of management's responsibilities. The club industry includes clubs with a strong profit orientation, but the majority are organized as not-for-profit. Even though these not-for-profit clubs are organized primarily to provide services to club members at minimal costs, still there is a need to earn positive bottom-line results to provide for club expansion and future major replacements of equipment, furniture, and so on. The focus of this section will be primarily from the perspective of a not-for-profit club.

The profitability ratios we are about to consider measure management's overall effectiveness, as shown by returns on sales (profit margin and operating efficiency ratio), return on assets, and return on members' equity.

Profit Margin. Clubs are often evaluated in terms of their ability to generate profits on sales. **Profit margin**, a key ratio, is determined by dividing increase in net assets by total income (these figures are taken from the statement of activities). Profit margin is an overall measurement of management's ability to generate income and control expenses, thus yielding the bottom line. In this ratio, the increase in net assets is the income remaining after all club expenses have been deducted, both those controllable by management and those directly related to decisions made by the club's board of directors.

Using figures from Exhibit 2, the 20X2 profit margin of the Grand Club can be determined as follows:

$$\text{Profit Margin} \quad = \quad \frac{\text{Increase in Net Assets}}{\text{Total Income}}$$

$$= \quad \frac{\$324,300}{\$5,210,000}$$

$$= \quad \underline{\underline{6.22\%}}$$

The Grand Club's 20X2 profit margin of 6.22 percent has increased considerably from the 20X1 figure of 3.77 percent.

If the profit margin is lower than expected, then expenses and other areas should be reviewed. Poor pricing and low sales volume could be contributing to the low margin. To identify the problem area, management should analyze both the club's overall profit margin and the profit margins for each club department that generates revenue. If the club's departmental margins are satisfactory, the problem would appear to be with the club's overhead expense.

Operating Efficiency Ratio. The **operating efficiency ratio** is a better measure of management's performance than the profit margin. This ratio is the result of dividing income before fixed expenses by total income. Income before fixed expenses is the result of subtracting expenses generally controllable by management from income. Non-operating expenses include fixed charges that are directly related to decisions made by a club's board of directors, not management. Fixed expenses are expenses relating to the capacity of the club, including rent, real estate taxes, insurance, depreciation, and interest expense. Although these expenses are the result of board of directors' decisions and thus beyond the direct control of active management, management can and should review tax assessments and insurance policies and quotations, and make recommendations to the board that can affect the club's total profitability.

Using figures from Exhibit 2, the 20X2 operating efficiency ratio of the Grand Club can be calculated as follows:

$$\text{Operating Efficiency Ratio} \quad = \quad \frac{\text{Income before Fixed Expenses}}{\text{Total Income}}$$

$$= \quad \frac{\$748,000}{\$5,210,000}$$

$$= \quad \underline{\underline{14.36\%}}$$

The operating efficiency ratio shows that just over $.14 of each $1 of income is available for fixed charges and bottom-line profits. The Grand Club's operating efficiency ratio was 12.5 percent for 20X1.

The next two profitability ratios compare profits to either assets or members' equity. The result in each case is a percentage and is commonly called a *return*.

Return on Assets. The **return on assets (ROA)** ratio is a general indicator of the profitability of a club in relation to its assets. Unlike the two preceding profitability ratios drawn only from statement of activities data, this ratio compares bottom-line profits to the total investment—that is, to the total assets. It is calculated by dividing result of operations by average total assets. This ratio, or a variation of it, is used by several large conglomerates to measure the performances of their subsidiary corporations.

Using figures from Exhibits 1 and 2, the Grand Club's 20X2 return on assets is calculated as follows:

$$\text{Return on Assets} = \frac{\text{Increase in Net Assets}}{\text{Average Total Assets}}$$

$$= \frac{\$324,300}{\$3,521,650^*}$$

$$= 9.21\%$$

$$^*\text{Average Total Assets} = \frac{\text{Total Assets at Beginning and End of Year}}{2}$$

$$= \frac{\$3,365,000 + \$3,678,300}{2}$$

$$= \$3,521,650$$

The Grand Club's 20X2 ROA means there was 9.21 cents of profit for every dollar of average total assets. The 20X1 ROA was 5.4 percent. Therefore, there was a major increase in ROA from 20X1 to 20X2.

A very low ROA may result from inadequate profits or excessive assets. A very high ROA may suggest that older assets require replacement in the near future or that additional assets need to be added to support growth in revenues. The determination of low and high is usually based on industry averages and the club's own ROA profile, developed over time.

ROA may also be calculated by multiplying the asset turnover ratio by the profit margin. For 20X2, the ROA for the Grand Club can be calculated as follows:

$$\text{ROA} = \text{Asset Turnover Ratio} \times \text{Profit Margin}$$

$$= 1.48 \times .0622$$

$$= 9.21\%$$

Return on Members' Equity. A key profitability ratio for clubs is the **return on members' equity (ROE)**. The ROE ratio compares the profits of the club to the members' investment. It is calculated by dividing the increase in net assets by the average net assets (in not-for-profit club) or members' equity (in profit-oriented clubs).

Using relevant figures from Exhibits 1 and 2, the 20X2 ROE for the Grand Club is calculated as follows:

$$
\text{Return on Members' Equity} = \frac{\text{Increase in Net Assets}}{\text{Average Net Assets}}
$$

$$
= \frac{\$324,300}{\$1,482,150^*}
$$

$$
= 21.88\%
$$

$$
^*\text{Average Net Assets} = \frac{\text{Net Assets at Beginning and End of Year}}{2}
$$

$$
= \frac{\$1,320,000 \ + \ \$1,644,300}{2}
$$

$$
= \$1,482,150
$$

In 20X2, for every one dollar of net assets, 21.88 cents was earned. The 20X1 ROE for the Grand Club was 14.72 percent. To club board members, this ratio represents the financial results of all of management's efforts. The ROE reflects management's ability to produce financial results for the members.

Operating Ratios

Operating ratios assist management in analyzing the operations of a club. Detailed information necessary for computing these ratios is normally not available to creditors or even to club members not actively involved in the club's management. These ratios reflect the actual mix of sales (revenues or income) and make possible comparisons to sales mix objectives. Further, operating ratios relate expenses to revenues and are useful for control purposes. For example, food cost percentage is calculated and compared to the budgeted food cost percentage to evaluate the overall control of food costs. Any significant deviation is investigated to determine the cause(s) for the variation between actual results and planned goals.

There are literally hundreds of operating ratios that could be calculated. Consider the following:

- Departmental revenues as a percentage of total revenue (sales mix)
- Expenses as a percentage of total revenue
- Departmental expenses as a percentage of departmental revenues
- Revenues per room occupied, meal sold, and so forth
- Revenues per club member
- Annual expenses per club member, and so forth

This section will consider only some of the most critical operating ratios, some relating to revenues and some relating to expenses. The two revenue ratios that will be discussed are mix of sales and average food service check. The expense ratios that will be discussed are food cost percentage, beverage cost percentage, and labor cost percentage.

Mix of Sales. Clubs, like enterprises in other industries, attempt to generate sales as a means of covering their expenses and producing profits. In a food service operation, the sales mix of entrées yields a given contribution. The same sales total in a different sales mix will yield a different (possibly lower) contribution toward overhead and profits. Therefore, it is essential for management to obtain the desired sales mix. To determine the sales mix, departmental revenues (income) are totaled and percentages of the total are calculated for each operated department.

Using figures from Exhibit 2, the 20X2 sales mix for the Grand Club is calculated as follows:

Income Sources	Amount	Percentage
Dues	$ 1,200,000	23.0%
Initiation fees	110,000	2.1
Food	2,400,000	46.1
Beverage	750,000	14.4
Golf	450,000	8.6
Other	300,000	5.8
Total	$ 5,210,000	100.0%

The sales mix of a given club is best compared with the club's objectives, as revealed in its budget. A second standard of comparison is the previous period's results. A third involves a comparison with industry averages.

An evaluation of revenue by department is accomplished by determining each department's average sale. For the food service department, this figure is the average food service check.

Average Food Service Check. A key food service ratio is the average food service check. This ratio is determined by dividing total food revenue by the number of food covers sold during the period.

Using figures from Exhibit 4, the average food service check for 20X2 for the Grand Club can be calculated as follows:

$$\text{Average Food Service Check} = \frac{\text{Total Food Sales}}{\text{Number of Food Covers}}$$

$$= \frac{\$2,400,000}{200,000}$$

$$= \$12.00$$

The $12 average food service check in 20X2 is best compared with the club's budgeted amount for 20X2. An additional comparison relates this ratio to club industry averages.

Additional average checks should be calculated for beverages. Management may even desire to calculate the average check by different dining areas and/or by various meal periods.

Food Cost Percentage. The **food cost percentage** is a key food service ratio that compares the cost of food sold to food sales. Most food service managers rely heavily on this ratio for determining whether food costs are reasonable.

Using figures from Exhibit 4, the 20X2 food cost percentage for the Grand Club is determined as follows:

$$\text{Food Cost Percentage} = \frac{\text{Cost of Food Sold}}{\text{Food Sales}}$$

$$= \frac{\$960,000}{\$2,400,000}$$

$$= 40.00\%$$

The Grand Club's 20X2 food cost percentage indicates that of every $1 of food sales, $.40 goes toward the cost of food sold. This is best compared with the club's budgeted percentage for the period. Management should investigate a significant difference in either direction. Management should be just as concerned about a food cost percentage that is significantly lower than the budgeted goal as it is about a food cost percentage that exceeds budgeted standards. A lower food cost percentage may indicate that the quality of food served is lower than desired, or that smaller portions are being served than are specified by the standard recipes. It also could indicate that expected cost increases are being passed along as menu price increases in advance of the cost increases occurring. A food cost percentage in excess of the objective may be due to poor portion control, excessive food costs, theft, waste, spoilage, and so on. Management and the club's board must keep in mind that this ratio (and all ratios) is the result of two numbers (the numerator and denominator). If a club chooses to keep its menu prices low to encourage members to use its dining facilities, the club's food cost percentage will be higher than the food cost percentage of a club with similar operating characteristics that charges higher menu prices. Thus, operating philosophies can affect this ratio.

Beverage Cost Percentage. A key ratio for beverage operations is the **beverage cost percentage**. This ratio results from dividing the cost of beverages sold by beverage sales. As with the food cost percentage ratio, this ratio is best compared with the budgeted goal set for that period. Likewise, managers should investigate any significant variances to determine the cause(s). Refinements of this ratio would be beverage cost percentage by type of beverage sold and by beverage outlet.

Labor Cost Percentage. The largest expense in clubs, hotels, motels, and many restaurants is labor. Labor expense includes salaries, wages, bonuses, payroll taxes, and fringe benefits. A general **labor cost percentage** is determined by dividing total labor costs by total revenue. This general labor cost percentage is simply a benchmark for making broad comparisons. For control purposes, labor costs must be analyzed on a departmental basis. The department labor cost percentage is determined by dividing department labor cost by the department revenue.

Using figures from Exhibit 4, the 20X2 operated department labor cost percentage of the food department for the Grand Club is determined as follows:

$$\text{Labor Cost Percentage} = \frac{\begin{array}{c}\text{Labor Cost for the Food Dept.}\\ \text{(payroll and related expenses)}\end{array}}{\text{Food Sales}}$$

$$= \frac{\$1,000,000}{\$2,400,000}$$

$$= \underline{\underline{41.7\%}}$$

The standards of comparison for these ratios are the budgeted percentages. Since labor costs are generally the largest expenses, they must be tightly controlled. Management must carefully investigate any significant differences between actual and budgeted labor cost percentages.

Ratios for other expenses are usually computed as a percentage of revenues. If the expenses are operated department expenses, then the ratio is computed with the operated department revenues in the denominator and the expense in the numerator. An overhead expense ratio will consist of the overhead expense divided by total revenue. For example, the administrative and general expense (A&G) percentage is determined by dividing the A&G expenses by total revenue. Using figures for the Grand Club in 20X2 found in Exhibit 2, the A&G expense percentage is 9.6 percent (A&G expenses of $500,000 ÷ total income of $5,210,000).

Limitations of Ratio Analysis

Exhibit 5 contains a list of the ratios presented in this chapter. Ratios are extremely useful to board members, creditors, and managers in evaluating the financial condition and operations of a club. However, ratios are only indicators. Ratios do not resolve a problem or even reveal exactly what the problem is. At best, when they vary significantly from past periods, budgeted standards, or industry averages, ratios only indicate that there *may* be a problem. Much more investigation and analysis are required.

Ratios are meaningful when they result from comparing two *related* numbers. Food cost percentage is meaningful because of the direct relationship between food costs and food sales. A goodwill to cash ratio is meaningless due to the lack of any direct relationship between goodwill and cash.

Ratios are most useful when compared with a standard. A food cost percentage of 32 percent has little usefulness or meaning until it is compared with a standard such as past performance, industry averages, or the club's budgeted percentages.

Ratios may be used to compare clubs. However, many ratios, especially operating ratios, will not result in meaningful comparisons if the two clubs are in completely different segments of the club industry. For example, comparing ratios for a golf club to ratios for a city club would probably not serve any meaningful purpose.

Exhibit 5   List of Ratios

Ratio	Formula
1. Current ratio	Current assets/current liabilities
2. Acid-test ratio	Cash, marketable securities, notes, and accounts receivable/current liabilities
3. Operating cash flows to current liabilities ratios	Operating cash flows/average current liabilities
4. Accounts receivable turnover	Revenue/average accounts receivable
5. Average collection period	365/accounts receivable turnover
6. Solvency ratio	Total assets/total liabilities
7. Debt-equity ratio	Total liabilities/total net assets
8. Long-term debt to total capitalization ratio	Long-term debt/long-term debt and net assets
9. Number of times interest earned ratio	Increase in net assets + interest expense/interest expense
10. Fixed charge coverage ratio	Increase in net assets + interest expense + lease expense/interest expense + lease expense
11. Operating cash flows to total liabilities ratio	Operating cash flows/average total liabilities
12. Food inventory turnover	Cost of food used/average food inventory
13. Property and equipment turnover	Total income/average net book value of property and equipment
14. Asset turnover	Total income/average total assets
15. Paid occupancy percentage	Rooms sold/rooms available
16. Profit margin	Increase in net assets/total revenue
17. Operating efficiency ratio	Income before fixed expenses/total revenue
18. Return on assets	Increase in net assets/average total assets
19. Return on members' equity	Increase in net assets/average net assets
20. Mix of sales	Departmental revenues are totaled; percentages of total revenue are calculated for each
21. Average food service check	Total food revenue/number of food covers
22. Food cost percentage	Cost of food sold/food sales
23. Beverage cost percentage	Cost of beverages sold/beverage sales
24. Labor cost percentage	Labor cost by department/department revenues

In addition, if the accounting procedures used by two separate clubs differ in several areas, then a comparison of their ratios will likely show differences related to accounting procedures as well as to financial positions or operations.

No single ratio tells the entire story; often, many ratios must be used to understand the financial picture of a club. Generally, the same ratios should be viewed over a series of time periods.

Finally, financial ratios are generally computed from figures in the financial statements. These figures are based on historical costs. Over time, the effects of inflation render some of these figures less useful. For example, an average food service check of $15 in 20X9 for a given club is not necessarily a better performance than $12 in 20X1; if the inflation rate was greater than 25 percent for the 20X1–20X9 time period, $15 in 20X9 is worth less than $12 in 20X1. Ratios that are most affected by inflation include those that contain property, equipment, or members' equity in either the numerator or denominator. In addition, depreciation, since it relates to the historical cost of property and equipment, is often "understated," so income figures involving depreciation expense are often "overstated."

Accountants have used some fairly sophisticated techniques, such as restating the financial statements in constant dollars of equal purchasing power, to overcome this limitation in ratio analysis. However, as desirable as this correction is, it is often not used because of the major effort and time required to use it. An alternative approach is to apply an inflation correction factor to ratios that are affected by inflation. For example, using the just-mentioned food service example, assume that inflation for the 20X1–20X9 period was 50 percent. The comparison of average food service for 20X1 and 20X9 would be as follows:

20X1 (historical)	$12
20X1 (adjusted)	$18*
20X9	$15

*$12 × 150% = $18

Thus, it is clear that the 20X1 food service check is preferred to the 20X9 food service check when inflation is considered.

Even though these limitations are present, a careful use of ratios that acknowledges their shortcomings will result in an enhanced understanding of a club's operations and overall financial position.

Endnotes

1. This may be determined mathematically using the following formula:

$$\frac{CA - x}{CL - x} = \text{desired current ratio where } x \text{ indicates the amount of current assets that would be used to retire current liabilities. The calculation for the Grand Club is as follows:}$$

$$\frac{1,140,000 - x}{614,500 - x} = 2; \quad x = 89,000; \quad \frac{1,051,000}{525,500} = 2 \text{ times}$$

Key Terms

accounts receivable turnover—A measure of the rapidity of conversion of accounts receivable into cash; calculated by dividing revenue by average accounts receivable.

acid-test ratio—Ratio of total cash and near-cash current assets to total current liabilities.

activity ratios—A group of ratios that reflect management's ability to use the club's assets and resources.

asset turnover—An activity ratio, calculated by dividing total revenues by average total assets.

average collection period—The average number of days it takes a club to collect its accounts receivable; calculated by dividing the accounts receivable turnover into 365 (the number of days in a year).

beverage cost percentage—A ratio comparing the cost of beverages sold to beverage sales; calculated by dividing the cost of beverages sold by beverage sales.

current ratio—Ratio of total current assets to total current liabilities, expressed as a coverage of so many times; it is calculated by dividing current assets by current liabilities.

debt-equity ratio—Compares the debt of a club to its net worth (net assets or members' equity) and indicates the club's ability to withstand adversity and meet its long-term obligations; calculated by dividing total liabilities by total members' equity.

fixed charge coverage ratio—A variation of the number of times interest earned ratio that considers leases as well as interest expense. It is calculated by dividing lease expenses and earnings before interest expenses by interest expense and lease expense.

food cost percentage—A ratio comparing the cost of food sold to food sales; calculated by dividing the cost of food sold by total food sales.

inventory turnover—A ratio showing how quickly inventory is moving from storage to productive use; calculated by dividing the cost of food or beverages used by the average food or beverage inventory.

labor cost percentage—A ratio comparing the labor expense for each department by the total revenue generated by the department; total labor cost by department divided by departmental revenues.

liquidity ratios—A group of ratios that reveal the ability of a club to meet its short-term obligations.

long-term debt to total capitalization ratio—A solvency ratio showing long-term debt as a percentage of the sum of long-term debt and net assets; it is calculated by dividing long-term debt by long-term debt and net assets.

number of times interest earned ratio—A solvency ratio expressing the number of times interest expense can be covered; it is calculated by dividing earnings before interest expenses by interest expense.

operating cash flows to current liabilities ratio—A liquidity ratio that compares the cash flow from the club's operating activities to its obligations at the statement of financial position date that must be paid within 12 months. It is calculated by dividing operating cash flows by average current liabilities.

operating cash flows to total liabilities ratio—A solvency ratio that uses figures from both the statement of cash flows and the balance sheet. Operating cash flows divided by average total liabilities.

operating efficiency ratio—A measure of management's ability to generate sales and control expenses; calculated by dividing income before fixed charges expense by total income.

operating ratios—A group of ratios that assist in the analysis of a club's operations.

profit margin—An overall measure of management's ability to generate sales and control expenses; calculated by dividing results of operations by total revenue.

profitability ratios—A group of ratios that reflect the results of all areas of management's responsibilities.

property and equipment turnover—A ratio measuring management's effectiveness in using property and equipment to generate revenue; it is calculated by dividing average total net book value of property and equipment into total revenue generated for the period. Sometimes called fixed asset turnover.

ratio analysis—The comparison of related facts and figures.

return on assets (ROA)—A ratio providing a general indicator of the profitability of a club by comparing net income to total investment; it is calculated by dividing net income by average total assets.

return on members' equity (ROE)—A ratio providing a general indicator of the profitability of a club by comparing results of club operations to the members' investment; it is calculated by dividing results of operations by average members' equity (or net assets).

seat turnover—An activity ratio measuring the rate at which members are served within a club's main dining room or other food outlet; it is calculated by dividing the number of people served within the outlet by the number of seats available.

solvency ratio—A measure of the extent to which a club is financed by debt and is able to meet its long-term obligations; calculated by dividing total assets by total liabilities.

solvency ratios—A group of ratios that measure the extent to which a club has been financed by debt and is able to meet its long-term obligations.

 # Review Questions

1. How does ratio analysis benefit creditors?
2. If you are joining a club, which ratios would be most useful to you? Why?
3. What are the limitations of ratio analysis?
4. How do the three user groups of ratio analysis react to solvency ratios?

5. Why is the labor cost percentage considered to be a critical operating ratio for management?

6. What do activity ratios highlight?

7. How is profit margin calculated? How is it used?

8. Which standard is the most effective for comparison with ratios?

9. What does the ratio expression "turnover" mean?

10. Of what value is the food sales/total sales ratio to the manager of a club? To a creditor?

 **Problems** ─────────────────────────────

Problem 1

Indicate the effects of the transactions listed below on each of the following: total current assets, working capital (CA − CL), and current ratio. Indicate increase with "+," indicate decrease with "−" and indicate no effect or effect cannot be determined with "0." Assume an initial current ratio of greater than 1.0.

	Total Current Assets	Working Capital	Current Ratio
1. Food is sold for cash.	_____	_____	_____
2. Equipment is sold at less than its net book value.	_____	_____	_____
3. Beverages are sold on account.	_____	_____	_____
4. Accrued payroll is paid.	_____	_____	_____
5. A fully depreciated fixed asset is retired.	_____	_____	_____
6. Equipment is purchased with long-term notes.	_____	_____	_____
7. Utility expenses are paid (they were not previously accrued).	_____	_____	_____
8. Cash is borrowed on a long-term basis from a bank.	_____	_____	_____

Problem 2

Selected financial ratios of the Razorback Club for 20X1 through 20X3 are as follows:

	20X1	20X2	20X3
Current ratio	1.6	1.7	1.8
Acid-test ratio	1.3	1.35	1.4
Accounts receivable turnover	24	20	16
Inventory turnover	20	22	24

Required:

Comment on the changing liquidity of the Razorback Club from 20X1 to 20X3. Be specific and use the ratios listed in this problem.

Problem 3

The Bruner Club has a 200-seat dining facility. Selected information is provided from operations in four short scenarios.

Required

Answer the question for each scenario.

1. The club had a beginning food inventory of $25,000 and an ending food inventory of $27,000 for 20X2. The inventory turnover was 24, and employee food expense was $9,000 for the year. What was the total cost of food sold?

2. The club had food sales during June 20X2 of $100,000, of which 40 percent were during lunch. If the club was open 26 days of the month and the average seat turnover was 1.5 per lunch period, what was the average lunch food service check?

3. The club's cost of food sold percentage was 40 percent during April 20X2. Total food sales in April were $90,000. The cost of employee meals for April totaled $1,000. What was the cost of food used?

4. The cost of food sold during July totaled $38,000. The beginning food inventory equaled $22,000 and the food inventory turnover was 3.1 times. If the cost of employee meals was $1,200 for the month, what was the ending food inventory?

Chapter 6 Outline

Competencies

1. Identify and distinguish between different types of costs and give an example of each. (pp. 139–143)

2. Describe how managers use cost–volume–profit analysis, identifying major assumptions and equations on which CVP analysis is based. (pp. 143–148)

3. Explain and apply the concept of cost approaches to pricing, including price elasticity of demand, informal pricing approaches, modifying factors, and mark–up approaches. (pp. 148–153)

4. Explain food sales mix and the menu engineering approach to pricing food and beverage items, including the value of the integrated pricing approach. (pp. 153–157)

6

Understanding and Applying Cost Concepts

A COST IS BEST DESCRIBED as something of value sacrificed or given up in order to achieve a specific objective. The term *cost* is often used interchangeably with the term *expense*. Technically, there is a difference between the two terms. An expense is appropriately described as an asset consumed or a service used in the process of achieving an objective. For purposes of this chapter, however, we will use the terms cost and expense interchangeably.

Costs are a huge issue for clubs. For a club that does not plan on having a reserve of cash at the end of the year, costs are equal to 100 percent of the revenues that the organization generates. Both general and financial managers need to know the many aspects of the costs that are likely to be encountered.

This chapter discusses cost behavior and explains the concepts of fixed and variable costs, direct and indirect costs, overhead costs, relevant costs, opportunity costs, sunk costs, and controllable and uncontrollable costs. Cost–volume–profit analysis is discussed, as well as cost and informal approaches to pricing. In addition, there is a brief discussion of sales mix and menu engineering.

Cost Behavior

An important aspect of a cost is the way it varies *in total* in relation to some activity. If a particular cost does not change in total as activity changes, it is called a **fixed cost**. For example, the rent that a club pays on its building would normally not change as the number of members increased, therefore it would be labeled a fixed cost. Other typical fixed costs include property taxes, insurance, salaried staff wages, and depreciation on equipment.

Costs that vary in total as activity changes are labeled **variable costs**. Food costs for a club's dining facility would increase as activity (the number of meals served) increased. Other typical examples of variable costs include wages paid to hourly employees and supplies used.

Another cost perspective focuses on costs *per unit*, rather than total cost. Many decisions (for example, pricing) revolve around unit costs. Assume that the monthly salary of the club's food and beverage manager is $2,500 and that the club served 3,000 meals for the month of June. The fixed cost per meal (to cover the manager's salary) for the month of June would be $.833. If the number of meals served in July were only 2,500, the fixed cost per meal would be $1.00. There is an inverse relationship between unit fixed cost and the level of activity. The higher the

Exhibit 1   Fixed Costs: Total and Per Unit

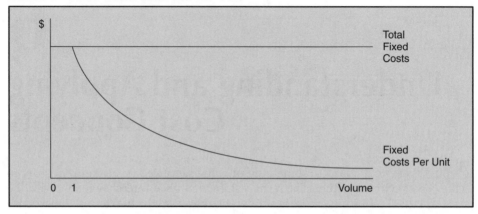

Exhibit 2   Variable Costs: Total and Per Unit

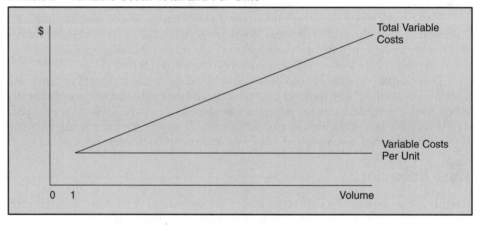

level of activity, the lower the fixed cost per unit, and vice versa. Exhibit 1 shows graphically both total fixed cost and unit fixed cost.

While fixed costs per unit may vary, variable cost per unit remains the same, at least in the short term. If, for example, the cost of preparing and serving a meal is $2.00 and the ingredient costs of the meal are $4.00, the unit variable cost of the meal is $6.00 regardless of the number of meals served. Total variable costs of meals served would, of course, vary directly with the number of meals served. Exhibit 2 illustrates graphically both the total variable and unit variable cost function.

Some costs have both variable and fixed components. These are referred to as **mixed costs**. Common examples of mixed costs include maintenance costs and the general manager's total compensation package (salary and bonus). In the case of maintenance, a certain amount of painting and plumbing work would be done on a regular basis regardless of volume of activity at the club. If, however, the club decided to rent out part of the facility for non–club members to use for receptions,

Exhibit 3 Step Costs

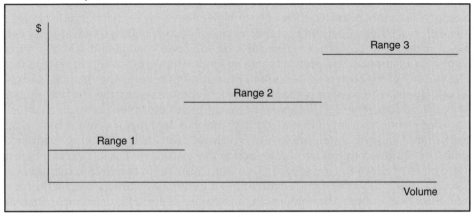

it would be reasonable that maintenance costs would increase. When compiling a budget, it is necessary to break down the mixed costs into the variable and fixed elements in order to accurately predict the future cost of maintenance. (Discussion of the methods for breaking down mixed costs is beyond our scope here.)

Another type of cost, the **step cost**, is one that increases in stair–step fashion over increasing amounts of activity. That is, step costs are constant within a range of activity but different among ranges of activity. An example of this would be rangers on the golf course. If there is little activity on the course, there would be no need for a ranger; however, at some level of activity, the cost of a ranger would be added to the budget. With enough additional activity, another ranger would be added. Exhibit 3 illustrates the nature of a step cost.

Direct and Indirect Costs

Costs can also be classified as either direct or indirect. Costs are considered direct if they are traceable to a given cost object. Indirect costs are related to a cost object, but cannot be traced to it; indirect costs must be allocated to the cost object on some reasonable basis. In order to determine if a cost is direct or indirect, the cost object must first be identified. A **cost object** is anything for which a separate accumulation of costs is desired. Consider, for example, the salary of the food and beverage manager of a club versus the salary of the general manager of the same club. If the cost object is defined as the food and beverage department of the club, then the salary of the F&B manager would be direct to that cost object, but the salary of the GM would be indirect to that cost object.

Granted, some of the GM's salary could normally be absorbed by the F&B department, but it would be tacked on to the F&B department through a process called allocation. The GM's salary would be an indirect cost of the F&B department. On the other hand, if the entire club was selected as the cost object, then the GM's salary would be considered a direct cost of that cost object.

Accountability for cost control is possible only if all costs in the club are identified with a specific cost object before a fiscal period begins.

Overhead Costs

Some costs cannot be traced directly to any given revenue center, but rather benefit the club as a whole. Costs that are indirect to all departments are considered **overhead costs**. Typical overhead costs for a club include general and administrative expenses, insurance, and promotional expenses. These costs could be allocated to the various profit centers of the club to provide a more complete financial picture of operations. The basic operations schedule as prescribed by the *Uniform System of Financial Reporting for Clubs* does not include the allocation of overhead costs.

For example, assume that a country club has two major profit centers—the golf course and the dining room. An overhead cost, such as liability insurance, could be allocated to the two centers on some reasonable basis. Two commonly used bases of allocation are square footage and number of employees. In this situation, it would probably be more equitable to allocate the insurance cost on the basis of the relative number of employees in the two cost centers. If, for example, the golf course had 60 percent of the total employees of the two cost centers, then the golf course should absorb 60 percent of the insurance expense, with the other 40 percent allocated to the dining facility.

A key principle of responsibility accounting is to make individuals responsible only for the costs that they can control. By allocating overhead costs to departments, frustration can develop among the department heads who see uncontrollable costs appear on their individual financial reports. The benefit of placing allocated costs on departmental reports is in making managers and board members aware that certain costs of the organization benefit the club's individual departments in an indirect way.

It is possible to use a system of dual reporting whereby general managers and board members receive two sets of periodic financial reports—one without allocated costs and the other with allocated costs.

Relevant Costs

Management must often decide between alternative courses of action. For example, a golf course superintendent may need to decide whether to buy a new greens mower or repair the old mower. The decision must be made on the basis of the relevant costs of the two options. **Relevant costs** are those that are future and that differ between alternative courses of action. To be relevant to a given decision, a cost must meet both of these criteria. For example, the cost of a new dishwashing machine the club is considering purchasing is relevant, but the (past) cost of the old machine currently in use is not. If the new dishwasher is being considered because it will have a labor savings of $4,000 annually over the old machine, the $4,000 is a relevant cost. If, on the other hand, the energy costs are $600 annually for both the old and the new machines, the energy costs are not relevant to the decision since they do not differ between alternatives.

Opportunity Costs

Opportunity costs represent profit that is foregone on a project due to acceptance of an alternative project. For example, assume that a country club currently owns

60 acres of undeveloped land that can be sold for $120,000, net of taxes. If the club decides not to sell the land and instead builds another nine-hole golf course, the club should consider the $120,000 of "lost profit" on the land as an additional opportunity cost of the golf course for decision-making purposes. Opportunity costs are relevant for decision-making purposes, but do not show up on the financial statements of the organization.

Sunk Costs

Sunk costs are costs that have been expended in the past and have no relevance for current or future decision-making purposes. An example of a sunk cost would be the cost of software purchased by the club two years ago for $1,500. If that software is now outdated and inefficient for the club's purposes, even though it is not fully depreciated, it may need to be replaced by newer, more efficient software. In making the decision to purchase the new software, only the cost of the new software and its cost savings should be considered relevant to this decision.

Controllable and Uncontrollable Costs

A cost is considered controllable if an individual has the ability to influence that particular cost. It would be reasonable to assume that the manager of the club's pro shop should be able to influence the labor costs and cost of merchandise sold in the pro shop. These costs would therefore be considered **controllable costs** for this manager. On the other hand, suppose that the general manager of the club insists that an employee be available during the day outside the pro shop to deliver beverages to members at a cost of $800 per month chargeable to the pro shop. This cost is not controllable to the manager of the pro shop, even though it has been determined that it is to be a direct cost of the pro shop. The cost of this labor is an uncontrollable cost to the manager of the pro shop. This labor cost is controllable, however, by the general manager of the club. A cost that may not be controllable at one level is often controllable at the next level of the organization. All costs are controllable at some level of the organization.

Cost-Volume-Profit Analysis

Cost-volume-profit (CVP) analysis is a powerful tool that allows managers to study the interrelationships among revenue, fixed costs, variable costs, and volume. CVP analysis is often referred to as *breakeven analysis*, although this term is not as descriptively accurate—the breakeven point is only one point on an infinite spectrum that can be determined using CVP analysis. Still, it is an important point, and our discussion will begin with the breakeven point. We will then go on to solve for certain profit levels above the breakeven point.

The breakeven point can be determined by either the graphic approach or the equation approach. Exhibit 4 shows graphically the relationship among revenues, fixed costs, variable costs, and volume. The breakeven point is the point where the revenue line intersects the total cost line. At this point, the club has neither a profit nor a loss. Revenue is just enough to cover total costs. The area above the breakeven point between the revenue line and the total cost line is the profit area. The

Exhibit 4   Cost-Volume-Profit Graph

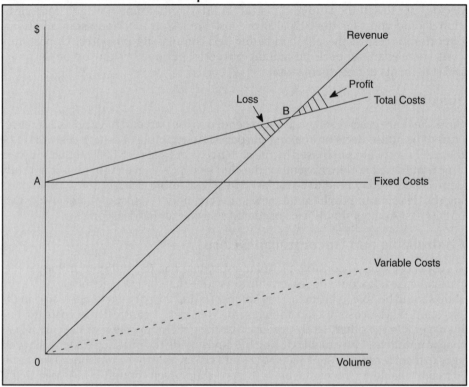

area below the breakeven point between the revenue line and the total cost line is the loss area. This chart illustrates a key concept: once the fixed costs of the club are covered, as long as variable costs are covered, a profit will be generated.

CVP Assumptions

Although CVP is a powerful tool, it is important to understand that there are certain assumptions that must be in place for it to be an effective tool. The following is a list of the basic CVP assumptions.

1. Unit food and beverage revenue is known and is a fixed amount; therefore, revenue increases in linear fashion and proportionally to volume.

2. Unit variable cost is known and is a fixed amount; therefore, total variable cost increases in linear fashion and proportionally to volume.

3. Fixed costs are constant in total over the period under consideration.

4. Any mixed costs can be broken down into their fixed and variable components.

Exhibit 5   Cost-Volume-Profit Analysis Equation—Single Product

A CVP analysis equation expresses the cost-volume-profit relationships as follows:

$$I_n = SX - VX - F$$

where:
I_n = Net income
S = Selling price
X = Units sold
V = Variable cost per unit
F = Total fixed cost

therefore:
SX = Total revenue
VX = Total variable costs

5. There is a single product involved in the analysis or, if there are multiple products, then the revenue mix stays constant over time.

6. Dues and initiation fee revenues are fixed in the short run.

CVP Equations

The CVP chart is useful in visually expressing the relationships among the revenue and cost functions. However, the equation approach is easier to use and more accurate. The basic CVP equation is shown in Exhibit 5. Using this equation to solve for the breakeven point, we get:

$$0 = SX - VX - F$$

It simply says that there is no profit or loss at the point where total revenue equals total variable and fixed costs. This formula can be rearranged to solve for any of the four variables as follows:

Equation	Determines
$X = \dfrac{F}{S - V}$	Units sold at breakeven
$F = SX - VX$	Fixed costs at breakeven
$S = \dfrac{F}{X} + V$	Selling price at breakeven
$V = S - \dfrac{F}{X}$	Variable cost per unit at breakeven

For example, if a dining facility had monthly fixed costs of $6,000, revenue per meal of $12, and variable cost per meal of $6, the breakeven point in meals served per month would be 1,000 as the following shows:

$$X = \frac{\$6,000}{\$12 - \$6}$$

$$= \underline{1,000} \text{ meals}$$

The dollar amount of monthly revenue needed to break even could be calculated in one of two ways. First, simply multiply the number of meals times $12 to get $12,000. A second approach uses the following formula:

$$\text{Total Revenue at the Breakeven Point} = \frac{F}{\dfrac{S - V}{S}}$$

$$= \frac{\$6,000}{\dfrac{\$12 - \$6}{\$12}}$$

$$= \underline{12,000}$$

Contribution Margin

Notice that the denominator of the above equation is revenue minus variable cost divided by revenue. The name for this denominator is the *contribution margin ratio (CMR)*. The **contribution margin** is the difference between revenue and variable cost. Contribution margin ratio is simply the contribution margin divided by revenue. (Since revenue and variable costs are both linear, the use of unit dollars and total dollars results in the same percentage.)

The above formula solves for the breakeven point in single product situations. Since most clubs sell more than one product, the formula must be adjusted to address multiple product situations. For example, if a club with a golf course and a restaurant was attempting to determine its breakeven point, the only rational breakeven point to solve for would be breakeven point in total dollars.

This would be done by calculating the **weighted average contribution margin ratio (CMR$_w$)** of the two profit centers and dividing that ratio into total fixed costs. In order to calculate the overall breakeven point for a club, the total fixed costs of the club would be divided by the weighted average contribution margin ratio for the profit centers.

For example, assume a country club had two profit centers, a dining facility and a riding stable, with the following revenue and cost data:

	Dining Facility	Riding Stables	Total
Sales	$1,500,000	$500,000	$2,000,000
Variable Costs	900,000	400,000	1,300,000
Contribution Margin	$600,000	$100,000	700,000
Fixed Costs			600,000
Net Profit			$100,000

The weighted average contribution margin ratio would be .35, calculated as follows:

$$\text{CMR}_\text{w} = \frac{\text{Total Contribution Margin}}{\text{Total Sales}}$$

$$= \frac{\$700,000}{\$2,000,000}$$

$$= .35$$

Another way to calculate the CM percentage would be to weight the two profit centers' relative sales and multiply the weights (75 percent for dining, 25 percent for stables) by the respective contribution margin percentages (40 percent for dining, 20 percent for stables):

$$\text{CMR}_\text{w} = (.75)\,(.4) + (.25)\,(.2)$$

$$= .35$$

Target Profit

Another useful manipulation of the CVP equation is to use it to solve for some point above breakeven. This is done simply by adding the desired profit to the numerator of the dollars equation. For example, if the desired profit above breakeven is $3,000 per month, the monthly fixed costs are $6,000, and the marginal contribution percentage is 45 percent, the revenue necessary to make the target profit of $3,000 is $20,000 as shown below:

$$\text{Total Revenue at \$3,000 Profit} = \frac{\text{F} + \$3,000}{\text{CMR}}$$

$$= \frac{\$6,000 + \$3,000}{.45}$$

$$= \$20,000$$

This equation does not consider the effect of income taxes, which we will return to below.

Because club members typically pay dues and initiation fees, the analysis becomes more complicated. Assume, for example, that a club has 1,000 members who pay $200 per month in dues. In addition, assume that 100 new members join on January 1 of this year and pay $2,000 in initiation fees. The club has a CMR_w of .6, fixed costs of $5,000,000, and a before-tax profit goal of $500,000. The amount of revenue needed to meet this profit goal can be calculated using the following equation where F = fixed costs, D = annual dues, IF = initiation fees, and CMR_w = weighted average contribution margin ratio.

$$\text{Revenue} = \frac{\text{F} - \text{D} - \text{IF} + \text{Profit}}{\text{CMR}_\text{w}}$$

$$= \frac{\$5,000,000 - \$2,400,000 - \$2,000,000 + \$500,000}{.6}$$

$$= \$1,833,333$$

The proof of this is shown below:

Dues	$ 2,400,000
Initiation Fees	2,000,000
Sales	1,833,333
Total Revenue	6,233,333
Less: Variable Costs (1,833,333 × .4)	733,333
Contribution Margin	5,500,000
Less: Fixed Costs	5,000,000
Pretax Profits	$ 500,000

The Effect of Income Taxes

Another useful manipulation of the basic equation involves adjusting it for income taxes. A club subject to income taxes may state its financial goal in terms of after-tax profits. To determine the revenue needed in order to achieve after-tax goals, we must adjust the equation used earlier to account for income taxes. Rather than add desired profit to fixed costs, we must add the amount of pre-tax revenue that will generate the desired after-tax profit. This amount is determined by dividing the desired profit by 1 minus the tax rate. For example, assume a club with an income tax rate of 20 percent desires after-tax profit of $6,000. If this club has a contribution margin ratio of .45 and fixed costs of $6,000, the revenue needed would be calculated as follows:

$$\text{Total Revenue at \$6,000 After-Tax Profit} = \frac{F + (\$6,000/.8)}{CMR}$$

$$= \frac{\$6,000 + \$7,500}{.45}$$

$$= \$30,000$$

Cost Approaches to Pricing ─────────────────

A club's dues structure and the prices it charges in its profit centers are major determinants of the club's financial health. When prices are too high, members are unhappy and revenue is lost. On the other hand, when prices are too low, the club may fail to break even. Revenue must cover expenses. Another factor affecting pricing is the "positioning" of the dues or prices charged within the local marketplace. Dues or prices set too low may tend to degrade the perceived quality of the club, whereas inflated dues or prices may tend to reduce the perceived value of the club's offerings from members' perspective. In the following discussion, we look at pricing from a cost perspective. However, this is not meant to suggest that noncost factors such as market demand and competition are not relevant to the pricing decision.

Clubs must make a profit (or increase their net assets) for expanding operations, replacing fixed assets, and upgrading services. Profit should not result simply because revenues happened to exceed expenses by chance. A healthy bottom

Exhibit 6   Price Elasticity of Demand Formula

$$\text{Price Elasticity of Demand} = \frac{\dfrac{\Delta Q}{Q_o}}{\dfrac{\Delta P}{P_o}}$$

where:

ΔQ	=	Change in quantity demanded
Q_o	=	Base quantity demanded
ΔP	=	Change in price
P_o	=	Base price

line should result from a concerted effort to have revenues exceed expenses for the fiscal period. Pricing is a key element.

Price Elasticity of Demand

The concept of **price elasticity of demand** provides a means for measuring how sensitive demand is to changes in price. In general, as the selling price of a product or service decreases, everything else being the same, more will be sold. When the price of a product is increased, only rarely is more of the product sold, everything else being the same, and even then there may be factors which account for the increased demand.

The demand for a product may be characterized as elastic or inelastic. Exhibit 6 illustrates the price elasticity of demand formula for determining whether the demand is elastic or inelastic. The base quantity demanded (Q_o) is the number of units sold during a given period before changing prices. The change in quantity demanded (ΔQ) is the change in the number of units sold during the period the prices were changed in comparison to the prior period. The base price (P_o) is the price of the product and/or service for the period prior to the price change. The change in price (ΔP) is the change in price from the base price. Strictly speaking, this equation will virtually always yield a negative number, since it is the result of dividing a negative change in quantity demanded by a positive price change or vice versa. (In other words, as price goes up, quantity demanded goes down and vice versa.) By convention, however, the negative sign is ignored.

If the elasticity of demand exceeds 1.0, the demand is said to be elastic. That is, demand is sensitive to price changes. With an elastic demand, the percentage change in quantity demanded exceeds the percentage change in price. In other words, any additional revenues generated by the higher price are more than offset by the decrease in demand. When demand is elastic, price and total revenues are inversely related, so a price increase will decrease total revenues. Up to a point, price decreases will increase total revenues.

If elasticity of demand is less than 1.0, demand is said to be inelastic. That is, a percentage change in price results in a smaller percentage change in quantity demanded. Every club desires an inelastic demand for its offerings. When prices are increased, the percentage reduction in quantity demanded is less than the percentage of the price increase. Therefore, revenues and generally profits increase despite some decrease in the quantity demanded.

Let's look at an example illustrating the calculation of price elasticity of demand. A country club opens one of its two 18-hole golf courses to the public. It sells 1,000 rounds of golf during a recent 30-day period at $20 per round. For the next 30-day period, the price was increased to $22, and 950 rounds were sold. The demand for the golf rounds over this time period is considered to be inelastic, since the calculated price elasticity of demand is less than 1. The calculation of price elasticity of demand is as follows:

$$\text{Price Elasticity of Demand} \quad = \quad \frac{50}{1,000} \quad \div \quad \frac{2}{20}$$

$$= \quad .05 \quad \div \quad .1$$

$$= \quad \underline{\underline{.5}}$$

In general, demand in the club segment of the hospitality industry is considered to be elastic. Generally, demand will be elastic where competition is high. Where the competition is low or nonexistent, or where a club has greatly differentiated its offerings, then demand may be inelastic.

Informal Pricing Approaches

There are several informal approaches to setting prices for membership dues, food, and beverages. Since each of these approaches ignores the cost of providing the product, they are only briefly presented here as a point of departure for our discussion of more scientific approaches to setting prices.

Several managers price their products on the basis of what the competition charges. If the competition charges $1,500 for a club membership, or an average of $20 for a dinner, then managers using competitive pricing set those prices as well. When the competition changes its prices, managers using this pricing approach follow suit. Although this approach may seem reasonable when there is much competition in a market, it ignores the many differences that exist among club operations, such as location, amenities, atmosphere, and so forth. In addition, it ignores the cost structure of the club. Clubs must consider their own cost structures when making pricing decisions. A dominant club with a low cost structure may "cause" competitors to go bankrupt if those competitors ignore their own costs and price their products following the competitive approach.

Another informal pricing approach used by some managers is intuition. Intuitive pricing is based on what the manager feels the member is willing to pay. Generally, managers using this approach rely on their experience regarding members' reactions to prices. However, as with competitive pricing, intuition ignores costs and may result in a failure not only to generate a reasonable profit, but even to recover costs.

A third approach is psychological pricing. Here, prices are established on the basis of what the member "expects" to pay. This approach may be used by relatively exclusive clubs and by club members who think that their members believe "the more paid, the better the product." Although psychological pricing does possess a certain merit, it fails to consider costs and, therefore, may not result in profit maximization.

Finally, the trial and error pricing approach first sets a product price, monitors member reactions, and then adjusts the price based on these reactions. This approach appears to consider fully the club members. However, problems with this method include:

- Monitoring members' reactions may take longer than the manager would like to allow.

- Frequent changes in prices based on members' reactions may result in price confusion among members.

- The trial and error approach fails to consider costs.

Although all of the informal price approaches have some merit, they are most useful only when coupled with the cost approaches we are now going to consider.

Cost Approaches: Four Modifying Factors

Before looking at specific cost approaches to pricing, however, we need to set the stage. When pricing is based on a cost approach, four modifying factors to consider are historical prices, perceived price/value relationships, competition, and price rounding. These price modifiers relate to the pricing of nearly all products and services.

First, prices that have been charged in the past must be considered when pricing the club's products. A dramatic change dictated by a cost approach may seem unrealistic to the members. For example, if a breakfast meal in the club's restaurant with a realistic price of $8.49 was mistakenly priced at $4.49 for five years, the club may be "forced" to move slowly from $4.49 to $8.49 by implementing several price increases over a period of time.

Second, the member must perceive that the product and/or service is reasonably priced in order to feel that he or she is getting a good value. Many individuals in the first decade of the 21st century appear to be more value-conscious than ever. Most are willing to pay prices much higher than a few years ago, but they also demand value for the price paid. The perceived value of a meal includes not only the food and drink but also the atmosphere, location, quality of service, and many other often intangible factors.

Third, the competition cannot be ignored. If a club's product is viewed as substantially the same as a competitor's, then, everything else being equal, the prices would have to be similar.

Finally, the price may be modified by price rounding. That is, the item's price will be rounded up to the nearest $.25 or possibly up to $X.95.

Exhibit 7   Chicken Dinner Ingredients and Cost

Ingredient	Cost
Chicken—2 pieces	$1.80
Baked potato with sour cream	.50
Roll and butter	.20
Vegetable	.45
Salad with dressing	.35
Coffee—refills free	.25
Total cost	$3.55

Mark-Up Approaches to Pricing. A major method of pricing is marking up the cost of goods sold. The **mark-up** is designed to cover all nonproduct costs, such as labor, utilities, supplies, interest expense, and taxes, and also to provide the desired profit. This approach is often used with food and beverages.

Under the mark-up approaches to pricing are **ingredient mark-up** and **prime ingredient mark-up.** The ingredient mark-up approach considers all product costs. The prime ingredient mark-up considers only the cost of the major ingredient. The four steps of the ingredient cost approach are as follows:

1. Determine the ingredient costs.

2. Determine the multiple to use in marking up the ingredient costs.

3. Multiply the ingredient costs by the multiple to get the desired price.

4. Determine whether the price seems reasonable based on the market.

The multiple determined in Step 2 is generally based on the desired product cost percentage. For example, if a product cost percentage of 40 percent is desired, the multiple would be 2.5, determined as follows:

$$\text{Multiple} = \frac{1}{\text{Desired Product Cost Percentage}}$$

$$= \frac{1}{.4}$$

$$= \underline{\underline{2.5}}$$

The ingredient cost approach can be illustrated using ingredient cost figures for a chicken dinner listed in Exhibit 7. Assuming a desired multiple of 2.5, the price of the chicken dinner is determined as follows:

$$\text{Price} = \text{Ingredients' Cost} \times \text{Multiple}$$

$$= \$3.55 \times 2.5$$

$$= \underline{\underline{\$8.88}}$$

Exhibit 8   Sales Mix Alternatives and Number of Meals

		Sales Mix Alternatives	
	#1	#2	#3
Chicken	500	300	200
Fish	200	300	300
Steak	300	400	500
Total	1,000	1,000	1,000

If the result appears reasonable based on the market for chicken dinners, then the chicken dinner is sold for about $8.88. (In this instance, price rounding might set the price at $8.95.)

The prime ingredient approach differs only in that the cost of the prime ingredient is marked up rather than the total cost of all ingredients. The multiple used, all other things being equal, would be greater than the multiple used when considering the total cost of all ingredients. The multiple used would generally be based on experience—that is, what multiple has provided adequate cost coverage and desired profit. Using the same chicken dinner example, the prime ingredient cost is chicken with a cost of $1.80. Using an arbitrary multiple of 4.9, the chicken dinner is priced at $8.82, calculated as follows:

$$\text{Price} = \text{Prime Ingredient Cost} \times \text{Multiple}$$
$$= \$1.80 \times 4.9$$
$$= \underline{\underline{\$8.82}}$$

If the cost of chicken in the above example increases to $2.00 for the dinner portion, then the new price would be $9.80 ($2.00 × 4.9). The prime ingredient approach assumes that the costs of all other ingredients change in proportion to the prime ingredient; that is, when the prime ingredient's cost increases 10 percent, then other ingredients' costs have also increased 10 percent. When changes in the other ingredients' cost percentage differ from the prime ingredient's, then the product cost percentage will differ from the established goal.

Food Sales Mix and Gross Profit

Traditionally, restaurant operations have placed heavy emphasis on food cost percentage. The multiple in the mark-up approach used to price meals for many restaurants has been set at 2.5 times, so that a 40 percent cost of food sold could be achieved. This emphasis resulted in many managers evaluating the profitability of their food service operations by reviewing the food cost percentage. However, the food cost percentage may not be the best guide to evaluating food sales, as will be shown below.

Consider a club restaurant that may sell one of three alternative sales mixes for the week as listed in Exhibit 8. Notice in each sales mix, the same number of

Exhibit 9   Profitability of Three Sales Mix Alternatives

	Selling Price	Cost Per Meal	Menu Item Food Cost Percentage	Meals Sold	Revenue	Total Cost of Food	Gross Profit
Alternative #1							
Chicken	$7.95	$2.49	31.32%	500	$3,975	$1,245	$2,730
Fish	10.95	4.15	37.90	200	2,790	830	1,960
Steak	14.95	6.65	44.48	300	4,485	1,995	2,490
Total				1,000	$11,250	$4,070	$7,780

$$\text{Food cost \%} = \frac{4,070}{11,250} = 36.18\%$$

	Selling Price	Cost Per Meal	Menu Item Food Cost Percentage	Meals Sold	Revenue	Total Cost of Food	Gross Profit
Alternative #2							
Chicken	$7.95	$2.49	31.32%	300	$2,385	$747	$1,638
Fish	10.95	4.15	37.90	300	3,285	1,245	2,040
Steak	14.95	6.65	44.48	400	5,980	2,660	3,320
Total				1,000	$11,650	$4,652	$6,998

$$\text{Food cost \%} = \frac{4,652}{11,650} = 39.93\%$$

	Selling Price	Cost Per Meal	Menu Item Food Cost Percentage	Meals Sold	Revenue	Total Cost of Food	Gross Profit
Alternative #3							
Chicken	$7.95	$2.49	31.32%	200	$1,590	$498	$1,092
Fish	10.95	4.15	37.90	300	3,285	1,245	2,040
Steak	14.95	6.65	44.48	500	7,475	3,325	4,150
Total				1,000	$12,350	$5,068	$7,282

$$\text{Food cost \%} = \frac{5,068}{12,350} = 41.04\%$$

Exhibit 10   Comparison of Sales Mix Alternatives

Sales Mix Alternative	Total Revenue	Total Cost of Food	Gross Profit	Food Cost %
1	$11,250	$4,070	$7,780	36.18%
2	11,650	4,656	6,998	39.93
3	12,350	5,068	7,282	41.04

meals is served. Exhibit 9 shows the total revenue, total cost of food sold, the gross profit, and food cost percentage for each alternative. The selling price and cost per meal remain constant for each menu item across the three alternative sales mixes. Exhibit 10 compares the three options. The sales mix with the lowest total food cost percentage is mix #1 at 36.18 percent, while mix #3 has the highest at 41.04 percent, or nearly five percent greater than mix #1. If the most desirable mix is based on food cost percentage, then mix #1 would be first followed by mix #2 with mix #3 last. However, the decision should be made based on gross profit generated. In this example, mix #1 would still rank first at $7,780, but that will not always be the case. Note, for example, that mix #3 (with the highest food cost

Exhibit 11   Profitability/Popularity Classification of Menu Items

Profitability	Popularity	Classification
High	High	Stars
High	Low	Puzzles
Low	High	Plow Horses
Low	Low	Dogs

percentage) would be more profitable than mix #2. A higher gross profit will result in a higher net income.

Menu Engineering

An interesting method of menu analysis and food pricing is called **menu engineering**. This sophisticated and fairly complex approach considers both the profitability and popularity of competing menu items. The emphasis is on gross margin (often called contribution margin). For all practical purposes, food cost percentages are ignored. The emphasis on gross margin rather than food cost percentage is based on the fact that managers bank dollars, not percentages.

Menu engineering requires the manager to know each menu item's food cost, selling price, and quantity sold over a specific period of time. The menu item's gross margin (selling price minus food cost) is characterized as either high or low in relation to the average gross margin for all competing menu items sold.

For example, if a menu item has a gross margin of $3.00 when the average gross margin for the menu is $3.50, then the menu item is classified as having a low gross margin. If the menu item has a gross margin of $4.50, then it is classified as high for profitability purposes.

Each menu item is further classified by popularity (high or low) based on the item's menu mix percentage, that is, the menu item count for each menu item as a percentage of the total menu items sold. When n equals the number of competing menu items, the dividing point for determining high and low popularity is calculated as follows:

$$70\% \times \frac{1}{n}$$

Therefore, if there are 10 competing items on a menu, the dividing point is seven percent, determined as follows:

$$70\% \times \frac{1}{10} = \underline{\underline{.07}} \text{ or } \underline{\underline{7\%}}$$

Given a ten-item menu, any menu items with unit sales of less than seven percent of the total items sold would be classified as having a low popularity, while any equal to or greater than seven percent would be classified as having high popularity.

The profitability and popularity classifications for each menu item result in four categories of menu items as shown in Exhibit 11. In general, stars should

Exhibit 12   Graph of Menu Engineering Results

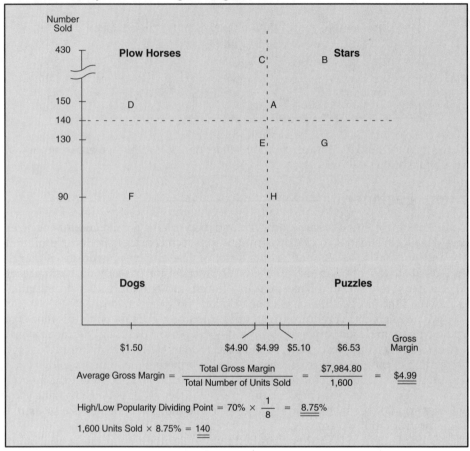

be retained, puzzles repositioned, plowhorses repriced, and dogs removed from the menu.

Exhibit 12 is a graphic illustration of menu engineering results, which contains menu items in the four classifications. Eight menu items, identified by letters corresponding to the following table, are shown on the graph.

Menu Item	Item Contribution Margin	Number Sold	Classification
A	$5.10	150	Star
B	$6.53	430	Star
C	$4.90	430	Plow Horse
D	$1.50	150	Plow Horse
E	$4.90	130	Dog
F	$1.50	90	Dog
G	$6.53	130	Puzzle
H	$5.10	90	Puzzle

In general, one prefers stars to dogs, puzzles, and plowhorses. However, are stars *always* preferred to puzzles and plowhorses? Specifically, is menu item A preferred to items C and G? Using the information for these menu items, we determine the following:

Menu Item	Classification	Item Contribution Margin	Number Sold	Total Item Contribution Margin
A	Star	$5.10	150	$ 765.00
C	Plow Horse	$4.90	430	$2,107.00
G	Puzzle	$6.53	130	$ 848.90

Menu items C and G provide $2,107 and $848.90 of contribution margin, respectively, compared to only $765 for item A. Thus, in this case, both items C and G (nonstar items) are preferred to the star menu item A. Further, as can be seen on Exhibit 12, the dog item E, with a total item contribution margin of $637, is nearly as profitable as the star menu item A.

The key to this analysis is not simply to classify menu items, but rather to consider total contribution margin. A menu may be analyzed using menu engineering and revised to eliminate all dogs. However, if the total contribution margin is not increased, little, if anything, has been accomplished. Exhibit 13 is a menu engineering worksheet useful for determining the classification of each menu item.

Integrated Pricing

Most clubs have several revenue-producing departments (profit centers). Allowing each profit center to price its products independently may fail to optimize the operation's profits. For example, a dining manager may decide to institute a direct charge to members. This new pricing policy may maximize dining revenues, but at the same time, members may opt not to be a part of the dining portion of the club.

Prices for all departments should be established so that they optimize the operation's net income. This will generally result in some profit centers *not* maximizing their revenues and thus their departmental incomes. This **integrated pricing** approach is essential and can only be accomplished by the general manager and profit center managers coordinating their pricing.

Summary

Cost management is a major issue for club managers, since costs normally amount to over 90 percent of club revenues. Cost behavior refers to the manner in which the total cost of an item changes in relation to volume. Total variable costs increase as volume increases, while total fixed costs remain constant as volume changes. On the other hand, unit variable costs are constant per unit, while unit fixed costs vary with volume.

Direct costs are those that are traceable to a given cost object, while indirect costs are related to the cost object but cannot be traced to the object and must therefore be allocated to it on some reasonable basis. Overhead costs of the club are

Exhibit 13 Menu Engineering Worksheet

Menu Engineering Worksheet

Restaurant: _____

Date: _____

Meal Period: _____

(A) Menu Item Name	(B) Number Sold (MM)	(C) Menu Mix %	(D) Item Food Cost	(E) Item Selling Price	(F) Item CM (E–D)	(G) Menu Costs (D*B)	(H) Menu Revenues (E*B)	(L) Menu CM (F*B)	(P) CM Category	(R) MM% Category	(S) Menu Item Classification	(T) Decision
Column Totals:	N					I	J	M				
						K = I/J	O = M/N			Q = (100%/items)(70%)		

Additional Computations:

general costs that benefit all of the profit centers of the club. These costs may be allocated to the respective departments.

Relevant costs are those that are future and differ between alternative courses of action. Opportunity costs are foregone profit due to the choice of an alternative course of action. Sunk costs are past costs that are irrelevant in decision making. A controllable cost is one that can be influenced by a given manager. All costs are controllable at some level in the club.

CVP analysis is a tool that examines the relationships among revenues, fixed costs, variable costs, and volume. Pricing is critical to the financial health of every club. The cost approach to pricing is an effective one that adds an amount or percent to cost in order to determine price.

Key Terms

contribution margin—Sales less costs of sales for either an entire operating department or for a given product; represents the amount of sales revenue that is contributed toward fixed costs and/or profits.

controllable costs—Costs over which a manager is able to exercise judgment and hence should be able to keep within predefined boundaries or limits.

cost object—Anything for which a separate accumulation of costs is desired.

cost-volume-profit (CVP) analysis—A set of analytical tools used by managers to examine the relationships among various costs, revenues, and sales volume in either graphic or equation form, allowing one to determine the revenue required at any desired profit level. Also called breakeven analysis.

fixed cost—Costs that remain constant in the short run even though sales volume varies; examples include salaries, rent expense, and insurance expense.

ingredient mark-up—See mark-up.

integrated pricing—An approach to pricing in an operation having several revenue-producing departments that sets prices for goods and/or services in each profit center so as to optimize the entire operation's net income.

mark-up—An approach that determines retail prices by adding a certain percentage to the cost of goods sold. The mark-up is designed to cover all nonproduct costs (for example, labor, utilities, supplies, interest expense, taxes, and so forth) as well as desired profit. Ingredient mark-up is based on all ingredients. Prime ingredient mark-up bases the mark-up solely on the cost of the main ingredient.

mixed costs—Costs that include both fixed and variable components.

menu engineering—A method of menu analysis and food pricing that considers both the profitability and popularity of competing menu items.

opportunity cost—Cost of foregoing the best alternative opportunity in a decision-making situation involving several alternatives.

overhead costs—All expenses other than the direct costs of profit centers; examples include undistributed operating expenses, management fees, fixed charges, and income taxes.

price elasticity of demand—An expression of the relationship between a change in price and the resulting change in demand.

prime ingredient mark-up—See mark-up.

relevant costs—Costs that must be considered in a decision-making situation; must be differential, future, and quantifiable.

step costs—Costs that are consistent within a range of activity, but different among ranges of activity.

sunk costs—Irrelevant past costs relating to a past decision; for example, the net book value of a fixed asset.

variable costs—Costs that change proportionately with sales volume.

weighted average contribution margin ratio—In a multiple product situation, an average contribution margin for all operated departments that is weighted to reflect the relative contribution of each department to the establishment's ability to pay fixed costs and generate profits.

Review Questions

1. What are the two important criteria for a cost to be relevant?

2. What is the difference between direct and indirect costs? Controllable and uncontrollable costs? Give examples of each.

3. What is a sunk cost? Are sunk costs relevant in managerial decision making?

4. What are opportunity costs? When are they included on financial reports?

5. What is the purpose of CVP analysis?

6. What is price elasticity of demand?

7. What are the four modifying factors to consider when pricing based on a cost approach?

8. Which pricing method is the most applicable for restaurants? Why?

9. What does menu engineering consider in its review of menu items?

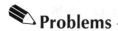

Problems

Problem 1

L.A. Gant Club is analyzing its pro shop and dining operations using the monthly data below.

Pro shop:	average sale: $80.00
	average variable cost / sale: $40.00
	fixed cost: $7,000
Dining:	average sale: $32
	average variable cost / sale: $15.40
	fixed cost: $12,000

Required:

Calculate the following amounts.

1. Breakeven number of meals for the dining facility

2. Breakeven dollar volume for the dining facility

3. Total breakeven point in dollars for the combined profit centers

4. Total dollar volume to make a before-tax profit of $40,000

5. Total dollar volume to make an after-tax profit of $30,000 with a 20 percent tax rate

Problem 2

Highland Hills Club has two profit centers, an 18-hole golf course and a dining facility. Classify the various costs below as either direct or indirect costs with respect to the type of profit center (golf course or dining facility). Classify each cost below as fixed or variable with respect to how the total costs of the club change as the number of members increases.

1. Property taxes on the 18-hole golf course

2. Electricity bill (one bill covers the entire club)

3. Wages for the dining room wait staff

4. The salary of the club's general manager

5. Annual recognition dinner for the golf course employees

6. Food costs for the dining room

7. Golf course superintendent's salary

8. Supplies for the dining room

Problem 3

The food and beverage manager of the Epicurean Delights Dinner Club is attempting to price out a steak dinner and has complied the following cost data:

Ingredient	Cost
Steak	$3.85
Baked potato	.45
Vegetable	.50
Soup	.30
Roll and butter	.20
Salad with dressing	.35
Coffee	.25
Total cost	$5.90

The desired product cost percentage is 50 percent.

Required:

1. Using the ingredient cost approach, determine the multiple to use in making up the ingredient costs.

2. Use the multiple to determine the menu price of the steak dinner.

3. Assuming a multiple of 5.0, determine the menu price of the steak dinner using the prime ingredient approach.

Chapter 7 Outline

Types of Budgets
Budgeting Horizons
Reasons for Budgeting
Personnel Responsible for Budget
    Preparation
The Budget Preparation Process
    Forecasting Revenue
    Estimating Expenses
    Projecting Fixed Expenses
    Budget Formulation Illustrated
    Flexible Budgets
Budgetary Control
    Determination of Variances
    Determination of Significant Variances
    Variance Analysis
    Determination of Problems and
        Management Action
    Reforecasting

Competencies

1. Describe the purposes of budgeting for operations and identify the roles and responsibilities of those involved in the budgeting process. (pp. 165–168)

2. Explain the process of preparing an operations budget in terms of establishing financial objectives, forecasting revenue, estimating expenses, and projecting fixed charges. (pp. 168–179)

3. Describe the budgeting control process and explain how significant variances are determined. (pp. 179–184)

4. Use information from budget reports to calculate and analyze revenue variances, cost of goods sold variances, and variable labor variances, and describe the process of correcting problems and reforecasting. (pp. 184–189)

7

Operations Budgeting

Every rational manager plans for the future. Some plans are formal and others are informal. Budgets are formal plans reduced to dollars. Budgets provide answers to many questions, including the following:

- What are the forecasted revenues for the month?

- What is the budgeted labor for the year?

- How many meals are expected to be sold during any given month, and what is the expected average foodservice price?

- What is the budgeted maintenance expense for the month?

- What is the estimated depreciation for the year?

- How close were actual food and beverage revenues to the budgeted amounts for the month?

- What is the projected bottom line from operations for the year?

This chapter is divided into two major sections. The first section investigates reasons for budgeting, the process of preparing the operations budget, and the idea of budgeting horizons. The second section focuses on budgetary control and on how club operations use budget reports in the budgetary control process. The Green Club, a hypothetical small club, is used to illustrate both budget preparation and control.

Types of Budgets

Clubs prepare several types of budgets. The **operations budget**, the topic of this chapter, is also referred to as the *revenue and expense budget*, because it includes management's plans for generating revenues and incurring expenses for a given period. The operations budget includes not only operated department budgets (budgets for food, beverage, golf, tennis, and other departments), but also budgets for service centers such as accounting and human resources. In addition, the operations budget includes the planned expenses for depreciation, interest expense, and other fixed charges. Thus, the operations budget is a detailed operating plan by profit centers, cost centers within profit centers (such as the golf course maintenance department within the golf department), and service centers. It includes all revenues and all expenses that appear on the statement of activities and related subsidiary schedules. Annual operating budgets are normally subdivided into monthly periods. Certain information is reduced to a daily basis for management's use in controlling operations. The operations budget enables management to accomplish three of its major functions: planning, execution, and control.

Two other types of budgets are the cash budget and the capital budget. The cash budget is management's plan for cash receipts and disbursements. Capital budgeting pertains to planning for the acquisition of equipment, land, buildings, and other property and equipment.

Budgeting Horizons

The annual operations budget must be subdivided into monthly plans in order for management to use it effectively as an aid in monitoring operations. Monthly plans allow management to measure the operation's overall performance several times throughout the year. Certain elements of the monthly plan are then reduced to weekly and daily bases. For example, clubs have daily revenue plans that differ by day of the week and by season. The daily revenue is compared to these daily revenue goals on the daily report of operations. Any significant differences (variances) require analysis, determination of causes, and, if necessary, corrective action. (Variance analysis will be discussed later in this chapter.) In addition, every month all revenue and expense amounts are compared to the budgeted amounts, and all significant variances are analyzed and explained.

An alternative to the monthly breakdown of annual budgets is using 13 four-week segments or the four-four-five quarterly plan. The four-four-five plan consists of two four-week plans followed by one five-week, equaling the 13 weeks in a quarter. Four of these quarterly plans serve as the annual operations budget.

Many clubs also prepare operations budgets on a long-range basis. In a survey of club executives, 36 percent of the respondents indicated that long-range operating budgets are prepared at their clubs.[1] The most common long-range period is five years. This survey found that, generally, the larger the club the more likely the operations budget is prepared for several years in the future. A brief breakdown of club size based on revenue and the percentage preparing long-range operating budgets is as follows:

Annual Revenues	%
< $1,000,000	0
$1–2 million	18
$2–3 million	34
$3–5 million	40
> $5,000,000	45

A five-year plan consists of five annual plans. The annual plans for the second through fifth years are much less detailed than the current year's annual plan. When long-range budgets are used, the next year's budget serves as a starting point for preparing the operations budget. The long-range budget procedure is used to review and update the next four years and add the fifth year to the plan.

Reasons for Budgeting

Virtually all clubs prepare operating budgets—and for several good reasons:

1. Budgeting requires management to examine alternatives before selecting a particular course of action. For example, there are pricing alternatives for each product and/or service sold. Also, there are many different marketing decisions that must be made, such as how to promote, when to promote, and so on. There are also several approaches to staffing, each of which will affect the quality of service provided. In nearly every revenue and expense area, several courses of action are available to the club. Budgeting provides management with an effective means of evaluating these alternatives.

2. Budgeting provides a standard of comparison. At the end of the accounting period, management is able to compare actual operating results to a formal plan. Significant variances may be analyzed to suggest the probable cause(s) that require additional investigation and, possibly, corrective action. While budget preparation is independent of budgetary control, it is inefficient not to use budgets for control purposes. The focus of the last part of this chapter is on the control process.

3. Budgeting enables management to look forward, especially when strategic planning is concerned. Too often, management is either solving current problems or reviewing the past. Budgeting requires management to anticipate the future. Future considerations may be both external and internal. External considerations include the economy, inflation, and major competition. Internal considerations are primarily the club operation's reactions to external considerations. Club operators should aggressively attempt to shape their environment rather than merely react to it.

4. When participative budgeting is practiced, the budget process involves all levels of management. This involvement motivates the lower level managers because they have real input in the process rather than being forced to adhere to budget numbers that are imposed upon them. Too often, autocratic budgeting approaches result in unsuccessful managers who blame the budget preparers (higher level managers) instead of accepting responsibility for poor operating results.

5. The budget process provides a channel of communication whereby the club's objectives are communicated to the lowest managerial levels. In addition, lower level managers are able to react to these objectives and suggest operational goals such as food sales, cost of food sales, food labor expense, and so on. When the budget is used as a standard of comparison, the operating results are also communicated to lower level managers. This allows for feedback to these managers. Further, lower level managers are required to explain significant variances—why they exist, what the causes are, and what action is to be taken.

6. Finally, to the degree that prices are a function of costs, the budget process (which provides estimates of future expenses) enables managers to set their

prices in relation to their expenses. Price changes can be the result of planning, thereby allowing such changes to be properly implemented. Price changes made on the spur of the moment often result in unprofessional price execution, such as poorly informed service staff who misquote prices and other similar situations.

The survey mentioned earlier asked club executives the major reason for preparing operating budgets. The major reason (at 56 percent of respondents) was to use the operations budget as a standard of comparison. Thirty-seven percent prepare the operations budget mainly for planning purposes.

Personnel Responsible for Budget Preparation

The complete budget process includes both budget preparation and budgetary control. The major purpose of budgeting is to allow management to accomplish three of its functions: planning, execution, and control.

In most clubs, the board of directors approves the operating budget, the preparation of which has been delegated to the general manager and controller. The GM usually enlists the controller to coordinate the budget preparation process. However, budgeting is not a financial function where bookkeepers, accountants, and the controller have the sole responsibility. The controller facilitates the budget preparation process by initially providing information to operating managers. The major input for the budget should come from operated department (profit center) managers working with their lower level managers and from service department managers.

The controller receives the department managers' operating plans and formulates them into a comprehensive operating budget. This is then reviewed by the GM and a budget committee (if one exists). If the comprehensive operating budget is satisfactory in meeting financial goals, the GM presents it to the board of directors. If it is not satisfactory, then the elements requiring change are returned to the appropriate department heads for review and change. This process may repeat several times until a satisfactory budget is prepared.

The final budget should ideally be the result of an overall team effort rather than a decree dictated by the GM. This participative management approach should result in maximizing departmental managers' motivation.

The Budget Preparation Process

The major elements in the budget preparation process are as follows:

- Overall objectives

- Revenue forecasts

- Expense forecasts

- Net income forecasts

The operations budget process begins with the board of directors establishing the major objectives of the club—including the financial objectives. Nearly half of the club executives surveyed in the late 1990s indicated a financial goal is established before the preparation of the operations budget. The most common financial goal set by clubs is achieving a positive bottom line.

Another objective may be to provide high quality service, even if it means incurring higher labor costs than allowable to maximize profits. Other objectives include being the top club in a given area or increasing membership by a stated percentage. Many more objectives could be listed. The critical point is that the board must establish major objectives. These are then communicated to the GM and are the basis for formulating the operations budget.

When a management company operates a club, the owners' expectations for both the long and short term must be fully considered. Generally, the club's board reserves the right to approve the operating budget. Therefore, failure to consider views of the club members as represented by the board will most likely result in their rejection of the plan, as well as damaged relationships and the need to redo the budget. Management teams overseeing clubs must work closely with the owners of each club.

Forecasting Revenue

Forecasting revenue is the next step in preparing the operations budget. In order for profit center managers (for example, food department managers) to be able to forecast revenue for their departments, they must have information regarding the economic environment, promotional plans, capital budgeting, and detailed historical financial operating results of their departments.

Information regarding the economic environment includes such items as:

- Expected inflation for the next year

- Ability of the club to pass on cost increases to members

- Changes in competitive conditions—for example, the emergence of new competitors, the closing of former competitors, change in aggressive marketing of a nearby club and so on

- Expected levels of member spending for products/services offered by the club

- Expected changes in employee wages and fringe benefits

In order for this information be useful, it must be expressed in usable numbers. For example, regarding inflation and the ability of the club to increase its prices, the information received by department heads may be phrased as follows: "Inflation is expected to be three percent for the next year. Prices of all products and services may be increased by an average maximum of four percent, with a two percent increase effective January 1 and July 1."

Promotion plans include, but are not limited to, membership drives. What promotion will be used—and when—during the budget year? What results are expected? Answers to these questions and many others must be provided in order for managers to be able to prepare their budgets.

Capital budgeting information includes the timing of the addition of property and equipment. For an existing club, the completion date of a dining room

Exhibit 1   Food Revenue Increases, 20X1–20X4

Year	Amount	Increase over prior year	
		Amount	**%**
20X1	$1,000,000	—	—
20X2	1,100,000	100,000	10
20X3	1,210,000	110,000	10
20X4	1,331,000	121,000	10

Exhibit 2   Food Revenue 20X1–20X4

Year	Covers	Price Per Cover	Food Revenue
20X1	50,000	$ 20	$1,000,000
20X2	52,000	21	1,092,000
20X3	55,000	22	1,210,000
20X4	57,000	23	1,311,000

renovation must be projected in order to effectively estimate food sales. The renovation of a golf course, the addition of tennis courts, and so forth must be covered before projecting sales and expenses for the upcoming year.

Historical financial information should be detailed by department. The breakdown should be on at least a monthly basis, and in some cases, more frequently. Quantities and prices should both be provided (for example, the number of covers sold and the average selling price by segment, by dining areas as well as banquets). Generally, financial information for at least the two prior years is provided. The controller should be prepared to provide additional prior information as requested.

Historical financial information often serves as the foundation on which managers build their revenue forecasts. This type of budgeting is called **incremental budgeting**. For example, food revenue of a club for 20X1 through 20X4 is shown in Exhibit 1. From year 20X1 to 20X4, the amount of revenue increased 10 percent for each year. Therefore, if future conditions appear to be similar to what they were in prior years, the food revenue for 20X5 would be budgeted at $1,464,100, which is a 10 percent increase over food revenue earned in 20X4.

An alternative approach to budgeting revenue based on increasing the current year's revenue by a percentage is to base the revenue projection on unit sales and prices. This approach considers the two variables of unit sales and prices separately. For example, an analysis of the past financial information in Exhibit 2 shows that covers increased 2,000 units from 20X1 to 20X2, 3,000 units from 20X2 to 20X3, and 2,000 units from 20X3 to 20X4. The average foodservice check has increased by $1, each year over the past three years. Therefore, assuming the future prospects appear similar, the forecaster may use an increase in covers of 2,000 and a $1 increase in average price per cover as the basis for forecasting 20X5 food revenue. The formula for forecasting food revenue is:

Covers		Price Per Cover		Forecasted Food Revenue
	×		=	
59,000	×	$24	=	$ 1,416,000

This simplistic approach to forecasting food revenue is meant only to illustrate the process. A more detailed (and proper) approach would include further considerations, such as different meal periods and related average prices per cover, as well as banquets and the related number of covers and average prices. In addition, managers of other profit centers, such as beverage, golf, and the pro shop, must forecast their revenue for the year.

Although sales forecasting is often used for short-term forecasts, many of its concepts are relevant to forecasting revenue for the annual budget. In addition to relying on historical information, many clubs book some events—such as wedding receptions and anniversary parties—a year or more in advance. In these cases, they are able to rely in part on the banquet reservations in forecasting part of their food and beverage sales.

Though two distinct forecasting techniques are presented above, there are many more approaches. Club executives were surveyed regarding the approaches they use to forecast the various major sales of their clubs (in particular, dining room, banquets, beverages, golf course, and tennis). Seven forecasting techniques were provided to potential respondents as shown in Exhibit 3. The techniques listed in Exhibit 3 are abbreviated in the matrix shown in Exhibit 4.

Across all sales areas, "last year's actual revenues adjusted subjectively" is the most commonly used technique. Approximately 40 percent of the clubs use this technique for the various sales areas. Just over 46 percent of the clubs use it to forecast tennis revenues, while 37 percent use it to forecast banquet food sales. The second most common choice for forecasting banquet food revenues is advanced bookings. Last year's actuals were used by nearly one of every four clubs for forecasting tennis revenues and by nearly one of every five clubs for forecasting golf revenues. Other techniques for other sales areas were used by less than 15 percent of the respondents.

The next two most common approaches across all sales areas clearly appear to be the prior year's budgeted dollar amounts multiplied by 1 plus x percent and the average of several past years' revenues multiplied by 1 plus x percent.

A review of techniques by size of club did not reveal any differences in forecasting techniques used. Each club differs yet some common subjective adjustments most likely provide better forecasts than others. Though some techniques may appear to be more sophisticated than others, the best technique is one that provides a forecast that is closest to the results that subsequently occur.

Estimating Expenses

The next step in the budget formulation process is estimating expenses. Since expenses are categorized both in relation to profit centers (direct/indirect) and

Exhibit 3   Seven Forecasting Techniques

Technique	Example
1. Prior year's budgeted dollar amounts multiplied by 1 + x percent	Green fees for March 20X1 were budgeted at $10,000. The budget for green fees for March 20X2 is set at a 10 percent increase. The budgeted amount is $11,000 ($10,000 + .10 × $10,000 = $11,000).
2. Number of members by expected spending per member	A club's 1,000 members spent an average of $25.00 each for lunches during January, 20X1. The expected spending by members in January of 20X2, on average, is $27.50 and membership has stabilized at 1,000. Therefore, luncheon sales for January 20X2 is budgeted to be $27,500 (1,000 × $27.50 = $27,500).
3. Expected units to be sold multiplied by expected selling price	A club budgets its dinner sales based on the forecasted number of covers and expected average dinner prices. The number of covers and the average dinner price during January 20X1 were 3,000 and $15.00, respectively. The forecast for January 20X2 is $49,600, based on 3,100 forecasted covers and an average expected selling price of $16.00.
4. Change in advance bookings from prior year.	A club's advance banquet bookings in November 20X0 for January 20X1 totaled 20 events at an average of $5,000 per event, The club's advance bookings in November 20X1 for January 20X2 (when the 20X2 budget is being prepared) total 25 events; the average expected sales per booking is $5,500. Therefore, the banquet food sales are forecasted to be $137,500 (25 × $5,500 = $137,500).
5. Last year's actual revenues	A club's green fees for May 20X1 were $15,000. The same figure is used as the forecast for May 20X2, since green fees have not changed and the membership is stable at 400 golf members.

Exhibit 3 *(Continued)*

Technique	Example
6. Last year's actual revenues are adjusted subjectively	A club's 20X1 tennis revenues were $5,000 during May. The forecast for May 20X2 is $6,000, based on the tennis pro's subjective consideration of expected participation, weather conditions, and anticipated changes in tennis fees.
7. Average of several past year's revenues multiplied by 1 + x percent	A club's beverage sales for the past three Aprils—20X1, 20X2, and 20X3—have been $16,000, $13,000, and $16,000, respectively. The average is $15,000. The manager forecasts the beverage sales to be $16,500 for April 20X4 based on the three–month average, plus a 10 percent increase ($15,000 + $15,000 × .1 = $16,500).

Exhibit 4   Forecasting Techniques Matrix

Forecasting Technique	Sales Areas (%)				
	Dining Room	Banquet	Beverage	Golf Course	Tennis
(1) Prior budget × 1 + x precent	3.8%	9.3%	12.4%	4.5%	13.9%
(2) Number of members × expected spending per member	11.0	3.1	6.7	7.2	6.2
(3) Units × selling price	6.4	3.1	6.7	3.6	3.1
(4) Advanced bookings	0.9	29.9	3.8	2.4	1.5
(5) Last year's actuals	7.3	6.2	10.5	18.1	24.6
(6) Last year's actuals, adjusted	45.0	37.0	43.7	42.1	46.1
(7) Average of past years × 1 + x percent	13.8	9.3	13.3	12.1	4.6
(8) Other	1.8	2.1	2.9	0.0	0.0
TOTAL	100.0%	100.0%	100.0%	100.0%	100.0%
Number of respondents	109	97	105	83	65

how they react to changes in volume (fixed/variable), the forecasting of expenses is similar to the approach used in forecasting revenue. However, before department heads are able to estimate expenses, they must be provided with information regarding the following:

- Expected cost increases for supplies, food, beverages, and other expenses
- Labor cost increases, including the cost of benefits and payroll taxes

Department heads of profit centers estimate their variable expenses in relation to the projected revenues of their departments. For example, historically, the food department may have incurred food costs at 40 percent of food sales. For the next year, the food department manager decides to budget at 40 percent. Therefore, multiplying projected food sales by 40 percent results in the projected cost of food sales. Other variable expenses may be estimated similarly.

An alternate way to estimate expense is based on standard amounts. For example, a club with overnight rooms for its members may have a work standard that requires room attendants to clean an average of two rooms per hour. Given this standard, if 400 rooms sales are budgeted during a month, 200 labor hours would be budgeted for room attendants' labor. If the average hourly wage is $10.00 per hour, $2,000 in wages is budgeted for room attendants for the period. Employee benefits related to room attendants are additional costs that also must be considered.

Fixed expenses are projected on the basis of experience and expected changes. For example, assume that supervisors in the food department were paid salaries of $85,000 for the past year. Further assume that the new salary level of the supervisors is $90,000 plus another half-time equivalent to be added at a cost of $15,000 for the next year. Thus, the fixed cost of supervisor salaries for the next year is set at $105,000. Other fixed expenses are similarly projected.

The service center department heads also estimate expenses for their departments. The service departments in a club comprise the general expense categories of clubhouse locker rooms, administrative and general, and energy costs. Service center department heads will estimate their expenses based on experience and expected changes. Generally, the historical amounts are adjusted to reflect higher costs. For example, assume that the accounting department salaries of a club for 20X1 were $80,000. Further assume that salary increases for 20X2 are limited to an average of five percent. Therefore, the 20X2 accounting department salaries budget is set at $84,000.

A different budgeting approach, **zero-base budgeting (ZBB)**, is applicable in budgeting for service departments. ZBB, unlike the incremental approach, requires all expenses to be justified. In other words, the assumption is that each department starts with zero dollars (zero base) and must justify all budgeted amounts. Let's look at an example that illustrates the differences between the incremental and ZBB approaches to budgeting.

Assume that the accounting department of a club had a total departmental budget of $120,000 in 20X1. In 20X2, cost increases are expected to average five percent, and a new half position is expected to cost $1,000 per month. Under the incremental approach, the budget would be set at $138,000, determined as follows:

$$\$120,000 + (\$120,000 \times .05) + (\$1,000 \times 12) = \$138,000$$

Under ZBB, the accounting department would have to justify every dollar budgeted. That is, documentation would be required showing that all budgeted amounts are cost-justified. This means all payroll costs, supplies, and so forth would have to be shown to yield greater than their cost.

Exhibit 5   Interest Expense Budget for 20X2

Debt	Principal	Interest Rate %	Time	Amount
Mortgage	$2,000,000	8	Year	$160,000
Working capital loans	200,000	7	6 mo.	7,000
			Total	$167,000

The ZBB approach to budgeting in clubs appears to be limited to the service departments. However, since the total cost of these departments is approximately 44 percent of the average club's total sales, the total amount can be considerable.[2]

Projecting Fixed Expenses

The next step in the budget formulation process is projecting fixed expenses. Fixed expenses include depreciation and amortization, insurance expense, real estate taxes, and interest expense. These expenses are fixed and are projected on the basis of experience and expected changes for the next year.

Exhibit 5 illustrates how the interest expense budget for 20X2 is determined by estimating interest expense based on current and projected borrowings. Based on calculations in Exhibit 5, the interest expense budgeted for 20X2 is $167,000.

Even though these expenses are considered fixed, management and/or the board may be able to affect the fixed amounts for the year. For example, property taxes are generally based on assessed valuation and a property tax rate. A reduction in the assessed valuation will result in a reduction in the club's property taxes. Thus, if the property is over-assessed, management should pursue a reduction that, if successful, will lower the property tax expense. Some clubs have been successful in obtaining reductions in their assessments, thus reducing this "fixed" expense for the year.

The final step of the budget formulation process is for the controller to formulate the entire budget based on submissions from operated departments and service departments. The forecasted bottom line is a result. If this bottom line is acceptable to the board of directors and/or the owners, then the budget formulation is complete. If the bottom line is not acceptable, then department heads are required to rework their budgets to provide a budget acceptable to the board and/or owners. Many changes may be proposed, including price changes and cost reductions. Often, the board or owner will provide a targeted bottom line number before the budget is prepared. More often than not, budgets must be reworked several times before an acceptable budget is produced.

Budget Formulation Illustrated

A very simplified club example will be used to illustrate the preparation of an operations budget. The Green Club is a 500-member dinner club—that is, it is open only at dinner Monday-Saturday each week. The Green Club also has two service centers, administration and a combined maintenance and utility cost department.

The board of directors has established the major financial goal of generating a minimum net income of four percent of food sales and membership income. The

Exhibit 6   Statement of Activities

	20X1	20X2	20X3
Green Club **Statement of Activities** **For the Years 20X1–20X3**			
Membership Income:			
Membership Dues	$ 259,200	$ 279,300	$ 300,000
Initiation fees	19,000	20,000	20,000
Total membership income	$ 278,200	$ 299,300	$ 320,000
Food operations:			
Sales	299,520	331,240	364,000
Cost of food sold	119,808	132,496	141,960
Payroll and related	119,904	144,560	146,440
Other expenses	59,904	66,248	72,800
Food operating income	(96)	(2,064)	2,800
Undistributed operating expenses:			
Administrative and general	$ 136,762	$ 151,540	$ 168,400
Energy costs	18,554	29,211	21,680
Total U.O.E.	155,316	171,751	190,080
Income before fixed expense	122,788	125,485	132,720
Real estate taxes	15,000	16,000	17,000
Insurance	7,500	8,000	8,000
Interest	30,000	28,000	26,000
Depreciation	40,000	45,000	50,000
Total fixed expenses	92,500	97,000	101,000
Increase in net assets	$ 30,288	$ 28,485	$ 31,720

statements of activities for the past three years are presented in Exhibit 6. An analysis of this financial information appears in Exhibit 7. Economic environment information relevant to the Green Club in 20X4 is summarized as follows:

- No new clubs are expected to compete with the Green Club.

- Overall member demand for dinner at the club is expected to remain relatively constant.

- Inflation is expected to be about three percent in the next year.

   The major findings and projections for 20X4 are as follows:

Item	Analytical Findings	Projections for 20X4
1. Membership income:		
Membership dues	10 members are expected to be added, as in past	510 members

Exhibit 7   Analysis of Statement of Activities

	20X1	20X2	20X3
Green Club			
Analysis of Statement of Activities			
For the Years 20X1–20X3			
Membership dues:			
Number of members	480	490	500
Monthly dues	$ 45	$ 47.50	$ 50
Initiation fees:			
Number of new members	10	10	10
Initiation fee	$ 1900	$ 2000	$ 2000
Food revenue:			
Covers	24,960	25,480	26,000
Price per cover	$ 12	$ 13	$ 14
Food department expense:			
Cost of food sold	40%	40%	39%
Payroll:			
Fixed	$ 60,000	$ 65,000	$ 70,000
Variable	20%	21%	21%
Other expense	20%	20%	20%
Administrative and general:			
Fixed	$ 80,000	$ 90,000	$ 100,000
Variable	10%	10%	10%
Energy costs:			
Fixed	$ 7,000	$ 8,000	$ 9,000
Variable	2%	2%	2%
Real estate taxes:	$ 15,000	$ 16,000	$ 17,000
Insurance	7,500	8,000	8,000
Interest	30,000	28,000	26,000
Depreciation	40,000	45,000	50,000

Item	Analytical Findings	Projections for 20X4
Monthly dues	Dues have increased $2.50 per month in 20X2 and 20X3. Assume a $2.50 increase in 20X4.	$52.50
Initiation fees	Increased by $100 in 20X2 and maintained at $2,000 in 20X3. Assume a $50 increase in 20X4.	$2,050

Item	Analytical Findings	Projections for 20X4
2. Food revenue:		
Covers	Members on average dined once a week in each of last three years. Assume practice continues. 510 × 52 = 26,520	26,520 covers
Price	Average food service price per cover has increased by $1 each year. Assume the same will continue in 20X4.	$15
3. Cost of food sold:	Food costs as a percentage of food sales was reduced by one percent in 20X3 from two prior years. Assume food costs can be maintained at 39 percent during 20X4.	39 percent
4. Payroll and related:		
Fixed	Amount has increased by $5,000 each year for past two years. Assume a $5,000 increase for 20X4.	$75,000
Variable	The percentage based on food sales increased one percent from 20X1 to 20X2 and stabilized in 20X3. Assume it will continue to stabilize in 20X4.	21 percent
5. Other expenses	The percentage has been 20 percent across the last three years. Assume it will remain at 20 percent.	20 percent
6. Administrative and general:		
Fixed	The fixed portion of A&G has. increased $10,000 per year. Assume this will continue into 20X4	$110,000
Variable	The variable portion of A&G has remained at 10 percent of total food sales and membership income for the years of 20X1–20X3. Assume it will continue at 10 percent.	10 percent
7. Energy costs:		
Fixed	The fixed portion has increased $1,000 per year from 20X1–20X3. Assume a $1,000 increase for 20X4.	$10,000

Item	Analytical Findings	Projections for 20X4
Variable	The variable portion of energy cost has been two percent for the past three years. Assume it will continue at two percent of food sales and membership income.	two percent

8. Fixed expenses:

Item	Analytical Findings	Projections for 20X4
Real estate taxes	These taxes have increased $1,000 per year and assume in 20X4 it will increase by $1,000.	$18,000
Insurance	The insurance contract is a $8,000 per year for 20X2–20X4.	$8,000
Interest	The rate is 10 percent and the average outstanding mortgage debt is $240,000 for 20X4.	$24,000
Depreciation	The accountants' calculations of depreciation for 20X4 is $50,000. Depreciation expense for planned purchases during 20X4 is expected to be $5,000.	$55,000

The operations budget for 20X4 is shown in Exhibit 8. The projected 20X4 net income for the Green Club of $32,608 is 4.41 percent of food sales and membership income, which exceeds the minimum requirement of four percent.

Flexible Budgets

The budgets we have discussed so far have been fixed (sometimes called static) in that only one level of activity was planned. However, no matter how sophisticated the budget process, it is improbable that the level of activity budgeted will be realized exactly. Therefore, when a fixed budget is used, variances from several budget line items, specifically for revenues and variable expenses, can almost always be expected. An alternative approach is to budget for several different levels of activity. For example, a club may budget at three membership levels, such as 500, 525, and 550, even though it believes that the membership level is likeliest to be at the 525-member level. With flexible budgeting, revenues and variable expenses change with each level of activity, while fixed expenses remain constant.

Budgetary Control ————————————————————————

In order for budgets to be used effectively for control purposes, budget reports must be prepared periodically (generally monthly) for each level of financial

Exhibit 8 Sample Operations Budget Worksheet

	Green Club Operations Budget For the Year 20X4	
	Calculation	**Amount**
Membership income:		
Membership dues	510 × $52.50 × 12	$312,300
Initiation fees	10 × 2050	20,500
Total		341,800
Food operations:		
Sales	26,520 × $15	397,800
Cost of food sold	397,800 × .39	155,142
Payroll and related	75,000 + 397,800 × .21	158,538
Other expenses	397,800 × .20	79,560
Food operating income		4,560
Undistributed operating expenses:		
Administrative and general	110,000 + 739,600 × .10	$183,960
Energy costs	10,000 + 739,600 × .02	24,792
Total U.O.E.		208,752
Income before fixed expenses:		137,608
Real estate taxes		18,000
Insurance		8,000
Interest		24,000
Depreciation		55,000
Total		105,000
Increase in net assets		$ 32,608

responsibility. In a club, this would normally require budget reports for profit, cost, and service centers.

Budget reports may take many forms. Most commonly, a club's revenues and expenses on its monthly statement of activities will be compared to the budget numbers. Both monthly and year-to-date numbers are generally shown. The differences between the budget and actual numbers, known as budget variances, are also reflected in this monthly report. In addition to variances from budget, variances from last year's actual may also be shown in order to put the budget in perspective and to provide management with trend information.

Exhibit 9 is a departmental budget report for the food department. It provides a further breakdown of the elements that make up revenues, wages, benefits, and other expenses. This report, which is available to the club's board of directors, also goes to the next level of management below the general manager and controller.

In order for the reports to be useful, they must be timely and relevant. Budget reports issued weeks after the end of the accounting period are too late to allow managers to investigate variances, determine causes, and take timely action. Relevant financial information includes only the revenues and expenses for which the

Exhibit 9 Monthly Food Department Schedule

	June 20X1				Year-to-Date		
Actual	Budget	Last Year			Actual	Budget	Last Year
60,200	60,000	58,200	Food sales		370,100	365,000	361,500
24,152	24,000	23,315	Cost of food sold		147,360	146,000	144,600
36,048	36,000	34,885	Gross profit on food sales		222,740	219,000	216,900
			Department Expenses:				
			Payable and related expenses:				
18,150	18,000	17,490	Salaries and wages		112,200	109,500	110,258
5,550	5,400	5,208	Payroll taxes and benefits		32,600	32,850	32,250
23,700	23,400	22,698	Total payroll and related		144,800	142,350	142,508
			Other Expenses:				
450	500	420	China, glassware & linen		3,112	3,000	2,915
750	700	725	Contract cleaning		2,080	2,100	1,962
225	200	210	Kitchen fuel		1,156	1,200	1,015
320	300	293	Laundry and dry cleaning		1,915	1,800	1,962
100	100	100	Licenses		600	600	600
1,115	1,000	1,081	Operating supplies		6,073	6,000	5,914
985	1,000	1,113	Other operating expenses		5,814	6,000	6,073
180	200	156	Printing and stationery		1,192	1,200	1,315
4,315	4,000	3,923	Repairs and maintenance		25,814	24,000	23,460
8,440	7,000	8,021	Total other		47,756	42,000	45,216
32,140	30,400	30,719	Total departmental expense		192,556	184,350	187,724
3,908	5,600	4,166	Departmental income (loss)		30,184	34,650	29,176

individual department head is held responsible. For example, including allocated overhead expenses such as administrative and general salaries on a food department budget report is rather meaningless from a control viewpoint, because the food department manager is unable to influence these costs. Further, they detract from the expenses that the food department manager can control.

Relevant reporting also requires sufficient detail to allow reasonable judgments regarding budget variances. Of course, information overload (which generally results in management's failure to act properly) should be avoided.

There are five steps in the budgetary control process:

1. Determination of variances
2. Determination of significant variances
3. Analysis of significant variances
4. Determination of problems
5. Action to correct problems

Determination of Variances

Variances are determined by using the budget report to compare actual results to the budget. The budget report ideally should disclose both monthly variances and

Exhibit 10   Summary Budget Report

			Variance	
Green Club				
Summary Budget Report				
For January 20X4				
	Budget	**Actual**	**$**	**%**
Membership income:				
Membership dues	$ 26,775	$ 26,525	$ (250)	(0.93)%
Initiation fees	2,050	-0-	(2,050)	(100.0)
Total	28,825	26,525	(2,300)	(7.98)
Food operations:				
Sales	32,800	33,500	700	2.13
Cost of sales	12,800	12,250	550	4.30
Payroll and related	13,150	12,982	168	1.28
Other expenses	6,560	6,607	(47)	(0.72)
Food operating income	290	1,661	1,371	472.76
Undistributed operating expenses:				
Administrative and general	15,400	14,980	420	2.73
Energy costs	2,070	2,115	(45)	(2.17)
Total U.O.E.	17,470	17,095	375	2.15
Income before fixed expenses	11,645	11,091	(554)	(4.76)
Real estate taxes	1,500	1,500	-0-	0.00
Insurance	1,670	1,670	-0-	0.00
Interest	2,000	2,000	-0-	0.00
Depreciation	4,500	4,450	50	1.11
Total	8,070	8,020	50	0.62
Increase in net assets	$ 3,575	$ 3,071	$ (504)	(14.10)

year-to-date variances. Variance analysis generally focuses on monthly variances, because the year-to-date variances are essentially the sum of monthly variances.

Exhibit 10 is the January 20X4 summary budget report for the Green Club. This budget report contains only monthly financial information and not separate year-to-date numbers, as January is the first month of the fiscal year for the Green Club.

Variances shown on this report include both dollar variances and percentage variances. The dollar variances result from subtracting the actual results from the budget figures. For example, food sales for the Green Club was $33,500, while the budgeted food sales revenue was $32,800, resulting in a difference of $700. The difference is a favorable variance since the actual exceeded the budget.

Percentage variances are determined by dividing the dollar variance by the budgeted amount. For food sales, the 2.13 percent for food sales is the result of dividing $700 by $32,800.

Variances should be determined for all line items on budget reports along with an indication of whether the variance is favorable or unfavorable. The kind of variance can be indicated by labeling it "F" for favorable and "U" for unfavorable, or placing parentheses around unfavorable variances and showing favorable variances without parentheses. Some clubs simply asterisk unfavorable variances.

Determination of Significant Variances

Virtually all budgeted revenue and expense items on a budget report will differ from the actual amounts, with the possible exception of fixed expenses. This is only to be expected, because no budgeting process, however sophisticated, is perfect. However, simply because a variance exists does not mean that management should analyze the variance and follow through with appropriate corrective actions. Only significant variances require this kind of management analysis and action.

Criteria used to determine which variances are significant are called **significance criteria**. They are generally expressed in terms of both dollar and percentage differences. Dollar and percentage differences should be used jointly due to the weakness of each when used separately. Dollar differences fail to recognize the magnitude of the base. For example, a large club may have a $1,000 difference in dues revenue from the budgeted amount. Yet the $1,000 difference based on a budget of $1,000,000 results in a percentage difference of only .1 percent. Most managers would agree this is insignificant. However, if the dues revenue budget for the period was $10,000, a $1,000 difference would result in a percentage difference of 10 percent, which most managers would consider significant. This seems to suggest that variances should be considered significant based on the percentage difference. However, the percentage difference also fails at times. For example, assume that the budget for an expense is $10. A dollar difference of $2 results in a 20 percent difference. The percentage difference appears significant, but generally little (if any) managerial time should be spent analyzing and investigating a $2 difference.

Therefore, the dollar and percentage differences should be used jointly in determining which variances are significant. The size of the significance criteria will differ among club properties in relation to the size of the operation and the controllability of certain revenue or expense items. In general, the larger the operation, the larger the dollar difference criteria. Also, the greater the control exercised over the item, the smaller the criteria. For example, a large operation may set significance criteria as follows:

Revenue	$1,000 and four percent
Variable expense	$500 and two percent
Fixed expense	$100 and one percent

A smaller club may set significance criteria as follows:

Revenue	$200 and four percent
Variable expense	$100 and two percent
Fixed expense	$50 and one percent

Notice that the change in criteria, based on size of operation, is generally the dollar difference. Both significance criteria decrease as the item becomes more controllable.

To illustrate the determination of significant variances, the significance criteria above for a small club will be applied to the Green Club's January 20X4 budget report (see Exhibit 10). The following revenue and expense items have significant variances:

1. The unfavorable $2,050 difference between the budgeted initiation fees and the actual initiation fees exceeds the dollar difference criterion of $200 and the unfavorable 100 percent difference exceeds the percentage criterion of four percent.

2. The favorable $550 difference between the budgeted cost of food sales and the actual cost of food sales exceeds the dollar difference criterion of $100, and the favorable 4.3 percent difference exceeds the percentage difference criterion of two percent.

Variance Analysis

Variance analysis is the third step in the five-step control process. It is the process of identifying and investigating significant differences between budgets and actual results. With this additional information, management is better prepared to identify the causes of any variances.

We will look at variance analysis for three general areas: revenue, cost of food sold, and variable labor. The basic models presented in these areas can be applied to other similar areas. For each area, formulas and an example will be provided.

Revenue Variance Analysis. Revenue variances occur because of price and volume differences. Thus, the variances relating to revenue are called *price variance* (PV) and *volume variance* (VV). The formulas for these variances are as follows:

$$\frac{\text{Price}}{\text{Variance}} = \frac{\text{Budgeted}}{\text{Volume}} \times \left(\frac{\text{Actual}}{\text{Price}} - \frac{\text{Budgeted}}{\text{Price}} \right)$$

$$PV = BV(AP - BP)$$

$$\frac{\text{Volume}}{\text{Variance}} = \frac{\text{Actual}}{\text{Price}} \times \left(\frac{\text{Actual}}{\text{Volume}} - \frac{\text{Budgeted}}{\text{Volume}} \right)$$

$$VV = AP(AV - BV)$$

These formulas are illustrated by using the Sample Club, whose budget and actual monthly results for food sales appear in Exhibit 11. The budget variance of $6,600 is favorable. Variance analysis will be conducted to determine the general cause(s) of this variance—that is, price or volume. The price variance for the Sample Club is determined as follows:

$$
\begin{aligned}
PV &= BV(AP - BP) \\
&= (4,000)(\$13 - \$12) \\
&= \underline{\$4,000} \text{ (F)}
\end{aligned}
$$

Exhibit 11 Food Sales at the Sample Club: Budget and Actual

	Lunch Covers	Average Price	Total
Budget	4,000	$12	$ 48,000
Actual	4,200	13	54,600
Difference	200	$ 1	$ 6,600(F)

The price variance of $4,000 is favorable because the average price charged per cover of $13 was $1 more than the budgeted average price of $12.

The volume variance is computed as follows:

$$
\begin{aligned}
VV &= AP(AV - BV) \\
&= \$13(4{,}200 - 4{,}000) \\
&= \$2{,}600 \text{ (F)}
\end{aligned}
$$

The volume variance of $2,600 is favorable, because 200 more covers were sold than planned.

The sum of the two variances equals the budget variance of $6,600 for revenue as follows:

$$
\begin{aligned}
VV &= \$2{,}600 \text{ (F)} \\
PV &= 4{,}000 \text{ (F)} \\
\text{Total} &= \$6{,}600 \text{ (F)}
\end{aligned}
$$

Cost of Goods Sold Analysis. The **cost of goods sold variance** occurs because of differences due to cost and volume. That is, the amount paid for the goods sold (food and/or beverage) differs from the budget, and the total amount sold differs from the budgeted sales. The detailed variances related to the cost of goods are called the cost variance (CV) and the volume variance (VV). The formulas for these variances are as follows:

$$
\frac{\text{Cost}}{\text{Variance}} = \frac{\text{Budgeted}}{\text{Volume}} \times \left(\frac{\text{Budgeted}}{\text{Cost}} - \frac{\text{Actual}}{\text{Cost}} \right)
$$

$$
CV = BV(BC - AC)
$$

$$
\frac{\text{Volume}}{\text{Variance}} = \frac{\text{Actual}}{\text{Cost}} \times \left(\frac{\text{Budgeted}}{\text{Volume}} - \frac{\text{Actual}}{\text{Volume}} \right)
$$

$$
VV = AC(BV - AV)
$$

The analysis of the cost of goods sold variance formulas is illustrated by using a food service example. The Sample Club, open for lunch only, had cost of food sold results and budgeted amounts for January as shown in Exhibit 12. The unfavorable budget variance of $160 is analyzed using variance analysis as follows.

Exhibit 12   Cost of Food Sold at the Sample Club: Budget and Actual

	Covers	Average Cost Per Cover	Total Cost
Budget	4,000	$ 5.00	$20,000
Actual	4,200	4.80	20,160
Difference	200	$ .20	$ 160 (U)

The cost variance is determined as follows:

$$CV \;=\; BV(BC - AC)$$
$$=\; 4{,}000(\$5.00 - \$4.80)$$
$$=\; \underline{\$800}\ (F)$$

The cost variance of $800 is favorable because the average food cost per cover of $4.80 is $.20 less than the budgeted cost per cover of $5.00.

The volume variance is determined as follows:

$$VV \;=\; AC(BV - AV)$$
$$=\; \$4.80(4{,}000 - 4{,}200)$$
$$=\; -\underline{\$960}\ (U)$$

The volume variance of $960 is unfavorable because excessive volume results in greater costs than budgeted. Remember that this is from an expense perspective. Excessive volume from a revenue perspective is favorable.

The sum of the two variances is $160(U).

Cost Variance	$800 (F)
Volume Variance	960 (U)
Total	$160 (U)

This sum equals the $160 budget variance shown in Exhibit 12. These results show that from a cost perspective, the club beat the budget by $800. The unfavorable volume variance of $960 more than offsets the favorable cost variance for food sales.

Variable Labor Variance Analysis. Variable labor expense is labor expense that varies directly with activity. Variable labor increases as sales increase and decreases as sales decrease. In a food service situation, servers' wages are generally treated as variable labor expense. Again, the greater the number of members to be served food, the greater the number of servers and the greater the server expense. In the discussion that follows, we use the term labor expense to refer only to variable labor.

Labor expense variances result from three general causes: volume, rate, and efficiency. All budget variances for labor expense may be divided among these three areas. Volume variances (VV) result when there is a different volume of work

Exhibit 13   Labor Expenses at the Sample Club: Budget and Actual

	Covers	Time/Cover (minutes)	Total Time (hours)	Hourly Wage (dollars)	Total
Budget	4,000	5.0 min.	333.33	$ 6.00	$ 2,000.00
Actual	4,200	5.2 min.	364.0	6.05	2,202.20
Difference	200	.2 min.	30.66	$ .05	$ 202.20 (U)

than forecasted. Rate variances (RV) result when the average wage rate is different than planned. Efficiency variances (EV) result when the amount of work performed by the labor force on an hourly basis differs from the forecast.

$$VV = AR(BT - ATAO)$$
$$RV = BT(BR - AR)$$
$$EV = AR(ATAO - AT)$$

The elements in these formulas are defined as follows:

- BR (Budgeted Rate)—the average wage rates budgeted per hour for labor services.

- BT (Budgeted Time)—the hours required to perform work according to the budget. For example, if the work standard for serving meals is 12 members/hour per server, then a club would require 50 server hours (600 ÷ 12) to serve 600 meals.

- ATAO (Allowable Time for Actual Output)—the hours allowable to perform work based on the actual output. This is determined in the same way as budgeted time, except that the work is actual versus budget. For example, if 660 meals were actually served, the allowable time given a work standard of 12 meals/hour would be 55 hours (660 ÷ 12).

- AR (Actual Rate)—the actual average wage rate paid per hour for labor services.

- AT (Actual Time)—the number of hours actually worked.

The calculation of these formulas is illustrated in Exhibit 13. The work standard for servers of the Sample Club is serving 12 meals per hour. Therefore, on the average, a meal should be served every five minutes (60 ÷ 12).

The volume variance is determined as follows:

$$VV = AR(BT - ATAO)$$
$$= \$6.05(333.33 - 350)$$
$$= -\$100.85 \text{ (U)}$$

Note: The ATAO of 350 is determined by dividing the work standard of 12 covers per hour into the 4,200 covers served.

The volume variance of $100.85 is unfavorable because more covers were served than budgeted. Normally, the volume variance is beyond the control of the supervisor to which the labor expense pertains. Therefore, this should be isolated and generally not further pursued from an expense perspective. In addition, an unfavorable volume variance should be more than offset by the favorable volume variance for the related food sales.

The rate variance for the Sample Club is determined as follows:

$$
\begin{aligned}
RV &= BT(BR - AR) \\
&= 333.33(\$6.00 - \$6.05) \\
&= -\underline{\$16.67} \text{ (U)}
\end{aligned}
$$

The rate variance of $16.67 is unfavorable because the average pay rate is $.05 per hour more than the budgeted $6 per hour. The labor supervisor responsible for scheduling and managing labor should be held responsible for this minor variance.

The efficiency variance for the Sample Club is determined as follows:

$$
\begin{aligned}
EV &= AR(ATAO - AT) \\
&= \$6.05(350 - 364) \\
&= -\underline{\$84.70} \text{ (U)}
\end{aligned}
$$

The efficiency variance of $84.70 is unfavorable because an average of 12 seconds more were spent serving a cover than was originally planned. The supervisor must determine why this occurred. It could have been due to new employees who were inefficient because of work overload, or perhaps there were other factors. Once the specific causes are determined, the manager can take corrective action to ensure a future recurrence is avoided.

The sum of the three variances equals the budget variance of $202.20 (the two-cent difference is due to rounding) as follows:

Volume Variance	$ 100.85 (U)
Rate Variance	16.67 (U)
Efficiency Variance	84.70 (U)
Total	$202.22 (U)

Determination of Problems and Management Action

The next step in the budgetary control process is for management to investigate variance analysis results in an effort to determine the cause(s) of the variance. This is needed because the analysis of a revenue variance will reveal differences due to price and/or volume, but not why the price and/or volume variances exist. Similarly, the analysis of variable labor expense will reveal differences due to rate, efficiency, and volume but, again, not the exact cause(s) of the variances. Additional investigation by management is required.

For example, assume that the analysis of the servers' labor variance reveals that a significant portion of an unfavorable variance is due to rate. Management must investigate the rate variance to determine why the average rate paid was higher than budgeted. An unfavorable labor rate variance may be due to staffing problems, excessive overtime pay, or a combination of these two factors. Each significant variance requires further management investigation to determine the cause(s).

The final step to complete the budgetary control process is taking action to correct a problem. For example, if a major cause of the rate variance for servers wages is excessive overtime, this may be controlled by requiring all overtime to be approved in advance.

Reforecasting

Regardless of the extensive efforts and the sophisticated methods used in formulating operations budgets, some clubs reforecast their expected operations as they progress through the budget year. This reforecasting is necessary only when the actual results begin to vary significantly from the budget. Some organizations will start reforecasting at the beginning of the budget year and continue to reforecast every month for the entire year. In the recent study of clubs' operating budgeting practices, 32 percent of the respondents indicated their operating budgets were revised as the year progresses. The frequency of revision varies from 19 percent revising on a monthly basis to 20 percent revising semi-annually. Most responding clubs—36 percent—reported that they reforecast "when club performance indicates a need."

Summary

The budgetary process is valuable to the operation of a club. In order to formulate a budget, the club's goals must be stated and each department must look ahead and estimate future performance. As the actual period progresses, management can compare operating results to the budget, and significant differences can be studied. This process forces management to set future goals and to strive to see that they become realized.

In order to formulate a budget, each department estimates its revenues and expenses. This is done by observing past trends and projecting them for another year. The manager must also take into account forces in the economy, new developments in the market, and other significant events that will affect the operation. These projections are then combined to form a budget for the next period's operations. At this point, the budgeted results are compared with the club's goals, and the budget is adjusted until these goals are met.

Once completed, the budget becomes a control tool. As the period progresses, management compares the budget with actual performance. The differences between each line item are calculated, and any significant differences are analyzed. Significance depends on both absolute dollar differences and percentage differences. The analysis includes dividing each line item into its components, including price and volume for revenues and rate, volume, and efficiency for labor. Management can then address any deficiencies and take corrective action to keep the operation heading toward the defined goals.

Endnotes

1. See also Raymond S. Schmidgall, "Operating Budgets Preparation," *Club Management,* November–December, 1997.

2. For more information on zero-base budgeting, see Peter A. Pyrrh, *Zero-Base Budgeting* (New York: John Wiley & Sons, 1973) and Lee M. Kruel, "Zero-Base Budgeting of Hotel Indirect Expense," *The Cornell Hotel & Restaurant Administration Quarterly,* November 1978, pp. 11–14.

Key Terms

cost of goods sold variance—A group of variances used to examine differences between budgeted and actual amounts paid for goods sold and the total amount sold.

incremental budgeting—Forecasting budgets based on historical financial information.

operations budget—Management's detailed plans for generating revenue and incurring expenses for each department within the operation; also referred to as the revenue and expense budget.

revenue variances—A group of variances used to examine differences between budgeted and actual prices and volumes.

significance criteria—Criteria used to determine whether variances are significant. Generally expressed in terms of both dollar and percentage differences.

variable labor variances—A group of variances used to examine differences between budgeted and actual variable labor expense.

variance analysis—Process of identifying and investigating causes of significant differences (variances) between budgeting plans and actual results.

zero-base budgeting (ZBB)—An approach to preparing budgets that requires the justification of all expenses; assumes that each department starts with zero dollars and must justify all budgeted amounts.

Review Questions

1. What are four future items that should be considered when formulating a budget?

2. How does a budget help a club to realize its operating goals?

3. How is the budget formulated?

4. Why should budgets be prepared at various levels of sales?

5. What constitutes a "significant" variance?

6. What do volume variances highlight for management?

7. Why is an increase in volume favorable in revenue analysis and unfavorable in cost analysis?

8. What does the formula EV = AR(ATAO – AT) reflect?

9. What items should be considered when preparing the food revenue section of the budget?

10. What are three possible goals a club could set for its operations?

 **Problems**

Problem 1

The Runners Club projected 3,000 lunches to be sold for September at an average price of $9.50. The actual sales were 3,200 meals and food revenue of $32,000.

Required:

1. Determine the budget variance.

2. Determine the volume variance.

3. Determine the price variance.

Problem 2

Jackie Jackson, the overnight rooms department manager of the Waverly Club, is preparing a condensed 20X1 annual budget. She has the following information upon which to base her estimates.

- Estimated occupancy percentage: 75 percent

- Rooms: 40

- Average rate: $80.00

- Labor: Fixed: $80,000 (annual)   Variable: $5.00/room

- Other operating expenses: $5.00/room

Required:

1. Prepare a condensed budget for the rooms department. (Assume that the club is open 300 days a year.)

2. The Waverly's general manager desires that the department have a departmental profit of at least $300,000 and 65 percent of revenue. Will Ms. Jackson's condensed budget projections be acceptable to the hotel's management?

Problem 3

Amy Howe is the dining room manager of the Marathon Club. The wages budget for her department is divided between fixed and variable expenses. The work standard for waitpersons is to serve 12 members per hour. The average wage rate per hour is $6.00. The variable wages budget for waitpersons for June is $14,400 based on $6.00 per hour, eight-hour shifts, 30 days in the month, and 10 waitpersons. Given the work standard, this is also based on serving 28,800 people. During the month of June, the waitperson wages totaled $15,600. During June, 2,500 hours were worked, and the average hourly pay was $6.24 per hour. In addition, 29,200 members were served by the waitpersons.

Required:

1. Determine the budget variance for waitperson variable wage expense.

2. Is the budget variance determined (in #1 above) significant? Explain.

3. Rate Amy Howe's performance in managing the waitpersons. Support your discussion with specific numbers.

4. What is the efficiency variance for waitperson wage expense for the month of June?

Chapter 8 Outline

Working Capital Components
Cash Budgets
    Various Budgeting Strategies
    Two Approaches to Presenting Cash
      Budgets
Inventory Management
    Estimating Ending Inventory and Cost
      of Goods Sold
Managing Accounts Receivable
Managing Current Liabilities
    Trade Payables
    Short-Term Bank Loans

Competencies

1. Identify the various components of working capital, explain the function of cash budgeting, and identify factors club managers should consider when managing cash budgets. (pp. 195–199)

2. Distinguish the cash receipts and disbursements approach to cash budgeting from the adjusted net income approach. (pp. 199–201)

3. Describe how inventory management, accounts receivable, trade payables, and short-term bank loans affect cash management. (pp. 202–207)

8

Current Asset Management

DRAW A LINE on a club's statement of financial position just below the total current asset section and the total current liability section. Because current assets and current liabilities are known collectively as **working capital**, this line could be called the working capital line. Working capital includes items such as cash, accounts receivable, inventory, and accounts payable. **Net working capital** is the difference between current assets and current liabilities.

The items above the working capital line are very important to the club, and the manager or controller spends most of his or her time managing these items. In this chapter we will examine the various elements of working capital and the management of those elements.

Working Capital Components

Exhibit 1 is a sample statement of financial position for a club, the top portion of which shows the various elements of working capital. Although there are many individual items of working capital, we will describe the most commonly encountered items. Cash includes cash on hand, such as undeposited cash receipts and cash banks, demand deposits, and certificates of deposit. Cash is the most liquid current asset and must have the most stringent controls.

Accounts receivable include dues, fees, assessments, and sales due to the club from members on open account. Inventory consists of food and beverages available for sale. In addition, some clubs have pro shop merchandise and fertilizer inventories. Since inventory is susceptible to both waste and theft, it too must be controlled very carefully.

Current liabilities are obligations due at the statement of financial position date that must be paid within 12 months. Accounts payable include amounts due to creditors for food and beverages purchased for resale, as well as other merchandise, services, and equipment. Payroll taxes related to the club's employees are recorded under "taxes payable and accrued." Other accrued expenses are accrued salaries and wages, interest expense, and workers' compensation insurance.

A club must closely monitor net working capital (current assets less current liabilities). Generally, the current ratio (current assets divided by current liabilities) should be two to one. That is, for every $1 of current liabilities, a club should have $2 of current assets. This provides a cushion of safety, or liquidity, for the club in meeting its current obligations. Exhibit 2 illustrates the effect of various transactions on net working capital.

Exhibit 1 Sample Statement of Financial Position

Assets

	December 31 Current Year	December 31 Prior Year
Current Assets:		
Cash:		
In bank	$	$
On hand		
Accounts receivable:		
House		
Dues, fees and assessments		
Other		
Total		
Less: Allowance for doubtful accounts		
Inventories, at cost:		
Food		
Beverages		
Other		
Prepaid expenses		
Insurance		
Real estate taxes		
Other		
Total current assets		
Cash Restricted for Capital Improvements		
Fixed Assets:		
Land and improvements		
Buildings and improvements		
Furniture, fixtures and equipment		
Total		
Less: Accumulated depreciation		
Total Assets	$	$

Liabilities and Members' Equity

	December 31 Current Year	December 31 Prior Year
Current Liabilities:		
Accounts payable:		
Trade	$	$
Other		
Taxes payable and accrued:		
Payroll		
State sales		
Accrued expenses		
Salaries and wages		
Workmen's compensation		
Insurance		
Interest		
Other		
Portion of long-term debt due within one year		
Special purpose funds		
Unearned income:		
Dues		
Special fees		
Scrip		
Rentals		
Total Current Liabilities		
Long-Term Debt:		
Mortgage note payable		
Less: Portion due within one year		
Total Liabilities		
Capital Improvement Fund		
Members' Equity:		
Membership certificates:		
Issued and outstanding		
Retained earnings:		
Balance, beginning		
Net income for the year		
Balance, end		
Total Liabilities and Members' Equity	$	$

Exhibit 2   Effect of Transactions on Net Working Capital

Transaction	Effect on Net Working Capital
Purchased inventory for cash	No effect
Purchased land for cash	Decrease
Purchased supplies on account	No effect
Sold used equipment for cash	Increase
Borrowed cash from bank, payable in one year	Increase

Exhibit 3   Top Five Practices in Cash Collection

Practices	Frequency (%)
Send collection letters in 60 days	69
Suspend privileges after 90 days	48
Send collection letters in 30 days	46
Send reminders with monthly statements	45
Post names of delinquent members	45

Cash Budgets

Of all of the working capital items, cash is the lifeblood of a club. A club may incur and survive operating losses (expenses in excess of revenue) for several periods, but it cannot operate without cash. Therefore, it is critical that sufficient cash be available to pay bills as they come due. This cash planning can be accomplished by using cash budgets.

Managing cash involves forecasting cash flows, accelerating cash flows, investing excess cash, and borrowing cash for working capital purposes. Today, greater emphasis is being placed on cash at private clubs than ever before. Managers are seeking ways to accelerate cash inflows and to conserve cash outflows, resulting in the more efficient use of cash. A survey of 200 financial executives associated with the club industry revealed the top five cash collection practices (Exhibit 3) and common cash payment practices (Exhibit 4).[1] Club managers are receiving more frequent and more detailed cash reports than in the past and a number of clubs are providing more detailed and more frequent information to their lenders.

Various Budgeting Strategies

Not all clubs have formalized (written) cash budgets covering at least a year. One survey found 46 percent of club executives indicating their clubs have a written cash budget for a year, while 54 percent indicated their clubs do not prepare cash budgets for a year.[2] These latter clubs may have written cash budgets for periods

Exhibit 4   Practices in Cash Payments

Practices	Frequency (%)
Take 30-day terms	77
Utilize all cash discounts	66
Use computers to monitor payables	61
Lengthen payroll periods	17

of less than a year or may use informal cash budgets. One club manager indicated that his club prepares a cash budget on a monthly basis for 18 months into the future; another club prepares an annual cash budget in monthly segments. A club in Nevada prepares a monthly cash budget for a year and quarterly cash budgets for the following year.

The survey results clearly show that the larger the club, the more likely it is to prepare a cash budget: cash budgets were prepared by 29 percent of the clubs with less than $2,000,000 in annual revenues, 47.8 percent of the clubs with annual revenues between $2,000,000 and $5,000,000, and 61.9 percent of the clubs with annual revenues of more than $5,000,000.

Several respondents who indicated they did *not* use formalized cash budgets revealed how they control cash. The following is a sample of responses:

- A northeastern country club: "Cash flows are monitored by making informal projections of cash inflows and outflows on a monthly basis. Bills due during the month are paid, and funds are borrowed from the bank to cover cash shortfalls."

- A city club in the upper Midwest: "Cash flows are monitored on a daily to weekly basis by tracking the amount of cash on hand and the levels of accounts receivable and accounts payable."

- A country club in Texas: "The club has always had an excess of cash and we are always looking for places to invest excess cash."

- A country club in a retirement community: "Cash is tracked informally by checking the amounts of cash receipts and disbursements. Members pay almost immediately when they receive their monthly bill, thus the timing on cash receipts is very close to the recording of revenue of the club."

Finally, respondents were queried as to why a cash budget was prepared. A majority (54 percent) indicated their cash budgets were prepared to monitor cash flow. Nearly two out of every five respondents (38 percent) indicated their cash budgets were prepared in order to plan operations and acquisitions requiring cash. The remaining eight percent indicated other choices.

Comments from two respondents reflected totally different uses of a cash budget. A Las Vegas club prepares cash budgets to finance capital acquisitions and to invest excess cash. On the other hand, a Georgia country club uses the cash budget to determine if sufficient cash is available to make payroll.

The most likely person to prepare the club's cash budget is the financial executive. Still, at many clubs, the general managers choose to prepare this budget, in part because:

- They believe they have a broader view of the club's cash needs.
- They believe they can prepare a more accurate cash budget.
- They simply prefer to do it.

Two Approaches to Presenting Cash Budgets

There are two basic approaches to cash budgeting: the cash receipts and disbursements approach and the adjusted net income approach. The method used depends primarily on the length of time for which the cash budget is prepared.

Cash Receipts and Disbursements Approach. The **cash receipts and disbursements approach** is useful when forecasting cash receipts for periods of up to six months, though it can be used for longer periods. It shows the direct sources of cash receipts, such as occasional cash sales, collection of accounts receivable, proceeds from bank loans, sale of membership certificates, and so forth. It also reveals the direct uses of cash, such as payment of food purchases, payroll, and mortgage payments.

Because the cash receipts and disbursements method reflects the direct sources and uses of cash, it is easy to understand. Care should be exercised when using this approach for periods exceeding six months, since projected figures beyond this point become increasingly unreliable, especially when actual operations differ significantly from the operations budget.

Exhibit 5 illustrates the basic format of a cash budget based on the cash receipts and disbursements approach. This format contains two major sections: estimated cash receipts and estimated cash disbursements. Estimated cash receipts are added to the estimated beginning cash to find the estimated cash available for the period. Estimated cash disbursements are subtracted from estimated cash available to determine estimated ending cash. This figure is then compared to the minimum cash required to identify any shortage or excess.

Adjusted Net Income Approach. The **adjusted net income approach** is generally preferable for budgeting cash for periods longer than six months. In addition, it emphasizes external, as opposed to internal, sources of funds. It also provides the estimated cash balance for management's evaluation. Exhibit 6 illustrates the format of a prepared cash budget using the adjusted net income approach.

The adjusted net income method is an indirect approach to cash budgeting because the direct sources and uses related to operations—for example, cash sales and disbursements for payroll—are not shown.

This approach has two major sections: sources and uses. The sources section consists of internal and external sources. Internal sources are primarily cash from operations (chiefly reflected by the increase in net assets from the statement of

Exhibit 5   Cash Budget: Cash Receipts and Disbursements Approach

Cash Budget
Cash Receipts and Disbursements Approach
For the months of Jan.–June, 20X1

	January	February	March	April	May	June
Estimated Cash— Beginning	$	$	$	$	$	$
Estimated Cash Receipts:						
Cash Sales						
Collection of Accounts Receivable						
Proceeds from Bank Loans						
Proceeds from Sale of Fixed Assets						
Other						
Total						
Estimated Cash Available						
Estimated Cash Disbursements:						
Inventory						
Payroll						
Operating Expenses						
Insurance						
Mortgage Payments						
Other						
Total						
Estimated Cash Ending						
Minimum Cash Required						
Cash Excess or Shortage	$	$	$	$	$	$

activities plus depreciation and other expenses that do not require cash). External sources of funds include proceeds from bank loans and the sale of membership certificates. The sum of the beginning cash and the sources of cash is the estimated cash available.

The uses of cash are subtracted from cash at the beginning of the year plus sources of cash to find the estimated cash at the end of the year. This figure is compared with the minimum cash requirement to determine any excess or shortage.

Exhibit 6   Cash Budget: Adjusted Net Income Approach

Cash Budget
Adjusted Net Income Approach
For the year ended December 31, 20X1

Cash—Beginning of Year $

Sources of Cash:
   Increase in Net Assets $
   Add: Depreciation
          Amortization
          Other   _____

Other Sources:
   Proceeds from Bank Loans
   Sale of Fixed Assets
   Sale of Membership Certificates
   Other   _____

          Total   _____

Uses of Cash:
   Increase in Accounts Receivable*
   Increase in Inventories*
   Decrease in Current Liabilities*
   Purchase of Fixed Assets
   Reduction in Long-Term Debt
   Other   _____

          Total   _____

Estimated Cash—End of Year   _____

Minimum Cash Requirement   _____

Cash Excess or Shortage $ _____

*Decreases in accounts receivable and inventories and increases in current liabilities would be sources of cash.

The adjusted net income approach, much like the statement of cash flows prepared on an indirect basis, focuses directly on changes in accounts receivable, inventories, and current liabilities. This requires management to consider the amount of cash tied up in accounts receivable and inventory and cash "provided" by current liabilities. Therefore, this approach encourages closer management review of these working capital accounts.

From a practical viewpoint, both cash budgeting approaches are useful. The cash receipts and disbursements approach is recommended for short-term budgets prepared on a monthly or weekly basis; the adjusted net income approach is recommended for long-term projections. Many clubs prepare a cash budget corresponding to each annual operations budget prepared for several years into the future.

Inventory Management

Inventory is viewed by some as a necessary evil. Fortunately, the inventory of most clubs is fairly low as a percentage of their total assets.

Clubs maintain an inventory of food and beverages, fertilizer and lawn chemicals, and, in some cases, pro shop merchandise, even though there is a relatively high cost to store this inventory. The benefits of having food, beverages, and merchandise for sale is reasonably obvious since these items are generally sold at three to four times their cost.

However, the non-product costs of inventory need to be considered so that management will appreciate the need to exercise tight control in this area. Several costs directly related to inventory include—but are not limited to—storage, insurance, and personnel. Storage space is required for keeping inventory, and many inventory items must be stored in temperature-controlled environments. Certain inventory items have a limited shelf life; thus, personnel should closely monitor these items. Inventory must be counted periodically, which also requires personnel and thus payroll dollars. Overall costs increase when, in spite of management's best efforts, some inventory spoils and must be discarded. Insurance to cover inventory, although not expensive, is still another cost. In addition to these costs, there is the opportunity cost of inventory. That is, if funds were not tied up in inventory, they could be invested to provide additional returns to the club. Therefore, management must track inventory closely to keep it at the lowest level that still allows the club to meet the members' desires.

Common means of monitoring inventory include inventory ratios. The most common inventory ratio is inventory turnover, calculated by dividing average inventory into cost of sales. This ratio should be computed not only for food and beverage, but also for each category of pro shop merchandise, if applicable. The results are most meaningful when compared to the planned ratios and to ratios for past periods. The ratios can assist management in detecting unfavorable trends. For example, successive food inventory turnovers of 2, 1.8, and 1.6 suggest a major change in food inventory. Management should determine if the inventory is excessive and take appropriate actions to correct the situation.

Estimating Ending Inventory and Cost of Goods Sold

Inventory is accounted for through either the perpetual or the periodic system. Under a perpetual inventory system, each item of inventory is continuously tracked in terms of both purchase and sale. Hence, a manager can look at the inventory records at any time to find the number of items of a particular type of inventory. Under a periodic inventory system, there is no continuous record of sales and purchases of inventory items. Instead, it is necessary to count the inventory in order to determine the exact inventory and gross profit for the period.

Clubs always take a physical inventory at the end of each fiscal year whether they use the periodic or the perpetual inventory method. They do this to accurately compile financial statements and to comply with Internal Revenue Service regulations. On a monthly basis, however, it may be too costly or inconvenient to take a physical inventory, and sometimes it may be impossible to do so, such as when a

Exhibit 7   The Retail Method of Inventory Valuation

	Cost Price ($)	Retail Selling Price ($)
Estimate of Ending Inventory **July 31, 20X1**		
Beginning Inventory	12,376	22,277
Purchases	+ 76,840	+138,312
Cost of Goods Available	89,216	160,589
Cost Percentage: $\dfrac{\$\ 89,216}{\$160,589} = 56\%$		
Subtract Net Sales at Retail		−132,068
Ending Inventory at Retail		28,521
Ending Inventory at Cost:		
$28,521 × .56	$ 15,972	

club is destroyed by a fire or flood. However, clubs still need to produce financial statements. In lieu of taking a physical inventory, clubs can use one of two methods to estimate ending inventory. They are the retail method and the gross profit method.

Although the **retail method of inventory valuation** is used primarily by department stores, clubs can also use it effectively. To implement this method, a club must maintain records of both cost and retail prices for beginning inventory and purchases. (The retail price is the amount at which the item is priced for sale.)

Since a controller would have a record of both beginning inventory and purchases, he or she should therefore know the amount of the cost of goods available for sale at both cost and retail; at the end of a fiscal period, the items included in cost of goods available must either be sold or in ending inventory. With that information and a record of sales for the period, the accountants can subtract cost of goods available at retail from sales at retail and end up with ending inventory at retail.

The books list ending inventory at cost, not retail, so there is one more step in the computation. It involves finding the percentage relationship between cost and retail for the business. This is accomplished by simply dividing the cost of goods available for sale *at cost* by the cost of goods available for sale *at retail*. The resulting percentage is then multiplied by the ending inventory at retail. The result is ending inventory at cost. Exhibit 7 shows the estimate of ending inventory at July 31, 20X1.

The basic assumption under the **gross profit method of inventory valuation** is that the gross profit percentage is fairly constant from period to period. Therefore, if a club's gross profit percentage was 53 percent over the past five years, it can assume that the current period's gross profit percentage is also 53 percent. Recall the relationship between the gross profit percentage and the cost of gross sold percentage: added together, they must equal 100 percent.

Once the controller obtains the gross profit percentage, he or she goes to the general ledger and adds beginning inventory and purchases to get cost of goods available for sale. Next, the controller estimates cost of goods sold by multiplying sales by 1 minus the gross profit percentage. Finally, the controller determines ending inventory by subtracting cost of goods sold from cost of goods available for sale.

The following example illustrates the gross profit method:

Beginning inventory, August 1, 20X1	$ 16,586
Purchases in August	48,522
Sales in August	93,407
Gross profit percentage	53%

Using these account balances and the gross profit ratio of 53 percent, the ending inventory would be $21,207, computed as follows:

Beginning inventory, August 1, 20X1		$ 16,586
Purchases in August		+48,522
Cost of goods available for sale		65,108
Subtract estimated cost of goods sold:		
Sales in August	$ 93,407	
Cost of goods sold % (1.00 − .53)	× .47	43,901
Estimated ending inventory, August 31, 20X1		$ 21,207

Managing Accounts Receivable

A major current asset of many clubs is accounts receivable. If all sales were cash sales, there would be no need to manage accounts receivable. This, however, is not the case for clubs, where credit sales are expected. Credit commences when the member receives a product or service without paying for it and continues until the member pays the bill, which generally occurs at the end of the month. Statements should be mailed monthly to member accounts, and the general manager should attend to delinquent accounts. Initially, collection letters are used, followed by telephone calls and eventually member suspension. Vigilant action is required to minimize uncollected accounts.

Accounts receivable are monitored by the preparation and review of an **aging of accounts receivable**, as shown in Exhibit 8. A review of the total of delinquent accounts by days outstanding will suggest the quality of the overall accounts receivable. Further, the aging lists specific accounts, and the most delinquent accounts can be quickly identified for follow-up collection efforts. Ratios are another tool to monitor accounts receivable.

Since clubs generally do not charge interest on current accounts, it is imperative that accounts be collected promptly. The real cost of receivables is the opportunity cost of the amounts "invested" in those accounts.

Exhibit 8   Aging of Accounts Receivable

Aging of Accounts Receivable
City Club
December 31, 20X1

Days Outstanding

Member Name	Total	0–30	31–60	61–90	91–120	Over 120 days
Adams	$ 600	$ 400	$ 200	$ -0-	$ -0-	$ -0-
Brown	400	100	-0-	300	-0-	-0-
Chilos	100	100	-0-	-0-	-0-	-0-
Dumas	1,000	950	-0-	-0-	-0-	50
Franks	50	-0-	-0-	-0-	50	-0-
Gordon	80	80	-0-	-0-	-0-	-0-
TOTAL	$145,000	$115,000	$18,000	$7,000	$4,000	$1,000
Percentage	100%	79.3%	12.4%	4.8%	2.8%	.7%

Managing Current Liabilities

A large portion of current assets is financed by current liabilities in clubs. The current ratio of approximately two to one for clubs reflects this situation. While trade credit *appears* to be free (that is, suppliers do not charge interest to clubs for amounts owed in the normal course of business), the cost to carry customers is included in the price of the goods. That is, food, beverages, and so forth are priced higher than they would be if interest were charged on payable accounts. Everything else being the same, the longer a club has to pay its bills, the greater its reliance on trade credit to finance its operations.

Current liabilities consist of trade payables, taxes payable, notes payable, accrued wages, and the current portion of long-term debt. The remainder of this section focuses on trade payables and bank loans (notes payable), as the other payables generally must be paid on stipulated dates.

Trade Payables

Trade payables resulting from purchases on account generally require payment in 30 days. However, suppliers may offer cash discounts to encourage customers to pay their accounts early. For example, a supplier may provide a two percent cash discount if the invoice is paid within 10 days of the invoice date. Thus, the terms of sale per the invoice are simply shown as 2/10, *n*/30. The *n*/30 means that if the invoice is not paid within 10 days of the invoice date, then the entire amount is due within 30 days of the invoice date.

The **effective interest rate** of the cash discount is determined as follows:

$$\text{Effective interest rate} = \frac{\text{Cash discount}}{\text{Invoice amount} - \text{Cash discount}} \times \frac{\text{Days in year}}{\text{Difference between end of discount period and "final" due day}}$$

The following example illustrates the calculation of the effective interest rate. Assume that a club purchases furniture for $10,000 and is offered terms of 2/10, $n/30$. The effective interest rate is determined as follows:

$$\text{Effective interest rate} = \frac{\$200^*}{\$10,000 - \$200} \times \frac{365}{20}$$

$$= \underline{\underline{37.24\%}}$$

$$^*\text{Cash discount} = \$10,000 \times .02 = \$200$$

In other words, the club would be wise to borrow funds to pay the invoice within the cash discount period as long as the interest rate was less than 37.24 percent. The effective interest rate of cash discounts is usually much higher than the firm's marginal cost of capital.

In general, management should pay bills only when they are due, except when cash discounts are available for early payments. The early payment of invoices results in a higher cost of doing business, since the cash expended could have been invested. However, management must also consider the intangible factor of supplier relations. Maintaining favorable relations with suppliers is especially advantageous when the club desires special favors, such as receiving food supplies two days sooner than normally available for a special event, and so on.

Short-Term Bank Loans

The short-term solution to a temporary cash shortage is to arrange an unsecured bank loan (that is, a loan for which no collateral is pledged). Unsecured bank loans are based on the club's ability to pay off the loan from future cash flows from operations. Because the loan is unsecured, cash flow projections must provide the promise of future payback. Such a loan is available to bank clients who have developed a history of bank loyalty and whose operations are familiar to the bank officials.

The interest on a short-term loan of less than one year is generally pegged to the prime rate (historically, the rate available to the bank's best customers). For example, if a club borrows $100,000 at one plus prime, where the prime rate is 8.5 percent, the interest rate is 9.5 percent.

Clubs that frequently use short-term bank loans can request a line of credit from their bank. The bank's agreement is usually informal and continues for an indefinite span of time. The loan is limited, not to exceed a specified amount. To continue the line of credit, the club generally must maintain in its checking account a compensating balance equal to a fraction of the loan. The bank generally reserves the right to refuse additional credit if the borrower's financial position deteriorates significantly; thus, it is necessary to provide the bank with periodic financial reports. Loans extended under this arrangement must generally be repaid within a year, thereby precluding clubs from using short-term financing for long-term needs.

A compensating balance requirement fixed to a loan effectively increases the interest rate. For example, consider a club that borrows $100,000 for one year at a stated interest rate of 12 percent. Further, assume that the bank requires a compensating balance of 10 percent of the loan. The effective interest rate is determined as follows:

$$\text{Effective interest rate} \quad = \quad \frac{\text{Annual interest on loan}}{\text{Loan} \; - \; \text{Compensating balance requirement}}$$

$$= \quad \frac{\$12,000\,{}^{*}}{\$100,000 \; - \; \$10,000}$$

$$= \quad \underline{\underline{13.33\%}}$$

$$^{*}\text{Annual interest} \quad = \quad \text{principal} \times \text{rate} \times \text{time}$$

$$= \quad 100,000 \times .12 \times 1$$

$$= \quad \underline{\underline{\$12,000}}$$

If the club desires an unconditional guarantee that funds will be available, a formal commitment must be secured. In this case, the bank commonly charges an additional standby fee. For example, if a $100,000 formal line of credit is secured and the standby fee is two percent per year, the borrower must pay $2,000 for the year, even if the line is not used.

Endnotes

1. Agnes DeFranco and Raymond S. Schmidgall, "Hotels and Clubs: How Cash Is Handled," *The Bottomline* (December 1998/January 1999), pp. 11–13.

2. Raymond Schmidgall, *Club Management* (May/June 1998), p. 40.

Key Terms

adjusted net income approach—An indirect method of cash budgeting that determines cash flow by adjusting net income to a strictly cash basis. The method is generally preferred for cash budgeting over periods longer than six months.

aging of accounts receivable—A listing of the accounts receivable showing days outstanding. Used by management to identify delinquent accounts for follow-up collection efforts.

cash receipts and disbursements approach—A cash budgeting method that shows direct sources and uses of cash. It is best used for short-term budgeting (less than six months), since the reliability of distant operational numbers decreases rapidly.

effective interest rate—Interest that has been effectively charged, based on interest paid and the actual amount borrowed.

gross profit method of inventory valuation—A method of estimating ending inventory based on a historical gross profit percentage for the club.

net working capital—Current assets less current liabilities.

retail method of inventory valuation—A method of estimating ending inventory that is based on the relationship between cost and retail price.

working capital—Collective term for current assets and current liabilities.

 # Review Questions

1. What are the components of working capital? How is the current ratio calculated?

2. What is the cash receipts and disbursements approach to cash budgeting? For what time period is it useful?

3. What is the adjusted net income approach to cash budgeting? For what time period is it useful?

4. What is the most common inventory ratio and how is it calculated?

5. What is the usefulness of an aging of accounts receivable schedule?

6. What are trade payables and when is payment generally required for their liabilities?

7. How is the effective interest on a cash discount calculated?

8. What effect does a compensating balance have on a bank loan?

9. What specific items are generally included in "cash" on a club's statement of financial position?

 # Problems

Problem 1

Indicate the effect of the following items on net working capital:

1. Purchased $5,000 supplies on account.

2. Borrowed $20,000 cash from bank, payable in three years.

3. Sold a $2,000 block of rooms on account.

4. Purchased $8,000 inventory for cash.

5. Purchased $1,500 of equipment for cash.

6. Sold $1,000 of used equipment for cash.

Problem 2

Calculate the effective interest rate in the following two situations:

1. A supplier offers a three percent discount on an equipment purchase if paid within 10 days of the invoice date, or the full amount is due in 60 days. (3/10, n/60). The cost of the equipment is $8,000.

2. A bank has agreed to loan the club $50,000 for 1 year at 10 percent. The bank requires a 10 percent compensating balance.

Problem 3

Gary Kelser, the general manager of the Downtown Club, has generated the following information about the club for January–March, 20X3. The cash balance on January 1 is $20,000, and the club's policy is to maintain a minimum cash balance of $20,000 at the end of each month.

	January	February	March
1. Dues Received:	$ 68,000	$ 72,000	$ 74,000
2. Cash Food & Beverage Sales:	4,200	4,500	6,000

In addition, food and beverage sales charged by members were $78,000 in January, $85,000 in February, and $92,000 in March. These house accounts are collected in the month following the sale. The house accounts receivable balance on December 31, 20X2, was $105,600. Food and beverages are paid for in the month following the sale and they average 40 percent of sales. Club employees are paid on the last day of the month, and total compensation is 35 percent of food and beverage sales. Food and beverage sales for December 20X2 totaled $125,700.

In March, $40,000 is expected to be spent on new equipment. Interest income of $5,000 will be collected in January. Administrative and general expenses are $70,000/month, and the monthly mortgage payment is $15,000.

Required:

Prepare the monthly cash budget for the Downtown Club for January–March 2000 using the cash receipts and disbursements approach.

Chapter 9 Outline

Characteristics of Internal Control
    Segregation of Duties or Separation of
        Incompatible Duties
    Establishment of Responsibility
    Maintaining Accurate Records and
        Documents
    Independent Checks for Performance
    Management Leadership
    Organizational Structure
    Sound Practices
    Competent and Trustworthy Personnel
    Authorization Procedures
    Procedure Manuals
    Physical Controls
    Budgets and Internal Reports
Basics of Internal Accounting Control
    Cash Control
    Accounts Receivable
    Accounts Payable
    Purchasing and Receiving
    Inventories
    Property and Equipment
Implementation and Review of Internal
    Controls
Internal Control in Small Operations
Additional Classification of Controls

Competencies

1. Explain the major objectives and identify general characteristics of an effective system of internal control. (pp. 211–215)

2. Describe specific procedures that meet basic requirements for the internal control of accounting functions. (pp. 215–222)

3. Implement and review internal controls and identify the key control duties of the owner or manager of a small hospitality operation. (pp. 222–225)

9

Internal Controls

ALL CLUBS NEED a strong system of internal control in order to monitor and maintain the quality of products and services offered to its members. All clubs should therefore develop an internal control system. The internal control system of a club is intended to accomplish the following four objectives.

1. *Safeguard assets.* A major objective of internal control is to protect club assets. This objective includes, but is not necessarily limited to, (1) the protection of existing assets from loss such as theft, (2) the maintenance of resources, especially equipment, to ensure efficient utilization, and (3) the safeguarding of resources, especially inventories for resale, to prevent waste and spoilage. This objective is achieved by various control procedures and safeguards that might include the proper use of coolers and freezers for storing food, the use of locks to secure assets, the use of safes or vaults for cash, limiting personnel access to various assets, and segregating the operating, custodial, and accounting functions.

2. *Check for accuracy and reliability of accounting data.* This objective consists of all the checks and balances within the accounting system to ensure the accuracy and reliability of accounting information. Accurate and reliable accounting information must be available not only for reports to members and governmental agencies, it is also necessary for management's own use in internal operations.

3. *Promote operational efficiency.* Operational efficiency results from providing products and services at a minimum cost. In a club, training programs and proper supervision promote operational efficiency. The use of mechanical and electronic equipment often improves operational efficiency.

4. *Encourage adherence to prescribed managerial policies.* Another major objective of internal control is to ensure that employees follow managerial policies. For example, most clubs have a policy that hourly employees must clock in and out themselves—one employee may not clock in another employee. Placing the time clock where managerial personnel can observe employees clocking in and out should encourage workers to adhere to the policy.

The four objectives of internal control may be divided between the accounting and administrative functions. The first two objectives, safeguarding assets and ensuring the accuracy and reliability of accounting data, are considered **accounting controls**. The last two objectives, promoting operational efficiency and encouraging adherence to managerial policies, are considered **administrative controls**.

Characteristics of Internal Control

Internal control measures will vary somewhat based on the size of the club; however, the following internal control principles generally apply to all clubs.

Segregation of Duties or Separation of Incompatible Duties

Generally, every business transaction involves several phases. For example, a club orders food from a local vendor, then goods arrive and are inspected and checked in. Approval is then made to pay for the inventory and a check is issued. Under a good system of internal control, the various phases of this transaction would be divided among several employees. The reasoning behind this is that the work of one employee should provide a basis for evaluating the work of another employee. Another example of **segregation of duties** involves the very portable asset—cash. As much as possible, the duties involving cash should be divided among the club's employees. For example, one person should make the bank deposit, with a different individual signing checks on the account, while a third individual does the monthly bank reconciliation.

In small clubs, it is often difficult to have enough employees to divide the phases of a transaction. The more division we are able to achieve, however, the better is the system of internal control. Division of the phases of a transaction does not ensure that fraud will never occur, but it makes fraud more difficult for someone acting alone. There is always the possibility of collusion (two or more people working together to defraud the club) among employees.

Establishment of Responsibility

Control is always enhanced when one person is responsible for a given task or for safeguarding a specific asset. A simple example involves the storage of golf carts for a club.

The club should have a policy that, by a certain time each day, all carts are to be put in a cart barn and locked up for the night. The responsibility for this task should be clearly assigned to one individual for each night. Only under this system can the responsibility for the golf carts be established.

Maintaining Accurate Records and Documents

Significant financial events of the club are recorded as accounting transactions. These transactions should be supported by proper documentation. A club's system of internal control is strengthened when documents are pre-numbered and when all documents are accounted for. Pre-numbering prevents a transaction from being recorded more than once and also helps ensure that all transactions are recorded. Source documents are the basis for accounting entries and therefore should be promptly forwarded to the accounting department of the club.

Independent Checks for Performance

Clubs are able to strengthen their system of internal control by providing independent checks on the performance of employees. This involves having an independent person who was not involved in the original transaction check the work of another employee.

In large organizations, an internal auditor often performs this check. Most clubs are not large enough to employ an internal auditor, hence this function is provided annually by the external auditors of the club. As part of the annual audit of the club, the external auditors do a test of transactions to determine the strength of the club's internal control system.

Additional internal performance checks may be done if the club is large enough to employ enough individuals. For example, one individual should deposit cash receipts while another should compare the amounts deposited with the receipts shown on the bank statement.

Management Leadership

Management's leadership is another key aspect of any club's system of internal control. The board of directors establishes the operation's highest-level policies, and management communicates and enforces these policies. These policies should be clearly stated and communicated to all management levels. In addition, the various management levels are responsible for ensuring that the internal control system is adequate. The tone they set in communicating and enforcing policies may determine the degree to which employees will accept them and carry them out. Although there may be exceptions to board and top-level management policies, these exceptions should be minimized so as not to render the policies useless.

Organizational Structure

Only in the smallest club is one person able to supervise all employees personally. In most clubs, the organizational structure is divided into the functional areas of club promotion to members, accounting/finance, and personnel. An organization chart represents the organizational structure of a club. Personnel must know the organizational chart and follow the chain of command. Management policies usually prevent employees from circumventing the chain of command by requiring them to discuss any complaints or suggestions with their immediate supervisors.

Each position on the organization chart usually has a corresponding written job description. A job description consists of a detailed list of duties for the position. The procedure manual indicates how a job or duty should be performed.

Sound Practices

Sound practices are policy measures generally set by the board of directors to create an environment conducive to excellent internal control. Several clubs have adopted the following practices:

- Bonding employees—Employees in a position of trust are covered by fidelity insurance. Some clubs carry a blanket bond for minimum coverage on all employees.

- Mandatory vacation policies—Employees are required to take annual vacations. This is rigidly enforced for employees in positions of trust. Other employees then perform the absent employees' duties. If the absent employees have engaged in dishonest practices, the replacements may discover them and management can take action.

Competent and Trustworthy Personnel

A key characteristic of internal control—perhaps the most important—is competent and trustworthy personnel. In clubs, the quality of service is often a result of staff competency. For example, excellent and friendly service may often be more important than the quality of the food served. Personnel must exhibit a caring attitude toward members in order for the club to be successful.

A club's system of internal control may be rendered useless if personnel are not competent and trustworthy. Generally, systems of internal control are not designed to prevent collusion. Therefore, the careful selection, training, and supervision of personnel is vital. The club must hire people with potential and train them properly in the work to be accomplished. This includes not only communicating what the jobs are and how to do them, but also following up to make sure that training has been effective. In addition, employees must understand the importance of their jobs in relation to the club's overall objective.

Finally, employees must be properly rewarded for work performed. This includes not only compensation but also praise for a job well done and a promotion when a person is ready and a position is available.

Authorization Procedures

Management must properly authorize every business transaction. Management's authorization may be either general or specific. Management provides general authorization for employees to follow in the normal course of performing their jobs. For example, children of club members are allowed to sign for food and beverages up to a certain dollar amount. No specific authorization is required in this case. Management may, however, state that certain transactions (such as purchase of equipment over a certain dollar amount) require the chief financial executive's approval.

Procedure Manuals

Each job within the club can be reduced to writing. The procedure manual should list the details of each position, including how and when to perform each task. The procedure manual encourages consistent job performance, especially for relatively new employees who may be unsure about the details of their jobs. In addition, the procedure manual enables personnel to temporarily fill another position during a regular employee's absence.

Physical Controls

Physical controls are a critical element of safeguarding assets. Physical controls include security devices and measures for protecting assets, such as safes and locked storerooms. In addition, forms and accounting records need to be secured through proper storage and limited access. Mechanical and electronic equipment used to execute and record transactions also helps to safeguard assets.

Budgets and Internal Reports

Budgets and other internal reports are essential elements of a system of internal control. These reports are an important part of a club's communications system. When budgets are used for control purposes, they help to ensure that management's goals will be attained. If actual performance falls short of these goals, management is informed and able to take corrective action.

Other reports also alert management to operating performance and enable management to take corrective action as necessary. These reports include those prepared daily (daily report of operations), weekly (weekly forecasts), monthly, and annually (long-range planning).

Basics of Internal Accounting Control

This section covers basic requirements of internal accounting control, including several methods of control for the various accounting functions. However, this list of methods is not exhaustive. Each club must review these areas and determine control methods best suited to its needs.

Cash Control

Most clubs do not accept cash from members, and the rest of the clubs tend to discourage cash payments. However, because cash is the most vulnerable of all assets, it is imperative to have an effective system of internal control over cash. The following is a list of suggestions commonly used for cash control procedures.

1. All bank accounts and check signers must be authorized by the board.

2. All bank accounts should be reconciled monthly, and the chief financial executive should review the bank reconciliation.

3. The person reconciling bank accounts should receive bank statements (including canceled checks) directly from the bank. Employees who sign checks or have other accounting duties in connection with cash transactions should not reconcile the bank accounts. The reconciliation procedure should include examination of signatures and endorsements and verification of the clerical accuracy of cash receipt and disbursement records. Exhibit 1 presents a sample bank reconciliation.

4. The custody of cash should be the responsibility of the chief financial executive.

5. Employees independent of the cash control function should count house banks and petty cash funds at unannounced intervals. Special attention should be give to the propriety of noncash items such as IOUs.

6. Cash register tapes, invoices, or other documents should support disbursements from petty cash funds. Such supporting data should be checked when funds are replenished and then canceled to prevent duplicate payments.

Exhibit 1 Bank Reconciliation—Hoosier Hotel

Bank Reconciliation
Hoosier Club
December 31, 20X2

Balance per bank statement—12/31/20X2		$14,622.18
Add: Deposit in Transit		3,641.18
Less: Outstanding checks		
Ck. 4315	$ 18.36	
Ck. 4422	156.14	
Ck. 4429	3,689.18	
Ck. 4440	172.47	
Ck. 4441	396.15	
Ck. 4442	100.00	
Ck. 4443	7.43	
Ck. 4444	799.18	−5,338.91
Other:		
Insufficient funds check received Dec. 31*		+ 324.32
Service charge—December 20X2**		+ 15.24
Cash balance per books—12/31/20X2		$13,264.01

Prepared by _____

Approved by _____

 * Redeposited January 1, 20X3
** Amount recorded on books in January 20X3, since it was minor in amount.

Cash Receipts. The following procedures are commonly used for internal control of cash receipts.

1. Accounting and physical control over cash receipts should be established when the cash is first received. In the case of a club, most cash receipts come through the mail. The person who opens the mail should make a list of the day's receipts and forward the list to the chief financial executive.

2. Restrictive endorsements, such as "For deposit only to Hoosier Club's account," should be placed on checks when first received to guard against the obstruction or illegal diversion of such cash receipts.

3. Cash received should be given to the chief financial executive as soon as is practical. Cash receipts should be deposited daily and intact. They should not be mixed with other cash funds used to pay invoices or incidental expenses.

4. The chief financial executive and his or her subordinates should not be responsible for any of the following activities:

   a.   Preparation or mailing of members' statements.

b. Posting accounts receivable records or balancing detail ledgers with general ledger control accounts.

c. Posting the general ledger.

5. General instructions for those handling cash (hereafter simply referred to as cashiers) often include the following:

a. The cash drawer must be closed after each sale.

b. Cashiers must circle and initial any overrings on the tape at the time of occurrence.

c. Cash registers must be locked and keys removed when unattended.

d. Cash sales must be rung up when they are made. Sales made on an honor system are prohibited.

e. Cashiers may not have briefcases, handbags, purses, cosmetic bags, and so forth at cash stations.

f. Cashiers should immediately inform the manager if they are experiencing problems with the cash register.

g. Cashiers should verify the amount of cash banks when they receive and sign for them and should not be allowed to count the banks after that time.

h. When feasible (or permitted by equipment), items should be rung up separately to allow the cash register to total the sale.

Cash Disbursements. There are several procedures that help to establish a strong system of internal control over cash disbursements.

1. Generally, all disbursements should be made by check. An exception is petty cash disbursements.

2. Checks should be pre-numbered and used in numerical sequence. In addition, it is a good idea to use a check protector (an imprinting device) to enter the amounts on the checks; this deters anyone from altering the amount.

3. Checks drawn in excess of a minimum amount (such as $50) should contain two signatures, while checks under this may require only one signature. Each check signer should carefully review supporting documents to ensure that the documentation has been properly audited and approved. Check signers should not be responsible for preparing checks and should not have custody of blank checks.

4. When a mechanical check-signing device is used, only the employee authorized to use it should have the key. The operation should maintain an independent record of the number of checks processed through the device, and that number should be reconciled with the numerical sequence of the checks used.

5. Vouchers, invoices, and other documents supporting cash disbursements should be canceled by stamping them "PAID" when the check is signed. This

procedure is designed to prevent duplicate payments should the document become detached from the check copy.

6. Signed checks and disbursement vouchers should not be returned to the check preparer but rather should be given to an employee independent of this function for immediate mailing.

7. Only authorized check preparers should have access to blank checks. Voided checks should be mutilated to prevent reuse by removing the signature line.

Accounts Receivable

Accounts receivable represent promises to pay the club. A critical control in this area is the segregation of duties to prevent accounts receivable employees from pocketing cash received in payment of accounts. Control procedures for accounts receivable include the following:

1. Accounts receivable employees should not handle cash received in payment of accounts. Posting to accounts receivable for cash received should be made from remittance advice or check listings. Control totals for posting should be made independently of accounts receivable employees for posting by the general ledger clerk to the accounts receivable control account.

2. At the end of the month, the total of member accounts should be reconciled with the independently determined balance in the general ledger control account. These procedures provide protection against manipulation by the accounts receivable employees. The failure to segregate cash handling and accounts receivable may facilitate **lapping**, a common fraudulent practice. Lapping occurs when an accounts receivable clerk steals cash received on an account, then posts cash received the next day on a second account to the first account. For example, assume that Member A pays $100 on his or her account and the accounts receivable clerk takes the $100. The following day, Member B pays $150. The accounts receivable clerk takes $50 for personal use and credits Member A's account for $100. At this point, the accounts receivable clerk has stolen $150. This fraudulent activity may continue for quite some time when there is no segregation of duties or other compensating controls.

3. Noncash entries to receivable accounts, such as writing off an account as uncollectable, should originate with employees or managers who do not handle cash and are not responsible for maintaining accounts receivable.

4. A key feature of control over receivables is an adequate system of internal reporting. Monthly, the accounts receivable should be aged, and special collection efforts should be applied to delinquent accounts. The trend of accounts receivable balances in relation to credit terms should be tracked over time.

5. All collection efforts should be carefully documented, and uncollectable accounts should be written off only with the approval of the treasurer.

Accounts Payable

There are several internal control procedures for accounts payable. These procedures include the following:

Exhibit 2 Voucher from Voucher System

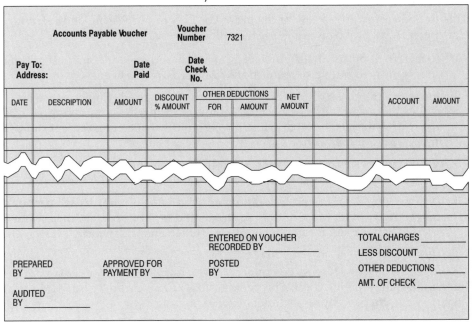

1. Vendors' invoices should be routed directly to the accounts payable department. Purchasing personnel should not handle or approve invoices.

2. Control should be established over vendors' invoices when received. This may be accomplished by the use of a voucher system (see Exhibit 2). The voucher system uses pre-numbered vouchers that are prepared from vendors' invoices and recorded in a voucher journal. Invoices should be reviewed for possible cash discounts, and the due dates noted to take advantage of any available discounts.

3. The terms of sale, prices, and list of goods received on vendors' invoices should be checked against purchase orders and receiving reports. All amount extensions and totals should be checked. The person auditing the vendors' invoices should initial these documents.

4. All vouchers, invoices, and supporting documents should be canceled when paid.

5. Only accounting personnel not responsible for the general ledger should maintain the accounts payable subsidiary ledger. The accounts payable subsidiary ledger should be reconciled monthly with the general ledger control account for accounts payable.

6. A monthly trial balance of accounts payable should be prepared for the treasurer's review. Suppliers should be paid on a timely basis in order to maintain good supplier relationships.

Purchasing and Receiving

This section covers only a few of the major controls of purchasing and receiving. Common control procedures include the following:

1. To the extent practical, the purchasing agent should make all purchases acting upon approved purchase requisitions from department heads.

2. A written purchase order (PO) system should be used. Copies of each PO should be sent to receiving and accounting. In this way, receiving will be aware of materials ordered, while the accounts payable department can use the PO to audit the vendor's invoice.

3. A receiving department, separate from the purchasing agent, should receive all incoming goods. All materials received should be carefully checked.

4. The receiving department should prepare a receiving report for each vendor's delivery. A copy of the receiving report should be forwarded to the accounts payable department for verification against the vendor's invoice.

Inventories

Purchasing and receiving control procedures apply to inventories also. Additional inventory control procedures include the following:

1. Accounting department employees should maintain inventory records. These employees should not have access to inventory, nor should employees with custody of inventory have access to inventory records.

2. Personnel independent of the storage function should periodically take a physical inventory. Accounting personnel should extend the physical inventory and compare it to the book inventory if a perpetual inventory record system is maintained. (*Extending* the physical inventory means listing the proper costs per unit and multiplying the counts of each item by the cost per unit.)

3. Taking physical inventory is best accomplished when:

   a. Like items are grouped together in the storeroom.
   b. Pre-printed inventory forms are used to list all inventory items.
   c. The inventory form is arranged in the same sequence as the inventory items are maintained in the storeroom
   d. Two individuals conduct the physical inventory; one can count the items while the other records the count. (As noted earlier, the personnel should be independent of the storing function.)

4. The inventory records must be adjusted for any differences between the books and the physical inventory. A key individual such as the treasurer must approve the inventory adjustment.

5. Any significant inventory overages or shortages should be investigated, the causes determined, and procedures designed to prevent recurrence of errors.

6. Other operating controls relating to inventory include the following:

a. Control must be maintained over the physical inventories. This is accomplished by storing inventory in the appropriate facilities; for example, food must be stored at proper temperatures.

b. Daily inventories and usage rates of high priced items should be monitored.

c. Access to inventory should be restricted to storage employees. Limiting access is accomplished, in part, by securing inventory in locked facilities.

d. Personnel handling inventory (storage and production personnel) should leave the facilities by an exit easily observed by management.

e. Records of spoilage, overcooked food, and so forth should be maintained for use in reconciling the physical inventory to the book inventory and for accounting for other discrepancies in food inventory.

Property and Equipment

Property and equipment generally constitute the largest percentage of most clubs' assets. These assets are not liquid; however, controls must still be established to maintain these resources for their intended use—providing services to members. Several common control procedures that could be used by clubs are listed below.

1. The board of directors usually issues formal policies establishing which individuals have the authority to purchase property and equipment.

2. A work order system should be established for the orderly accumulation of property costs when facilities are acquired. Each approved project is assigned a work order number, and all expenditures are charged to this number as the work progresses.

3. Accounting records maintained under a typical work order system include the following:

   a. An expenditure authorization that defines the project scope, purpose, cost justification, and budgeted amount.

   b. Cost sheets that summarize actual expenditures for comparison to budgeted amounts.

   c. Supporting evidence of costs charged to the project account. This evidence includes vendors' invoices, material requisitions, and labor time tickets.

4. General ledger control should be established for each principal classification of property cost and each related depreciation accumulation.

5. Personnel should take physical inventories of equipment periodically, independent of the person with custody of the assets and of the person maintaining the accounting records. The physical inventory should be compared to the equipment listed in the accounting records. Any discrepancies must be resolved and action taken to prevent recurrence of similar errors.

6. The sale, retirement, or scrapping of equipment requires formal board approval. Approval must be from individuals not having custody of the

equipment. Accounting department personnel must determine that retired assets are removed from the books and that proceeds received are properly accounted for.

Implementation and Review of Internal Controls

The club's board ultimately is responsible for implementing and maintaining the system of internal controls. However, day-to-day implementation is done through the chief financial executive. Since this system is critical to the well-being of the club, the board must regularly review it to ensure that it is adequate. The internal control system may break down periodically. New personnel may not understand or follow procedures. For example, a new employee may return disputed statements to the accounts receivable clerk for resolution, reasoning that the clerk can resolve such differences most efficiently.

The internal control system may also need restructuring due to changing business conditions and other circumstances. For example, ten years ago, a club may have established a policy stating that cash receipts had to be deposited when they reached $1,000. Due to inflation, the amount might now be raised to $2,000.

An operation's internal controls may be documented and reviewed by flowcharting and using internal control questionnaires. A **flowchart** diagrams the flow of documents through an organization, indicating the origin, processing, and final deposition of each document. In addition, the flowchart shows the segregation of duties. Exhibit 3 is a simplified flowchart of a club operation's payroll system. Flowcharting is useful because it provides a concise overview of the internal control system. It facilitates review of the internal control system, enabling management or the board to identify weaknesses for corrective action.

A second device for studying a club operation's system of internal control is the **internal control questionnaire (ICQ)**. The ICQ uses a series of questions about controls in each accounting area to identify weaknesses. ICQs generally provide complete coverage for each accounting area. However, they do not reveal document flows, as do flowcharts. From a practical viewpoint, both flowcharts and ICQs should be used in documenting and reviewing a club's system of internal control.

Once the review is completed, management must act to strengthen the internal control system. If a system is documented and reviewed without proper follow-up, then the real value of the review process is lost.

Internal Control in Small Operations

Some clubs are small and the elaborate control procedures presented thus far are not practical. Some clubs have only a few employees and there are simply not enough people for the proper segregation of duties.

The key person in internal control of a small club is the manager. Several duties, if performed by the manager, help to offset what might otherwise be weaknesses in the internal control system. These critical duties are outlined below.

1. Cash Receipts

Exhibit 3   Flowchart of a Payroll System

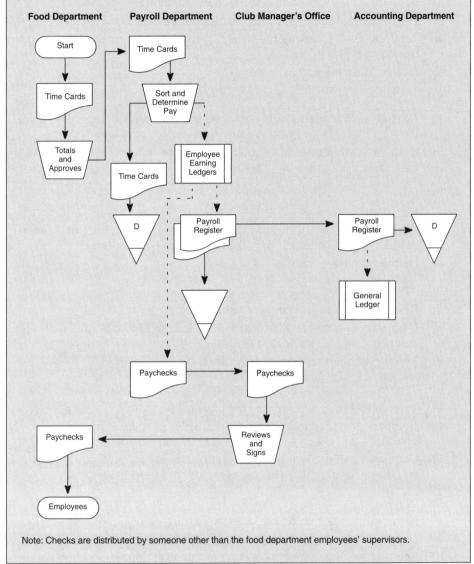

Note: Checks are distributed by someone other than the food department employees' supervisors.

a.   Open all mail and list cash receipts, retaining one copy of the list.

b.   Deposit all cash daily and compare the deposit with the cash receipts debit recorded by someone in the accounting office.

c.   Reconcile cash receipts with cash register tapes.

2. Cash Disbursements

   a. Have all checks signed by an officer, carefully review documentation, and verify that all supporting documentation is canceled.
   b. Use only pre-numbered checks and account for them as checks are signed.
   c. Total check disbursements periodically and compare the total to the bookkeeper's cash credit.
   d. Review the bank reconciliation.

3. Sales

   a. Keep all cash registers locked and remove cash register tapes when not in use.
   b. Compare cash register tape totals with the cash debit for the day and the cash receipts deposited.

4. Payroll

   a. Examine the payroll worksheet (or payroll journal), noting employees' names, authorized gross pay, hours worked, deductions, and net pay. Add the payroll and compare the net pay with the cash credit.
   b. Distribute payroll checks.

5. Accounts Receivable

   a. Review aging of accounts receivable.
   b. Compare statements with individual ledger accounts and mail statements.
   c. Resolve all disputed account balances.

6. Inventories

   a. Periodically supervise or take the physical inventory.
   b. Compare the physical inventory with the perpetual inventory on the books.
   c. Compare cost of goods sold with total sales each month, and investigate any major discrepancies in cost of goods sold percentages.

7. Purchases

   a. Randomly review price quotes for inventory items purchased.
   b. Use a purchase order system and account for all purchase orders.
   c. Randomly compare purchase orders with receiving reports, and vendors' invoices with vendors' statements.

8. General

   a. Review all general journal entries.
   b. Employ a competent, trustworthy controller.
   c. Engage an independent auditor to conduct an annual audit and to periodically conduct limited surprise audits of cash, inventory, and accounts receivable.

Additional Classification of Controls

At the beginning of the chapter, internal controls were classified as either accounting or administrative controls. Controls may also be classified based on whether they take effect before or after a problem occurs. **Preventive controls** are implemented before a problem occurs. They include such things as the use of locks to safeguard assets, the separation of duties to preclude operating personnel from controlling inventories, and general and specific authorization policies. Preventive controls are less expensive to establish than detective controls. **Detective controls** are designed to discover problems and to monitor preventive controls. Detective controls include external audits, surprise cash internal audits, and bank reconciliations. Detective controls may serve in part as preventive controls; for example, if employees know that audits will be conducted, they will be less likely to take advantage of access to cash and other assets.

Summary

An internal control system is critical to the proper operation of any club. A good system of internal control protects the club's assets, ensures the accuracy and reliability of the accounting records, promotes efficient operations, and encourages adherence to the club's policies.

There are four main objectives of every internal control system. The first two, checking the accuracy of accounting data and safeguarding assets, are known as accounting controls. These controls ensure that assets are recorded properly and are safe from loss through negligence or theft. The other two controls are administrative controls. Promoting operational efficiency means that the operation's products and/or services are produced efficiently. Adherence to managerial policies is important because established rules are only effective if they are followed.

There are several characteristics of a strong internal control system. These characteristics include the physical control of assets, the development of budgets, management leadership, and organizational structure. Competent and trustworthy personnel are necessary for operational efficiency and adequate physical control of the assets.

Management needs to examine every function of the club's operation and establish controls for each one. For example, the cash account must have adequate controls because it is highly vulnerable to theft. Management should consider physical controls, segregation of duties, management policies, proper authorization procedures, and adequate performance checks. These characteristics of internal control can help protect the operation's cash.

A perfect system—one that guarantees the safety of assets—would probably be cost prohibitive. The club's board must always consider the cost and benefits of all internal control policies.

Key Terms

accounting controls—Controls for safeguarding assets and ensuring the accuracy and reliability of accounting data.

administrative controls—Controls for promoting operational efficiency and encouraging adherence to managerial policies.

detective controls—Controls designed to discover problems and to monitor preventive controls. Detective controls include external audits, surprise cash internal audits, and bank reconciliations.

flow chart—A visual representation of the movement of information and documents within an operation.

internal control questionnaire (ICQ)—A series of questions about controls in each accounting area, used to identify weaknesses in an operation's system of internal control.

lapping—A type of theft that occurs when an accounts receivable clerk steals cash received on account, then posts cash received the next day on a second account to the first account.

preventive controls—Controls implemented before a problem occurs, including such things as the use of locks to safeguard assets, the separation of duties to preclude operating personnel from controlling inventories, and general and specific authorization policies.

segregation of duties—An element of internal control systems in which different personnel are assigned the different functions of accounting, custody of assets, and production; the purpose is to prevent and detect errors and theft.

 Review Questions —————————————————————————————

1. What are the four basic objectives of an internal control system for a club?

2. What are some common cash control procedures?

3. Who has the ultimate responsibility for the club's system of internal control? Who handles the day-to-day implementation of the system?

4. What are the major procedures for establishing a strong system of internal control over cash disbursements?

5. Explain the importance of segregation of duties to a system of internal control. Give two examples of segregation of duties for clubs.

6. What are the benefits of pre-numbering documents?

7. What is meant by the term *lapping*?

8. What should be the elements of a good policy for adequate control of inventory?

9. What are the three major aspects of safeguarding the club's assets?

10. What is the purpose of the bank reconciliation? Who should review the bank reconciliation?

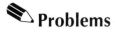

Problems

Problem 1

At the Suburban Country Club, checks are not pre-numbered because both the general manager and the treasurer are authorized to issue checks. Both of these individuals have access to un-issued checks, which are kept in an unlocked desk drawer.

The general manager pays all bills that are received from suppliers. Before paying the bills, the general manager checks to see that the goods have been received and checks the mathematical accuracy of the suppliers' invoices. After the bills are paid, the general manager files the paid invoices and records the payment in the club's cash payments journal. The club has only one checking account that is reconciled monthly by the treasurer.

Required:

Identify the weaknesses of the club's system on internal control. What would you recommend to improve the system?

Problem 2

The Pine Hills Golf Club uses the following internal control procedures:

1. Both the general manager and the treasurer are required to sign checks over $250.

2. The club's "outside" CPA prepares the monthly bank reconciliation.

3. All beverages over $100 per bottle are locked in a storeroom.

4. Accounting and cash activities are separated.

5. Time clocks are used for club employees.

Required:

Indicate the objective of internal control that each of the above is most likely directed toward.

Problem 3

Below is a list of internal control principles. For the items that follow the list, indicate which internal control principle was violated.

A. Segregation of duties

B. Establishment of responsibility

C. Maintaining accurate records

D. Independent checks for performance

E. Management leadership

F. Organizational structure

G. Sound practices

H. Competent and trustworthy personnel

I. Authorization procedure

J. Procedure manuals

K. Physical controls

L. Budgets and internal reports

_____ 1. Because a club feels that its employees are all trustworthy, it performs no annual external audit.

_____ 2. Job descriptions for the club are communicated verbally only.

_____ 3. Reports of the club's performance are compiled only on an annual basis.

_____ 4. Children of club members are allowed to sign for food and beverages without limit.

_____ 5. Source paperwork for accounting transactions is not pre-numbered.

_____ 6. One individual in the club signs all checks, makes the bank deposit, and does the bank reconciliation.

_____ 7. The general manager develops all key policies and forwards copies to the board of directors.

_____ 8. All cash is kept in an unlocked file cabinet to insure that all C.O.D. orders are received and paid for.

_____ 9. All personnel training sessions have been cut in half in order to cut costs.

_____ 10. All expensive beverages are kept in a locked storeroom, with all employees having keys.

_____ 11. All employee complaints are directed to the general manager.

_____ 12. Employees are given a choice of either taking their vacation or being paid double while working during their vacation.

Chapter 10 Outline

Time Value of Money
Capital Budgeting Models
    Payback
    Net Present Value Model
    Internal Rate of Return
    Accounting Rate of Return
Use of Capital Budgeting Models in the
    Club Industry

Competencies

1. Identify types of capital budgeting decisions. (pp. 231–232)

2. Explain the time value of money and, given relevant information, calculate the future value of a present amount and the present value of a future amount. (pp. 232–238)

3. Apply the payback model to capital budgeting decisions. (pp. 238–241)

4. Identify factors addressed by the net present value model for capital budgeting. (p. 241)

5. Identify factors addressed by the internal rate of return model for capital budgeting. (pp. 242–243)

6. Apply the accounting rate of return model to capital budgeting decisions. (pp. 243–245)

10

Capital Budgeting

THE CLUB INDUSTRY is very fixed-asset intensive. A much higher percentage of total assets are in fixed or (as they are often called) long-term assets than is the case in the manufacturing or retail sectors of the economy. Assets such as land, buildings, and equipment—rather than cash, receivables, and inventory—dominate the statement of financial position.

Expenditures for fixed assets are referred to as **capital expenditures**. Revenue expenditures (the other category of outlays) are typically smaller and have a shorter time horizon. The double-edged significance of capital expenditures is that these outlays are for relatively large dollar amounts and (by definition) for periods greater than one year.

Capital expenditures have far-reaching ramifications and may affect the success or failure of a club. Incurring indebtedness to finance capital expenditures commits future club revenue to repaying principal and interest on that indebtedness. Clubs typically assess members monthly for capital improvements, and large capital projects may require significant increases in those assessments. Accordingly, during poor economic times, club management may be reluctant to embark on capital expenditure programs. Conversely, failure to engage in an appropriate capital expenditure such as installation of a swimming pool could result in membership dissatisfaction or decline in club membership.

Preparation of the operating budget is a prerequisite for the capital budget. The operating budget will indicate the need for possible future expansion as well as the cash flow available to help finance major expenditures.

Capital budgeting decisions are made for a variety of reasons. Some are the result of meeting government requirements. For example, the Occupational Safety & Health Administration (OSHA) requires certain safety equipment and guards on meat-cutting equipment. The operation may spend several hundreds or even thousands of dollars to meet OSHA's requirements, regardless of the potential profit or cost savings (if any). A second capital budgeting decision might be to acquire a fixed asset to reduce the operation's costs, as in the case of a laborsaving dishwashing device in the kitchen. A third decision would be to acquire fixed assets to increase sales (for example, expanding the club's dining room to increase club revenues). A fourth capital budgeting decision would be to replace an existing fixed asset, such as obsolete equipment currently being used on the club's golf course.

All four kinds of capital budgeting decisions require significant expenditures resulting in fixed assets. The return on the expenditures will accrue over an extended period of time. The expenditures should generally be cost-justified in the sense that the expected benefits will exceed the cost. The more sophisticated capital budgeting models require a comparison of current cost expenditures for the fixed asset against a future stream of funds. In order to compare current year expenditures to future years' income, the future years' income must be placed on an equal basis. The process for accomplishing this recognizes the **time value of money**.

Time Value of Money

The saying, "$100 today is worth more than $100 a year from now" is true, in part because $100 today could be invested to provide $100 plus the interest for one year in the future. If the $100 can be invested at 12 percent annual interest, then the $100 can be worth $112 in one year. This is determined as follows:

Principal	+	(Principal	×	Time	×	Interest Rate)	=	Total
100	+	(100	×	1	×	.12)	=	$112

Principal is the sum of dollars at the beginning of the investment period ($100 in this case). Time is expressed in years, as long as an annual interest rate is used. The interest rate is expressed in decimal form. The interest of $12, plus the principal of $100, equals the amount available one year hence.

A shorter formula for calculating a future value is as follows:

$$F = A(1 + i)^n$$

$$\text{where } F = \text{Future Value}$$
$$A = \text{Present Amount}$$
$$i = \text{Interest Rate}$$
$$n = \text{Number of Years (or Interest Periods)}$$

One hundred dollars invested at 12 percent for two years will yield $125.44 determined as follows:

$$F = 100(1 + .12)^2$$
$$= 100(1.2544)$$
$$= \$125.44$$

An alternative to using this formula to calculate the future value of a present amount is to use a table of future value factors, such as that found in Exhibit 1. The future value factors are based on present amounts at the end of each period. For example, the future amount of $100 two years from now at 15 percent interest is $132.25. This is determined by finding the number in the 15 percent column and the period 2 row (1.3225) and multiplying it by $100.

The present value of a future amount is the present amount that must be invested at x percent interest to yield the future amount. For example, what is the present value of $100 one year hence when the interest rate is 12 percent? The formula to determine the present value of the future amount is as follows:

Exhibit 1 Table of Future Value Factors for a Single Cash Flow

$FV_{n,k} = (1 + k)^n$ where FV is future value, n is the number of periods, and k is the rate.

Number of Periods	1%	2%	3%	4%	5%	6%	7%	8%	9%	10%	12%	14%	15%	16%	18%	20%	22%	24%	26%	28%	30%	35%
1	1.0100	1.0200	1.0300	1.0400	1.0500	1.0600	1.0700	1.0800	1.0900	1.1000	1.1200	1.1400	1.1500	1.1600	1.1800	1.2000	1.2200	1.2400	1.2600	1.2800	1.3000	1.3500
2	1.0201	1.0404	1.0609	1.0816	1.1025	1.1236	1.1449	1.1664	1.1881	1.2100	1.2544	1.2996	1.3225	1.3456	1.3924	1.4400	1.4884	1.5376	1.5876	1.6384	1.6900	1.8225
3	1.0303	1.0612	1.0927	1.1249	1.1576	1.1910	1.2250	1.2597	1.2950	1.3310	1.4049	1.4815	1.5209	1.5609	1.6430	1.7280	1.8158	1.9066	2.0004	2.0972	2.1970	2.4604
4	1.0406	1.0824	1.1255	1.1699	1.2155	1.2625	1.3108	1.3605	1.4116	1.4641	1.5735	1.6890	1.7490	1.8106	1.9388	2.0736	2.2153	2.3642	2.5205	2.6844	2.8561	3.3215
5	1.0510	1.1041	1.1593	1.2167	1.2763	1.3382	1.4026	1.4693	1.5386	1.6105	1.7623	1.9254	2.0114	2.1003	2.2878	2.4883	2.7027	2.9316	3.1758	3.4360	3.7129	4.4840
6	1.0615	1.1262	1.1941	1.2653	1.3401	1.4185	1.5007	1.5869	1.6771	1.7716	1.9738	2.1950	2.3131	2.4364	2.6996	2.9860	3.2973	3.6352	4.0015	4.3980	4.8268	6.0534
7	1.0721	1.1487	1.2299	1.3159	1.4071	1.5036	1.6058	1.7138	1.8280	1.9487	2.2107	2.5023	2.6600	2.8262	3.1855	3.5832	4.0227	4.5077	5.0419	5.6295	6.2749	8.1722
8	1.0829	1.1717	1.2668	1.3686	1.4775	1.5938	1.7182	1.8509	1.9926	2.1436	2.4760	2.8526	3.0590	3.2784	3.7589	4.2998	4.9077	5.5895	6.3528	7.2058	8.1573	11.032
9	1.0937	1.1951	1.3048	1.4233	1.5513	1.6895	1.8385	1.9990	2.1719	2.3579	2.7731	3.2519	3.5179	3.8030	4.4355	5.1598	5.9874	6.9310	8.0045	9.2234	10.604	14.894
10	1.1046	1.2190	1.3439	1.4802	1.6289	1.7908	1.9672	2.1589	2.3674	2.5937	3.1058	3.7072	4.0456	4.4114	5.2338	6.1917	7.3046	8.5944	10.086	11.806	13.786	20.107
11	1.1157	1.2434	1.3842	1.5395	1.7103	1.8983	2.1049	2.3316	2.5804	2.8531	3.4785	4.2262	4.6524	5.1173	6.1759	7.4301	8.9117	10.657	12.708	15.112	17.922	27.144
12	1.1268	1.2682	1.4258	1.6010	1.7959	2.0122	2.2522	2.5182	2.8127	3.1384	3.8960	4.8179	5.3503	5.9360	7.2876	8.9161	10.872	13.215	16.012	19.343	23.298	36.644
13	1.1381	1.2936	1.4685	1.6651	1.8856	2.1329	2.4098	2.7196	3.0658	3.4523	4.3635	5.4924	6.1528	6.8858	8.5994	10.699	13.264	16.386	20.175	24.759	30.288	49.470
14	1.1495	1.3195	1.5126	1.7317	1.9799	2.2609	2.5785	2.9372	3.3417	3.7975	4.8871	6.2613	7.0757	7.9875	10.147	12.839	16.182	20.319	25.421	31.691	39.374	66.784
15	1.1610	1.3459	1.5580	1.8009	2.0789	2.3966	2.7590	3.1722	3.6425	4.1772	5.4736	7.1379	8.1371	9.2655	11.974	15.407	19.742	25.196	32.030	40.565	51.186	90.158
16	1.1726	1.3728	1.6047	1.8730	2.1829	2.5404	2.9522	3.4259	3.9703	4.5950	6.1304	8.1372	9.3576	10.748	14.129	18.488	24.086	31.243	40.358	51.923	66.542	121.71
17	1.1843	1.4002	1.6528	1.9479	2.2920	2.6928	3.1588	3.7000	4.3276	5.0545	6.8660	9.2765	10.761	12.468	16.672	22.186	29.384	38.741	50.851	66.461	86.504	164.31
18	1.1961	1.4282	1.7024	2.0258	2.4066	2.8543	3.3799	3.9960	4.7171	5.5599	7.6900	10.575	12.375	14.463	19.673	26.623	35.849	48.039	64.072	85.071	112.46	221.82
19	1.2081	1.4568	1.7535	2.1068	2.5270	3.0256	3.6165	4.3157	5.1417	6.1159	8.6128	12.056	14.232	16.777	23.214	31.948	43.736	59.568	80.731	108.89	146.19	299.46
20	1.2202	1.4859	1.8061	2.1911	2.6533	3.2071	3.8697	4.6610	5.6044	6.7275	9.6463	13.743	16.367	19.461	27.393	38.338	53.358	73.864	101.72	139.38	190.05	404.27
21	1.2324	1.5157	1.8603	2.2788	2.7860	3.3996	4.1406	5.0338	6.1088	7.4002	10.804	15.668	18.822	22.574	32.324	46.005	65.096	91.592	128.17	178.41	247.06	545.77
22	1.2447	1.5460	1.9161	2.3699	2.9253	3.6035	4.4304	5.4365	6.6586	8.1403	12.100	17.861	21.645	26.186	38.142	55.206	79.418	113.57	161.49	228.36	321.18	736.79
23	1.2572	1.5769	1.9736	2.4647	3.0715	3.8197	4.7405	5.8715	7.2579	8.9543	13.552	20.362	24.891	30.376	45.008	66.247	96.889	140.83	203.48	292.30	417.54	994.66
24	1.2697	1.6084	2.0328	2.5633	3.2251	4.0489	5.0724	6.3412	7.9111	9.8497	15.179	23.212	28.625	35.236	53.109	79.497	118.21	174.63	256.39	374.14	542.80	1342.80
25	1.2824	1.6406	2.0938	2.6658	3.3864	4.2919	5.4274	6.8485	8.6231	10.835	17.000	26.462	32.919	40.874	62.669	95.396	144.21	216.54	323.05	478.90	705.64	1812.78
26	1.2953	1.6734	2.1566	2.7725	3.5557	4.5494	5.8074	7.3964	9.3992	11.918	19.040	30.167	37.857	47.414	73.949	114.48	175.94	268.51	407.04	613.00	917.33	2447.25
27	1.3082	1.7069	2.2213	2.8834	3.7335	4.8223	6.2139	7.9881	10.245	13.110	21.325	34.390	43.535	55.000	87.260	137.37	214.64	332.95	512.87	784.64	1192.5	3303.78
28	1.3213	1.7410	2.2879	2.9987	3.9201	5.1117	6.6488	8.6271	11.167	14.421	23.884	39.204	50.066	63.800	102.97	164.84	261.86	412.86	646.21	1004.3	1550.3	4460.11
29	1.3345	1.7758	2.3566	3.1187	4.1161	5.4184	7.1143	9.3173	12.172	15.863	26.750	44.693	57.575	74.009	121.50	197.81	319.47	511.95	814.23	1285.6	2015.4	6021.15
30	1.3478	1.8114	2.4273	3.2434	4.3219	5.7435	7.6123	10.063	13.268	17.449	29.960	50.950	66.212	85.850	143.37	237.38	389.76	634.82	1025.9	1645.5	2620.0	8128.55
40	1.4889	2.2080	3.2620	4.8010	7.0400	10.286	14.974	21.725	31.409	45.259	93.051	188.88	267.86	378.72	750.38	1469.8	2847.0	5455.9	10347	19427	36118.9	*
50	1.6446	2.6916	4.3839	7.1067	11.467	18.420	29.457	46.902	74.358	117.39	289.00	700.23	1083.7	1670.7	3927.4	9100.4	20797.	46890.	*	*	*	*
60	1.8167	3.2810	5.8916	10.520	18.679	32.988	57.946	101.26	176.03	304.48	897.60	2595.9	4384.0	7370.2	20555.	56348.	*	*	*	*	*	*

*$FV_{n,k} > 99{,}999$

$$P = F \frac{1}{(1 + i)^n}$$

where P = Present Amount

F = Future Amount

i = Interest Rate

n = Number of Years

Therefore, the present value of $100 one year hence (assuming an interest rate of 12 percent) is $89.29, determined as follows:

$$P = 100 \frac{1}{(1 + .12)^1}$$

$$= 100(.8929)$$

$$= \underline{\underline{\$89.29}}$$

The present value of $100 two years hence (assuming an interest rate of 12 percent) is $79.72 determined as follows:

$$P = 100 \frac{1}{(1 + .12)^2}$$

$$= 100(.7972)$$

$$= \underline{\underline{\$79.72}}$$

An alternative to using this formula to calculate the present value of a future amount is to use a table of present value factors, such as that found in Exhibit 2. The present value factors in Exhibit 2 are based on future amounts at the end of a period. For example, the present value of $100 a year from now at 15 percent interest is $86.96. This is determined by finding the number in the 15 percent column and the period 1 row (0.8696) and multiplying it by $100. The present value of $100 today is $100.

Most capital investments provide a stream of receipts for several years. When the amounts are equal at equal intervals, such as the end of each year, the stream is referred to as an **annuity**. Exhibit 3 shows the calculation of the present value of an annuity of $10,000 due at the end of each year for five years. The present value factors used in the calculation are from the present value table in Exhibit 2.

The present value of an annuity will vary significantly based on the interest rate (also called the discount rate) and the timing of the future receipts. Everything else being the same, the higher the discount rate, the lower the present value. Likewise, everything else being the same, the more distant the receipt, the smaller the present value.

An alternative to multiplying each future amount by the present value factor from the present value table in Exhibit 2 is to sum the present value factors and make one multiplication. This is illustrated in Exhibit 4. Thus, the $33,522

Exhibit 2 Table of Present Value Factors for a Single Cash Flow

$PV_{n,k} = 1/(1 + k)^n$ where PV is present value, n is the number of periods, and k is the rate.

Number of Periods	1%	2%	3%	4%	5%	6%	7%	8%	9%	10%	12%	14%	15%	16%	18%	20%	22%	24%	26%	28%	30%	35%
1	.9901	.9804	.9709	.9615	.9524	.9434	.9346	.9259	.9174	.9091	.8929	.8772	.8696	.8621	.8475	.8333	.8197	.8065	.7937	.7813	.7692	.7407
2	.9803	.9612	.9426	.9246	.9070	.8900	.8734	.8573	.8417	.8264	.7972	.7695	.7561	.7432	.7182	.6944	.6719	.6504	.6299	.6104	.5917	.5487
3	.9706	.9423	.9151	.8890	.8638	.8396	.8163	.7938	.7722	.7513	.7118	.6750	.6575	.6407	.6086	.5787	.5507	.5245	.4999	.4768	.4552	.4064
4	.9610	.9238	.8885	.8548	.8227	.7921	.7629	.7350	.7084	.6830	.6355	.5921	.5718	.5523	.5158	.4823	.4514	.4230	.3968	.3725	.3501	.3011
5	.9515	.9057	.8626	.8219	.7835	.7473	.7130	.6806	.6499	.6209	.5674	.5194	.4972	.4761	.4371	.4019	.3700	.3411	.3149	.2910	.2693	.2230
6	.9420	.8880	.8375	.7903	.7462	.7050	.6663	.6302	.5963	.5645	.5066	.4556	.4323	.4104	.3704	.3349	.3033	.2751	.2499	.2274	.2072	.1652
7	.9327	.8706	.8131	.7599	.7107	.6651	.6227	.5835	.5470	.5132	.4523	.3996	.3759	.3538	.3139	.2791	.2486	.2218	.1983	.1776	.1594	.1224
8	.9235	.8535	.7894	.7307	.6768	.6274	.5820	.5403	.5019	.4665	.4039	.3506	.3269	.3050	.2660	.2326	.2038	.1789	.1574	.1388	.1226	.0906
9	.9143	.8368	.7664	.7026	.6446	.5919	.5439	.5002	.4604	.4241	.3606	.3075	.2843	.2630	.2255	.1938	.1670	.1443	.1249	.1084	.0943	.0671
10	.9053	.8203	.7441	.6756	.6139	.5584	.5083	.4632	.4224	.3855	.3220	.2697	.2472	.2267	.1911	.1615	.1369	.1164	.0992	.0847	.0725	.0497
11	.8963	.8043	.7224	.6496	.5847	.5268	.4751	.4289	.3875	.3505	.2875	.2366	.2149	.1954	.1619	.1346	.1122	.0938	.0787	.0662	.0558	.0368
12	.8874	.7885	.7014	.6246	.5568	.4970	.4440	.3971	.3555	.3186	.2567	.2076	.1869	.1685	.1372	.1122	.0920	.0757	.0625	.0517	.0429	.0273
13	.8787	.7730	.6810	.6006	.5303	.4688	.4150	.3677	.3262	.2897	.2292	.1821	.1625	.1452	.1163	.0935	.0754	.0610	.0496	.0404	.0330	.0202
14	.8700	.7579	.6611	.5775	.5051	.4423	.3878	.3405	.2992	.2633	.2046	.1597	.1413	.1252	.0985	.0779	.0618	.0492	.0393	.0316	.0254	.0150
15	.8613	.7430	.6419	.5553	.4810	.4173	.3624	.3152	.2745	.2394	.1827	.1401	.1229	.1079	.0835	.0649	.0507	.0397	.0312	.0247	.0195	.0111
16	.8528	.7284	.6232	.5339	.4581	.3936	.3387	.2919	.2519	.2176	.1631	.1229	.1069	.0930	.0708	.0541	.0415	.0320	.0248	.0193	.0150	.0082
17	.8444	.7142	.6050	.5134	.4363	.3714	.3166	.2703	.2311	.1978	.1456	.1078	.0929	.0802	.0600	.0451	.0340	.0258	.0197	.0150	.0116	.0061
18	.8360	.7002	.5874	.4936	.4155	.3503	.2959	.2502	.2120	.1799	.1300	.0946	.0808	.0691	.0508	.0376	.0279	.0208	.0156	.0118	.0089	.0045
19	.8277	.6864	.5703	.4746	.3957	.3305	.2765	.2317	.1945	.1635	.1161	.0829	.0703	.0596	.0431	.0313	.0229	.0168	.0124	.0092	.0068	.0033
20	.8195	.6730	.5537	.4564	.3769	.3118	.2584	.2145	.1784	.1486	.1037	.0728	.0611	.0514	.0365	.0261	.0187	.0135	.0098	.0072	.0053	.0025
21	.8114	.6598	.5375	.4388	.3589	.2942	.2415	.1987	.1637	.1351	.0926	.0638	.0531	.0443	.0309	.0217	.0154	.0109	.0078	.0056	.0040	.0018
22	.8034	.6468	.5219	.4220	.3418	.2775	.2257	.1839	.1502	.1228	.0826	.0560	.0462	.0382	.0262	.0181	.0126	.0088	.0062	.0044	.0031	.0014
23	.7954	.6342	.5067	.4057	.3256	.2618	.2109	.1703	.1378	.1117	.0738	.0491	.0402	.0329	.0222	.0151	.0103	.0071	.0049	.0034	.0024	.0010
24	.7876	.6217	.4919	.3901	.3101	.2470	.1971	.1577	.1264	.1015	.0659	.0431	.0349	.0284	.0188	.0126	.0085	.0057	.0039	.0027	.0018	.0007
25	.7798	.6095	.4776	.3751	.2953	.2330	.1842	.1460	.1160	.0923	.0588	.0378	.0304	.0245	.0160	.0105	.0069	.0046	.0031	.0021	.0014	.0006
26	.7720	.5976	.4637	.3607	.2812	.2198	.1722	.1352	.1064	.0839	.0525	.0331	.0264	.0211	.0135	.0087	.0057	.0037	.0025	.0016	.0011	.0004
27	.7644	.5859	.4502	.3468	.2678	.2074	.1609	.1252	.0976	.0763	.0469	.0291	.0230	.0182	.0115	.0073	.0047	.0030	.0019	.0013	.0008	.0003
28	.7568	.5744	.4371	.3335	.2551	.1956	.1504	.1159	.0895	.0693	.0419	.0255	.0200	.0157	.0097	.0061	.0038	.0024	.0015	.0010	.0006	.0002
29	.7493	.5631	.4243	.3207	.2429	.1846	.1406	.1073	.0822	.0630	.0374	.0224	.0174	.0135	.0082	.0051	.0031	.0020	.0012	.0008	.0005	.0002
30	.7419	.5521	.4120	.3083	.2314	.1741	.1314	.0994	.0754	.0573	.0334	.0196	.0151	.0116	.0070	.0042	.0026	.0016	.0010	.0006	.0004	.0001
35	.7059	.5000	.3554	.2534	.1813	.1301	.0937	.0676	.0490	.0356	.0189	.0102	.0075	.0055	.0030	.0017	.0009	.0005	.0003	.0002	.0001	*
40	.6717	.4529	.3066	.2083	.1420	.0972	.0668	.0460	.0318	.0221	.0107	.0053	.0037	.0026	.0013	.0007	.0004	.0002	.0001	.0001	*	*
45	.6391	.4102	.2644	.1712	.1113	.0727	.0476	.0313	.0207	.0137	.0061	.0027	.0019	.0013	.0006	.0003	.0001	.0001	*	*	*	*
50	.6080	.3715	.2281	.1407	.0872	.0543	.0339	.0213	.0134	.0085	.0035	.0014	.0009	.0006	.0003	.0001	*	*	*	*	*	*
55	.5785	.3365	.1968	.1157	.0683	.0406	.0242	.0145	.0087	.0053	.0020	.0007	.0005	.0003	.0001	*	*	*	*	*	*	*
60	.5504	.3048	.1697	.0951	.0535	.0303	.0173	.0099	.0057	.0033	.0011	.0004	.0002	.0001	*	*	*	*	*	*	*	*

*Rounds to zero

Exhibit 3   Present Value of a $10,000 Five-Year Annuity at 15%

Exhibit 4   Shortcut Calculations of the Present Value of a $10,000 Five-Year Annuity at 15%

Years Hence	Present Value Factors at 15%
1	.8696
2	.7561
3	.6575
4	.5718
5	+ .4972
	3.3522
3.3522 × $10,000 =	$33,522

calculated in Exhibit 4 equals the calculation performed in Exhibit 3. Rather than using the present value tables from Exhibit 2, present value tables of an annuity are provided in Exhibit 5. As a check on your understanding of the present value of an annuity table, locate the present value factor for five years and 15 percent. As you would expect, it is 3.3522. Thus, the present value of an annuity table is nothing more than a summation of present value factors from Exhibit 2. However, this table of present values of an annuity will save much time, especially when streams of receipts for several years must be calculated.

A problem that calls for the use of both present value factors (Exhibit 2) and present value of an annuity factor (Exhibit 5) is presented in Exhibit 6. This

Exhibit 5 Table of Present Value Factors for an Annuity

$$PVA_{n,k} = \frac{1 - \dfrac{1}{(1+k)^n}}{k}$$

where PVA is present value for an annuity, n is the number of periods, and k is the rate.

Number of Periods	1%	2%	3%	4%	5%	6%	7%	8%	9%	10%	12%	14%	15%	16%	18%	20%	22%	24%	26%	28%	30%	35%
1	0.9901	0.9804	0.9709	0.9615	0.9524	0.9434	0.9346	0.9259	0.9174	0.9091	0.8929	0.8772	0.8696	0.8621	0.8475	0.8333	0.8197	0.8065	0.7937	0.7813	0.7692	0.7407
2	1.9704	1.9416	1.9135	1.8861	1.8594	1.8334	1.8080	1.7833	1.7591	1.7355	1.6901	1.6467	1.6257	1.6052	1.5656	1.5278	1.4915	1.4568	1.4235	1.3916	1.3609	1.2894
3	2.9410	2.8839	2.8286	2.7751	2.7232	2.6730	2.6243	2.5771	2.5313	2.4869	2.4018	2.3216	2.2832	2.2459	2.1743	2.1065	2.0422	1.9813	1.9234	1.8684	1.8161	1.6959
4	3.9020	3.8077	3.7171	3.6299	3.5460	3.4651	3.3872	3.3121	3.2397	3.1699	3.0373	2.9137	2.8550	2.7982	2.6901	2.5887	2.4936	2.4043	2.3202	2.2410	2.1662	1.9969
5	4.8534	4.7135	4.5797	4.4518	4.3295	4.2124	4.1002	3.9927	3.8897	3.7908	3.6048	3.4331	3.3522	3.2743	3.1272	2.9906	2.8636	2.7454	2.6351	2.5320	2.4356	2.2200
6	5.7955	5.6014	5.4172	5.2421	5.0757	4.9173	4.7665	4.6229	4.4859	4.3553	4.1114	3.8887	3.7845	3.6847	3.4976	3.3255	3.1669	3.0205	2.8850	2.7594	2.6427	2.3852
7	6.7282	6.4720	6.2303	6.0021	5.7864	5.5824	5.3893	5.2064	5.0330	4.8684	4.5638	4.2883	4.1604	4.0386	3.8115	3.6046	3.4155	3.2423	3.0833	2.9370	2.8021	2.5075
8	7.6517	7.3255	7.0197	6.7327	6.4632	6.2098	5.9713	5.7466	5.5348	5.3349	4.9676	4.6389	4.4873	4.3436	4.0776	3.8372	3.6193	3.4212	3.2407	3.0758	2.9247	2.5982
9	8.5660	8.1622	7.7861	7.4353	7.1078	6.8017	6.5152	6.2469	5.9952	5.7590	5.3282	4.9464	4.7716	4.6065	4.3030	4.0310	3.7863	3.5655	3.3657	3.1842	3.0190	2.6653
10	9.4713	8.9826	8.5302	8.1109	7.7217	7.3601	7.0236	6.7101	6.4177	6.1446	5.6502	5.2161	5.0188	4.8332	4.4941	4.1925	3.9232	3.6819	3.4648	3.2689	3.0915	2.7150
11	10.3676	9.7868	9.2526	8.7605	8.3064	7.8869	7.4987	7.1390	6.8052	6.4951	5.9377	5.4527	5.2337	5.0286	4.6560	4.3271	4.0354	3.7757	3.5435	3.3351	3.1473	2.7519
12	11.2551	10.5753	9.9540	9.3851	8.8633	8.3838	7.9427	7.5361	7.1607	6.8137	6.1944	5.6603	5.4206	5.1971	4.7932	4.4392	4.1274	3.8514	3.6059	3.3868	3.1903	2.7792
13	12.1337	11.3484	10.6350	9.9856	9.3936	8.8527	8.3577	7.9038	7.4869	7.1034	6.4235	5.8424	5.5831	5.3423	4.9095	4.5327	4.2028	3.9124	3.6555	3.4272	3.2233	2.7994
14	13.0037	12.1062	11.2961	10.5631	9.8986	9.2950	8.7455	8.2442	7.7862	7.3667	6.6282	6.0021	5.7245	5.4675	5.0081	4.6106	4.2646	3.9616	3.6949	3.4587	3.2487	2.8144
15	13.8651	12.8493	11.9379	11.1184	10.3797	9.7122	9.1079	8.5595	8.0607	7.6061	6.8109	6.1422	5.8474	5.5755	5.0916	4.6755	4.3152	4.0013	3.7261	3.4834	3.2682	2.8255
16	14.7179	13.5777	12.5611	11.6523	10.8378	10.1059	9.4466	8.8514	8.3126	7.8237	6.9740	6.2651	5.9542	5.6685	5.1624	4.7296	4.3567	4.0333	3.7509	3.5026	3.2832	2.8337
17	15.5623	14.2919	13.1661	12.1657	11.2741	10.4773	9.7632	9.1216	8.5436	8.0216	7.1196	6.3729	6.0472	5.7487	5.2223	4.7746	4.3908	4.0591	3.7705	3.5177	3.2948	2.8398
18	16.3983	14.9920	13.7535	12.6593	11.6896	10.8276	10.0591	9.3719	8.7556	8.2014	7.2497	6.4674	6.1280	5.8178	5.2732	4.8122	4.4187	4.0799	3.7861	3.5294	3.3037	2.8443
19	17.2260	15.6785	14.3238	13.1339	12.0853	11.1581	10.3356	9.6036	8.9501	8.3649	7.3658	6.5504	6.1982	5.8775	5.3162	4.8435	4.4415	4.0967	3.7985	3.5386	3.3105	2.8476
20	18.0456	16.3514	14.8775	13.5903	12.4622	11.4699	10.5940	9.8181	9.1285	8.5136	7.4694	6.6231	6.2593	5.9288	5.3527	4.8696	4.4603	4.1103	3.8083	3.5458	3.3158	2.8501
21	18.8570	17.0112	15.4150	14.0292	12.8212	11.7641	10.8355	10.0168	9.2922	8.6487	7.5620	6.6870	6.3125	5.9731	5.3837	4.8913	4.4756	4.1212	3.8161	3.5514	3.3198	2.8519
22	19.6604	17.6580	15.9369	14.4511	13.1630	12.0416	11.0612	10.2007	9.4424	8.7715	7.6446	6.7429	6.3587	6.0113	5.4099	4.9094	4.4882	4.1300	3.8223	3.5558	3.3230	2.8533
23	20.4558	18.2922	16.4436	14.8568	13.4886	12.3034	11.2722	10.3711	9.5802	8.8832	7.7184	6.7921	6.3988	6.0442	5.4321	4.9245	4.4985	4.1371	3.8273	3.5592	3.3254	2.8543
24	21.2434	18.9139	16.9355	15.2470	13.7986	12.5504	11.4693	10.5288	9.7066	8.9847	7.7843	6.8351	6.4338	6.0726	5.4509	4.9371	4.5070	4.1428	3.8312	3.5619	3.3272	2.8550
25	22.0232	19.5235	17.4131	15.6221	14.0939	12.7834	11.6536	10.6748	9.8226	9.0770	7.8431	6.8729	6.4641	6.0971	5.4669	4.9476	4.5139	4.1474	3.8342	3.5640	3.3286	2.8556
26	22.7952	20.1210	17.8768	15.9828	14.3752	13.0032	11.8258	10.8100	9.9290	9.1609	7.8957	6.9061	6.4906	6.1182	5.4804	4.9563	4.5196	4.1511	3.8367	3.5656	3.3297	2.8560
27	23.3596	20.7069	18.3270	16.3296	14.6430	13.2105	11.9867	10.9352	10.0266	9.2372	7.9426	6.9352	6.5135	6.1364	5.4919	4.9636	4.5243	4.1542	3.8387	3.5669	3.3305	2.8563
28	24.3164	21.2813	18.7641	16.6631	14.8981	13.4062	12.1371	11.0511	10.1161	9.3066	7.9844	6.9607	6.5335	6.1520	5.5016	4.9697	4.5281	4.1566	3.8402	3.5679	3.3312	2.8565
29	25.0658	21.8444	19.1885	16.9837	15.1411	13.5907	12.2777	11.1584	10.1983	9.3696	8.0218	6.9830	6.5509	6.1656	5.5098	4.9747	4.5312	4.1585	3.8414	3.5687	3.3317	2.8567
30	25.8077	22.3965	19.6004	17.2920	15.3725	13.7648	12.4090	11.2578	10.2737	9.4269	8.0552	7.0027	6.5660	6.1772	5.5168	4.9789	4.5338	4.1601	3.8424	3.5693	3.3321	2.8568
35	29.4086	24.9986	21.4872	18.6646	16.3742	14.4982	12.9477	11.6546	10.5668	9.6442	8.1755	7.0700	6.6166	6.2153	5.5386	4.9915	4.5411	4.1644	3.8450	3.5708	3.3330	2.8571
40	32.8347	27.3555	23.1148	19.7928	17.1591	15.0463	13.3317	11.9246	10.7574	9.7791	8.2438	7.1050	6.6418	6.2335	5.5482	4.9966	4.5439	4.1659	3.8458	3.5712	3.3332	2.8571
45	36.0945	29.4902	24.5187	20.7200	17.7741	15.4558	13.6055	12.1084	10.8812	9.8628	8.2825	7.1232	6.6543	6.2421	5.5523	4.9986	4.5449	4.1664	3.8460	3.5714	3.3333	2.8571
50	39.1961	31.4236	25.7298	21.4822	18.2559	15.7619	13.8007	12.2335	10.9617	9.9148	8.3045	7.1327	6.6605	6.2463	5.5541	4.9995	4.5452	4.1666	3.8461	3.5714	3.3333	2.8571
55	42.1472	33.1748	26.7744	22.1086	18.6335	15.9905	13.9399	12.3186	11.0140	9.9471	8.3170	7.1376	6.6636	6.2482	5.5549	4.9998	4.5454	4.1666	3.8461	3.5714	3.3333	2.8571
60	44.9550	34.7609	27.6756	22.6235	18.9293	16.1614	14.0392	12.3766	11.0480	9.9672	8.3240	7.1401	6.6651	6.2492	5.5553	4.9999	4.5454	4.1667	3.8462	3.5714	3.3333	2.8571

Exhibit 6   Present Value of a Stream of Unequal Future Receipts

Problem:

Determine the present value of receipts from an investment using a 15% discount factor which provides the following stream of income.

Years Hence	Amount
0	$10,000
1	10,000
2	15,000
3	10,000
4	20,000
5	10,000

Solution:

Years Hence	Amount	Annuity	Excess of Annuity
0	$10,000	$10,000	$ 0
1	10,000	10,000	0
2	15,000	10,000	5,000
3	10,000	10,000	0
4	20,000	10,000	10,000
5	10,000	10,000	0

Calculation:

Present Value of amount due today	=	$ 10,000
Present Value of the $10,000 annuity for 5 years		
$10,000 × 3.3522	=	33,522
Present Value of $5,000 due 2 years hence		
$5,000 × .7561	=	3,781
Present Value of $10,000 due 4 years hence		
$10,000 × .5718	=	5,718
Total		$53,021

problem is solved by treating the stream of receipts as a $10,000 annuity and two separate payments of $5,000 and $10,000 due at the end of years two and four, respectively.

Capital Budgeting Models

Managers use several different models in making capital budgeting decisions. There are four commonly used approaches that vary from simple to sophisticated. The simple models are **accounting rate of return (ARR)** and **payback**, while more sophisticated models, which require the discounting of future cash flows, are **net present value (NPV)** and **internal rate of return (IRR)**. Three of the approaches use cash flow, while one uses accrual income in its implementation. In addition,

Exhibit 7 Capital Budgeting Models

Technique	Uses Cash Flow	Uses DCF	Uses Accrual Income
Payback	X		
Net present value	X	X	
Internal rate of return	X	X	
Accounting rate of return			X

two of the approaches employ the concept of discounted cash flow (DCF). Exhibit 7 is a good reference for the rest of the chapter.

Since three of the four techniques use cash flow rather than accrual income, a brief explanation of the difference is appropriate. Virtually all clubs maintain their books on an accrual rather than on a cash basis. This involves recording revenue when it is earned, not necessarily when the cash is received, and recording expenses when they are incurred rather than when they are actually paid. This also involves making periodic entries for depreciation and amortization.

Since the books are kept on an accrual basis, it is easy to use the accounting rate of return approach. The projected accrual income figures are related to the cost of the investment to determine the rate of return. The specifics of this technique will be discussed later in this chapter.

The other three methods use cash flow rather than accrual income. The reason for using the preferred cash flow figures rather than accrual income figures is that cash flow is better for project evaluation. The accrual income figure reflects non-cash items such as depreciation and amortization, with depreciation being by far the more significant of the two.

In this chapter, we will present a simple technique for converting accrual income to cash flow. This is done by simply adding back depreciation to net income. Hence for the three techniques that employ cash flow, the following equation will be employed:

$$\text{Cash Flow} \quad = \quad \text{Net Income} \quad + \quad \text{Depreciation}$$

Payback

The payback model to capital budgeting is simple and clubs commonly use it. As the name implies, it tells the number of years it takes for the project to pay for itself. Specifically, it tells the number of years it takes for the cash inflows on the project to pay for the initial investment.

In its simplest form, consider the construction of an additional nine-hole golf course for a country club that has an estimated cost of $2,750,000. If the projected annual cash flow from the new nine-hole course was $275,000, then the payback would be 10 years:

$$\text{Payback Period} \quad = \quad \frac{\text{Project Cost}}{\text{Annual Cash Flow}}$$

$$\text{10 Years} \quad = \quad \frac{\$2,750,000}{\$275,000}$$

If the annual cash flow on the project is different every year, then the payback is determined by summing the annual cash flows chronologically until the year before the investment is exceeded and taking the appropriate fraction of the following year. For example, consider a different nine-hole golf course project:

Cost of the project:	$2,700,000	
Annual cash flows:	Year	Amount
	1	$180,000
	2	240,000
	3	270,000
	4	300,000
	5	330,000
	6	360,000
	7	450,000
	8	670,000

The payback on the project would be 7.85 years–that is, the $2,130,000 cash flow for the first seven years plus $570,000 (or 85 percent) of the eighth year's $670,000.

The advantages of the payback method are that it is simple to use and it does give some insight into the riskiness of a project. The disadvantages are that it doesn't take into account cash flows that occur beyond the recovery period and it doesn't take into account the timing of the cash flows. For example, consider the two examples below.

Example 1		Project A	Project B
Cost:		$60,000	$60,000
Cash Flows:	Year 1	20,000	20,000
	Year 2	30,000	30,000
	Year 3	10,000	10,000
	Year 4	0	10,000

The payback for each project is three years. According to the basics of the payback approach, both projects are equal. However, Project B is the better project since there is additional cash flow in the fourth year. It is not always so easy to see this weakness of payback.

Example 2		Project A	Project B
Cost:		$100,000	$100,000
Cash Flows:	Year 1	60,000	10,000
	Year 2	30,000	30,000
	Year 3	10,000	60,000

The payback for both projects is three years. However, Project A is the superior project since the cost of the investment is recovered more quickly. Once again, this is an extreme and obvious example to illustrate the second weakness of the payback approach. It isn't always this easy to see the difference between two projects.

Net Present Value

The net present value (NPV) approach is a discounted cash flow method. The NPV is calculated by subtracting the cost of the investment from the present value of the cash inflows associated with the investment.

Present value of the cash inflows
− The cost of the investment
= The net present value

On a given project, the future cash flows are first scheduled out over its life, then they are discounted back to the present at an appropriate rate. Next, the cost of the investment is deducted from the total of the discounted cash flows to arrive at net present value. The criterion for acceptance or rejection of the project is the dollar value of the net present value. If the net present value is positive, the project is accepted; if it is negative, the project is rejected.

A good question at this point is where one obtains the appropriate discount rate. The rate is normally defined as the overall cost of capital for an organization. If a particular project is being financed entirely by a loan from a bank, it could be argued that the rate on the loan would be the appropriate discount rate.

Consider the following example of a club that is proposing the construction of a new dining facility. The club has secured a contractor's bid for a building in the amount of $1,275,000. The local bank has tentatively agreed to finance the construction at 10 percent, pending the club's submission of an appropriate business plan. Club management has estimated the annual cash flow for the dining room to be $175,000 for the next 15 years. Using the present value factor for 15 years at 10 percent (7.6061 as shown in Exhibit 5), the net present value of the project is calculated to be a positive $56,068 as shown below.

Present value of the cash inflows:	$175,000 × 7.6061 =	$1,331,068
Minus cost of the investment:		1,275,000
Net present value:		$ 56,068

Since the net present value is positive, it is an acceptable project.

Internal Rate of Return

The internal rate of return (IRR) approach solves for a rate rather than a dollar amount. The rate that is sought is the discount rate that equates the present value of the inflows on the project with the cost of the investment. Using the data from the building example above, the internal rate of return on the project would be calculated to be approximately 11 percent as shown below.

Cost of the Investment	=	Annual Cash Flow × Annuity Factor for 15 Years
$1,275,000	=	$175,000$x$

Solving for x (the annuity factor) in the above equation yields an annuity factor of 7.29. This number is between the factors for 10 and 12 percent for 15 years (see Exhibit 5). Therefore, the internal rate of return is approximately 11 percent. The exact rate on the project could be found through simple interpolation of the numbers in the table.

Calculation of the IRR on a project is simple in the case where the annual cash flow is the same every year, since there is only one unknown in the equation. Consider an identical project with the same cost, but assume that the annual cash flow for the first eight years is $180,000 while the annual cash flow for years 9–15 is $265,500. The internal rate of return is calculated to be approximately 14 percent by using the mathematical equation shown below.

$1,275,000 = (Cash Flow for Years 1–8 × 8 Year Factor) + (Cash Flow for Years 9–15 × [15 Year Factor − 8 Year Factor])

Plugging in the factors for 14 percent results in the following:

$1,275,000	=	$180,000(4.6389) + $265,500(6.1422 − 4.6389)
	=	$1,234,128

The amounts are not exactly even; hence, the rate is not exactly 14 percent. Once again, it is possible to calculate the exact rate through interpolation. Note that $265,500 is multiplied by the difference between the factor for 15 years and the factor for the first eight years since the $265,500 annuity comes in only during the last seven years. Problems like this one that involve an annuity followed by another annuity can be solved with a programmable calculator or by the tried and true "hit or miss" technique. Hit or miss involves estimating the rate by plugging in the factors for various rates until the actual rate is found. Alternatively, the IRR can be quickly and easily determined by using a computer spreadsheet program's IRR function, which allows the user to insert and calculate potential IRR values virtually instantaneously.

The criterion for acceptance of a project under the internal rate of return method of capital budgeting is whether the rate on the project exceeds the organization's target or **hurdle rate** of return. In the case of a club, an appropriate rate to compare the project to would be the cost of borrowing on the proposed project.

There is, admittedly, some ambiguity regarding the appropriate discount rate for the net present value method and the appropriate hurdle rate for the internal rate of return method. The issue of *exactly* which rate to use should not be focused on as long as the rate used is reasonable. The fact that these two discounted cash flow methods are used to justify a given project is the key, since bankers and accountants consider these two methods to be the best.

Of the two discounted cash flow methods of capital budgeting, the net present value approach is superior. It is better for a number of reasons, but the most important reason is the reinvestment rate assumption. Under the NPV method, it is assumed that the cash flows on a project can be reinvested at the same rate as the discount rate on the project. Under the IRR method, the assumption is that the cash flows are reinvested at the internal rate of return from the project being evaluated. It is safer to assume that cash flows can be reinvested at the club's hurdle rate rather than at what could be an unreasonably high rate on one given project.

Accounting Rate of Return

The last method to be discussed, the **accounting rate of return method**, is the only one that uses accrual income in its computation. An advantage of this method is that it is simple to use. The calculation of ARR is simply:

$$\text{ARR} \quad = \quad \frac{\text{Average Annual Project Income}}{\text{Project Cost}}$$

Assuming the project's cost is $275,000 with an average annual income on the project of $25,000, the accounting rate of return would be 9 percent as shown below.

$$\text{ARR} \quad = \quad \frac{\$25,000}{\$275,000}$$

$$= \quad \underline{\underline{9\%}}$$

The ARR would then be compared to a target rate of return set by the club to determine whether or not to go with the project. This method is generally considered to be the least favored method since it doesn't use discounted cash flows or even use cash flows in its implementation.

Use of Capital Budgeting Models in the Club Industry ——

Club executives were queried regarding their use of cost/benefit studies before acquiring property and equipment. Thirty-four percent of the respondents said they conducted cost justification informally. This suggests that they did not use the models discussed above, but that the respondents did consider future expected cash flows informally in comparison to the cost of their investments.

Fifty-one percent of the respondents used formal cost justification of fixed asset acquisitions. Approximately half indicated that these studies were conducted for all capital projects, while the other half indicated that a formal cost study was made only for major purchases.

Only 15 percent of the respondents indicated they did not conduct a cost/benefit study before acquiring property and equipment. By comparison, 30 percent of the respondents to a similar club study conducted in 1985 did not conduct a formalized cost/benefit study prior to making their capital purchases. As expected, the larger the club (based on number of members), the more likely formalized capital budgeting approaches are used as follows:

Size of Club	Percent
less than 501 members	43.9
501-750 members	56.8
751-1000 members	60.0
More than 1000 members	51.9

Another question dealt with defining how large an expenditure must be to be considered major. Of those respondents that conduct formalized study only for major acquisitions, 46.2 percent defined "major" as anything in excess of $1,000. Nearly 35 percent restricted their formal studies to items costing over $10,000; 12.8 percent to items costing over $50,000; and 1.3 percent to items costing over $100,000. The remaining five percent of the respondents defined major as amounts spent in excess of either $500, $5,000, or $25,000.

The most common capital budgeting approach used by clubs is payback; just over 42 percent of the club executives indicated this was their capital budgeting approach of choice. NPV and IRR were used by 35.2 percent and 17.6 percent of the respondents, respectively, compared with 28 percent and 18.5 percent in the 1985 study. Thus, a moderate increase in using discounted cash flow approaches has occurred in the club industry since 1985.

In anticipation of payback being the most popular approach, respondents were queried regarding the maximum payback period. In other words, how many years are allowable for a capital project to reach a breakeven point where cash flows from the project equal the project cost? The median response was three years. Nearly 35 percent of the respondents indicated three years, while another 14.3 percent indicated two years. The maximum payback period set by clubs varied as follows:

Maximum Payback Period	Percentage of Clubs
2 years	14
3 years	35
4 years	8
5 years	27
Other	16
Total	100

Exhibit 8   Selected Capital Projects

Project	Cost	Type of Club	Location of Club	Capital Budgeting Approach	Financing
Tennis Club	$220,000	Country	South Carolina	IRR	Operations—40 new tennis memberships
Golf Carts	$34,000	Country	Illinois	Payback	100% of initiation fees, 1% of dues of full-time members
Clubhouse Renovation	$2.2 million	Country	Texas	IRR	Operating funds— $500,000, special assessment—$1.7 million
Clubhouse	N/A	Residential/ Country	Illinois	Informal	Bank financing

A sampling of capital projects, including the project, its cost, the type of club, the capital budgeting approach used, and the method of financial reporting is shown in Exhibit 8. The projects vary in cost from $34,000 for golf carts to $2.2 million for the renovation of a clubhouse. The cost of the new clubhouse, listed as the last project, was not known by the general manager as the owner was handling this project.

Summary

Most of a club's financial decisions will relate to working capital management, which involves a short-term time horizon. However, when a capital budgeting decision needs to be made, it is very crucial due to its large dollar outlay and its long-term time horizon. Capital budgeting decisions involve buying land, purchasing equipment, construction of buildings, and making major improvements.

Several approaches to capital budgeting are presented in this chapter. Three of the approaches—payback, net present value, and internal rate of return—employ cash flow analysis, while accounting rate of return uses accrual income for its implementation. The NPV and IRR methods are more complex than the ARR and payback approaches, but they also provide more valuable results. They both examine cash flows and recognize the time value of money.

Key Terms

accounting rate of return (ARR)—An approach to evaluating capital budgeting decisions based on the average annual project income (project revenues less project expenses) divided by the original investment.

annuity—A stream of funds provided by a capital investment when the amounts provided are the same and at equal intervals (such as the end of each year).

capital expenditure—Expenditures for fixed assets.

internal rate of return (IRR) method—An approach to evaluating capital budget decisions based on the rate of return generated by the investment.

net present value (NPV) method—An approach to evaluating capital budget decisions based on discounting the cash flows relating to the project to their present value; calculated by subtracting the project cost from the present value of the discounted cash flow stream.

payback—An approach to evaluating capital budget decisions based on the number of years of annual cash flow generated by the fixed asset purchase required to recover the investment.

time value of money—The process of placing future years' income on an equal basis with current year expenditures in order to facilitate comparison.

 # Review Questions

1. What is the difference between a capital expenditure and a revenue expenditure?

2. What is generally considered to be the double-edged significance of capital budgeting?

3. Which of the four capital budgeting techniques uses cash flow? Which methods use discounted cash flow?

4. What are the advantages and disadvantages of the payback method?

5. Which method is conceptually better, the net present value method or the internal rate of return method?

6. What is the relationship between the operating budget and the capital budget?

7. What are some typical reasons for making capital budgeting decisions?

8. What are a strength and a weakness of the accounting rate of return approach?

9. How is the internal rate of return on a project defined?

10. What is the methodology of the net present value approach to capital budgeting?

 # Problems

Problem 1

The High Hills Club is considering the purchase of land and the construction of an 18-hole golf course with a clubhouse. The total cost is estimated to be $1,800,000. The estimated annual cash flow on the project is $160,000 while the average annual income is $130,000.

Required:

1. Calculate the payback on the project.
2. Calculate the accounting rate of return on the project.

Problem 2

The Broadway Athletic Club is evaluating an expansion that would include the addition of a bowling alley, squash courts, fitness center, and a swimming pool. The estimated cost of the addition is $3,000,000 and the appropriate discount rate is 12 percent. The annual cash inflows on the project are expected to be $400,000 per year for the first 10 years and $650,000 per year for the following 10 years.

Required:

1. Calculate the net present value on the project,
2. Calculate the internal rate of return on the project.

Problem 3

The Lakeside Country Club is considering adding nine holes to its golf course and constructing a new clubhouse with a large dining facility. The estimated cost is $2,300,000 and the appropriate discount rate is 10 percent. The average annual income on the project is $285,000 and the annual cash flow is expected to be $300,000 for the first 10 years, followed by $350,000 for the next 10 years.

Required:

1. Calculate the net present value on the project.
2. Calculate the internal rate of return on the project.
3. Calculate the payback on the project.
4. Calculate the accounting rate of return on the project.

Chapter 11 Outline

Initial Recording of Property and
    Equipment
Depreciation of Property and Equipment
    Methods of Depreciation
    Financial Versus Tax Reporting
Other Assets
Leasing

Competencies

1. Describe the process of recording property and equipment assets when purchased. (pp. 249–250)

2. Define depreciation and describe the four basic methods of depreciation, including the steps involved in recording changes to property and equipment assets as a result of occasional revisions, and disposal or exchange. (pp. 250–257)

3. List the items typically represented by the Other Assets category of the statement of financial position. (pp. 257–258)

4. Describe the general conditions under which a club should lease rather than buy property and equipment. (p. 258)

Property, Equipment, and Other Fixed Assets

Cᴌᴜʙꜱ, ʟɪᴋᴇ ᴏᴛʜᴇʀ segments of the hospitality industry, are fixed-asset intensive. This means that the majority of club assets are classified as fixed assets instead of current assets. Fixed assets include land, buildings, furniture, and equipment. This sets clubs apart from many manufacturing or retail firms, where a larger percentage of their assets are current assets such as cash, receivables, and inventory.

This chapter discusses the proper financial management of long-term assets, covering such procedures as the proper recording and depreciation of these assets. There is a discussion of lease-versus-buy decisions and a brief section on other assets such as security deposits and deferred charges.

Initial Recording of Property and Equipment

Property and equipment should be recorded at cost when purchased. The cost of these assets should include all reasonable and necessary expenditures required to get the asset into operating condition. Examples of expenditures that ought to be included with property and equipment assets are such items as freight charges, sales tax on the purchase, and installation charges. Charges that would not be considered reasonable and necessary include repairs due to damages in handling or a traffic ticket incurred by one of the club's employees during delivery.

The following illustrates the recording of an asset's purchase. Assume that the Oakdale Athletic Club has just purchased some exercise equipment from a supplier. The list price of the equipment is $40,000 with terms of $2/10, n/60$. The club, in this case, is able to pay within the cash discount period. Also assume that sales tax of $1,568 must be paid, along with freight charges of $650 and installation costs of $290. The club also purchases a two-year maintenance contract on the equipment at a cost of $1,000. Based on this information, the cost to be recorded for the asset is determined as follows:

List price of equipment	$ 40,000
Less two percent cash discount	800
Net price	39,200
Sales tax	1,568
Freight charges	650
Installation charges	290
Cost of equipment	$ 41,708

Notice that the maintenance contract is not added to the cost of the equipment and depreciated over the asset's life. Instead, the $500 for the next 12 months would be recorded as a prepaid expense, while the coverage for the second year would be deferred.

When land is purchased, all of the reasonable and necessary expenditures to buy the land are included in the purchase price. These expenditures include property taxes paid, title opinions, surveying costs, brokerage commissions, and any excavating expenses required to get the land into proper condition.

Occasionally the purchase of two or more assets is made for one price. This is referred to as a **lump sum purchase** or basket purchase. Sometimes this will include a building, which is depreciable, and land, which is nondepreciable. In this case, the procedure for placing individual assets on the books involves appraising both assets at their current market value. The values of the individual assets are then added up, and each asset is expressed as a percentage of the total appraised value. Next, those respective percentages are multiplied by the total purchase price of the combined assets, and the individual assets are then recorded at their respective amounts.

Assume that a club makes a lump sum purchase of land, building, and equipment for $500,000. The individual asset accounts would be increased for amounts based on the following computations:

Asset	Appraised Value	Percentage of Total (%)	Apportionment of Costs
Land	$300,000	50	$250,000*
Building	240,000	40	200,000
Equipment	60,000	10	50,000
	$600,000	100	$500,000

*50% of the $500,000 purchase price = $250,000

Depreciation of Property and Equipment

The process by which property or equipment is expensed over its life is called **depreciation**. The total amount of depreciation that can be taken over the life of an asset is equal to the cost of the asset less its salvage or residual value. Through the matching process, every year in the life of an asset an amount is placed in a contra-asset account called Accumulated Depreciation that carries a credit balance. Property and equipment assets are typically shown on the books at their book value or at what is sometimes called carrying value. Book value (also called net book value) is determined when the accumulated depreciation on the asset to date is subtracted from the cost of the asset. The accounting for fixed assets and related depreciation in the club industry is quite varied. There are conflicting philosophies on the question of whether or not clubs should provide for depreciation of fixed assets. The philosophy supporting depreciation is based on the concept that depreciation is an element of the cost of doing business; that the cost of an asset should be depreciated over its useful life, and that operations should be charged with a pro-rata portion of prior years' expenditures for capital additions.

The opposing philosophy is based on the premise that a club should be operated on a year-to-year, "pay as you go" basis, leaving new members in a position no better or worse than when the club started. Under this philosophy, depreciation is eliminated as a charge against the operations of the club; as new facilities are needed or desired, the active membership has the responsibility of financing the cost of such improvements by means of special assessments or borrowed funds, with the concomitant obligation to repay the amount borrowed. It is the view of the no-depreciation proponents that to assess the membership to raise funds for a new facility and then to provide for depreciation of the new asset would, in effect, have the present membership paying for the new facility twice if the dues structure were increased to cover the additional depreciation expense.

Because of these conflicting philosophies, one may find a wide range of policies related to the treatment of fixed assets and related depreciation in clubs (for example, the capitalization of all fixed assets purchased; the charging of all capital expenditures to expense as incurred; the charging of fixed assets purchased to special funds—for example, a capital improvement fund—and not capitalizing them). Since the purchase of fixed assets is afforded such a wide variety of treatment by membership clubs, it follows that the depreciation accounting methods are also diverse. Among the methods used are (1) depreciation in accordance with generally accepted accounting principals by providing for depreciation over the estimated useful lives of the various assets, (2) no depreciation at all, (3) providing for depreciation at a predetermined fixed amount, (4) providing for depreciation of only those assets acquired through general funds, and (5) not providing for depreciation of assets acquired through special funds. For the purposes of this chapter, we will assume that clubs are seeking to follow the first method.

It is generally an accepted accounting principle that fixed assets should be capitalized and depreciated over the period of their useful lives in a systematic and rational manner. In order to establish a simple depreciation schedule, assets are normally grouped together by year of purchase, type of asset, and estimated useful life, and then depreciated in a systematic manner.

It is important to realize that no one writes a check for depreciation. Depreciation is also not a fund of cash set aside by a company. Unlike most other expenses, it is a non-cash expense. However, depreciation can save cash in this way: it provides a tax shelter for the club subject to income taxes, since it, like other expenses, reduces taxable income.

For tax purposes, private clubs—whether or not exempt from income tax under Section 501(c)(7)—are required to compute depreciation under the rules prescribed in the Internal Revenue Code and its numerous amendments. The Internal Revenue Code stipulates prescribed times and methods in which to recover the cost of any asset that is used in a trade or business. If a club reports any unrelated business income (generally food, beverage, rooms, green fees, cart rentals, and investment income), the deduction allowable for depreciation against the unrelated business income has to be computed in accordance with the provisions of the tax law.

Methods of Depreciation

The four basic methods used to depreciate assets are straight-line, units of production, sum-of-the-years' digits, and double declining balance. The most commonly used methods are straight-line and double declining balance. Sum-of-the-years' digits and double declining balance are called **accelerated methods of depreciation** because they result in the highest charges in the first year, with lower and lower charges in successive years. These accelerated methods allocate the largest portion of an asset's depreciation costs to the early years of the asset's estimated useful life.

An important concept relating to depreciation is the **salvage value**, or residual value, of the asset. This is the estimated value of the asset at the end of its useful life. Most of the depreciation methods take salvage value into consideration; the double declining balance method does not.

Straight-line depreciation is the simplest of the four methods. Under this technique, the same amount of depreciation is taken on the asset in each year of its life. To compute the annual depreciation under straight-line, one simply takes the cost of the asset less its salvage value and divides that figure by the estimated life of the asset. For example, assume that a truck costs the club $34,000, and has a salvage value of $4,000 and a life of five years. As shown in the following illustration, the annual depreciation under straight-line would be $6,000 per year.

Cost of truck $ 34,000
Less salvage value   4,000
Depreciable cost $ 30,000 ÷ 5 Years = $6,000 annual depreciation
          Total depreciation over life: $6,000 × 5 = $30,000

Under the **units of production depreciation** method, depreciation taken is based on the usage of the asset. In the preceding example of the $34,000 truck with a $4,000 salvage value, the depreciation would be computed in the following way. First, the number of useful miles of the truck would be estimated. Assuming that this figure is 100,000, we would divide this into the cost less salvage value of $30,000. This would give a depreciation rate of $.30 per mile. If, in the first year of its use, the truck was driven 12,000 miles, the depreciation taken for the first year would be 12,000 miles times $.30, or $3,600.

Under the **sum-of-the-years' digits depreciation** method, the years of the asset's life are added together; the resulting total becomes the denominator in a fraction used to calculate each year's depreciation. For instance, using the truck example, we would sum the years of its life in this way: $5 + 4 + 3 + 2 + 1 = 15$. The following is a quick formula for figuring this:

$$\frac{n(n + 1)}{2}$$

The first year we would take $\frac{5}{15}$ of $30,000 (that is, cost less salvage value) and get $10,000 depreciation. Depreciation for the other years is shown in the following table:

Cost of truck	$34,000
Less salvage value	4,000
Depreciable cost	$30,000

Year	Depreciable Rate	Annual Cost	Depreciation
1	5/15	$30,000	$10,000
2	4/15	30,000	8,000
3	3/15	30,000	6,000
4	2/15	30,000	4,000
5	1/15	30,000	2,000
		TOTAL	$30,000

The **double declining balance depreciation** method ignores salvage value while computing annual depreciation. Under this method, the straight-line rate of depreciation is calculated first with the division of the life of the asset into 100 percent. In the example of the $34,000 truck, we would divide five (years) into 100 (percent) and get 20 percent per year. Then the straight-line rate of 20 percent would be multiplied by two to get the double declining rate, which is 40 percent. Thus, in the first year of depreciation for the truck, the depreciation would be $34,000 times .40, or $13,600. In the second year, the $34,000 cost minus the first year's depreciation for $13,600 would yield $20,400, which would be multiplied by .40 to get the second year's depreciation of $8,160. The remaining years' depreciation is illustrated in the following table. Notice that although the salvage value is not used in the computation of the annual depreciation under this method, one must be careful not to depreciate the asset below the salvage value in the later years. Also notice that the depreciation in year five is limited to $406 rather than 40 percent of $4,406 so that the asset is not depreciated below its $4,000 salvage value.

Cost of truck		$34,000	

Year	Rate (%)	Declining Balance	Annual Depreciation
1	40	$34,000	$13,600
2	40	20,400	8,160
3	40	12,240	4,896
4	40	7,344	2,938
5	40	4,406	406
		TOTAL	$30,000

Depreciation for Fractional Periods. If the $34,000 truck had been purchased on September 1, 20X3, the depreciation taken in 20X3 under the straight-line method would be $2,000 for the four months it was owned, as shown:

$$\text{Depreciable cost of } \$30,000 \div 5 \text{ Years} = \$6,000$$
$$\text{Depreciation for September–December 20X3} = \$6,000 \times \tfrac{4}{12} = \underline{\$2,000}$$

Calculation of the depreciation for the truck for September–December 20X3 and full-year 20X4 under the sum-of-the-years' digits method would be as follows:

Year 20X3

Depreciable cost of $30,000 $\times \tfrac{5}{15} \times \tfrac{4}{12} \times$ = $3,333

Year 20X4

Depreciable cost of $30,000 $\times \tfrac{5}{15} \times \tfrac{8}{12} \times$ = $6,667
+ $30,000 $\times \tfrac{4}{15} \times \tfrac{4}{12} \times$ = $\underline{2,667}$
Total Depreciation: $9,334

If the truck were being depreciated under the double declining balance method, the depreciation for the years 20X3 and 20X4 would be $4,533 and $11,787, as illustrated:

Year 20X3

Cost = $34,000 $\times$ .40 $\times \tfrac{4}{12}$ = $4,533

Year 20X4

Declining balance of $34,000 − $4,533 = $29,467 $\times$ .40 = $11,787

Revision of Useful Lives of Assets. Occasionally during the life of a depreciable asset, a revision is made regarding the asset's useful life. In this situation, the remaining depreciable cost of the asset is simply spread over its remaining life. Assume in the case of the $34,000 truck that, after three years of its life, it was determined that its total life was eight years instead of five years. The depreciation for year four would be computed as follows:

Depreciable cost	$30,000
Depreciation for years 1, 2, 3	$\underline{18,000}$
Remaining depreciable cost	12,000
Remaining life: five years	
Depreciation for year four: $12,000 ÷ 5 = $2,400	

Disposal of Property and Equipment. Occasionally a club will take a property and equipment asset off the books because it is being scrapped, sold, or traded in. If an asset is scrapped and has been fully depreciated, it is necessary to remove both the asset and related accumulated depreciation from the books. Assume that a truck with a cost of $34,000 and a salvage value of zero was fully depreciated. In this case, the following entry would be made:

| Accumulated Depreciation—Truck | $34,000 | |
| Truck | | $34,000 |

If the same asset is scrapped before it is fully depreciated, a different entry is made. Assuming that the same truck costing $34,000 has been depreciated in the amount of $28,000, the journal entry would be:

Accumulated Depreciation—Truck	$28,000	
Loss on Disposal of Asset	6,000	
Truck		$34,000

The loss on the disposal of this asset would be closed into the Income Summary account at the end of the next fiscal period.

Sometimes property and equipment assets are disposed of through a sale resulting in a gain or loss. Suppose the same truck had a book value of $6,000, based on a cost of $34,000 and an accumulated depreciation balance of $28,000. If this truck is sold for $8,000, the following journal entry would be made:

Cash	$ 8,000	
Accumulated Depreciation—Truck	28,000	
Truck		$34,000
Gain on Disposal of Asset		2,000

The gain of $2,000 is simply the difference between the selling price of $8,000 and the book value of $6,000.

Assume the same facts concerning the $34,000 truck, except that it is sold for $4,000. Since it has a book value of $6,000 and is sold for $4,000, a loss of $2,000 would result. The journal entry to record this transaction would look like this:

Cash	$ 4,000	
Accumulated Depreciation—Truck	28,000	
Loss on Disposal of Asset	2,000	
Truck		$34,000

Exchange of Property and Equipment Assets. Property and equipment assets, such as the truck, are commonly exchanged or traded in for similar assets. Assume that the $34,000 truck is exchanged along with $36,000 cash for a new truck that has a list price of $38,000. At the time of the exchange, the old $34,000 truck has accumulated depreciation of $28,000; hence, it has a book value of $6,000. Notice that, although the book value is $6,000, the firm is getting only $2,000 on the trade-in. Therefore, there is a loss of $4,000. The entry to record the exchange is:

Truck—New	$38,000	
Accumulated Depreciation—Old Truck	28,000	
Loss on Disposal of Asset	4,000	
Cash		$36,000
Truck—Old		34,000

Notice how this entry would change if, instead, the club is given $7,000 on the trade-in and consequently has to pay only $31,000 for the new truck. In this case, the journal entry would be:

Truck—New	$38,000	
Accumulated Depreciation—Old Truck	28,000	
Cash		$31,000
Truck—Old		34,000

The Financial Accounting Standards Board (FASB) has stated that no gains are to be recorded on exchanges. Instead, the gain is to be reflected in the value of the asset acquired. Two points should be noted concerning these two entries:

1. The generally accepted accounting principle of conservatism states that losses should be recorded, but not gains.

2. Tax reporting rules differ from financial reporting rules. In reporting for tax purposes, neither gains nor losses are recorded on exchanges of similar assets.

Financial Versus Tax Reporting

Any of the depreciation methods discussed here can be used for financial reporting purposes. Tax legislation in 1981 and 1982 liberalized tax depreciation rules with the enactment of an Accelerated Cost Recovery System (ACRS), which provided for faster recovery (depreciation) of capital expenditures. For clubs having income subject to the federal income taxes, all assets acquired after 1981, except for land, must be depreciated with either straight-line depreciation or ACRS. Under

ACRS, assets are arbitrarily placed into one of six property class lives. Predetermined rates are then applied to the asset's cost with salvage value ignored.

The Tax Reform Act of 1986 created the Modified Accelerated Cost Recovery System (MACRS), which provided for eight classes of property and lengthened the recovery periods. In financial accounting, a building may be depreciated over 30 years or more. MACRS currently allows, for tax purposes, recovery over 31.5 years. Similarly, furnishings and equipment may be depreciated over seven to ten years (or more) for financial accounting purposes, while the same items are depreciated for tax purposes over five years under MACRS. Thus, the timing of reported net income for financial purposes can be significantly different from that for taxable income.

This situation will be reversed in the later years of an asset's life; the deduction for depreciation, especially with furnishings and equipment, will be greater for financial accounting than for tax accounting. At the end of the asset's life, the deduction for depreciation will be the same in total for both financial reporting and tax accounting. The difference is in the timing of the deduction. Clubs can now choose to use optional straight-line depreciation with half-year convention instead of MACRS. ("Half-year convention" means that, regardless of the month of the year when an asset is purchased, one-half of a year's depreciation is taken in the year of purchase.)

Other Assets

The Other Assets category on the statement of financial position typically includes these four areas:

* Security deposits

* Deferred charges

* Deferred income taxes

* Other

Security deposits include funds deposited to secure occupancy or utility services (such as telecommunications, water, electricity, and gas) and any similar types of deposits.

Deferred charges, also called deferred assets or deferred expenses, are expenses that are prepaid yet are noncurrent. They are distinguished from prepaid expenses that would show up in the Current Assets section of the statement of financial position. Since they are noncurrent, they benefit future periods. Examples include maintenance expenses or financing costs related to long-term debt.

Deferred income taxes result from the tax effects of temporary differences between the bases of noncurrent assets and noncurrent liabilities for financial and income tax reporting purposes.

"Other" is a miscellaneous category for items that do not fit neatly into the other three categories. Items included here are the cash surrender value of life insurance on the officers of the company, organization costs such as legal fees, and any intangible assets carried on the books.

The *Uniform System of Financial Reporting for Clubs* requires that preopening expenses be expensed when incurred. Clubs outside the United States may be allowed to amortize preopening expenses, depending on local conventions and laws.

Leasing

Leasing is an alternative to purchasing property and equipment. A **lease** is an agreement that conveys the right to use a specific resource for a specific purpose for a set period of time. Leases can vary from hourly leases of specialized equipment to a very long-term lease, such as a 99-year lease of land. From a financial perspective, a club should enter into a lease if the cost of leasing is cheaper than owning the asset. The lease agreement governs the two parties to the lease, the lessor and the lessee. The lessor is the owner of the asset who allows the lessee to use the asset in exchange for rent.

There are both advantages and disadvantages of leasing for a club (though they are beyond our focus in this chapter). The decision to lease or buy a given asset should involve both qualitative and quantitative factors. The costs of owning the asset and the costs of leasing the asset should be discounted back to the present at an appropriate discount rate. The option that has the lowest present value of the costs should be the accepted option.

Key Terms

accelerated methods of depreciation—Depreciation methods that result in higher depreciation charges in the first year and gradually declining charges over the life of fixed assets—for example, sum-of-the-years' digits and double declining balance.

deferred income taxes—The excess that occurs for a business when the income taxes on the statement of income exceed the amount of tax liability.

depreciation—The systematic transfer of part of a tangible long-lived asset's cost to an expense. Usually associated with property and equipment, but not with land.

double declining balance depreciation—An accelerated method of depreciation that ignores salvage value in the computation of annual depreciation. One must be careful not to depreciate the asset below its salvage value in the later years.

lease—An agreement conveying the right to use resources (equipment, buildings, land) for specified purposes and limited periods of time in exchange for rent.

lump sum purchase—The purchase of two or more assets made for one price.

salvage value—The estimated market value of an asset at the time it is to be retired from use.

straight-line depreciation—A method of depreciation that distributes expense evenly throughout the estimated life of the asset. That is, the same amount of depreciation is taken on the asset in each year of its life.

sum-of-the-years' digits depreciation—An accelerated method of depreciation that uses a variable fraction as a multiplier. The years of the asset's life are added together, and the resulting total becomes the denominator used to calculate each year's deprecation. As with all accelerated methods of depreciation, more depreciation is taken in the early years and less in the later years.

units of production depreciation—A method of depreciation in which the depreciation taken is based on the use of the asset.

Review Questions

1. How is depreciation unlike most expenses? In what circumstances does depreciation affect the taxes a club pays? Are there times when depreciation does not affect a club's taxes?

2. What does accelerated depreciation mean? Which methods are considered accelerated?

3. What are some common expenditures included in the cost of a property and equipment asset?

4. How are the values of individual assets determined in the case of a lump-sum purchase?

5. How is the gain or loss on the sale of a property and equipment asset calculated?

6. What is salvage value or residual value? Which depreciation methods take the salvage value into account when the annual depreciation is calculated?

7. What is the proper procedure for the expensing of preopening expenses?

8. When might it be more appropriate for a club to lease property or equipment than to buy it?

## Problems

Problem 1

The Riviera Country Club has purchased a trolley bus that is available for members to use in shuttling people to and from the club. The cost of the bus is $40,000; its salvage value is $4,000; its life is five years with expected usable mileage of 100,000.

Required:

Calculate the first year's depreciation under each of the following methods:

    a. Straight line

    b. Units of production, assuming the bus traveled 15,000 miles in year 1.

    c. Sum-of-the-years' digits

    d. Double declining balance

Problem 2

Bay View Golf Club has purchased a new greens mower for the golf course. Various pieces of information concerning this purchase are as follows:

Invoice price of equipment	$22,000
Cash discount allowed	2% of invoice
Freight-in paid	300
Speeding ticket given to club's superintendent while driving the equipment	25
Sales tax on purchase	550
Repair of damages due to equipment being dropped off truck	200

Required:

Determine the proper amount to be capitalized in the asset account Equipment.

Problem 3

Rolling Hills Club recently purchased a parcel of land, a building, and some equipment for $2,400,000 cash. The land was appraised at $800,000, the building at $2,800,000, and the equipment at $400,000.

Required:

What amounts should be entered on the books of the club for the land, building, and equipment?

Chapter 12 Outline

Control Features
Payroll Records
    Regular Pay and Overtime Pay
Payroll Journal Entries
    The Entry to Record Payroll
    The Entry to Record Payroll Taxes
Reporting Tips
Determining Employee Status

Competencies

1. Describe the importance of managing payroll-related liabilities and the control features that clubs should have in place. (pp. 263–266)

2. List the elements involved in maintaining payroll records, including departmentalization, knowledge of applicable wage and tax acts, preparing appropriate files and forms, and evaluating overtime and part-time employment situations. (pp. 266–270)

3. Describe the two distinct journal entries involving payroll. (pp. 270–276)

4. Explain the importance of tip reporting and list the relevant tax forms and documents associated with claiming tip income. (pp. 276–277)

5. List the characteristics that distinguish employees from self-employed individuals for income tax reporting purposes. (pp. 277–280)

Accounting for Payroll-Related Liabilities

P AYROLL REPRESENTS THE LARGEST expense for any club. According to PKF Consulting research released in 2000, payroll and related costs for 1999 were 46 percent of income. Or consider payroll costs per golf course hole. In 1999, payroll, payroll taxes, and employee benefits for country clubs averaged nearly $38,000 per golf course hole across the United States. City clubs are also dealing with large and increasing payroll costs. In 1980, payroll and related costs came to $447 per member; by 1999, city clubs were spending $1,400 per member. Exhibit 1 provides detailed information on payroll percentages by geographic division and membership size for city clubs in 1999. Clearly, payroll-related liabilities for clubs are of great importance.

Control Features

To deal effectively with this major liability, clubs should have several important control features in place.

1. The following payroll functions should be segregated whenever possible.

   - Authorization of employment and establishment of wage rates for employees.

   - Reporting of hours worked by employees. Probably the most difficult timekeeping area to control is the golf course maintenance department. The crew reports for work to the maintenance building, usually located apart from the clubhouse where other employees report for work; therefore, generally the greens superintendent's duty is to record the number of hours his crew works. The other hourly employees generally use a time clock to keep track of their hours. But, if time clocks are not used, the department heads maintain a time book showing the hours that employees work daily. For control purposes, overtime hours should be approved in advance.

   - Actual preparation of the payroll.

   - Signing of the payroll checks.

   - Distribution of checks to employees. Checks should be distributed by individuals independent of the payroll department. Some larger clubs

Exhibit 1   Payroll Statistics for City Clubs

	Your Figures	All City Clubs	Geographic Divisions			Size (Membership)		
			East	Central	West	Under 750	750 to 1,500	Over 1500
1999 payroll ratios based on total sales and income - excluding dues	%	%	%	%	%	%	%	%
Payroll:								
Food and beverages		34.1	41.5	30.7	35.1	37.2	37.0	25.7
Rooms		1.0	2.2	*	1.7	1.9	0.6	5.2
All other income-producing departments		7.2	1.3	10.0	6.1	2.8	6.9	7.9
Subtotal		42.3	45.0	40.7	42.9	41.9	44.5	38.8
Clubrooms		.4.9	4.6	2.7	7.5	6.5	4.4	4.1
Administrative and general		13.8	16.4	13.3	13.5	17.7	12.2	12.3
Heat, light, and power		0.7	0.8	1.3	0.0	0.2	0.3	2.1
Repairs and maintenance		2.9	2.2	2.8	3.3	3.9	2.8	2.0
Total club payroll		64.6	69.0	60.8	67.2	70.2	64.2	59.3
Payroll taxes and employee benefits		9.1	6.7	5.3	14.5	15.2	9.7	1.6
Employees' meals		1.2	0.4	0.6	2.2	1.5	1.7	0.0
Total club payroll and related costs		74.9	76.1	66.7	83.9	86.9	75.6	60.9
Variations in total dollar payroll costs -- 1999 based on 1998	%	%	%	%	%	%	%	%
Payroll:								
Food and beverages		7.4	4.9	11.5	4.5	10.9	4.6	8.7
Rooms		19.2	12.8	*	22.7	36.7	7.4	1.8
All other income-producing departments		11.0	(43.1)	5.8	34.7	11.9	15.7	9.5
Subtotal		8.2	2.8	10.0	8.6	11.9	6.2	7.9
Clubrooms		34.1	27.6	6.4	53.3	5.0	139.7	2.5
Administrative and general		5.3	1.2	9.8	2.4	6.2	3.0	7.7
Heat, light, and power		13.1	5.6	14.6	0.0	8.7	2.4	16.3
Repairs and maintenance		11.0	(7.5)	10.3	18.1	39.6	0.6	(6.9)
Total club payroll		9.3	3.4	9.9	11.3	11.0	9.4	7.1
Payroll taxes and employee benefits		40.5	(5.6)	34.2	58.0	34.6	51.4	9.9
Employees' meals		52.3	1.2	24.0	70.9	11.7	94.1	(8.2)
Total club payroll and related costs		12.9	2.5	11.6	18.5	14.5	14.7	7.2

* No rooms data available.

Source: *Clubs in Town & Country* (New York: PKF Worldwide, 2000), p. 20.

with many employees will use what is called the *payoff test;* that is, they will require a periodic "shaking of hands" of employees receiving the checks to make certain the individuals actually exist. This procedure is decreasing due to direct deposit of employees' checks.

- Reconciliation of payroll bank accounts by an independent party.

Exhibit 2   Sample Employee Time Card

WEEK ENDING _____ 20 _____

Form No. 1212

No.

NAME

DAY	MORNING IN	NOON OUT	NOON IN	NIGHT OUT	EXTRA IN	EXTRA OUT	TOTAL

TOTAL TIME _____ HRS.

RATE _____

TOTAL WAGES FOR WEEK $ _____

2. The human resources manager, controller, or the general manager, as the case may be, should be the only person allowed to add individuals to, or delete them from, the labor force. In addition, he or she should be the only one that provides the payroll department with employees' wage rates.

3. Proper procedures should be in place for recording time worked, including the use of time clocks where possible. Exhibit 2 shows a sample employee time card.

4. Employees should be paid by check only, not in cash. In addition, a special **imprest payroll account** should be used. An imprest payroll account is one into which only the exact amount of a given payroll period is deposited. Once all of the checks clear the bank, there is nothing left in the account.

5. Payroll sheets and employee paychecks should be independently checked.

6. Any unclaimed payroll checks should be returned immediately to the controller or manager who will hold them until the employees return to work and pick up their checks directly from the controller or manager.

Payroll Records

Most clubs are completely departmentalized, and the payroll records should be arranged in departmental categories to simplify the distribution of payroll expense. Probably the simplest and oldest method of recording payroll is through the "one-write system." With this system, the payroll check, payroll sheet, and earnings card are prepared at the same sitting through the use of a check with a carbon stub and a pegboard. Although a few clubs may still use one-write systems, most clubs now use a computerized payroll system or they outsource this function.

The Fair Labor Standards Act (FLSA), commonly known as the Federal Wage and Hour Law, covers such things as equal pay for equal work, recordkeeping requirements, minimum wage rates, and overtime pay. Most clubs, except for certain very small operations, are subject to this act. The two tests to determine whether a club is required to pay minimum wage and overtime under the FLSA are:

1. If the club has revenues, or projects revenues, in excess of $500,000 per year, or if the club was operating prior to April 1, 1990, and revenues were in excess of $362,500 on that date, the club is subject to FLSA requirements.

2. Even if revenues are below $500,000 per year, a club may be required to pay minimum wage and overtime to some employees. For example, if any employee is engaged in interstate communications, he or she is covered by the law.

If neither of these tests is met, the club manager should still consult with the state government to determine whether state minimum wage and overtime laws apply to the club.

To comply with the FLSA, employers must keep records of the time worked by hourly employees. Time cards or time sheets are generally used to satisfy this requirement. The time cards or sheets can be completed manually or through an electronic time clock.

Clubs will typically keep a **master payroll file** of records that include important information on employees. The information in the file would include employees' full names, addresses with zip codes, dates of birth (if less than 19 years of age), sex, occupation, time and day when their workweek starts, rate of pay, hours worked each day and week, regular earnings, overtime earnings, other additions and deductions from pay, total wages paid, pay date, and pay period.

All employees need to complete Internal Revenue Service (IRS) Form W-4 and provide it to the employer.[1] This form helps the employer calculate the amount of taxes withheld from the individual employee's payroll check. The front of a W-4 form is shown in Exhibit 3. In addition, clubs are required to have employees complete the U.S. Department of Justice Employment Eligibility Verification Form I-9,

Exhibit 3 Form W-4: Employee's Withholding Allowance Certificate

Form W-4 (2001)

Purpose. Complete Form W-4 so your employer can withhold the correct Federal income tax from your pay. Because your tax situation may change, you may want to refigure your withholding each year.

Exemption from withholding. If you are exempt, complete only lines 1, 2, 3, 4, and 7, and sign the form to validate it. Your exemption for 2001 expires February 18, 2002.

Note: *You cannot claim exemption from withholding if (1) your income exceeds $750 and includes more than $250 of unearned income (e.g., interest and dividends) and (2) another person can claim you as a dependent on their tax return.*

Basic instructions. If you are not exempt, complete the **Personal Allowances Worksheet** below. The worksheets on page 2 adjust your withholding allowances based on itemized deductions, certain credits, adjustments to

income, or two-earner/two-job situations. Complete all worksheets that apply. They will help you figure the number of withholding allowances you are entitled to claim. **However, you may claim fewer (or zero) allowances.**

Head of household. Generally, you may claim head of household filing status on your tax return only if you are unmarried and pay more than 50% of the costs of keeping up a home for yourself and your dependent(s) or other qualifying individuals. See line **E** below.

Tax credits. You can take projected tax credits into account in figuring your allowable number of withholding allowances. Credits for child or dependent care expenses and the child tax credit may be claimed using the **Personal Allowances Worksheet** below. See **Pub. 919,** *How Do I Adjust My Tax Withholding?* for information on converting your other credits into withholding allowances.

Nonwage income. If you have a large amount of nonwage income, such as interest or dividends,

consider making estimated tax payments using **Form 1040-ES,** *Estimated Tax for Individuals.* Otherwise, you may owe additional tax.

Two earners/two jobs. If you have a working spouse or more than one job, figure the total number of allowances you are entitled to claim on all jobs using worksheets from only one Form W-4. Your withholding usually will be most accurate when all allowances are claimed on the Form W-4 for the highest paying job and zero allowances are claimed on the others.

Check your withholding. After your Form W-4 takes effect, use Pub. 919 to see how the dollar amount you are having withheld compares to your projected total tax for 2001. Get Pub. 919 especially if you used the **Two-Earner/Two-Job Worksheet** on page 2 and your earnings exceed $150,000 (Single) or $200,000 (Married).

Recent name change? If your name on line 1 differs from that shown on your social security card, call 1-800-772-1213 for a new social security card.

Personal Allowances Worksheet (Keep for your records.)

A Enter "1" for **yourself** if no one else can claim you as a dependent . . . . **A** _____

B Enter "1" if:
- You are single and have only one job; or
- You are married, have only one job, and your spouse does not work; or
- Your wages from a second job or your spouse's wages (or the total of both) are $1,000 or less. **B** _____

C Enter "1" for your **spouse.** But, you may choose to enter -0- if you are married and have either a working spouse or more than one job. (Entering -0- may help you avoid having too little tax withheld.) . . . . . . **C** _____

D Enter number of **dependents** (other than your spouse or yourself) you will claim on your tax return . . . . **D** _____

E Enter "1" if you will file as **head of household** on your tax return (see conditions under **Head of household** above) . **E** _____

F Enter "1" if you have at least $1,500 of **child or dependent care expenses** for which you plan to claim a credit . **F** _____

(**Note:** *Do not* include child support payments. See **Pub. 503,** *Child and Dependent Care Expenses, for details.*)

G **Child Tax Credit** (including additional child tax credit):
- If your total income will be between $18,000 and $50,000 ($23,000 and $63,000 if married), enter "1" for each eligible child.
- If your total income will be between $50,000 and $80,000 ($63,000 and $115,000 if married), enter "1" if you have two eligible children, enter "2" if you have three or four eligible children, or enter "3" if you have five or more eligible children. **G** _____

H Add lines A through G and enter total here. (**Note:** *This may be different from the number of exemptions you claim on your tax return.*) ▶ **H** _____

For accuracy, complete all worksheets that apply.
- If you plan to **itemize or claim adjustments to income** and want to reduce your withholding, see the **Deductions and Adjustments Worksheet** on page 2.
- If you are **single,** have **more than one job** and your combined earnings from all jobs exceed $35,000, **or** if you are **married** and have a **working spouse or more than one job** and the combined earnings from all jobs exceed $60,000, see the **Two-Earner/Two-Job Worksheet** on page 2 to avoid having too little tax withheld.
- If **neither** of the above situations applies, **stop here** and enter the number from line H on line 5 of Form W-4 below.

- - - - - - - - - - - - **Cut here and give Form W-4 to your employer. Keep the top part for your records.** - - - - - - - - - - - -

Form **W-4** Department of the Treasury Internal Revenue Service	**Employee's Withholding Allowance Certificate** ▶ **For Privacy Act and Paperwork Reduction Act Notice, see page 2.**	OMB No. 1545-0010 **2001**

1 Type or print your first name and middle initial Last name		**2** Your social security number
Home address (number and street or rural route)	**3** ☐ Single ☐ Married ☐ Married, but withhold at higher Single rate. **Note:** *If married, but legally separated, or spouse is a nonresident alien, check the Single box.*	
City or town, state, and ZIP code	**4** **If your last name differs from that on your social security card, check here. You must call 1-800-772-1213 for a new card.** ▶ ☐	

5 Total number of allowances you are claiming (from line **H** above **or** from the applicable worksheet on page 2) **5** ____

6 Additional amount, if any, you want withheld from each paycheck . . . . **6** $ ____

7 I claim exemption from withholding for 2001, and I certify that I meet **both** of the following conditions for exemption:
- Last year I had a right to a refund of **all** Federal income tax withheld because I had **no** tax liability **and**
- This year I expect a refund of **all** Federal income tax withheld because I expect to have **no** tax liability.

If you meet both conditions, write "Exempt" here . . . . ▶ **7** ____

Under penalties of perjury, I certify that I am entitled to the number of withholding allowances claimed on this certificate, or I am entitled to claim exempt status.

Employee's signature (Form is not valid unless you sign it.) ▶ _____ **Date** ▶ _____

8 Employer's name and address (Employer: Complete lines 8 and 10 only if sending to the IRS.)	**9** Office code (optional)	**10** Employer identification number

Cat. No. 10220Q

shown in Exhibit 4. IRS Form W-2, which employers must provide to employees annually for filing along with their income tax forms, is shown in Exhibit 5.

Another payroll record is the **payroll journal**. This lists a record of each payroll check issued by the club, along with the corresponding gross pay and various deductions for federal, state, city, and Social Security taxes; employee health care contributions; and miscellaneous contributions such as union dues. A file called an **employee's earnings record** is also kept for each individual employee of the club. This record is used to compile information for government reporting of employees' wages. Some taxes apply to earnings up to a certain dollar amount only; this record is used to make sure that those caps are not exceeded.

Regular Pay and Overtime Pay

According to the FLSA, regular pay for an employee is based on a 40-hour workweek. *Regular hourly rate* refers to the rate per hour that is used to compute regular pay. The FLSA also requires that overtime pay be given for any hours worked in excess of 40 hours in a week; *overtime hourly rate* refers to the rate per hour used to compute overtime pay. The FLSA requires that overtime be paid at the rate of 1.5 times the employee's regular hourly rate.

To calculate the overtime pay for some employees, it may be necessary to convert a weekly wage into an hourly rate. For example assume that an employee is hired at a weekly wage of $218 for a 40-hour workweek. The regular hourly rate for this employee would be $5.45:

$$\text{Regular Hourly Rate} = \frac{\text{Weekly Wage}}{\text{Number of Hours in Regular Workweek}}$$

$$= \frac{\$218}{40}$$

$$= \$5.45$$

Now that the regular hourly rate has been calculated, the overtime rate can easily be determined. Since the FLSA requires the overtime rate to be 1.5 times the regular hourly rate, this employee would have an hourly overtime rate of $8.175:

$$\text{Overtime Hourly Rate} = \text{Regular Hourly Rate} \times 1.5$$

$$= \$5.45 \times 1.5$$

$$= \$8.175$$

Occasionally, employees may ask to work extra days to earn additional wages, not expecting to get paid overtime premium pay. Sometimes a club will have them sign an agreement to that effect. However, the law states that the overtime premium cannot be waived by any such agreement.

Another situation that arises is when a club employee works (for example) 40 hours on the golf course and is then transferred to the dining room to work more hours that week. All of the hours worked in that week must be counted in determining whether overtime is due, despite the transfer from one department to another. A club cannot avoid overtime premium pay in this situation. In

Exhibit 4 Form I-9: Employment Eligibility Verification

U.S. Department of Justice
Immigration and Naturalization Service

OMB No. 1115-0136
Employment Eligibility Verification

Please read instructions carefully before completing this form. The instructions must be available during completion of this form. **ANTI-DISCRIMINATION NOTICE: It is illegal to discriminate against work eligible individuals. Employers CANNOT specify which document(s) they will accept from an employee. The refusal to hire an individual because of a future expiration date may also constitute illegal discrimination.**

Section 1. Employee Information and Verification. To be completed and signed by employee at the time employment begins.

Print Name: Last	First	Middle Initial	Maiden Name

Address *(Street Name and Number)*	Apt. #	Date of Birth *(month/day/year)*

City	State	Zip Code	Social Security #

I am aware that federal law provides for imprisonment and/or fines for false statements or use of false documents in connection with the completion of this form.

I attest, under penalty of perjury, that I am (check one of the following):
☐ A citizen or national of the United States
☐ A Lawful Permanent Resident (Alien # A_____
☐ An alien authorized to work until ___/___/___
(Alien # or Admission #) _____

Employee's Signature	Date *(month/day/year)*

Preparer and/or Translator Certification. *(To be completed and signed if Section 1 is prepared by a person other than the employee.) I attest, under penalty of perjury, that I have assisted in the completion of this form and that to the best of my knowledge the information is true and correct.*

Preparer's/Translator's Signature	Print Name

Address *(Street Name and Number, City, State, Zip Code)*	Date *(month/day/year)*

Section 2. Employer Review and Verification. To be completed and signed by employer. Examine one document from List A OR examine one document from List B and one from List C, as listed on the reverse of this form, and record the title, number and expiration date, if any, of the document(s)

List A	OR	List B	AND	List C
Document title: _____		_____		_____
Issuing authority: _____		_____		_____
Document #: _____		_____		_____
Expiration Date *(if any):* ___/___/___	___/___/___			___/___/___
Document #: _____				
Expiration Date *(if any):* ___/___/___				

CERTIFICATION - I attest, under penalty of perjury, that I have examined the document(s) presented by the above-named employee, that the above-listed document(s) appear to be genuine and to relate to the employee named, that the employee began employment on *(month/day/year)* ___/___/___ and that to the best of my knowledge the employee is eligible to work in the United States. (State employment agencies may omit the date the employee began employment.)

Signature of Employer or Authorized Representative	Print Name	Title

Business or Organization Name	Address *(Street Name and Number, City, State, Zip Code)*	Date *(month/day/year)*

Section 3. Updating and Reverification. To be completed and signed by employer.

A. New Name *(if applicable)*	B. Date of rehire *(month/day/year) (if applicable)*

C. If employee's previous grant of work authorization has expired, provide the information below for the document that establishes current employment eligibility.

Document Title:_____   Document #: _____   Expiration Date (if any): ___/___/___

I attest, under penalty of perjury, that to the best of my knowledge, this employee is eligible to work in the United States, and if the employee presented document(s), the document(s) I have examined appear to be genuine and to relate to the individual.

Signature of Employer or Authorized Representative	Date *(month/day/year)*

Form I-9 (Rev. 11-21-91)N Page 2

Exhibit 5   Form W-2: Wage and Tax Statement

a Control number	22222	Void ☐	For Official Use Only ▶ OMB No. 1545-0008		
b Employer identification number				**1** Wages, tips, other compensation $	**2** Federal income tax withheld $
c Employer's name, address, and ZIP code				**3** Social security wages $	**4** Social security tax withheld $
				5 Medicare wages and tips $	**6** Medicare tax withheld $
				7 Social security tips $	**8** Allocated tips $
d Employee's social security number				**9** Advance EIC payment $	**10** Dependent care benefits $
e Employee's first name and initial	Last name			**11** Nonqualified plans $	**12a** See instructions for box 12 $
				13 Statutory employee ☐ Retirement plan ☐ Third-party sick pay ☐	**12b** $
				14 Other	**12c** $
					12d $
f Employee's address and ZIP code					

15 State Employer's state ID number	16 State wages, tips, etc. $	17 State income tax $	18 Local wages, tips, etc. $	19 Local income tax $	20 Locality name
	$	$	$	$	

Form **W-2** Wage and Tax Statement   **2001**

Copy A For Social Security Administration—Send this entire page with Form W-3 to the Social Security Administration; photocopies are **not** acceptable.

Cat. No. 10134D

Department of the Treasury—Internal Revenue Service
For Privacy Act and Paperwork Reduction Act Notice, see separate instructions.

Do Not Cut, Fold, or Staple Forms on This Page — Do Not Cut, Fold, or Staple Forms on This Page

determining the overtime rate, where the two jobs involved different regular rates, the premium is calculated using a weighted average of the two rates. In some states, there is also a "seven day rule," where employees are paid time and one-half on the seventh consecutive day of work.

Payroll Journal Entries

There are two major journal entries involving payroll. These two separate and distinct entries are referred to as *the entry to record the payroll* and *the entry to record the payroll taxes.*

The Entry to Record Payroll

It may be useful to think of the payroll entry as a "check stub" entry; if we had only one employee and that employee's check stub were in front of us, we could use the stub's information to journalize the entry. The following items would be included in the payroll entry:

1. *Gross pay.* Gross pay is calculated by multiplying the hours the employee worked for the pay period by the hourly rate, including any overtime premium. In the case of salaried employees, for example, gross pay for a month would be $1/12$ of their annual salaries or earnings from lessons, clinics, etc.

2. *Federal income tax.* Exhibit 6 is an example of withholding tables employers refer to for this deduction. The withholding amounts for federal income tax vary depending on marital status and pay period.

3. *Social Security taxes.* Social Security taxes result from the **Federal Insurance Contributions Act (FICA)**. The current rate for FICA taxes is 7.65 percent. This rate is actually a combination of two rates: 6.2 percent on the first $76,200 of income (as of the year 2000), plus 1.45 percent on all income.

4. *State income tax.* States vary widely in the amount of state income tax assessed, ranging from zero percent in several states to North Dakota's rate of about 12 percent.

5. *Miscellaneous deductions.* Other deductions from an individual's pay might include local income tax, the employee's contribution to health care benefits, union dues taken by the employer and later remitted to the union, or a payroll deduction for items such as charitable contributions. All of these current liabilities are eventually remitted to the appropriate agencies. From the time they are deducted from employee wages until they are remitted to the agencies, they are considered current liabilities for the club.

6. *The amount of the employee's net pay.* Net pay is simply gross pay minus the various deductions. It is the amount the payroll check is written for.

Let us assume that for a given pay period a club had administrative salaries of $5,000. Let us also assume that the total federal income tax withheld for this pay period was $1,400, the state income tax withheld was $250, the FICA deduction was $383, and the health insurance deduction $150, making the net pay $2,817. The entry to record this transaction would be:

Administrative Salaries	$5,000	
Federal Income Tax Payable		$1,400
State Income Tax Payable		250
FICA		383
Health Insurance Payable		150
Salaries Payable		$2,817

This entry would be made on the date the payroll was computed. On the date the payroll was actually paid to the employees and the amount of net pay transferred into the payroll imprest fund, the journal entry would be:

Salaries Payable	$2,817	
Cash		$2,817

Exhibit 6 Publication 15: Income Tax Withholding from Gross Wages

(For Wages Paid in 2000)

Wage Bracket Percentage Method Table for Computing

Income Tax Withholding From Gross Wages

Biweekly Payroll Period

If the number of allowances is—	Single Persons				Married Persons			
	And gross wages are—		from gross wages [1]	Multiply result by—	And gross wages are—		from gross wages [1]	Multiply result by—
	Over	But not over			Over	But not over		
	A	B	C	D	A	B	C	D
0	$0.00	$1,071.00	subtract $102.00	15%	$0.00	$1,862.00	subtract $248.00	15%
	$1,071.00	$2,304.00	subtract $551.89	28%	$1,862.00	$3,885.00	subtract $997.36	28%
	$2,304.00	$5,162.00	subtract $721.45	31%	$3,885.00	$6,385.00	subtract $1,276.81	31%
	$5,162.00	$11,152.00	subtract $1,338.19	36%	$6,385.00	$11,265.00	subtract $1,986.28	36%
	$11,152.00	....	subtract $2,230.36	39.6%	$11,265.00	....	subtract $2,829.80	39.6%
1	$0.00	$1,178.69	subtract $209.69	15%	$0.00	$1,969.69	subtract $355.69	15%
	$1,178.69	$2,411.69	subtract $659.58	28%	$1,969.69	$3,992.69	subtract $1,105.05	28%
	$2,411.69	$5,269.69	subtract $829.14	31%	$3,992.69	$6,492.69	subtract $1,384.50	31%
	$5,269.69	$11,259.69	subtract $1,445.88	36%	$6,492.69	$11,372.69	subtract $2,093.97	36%
	$11,259.69	....	subtract $2,338.05	39.6%	$11,372.69	....	subtract $2,937.49	39.6%
2	$0.00	$1,286.38	subtract $317.38	15%	$0.00	$2,077.38	subtract $463.38	15%
	$1,286.38	$2,519.38	subtract $767.27	28%	$2,077.38	$4,100.38	subtract $1,212.74	28%
	$2,519.38	$5,377.38	subtract $936.83	31%	$4,100.38	$6,600.38	subtract $1,492.19	31%
	$5,377.38	$11,367.38	subtract $1,553.57	36%	$6,600.38	$11,480.38	subtract $2,201.66	36%
	$11,367.38	....	subtract $2,445.74	39.6%	$11,480.38	....	subtract $3,045.18	39.6%
3	$0.00	$1,394.07	subtract $425.07	15%	$0.00	$2,185.07	subtract $571.07	15%
	$1,394.07	$2,627.07	subtract $874.96	28%	$2,185.07	$4,208.07	subtract $1,320.43	28%
	$2,627.07	$5,485.07	subtract $1,044.52	31%	$4,208.07	$6,708.07	subtract $1,599.88	31%
	$5,485.07	$11,475.07	subtract $1,661.26	36%	$6,708.07	$11,588.07	subtract $2,309.35	36%
	$11,475.07	....	subtract $2,553.43	39.6%	$11,588.07	....	subtract $3,152.87	39.6%
4	$0.00	$1,501.76	subtract $532.76	15%	$0.00	$2,292.76	subtract $678.76	15%
	$1,501.76	$2,734.76	subtract $982.65	28%	$2,292.76	$4,315.76	subtract $1,428.12	28%
	$2,734.76	$5,592.76	subtract $1,152.21	31%	$4,315.76	$6,815.76	subtract $1,707.57	31%
	$5,592.76	$11,582.76	subtract $1,768.95	36%	$6,815.76	$11,695.76	subtract $2,417.04	36%
	$11,582.76	....	subtract $2,661.12	39.6%	$11,695.76	....	subtract $3,260.56	39.6%
5	$0.00	$1,609.45	subtract $640.45	15%	$0.00	$2,400.45	subtract $786.45	15%
	$1,609.45	$2,842.45	subtract $1,090.34	28%	$2,400.45	$4,423.45	subtract $1,535.81	28%
	$2,842.45	$5,700.45	subtract $1,259.90	31%	$4,423.45	$6,923.45	subtract $1,815.26	31%
	$5,700.45	$11,690.45	subtract $1,876.64	36%	$6,923.45	$11,803.45	subtract $2,524.73	36%
	$11,690.45	....	subtract $2,768.81	39.6%	$11,803.45	....	subtract $3,368.25	39.6%
6	$0.00	$1,717.14	subtract $748.14	15%	$0.00	$2,508.14	subtract $894.14	15%
	$1,717.14	$2,950.14	subtract $1,198.03	28%	$2,508.14	$4,531.14	subtract $1,643.50	28%
	$2,950.14	$5,808.14	subtract $1,367.59	31%	$4,531.14	$7,031.14	subtract $1,922.95	31%
	$5,808.14	$11,798.14	subtract $1,984.33	36%	$7,031.14	$11,911.14	subtract $2,632.42	36%
	$11,798.14	....	subtract $2,876.50	39.6%	$11,911.14	....	subtract $3,475.94	39.6%
7	$0.00	$1,824.83	subtract $855.83	15%	$0.00	$2,615.83	subtract $1,001.83	15%
	$1,824.83	$3,057.83	subtract $1,305.72	28%	$2,615.83	$4,638.83	subtract $1,751.19	28%
	$3,057.83	$5,915.83	subtract $1,475.28	31%	$4,638.83	$7,138.83	subtract $2,030.64	31%
	$5,915.83	$11,905.83	subtract $2,092.02	36%	$7,138.83	$12,018.83	subtract $2,740.11	36%
	$11,905.83	....	subtract $2,984.19	39.6%	$12,018.83	....	subtract $3,583.63	39.6%
8	$0.00	$1,932.52	subtract $963.52	15%	$0.00	$2,723.52	subtract $1,109.52	15%
	$1,932.52	$3,165.52	subtract $1,413.41	28%	$2,723.52	$4,746.52	subtract $1,858.88	28%
	$3,165.52	$6,023.52	subtract $1,582.97	31%	$4,746.52	$7,246.52	subtract $2,138.33	31%
	$6,023.52	$12,013.52	subtract $2,199.71	36%	$7,246.52	$12,126.52	subtract $2,847.80	36%
	$12,013.52	....	subtract $3,091.88	39.6%	$12,126.52	....	subtract $3,691.32	39.6%
9 [2]	$0.00	$2,040.21	subtract $1,071.21	15%	$0.00	$2,831.21	subtract $1,217.21	15%
	$2,040.21	$3,273.21	subtract $1,521.10	28%	$2,831.21	$4,854.21	subtract $1,966.57	28%
	$3,273.21	$6,131.21	subtract $1,690.66	31%	$4,854.21	$7,354.21	subtract $2,246.02	31%
	$6,131.21	$12,121.21	subtract $2,307.40	36%	$7,354.21	$12,234.21	subtract $2,955.49	36%
	$12,121.21	....	subtract $3,199.57	39.6%	$12,234.21	....	subtract $3,799.01	39.6%

Instructions

A. For each employee, use the appropriate payroll period table and marital status section, and select the subsection showing the number of allowances claimed.

B. Read across the selected subsection and locate the bracket applicable to the employee's gross wages in columns A and B.

C. Subtract the amount shown in column C from the employee's gross wages.

D. Multiply the result by the withholding percentage rate shown in column D to obtain the amount of tax to be withheld.

[1] If the gross wages are less than the amount to be subtracted, the withholding is zero.

[2] You can expand these tables for additional allowances. To do this, increase the amounts in this subsection by $107.69 for each additional allowance claimed.

The Entry to Record Payroll Taxes

The second major entry involving payroll is the one recording the employer's payroll taxes. **Payroll taxes** represent additional taxes paid by the employer based on employee wages. The three major elements of payroll taxes are the employer's FICA tax contribution and its contributions under the **Federal Unemployment Tax Act (FUTA)** and the **State Unemployment Tax Act (SUTA)**.

We have already discussed FICA taxes in relation to the first payroll entry. FICA also states that the employer must match the dollar amount of the credit to FICA Tax Payable in the first journal entry (that is, the entry to record the payroll will be the same dollar amount in this second journal entry). Employers are required to report the amounts of FICA taxes for employees on Federal Form 941, which is filed quarterly. The first page of Federal Form 941 is shown in Exhibit 7. Employers are now able to report FICA taxes electronically by touch-tone phone with Form 941 Telefile.

The Federal Unemployment Tax Act (FUTA) establishes a tax that pays unemployment wages to people who have lost their jobs. This fund is financed through taxes levied on employer payrolls. The 2000 federal unemployment tax is 6.2 percent on employee's wages up to $7,000. This tax is no longer levied on an employee's wages after the first $7,000.

States must contribute dollars into the federal unemployment fund. To do so, they levy their own state unemployment tax rates. These rates vary by state, but whatever that rate is, employers are allowed to use the state tax rate as a credit against the federal rate. For example, assume that a state levied a 5.4 percent state unemployment rate while the federal rate was 6.2 percent. This would result in a federal unemployment tax rate of 0.8 percent (that is, 6.2 percent minus 5.4 percent).

With the information given in the earlier example for the payroll of the club and using a federal unemployment rate of 6.2 percent and a state rate of 5.4 percent, the club would make the following journal entry (assuming no employee had earned $7,000 yet) to record its payroll taxes:

Payroll Tax Expense	$693	
FICA Tax Payable		$383
Federal Unemployment Tax Payable		
($5,000 × 0.8%)		40
State Unemployment Tax Payable		
($5,000 × 5.4%)		270

The amount of Payroll Tax Expense is simply the total of the three credits to the liability accounts. (The annual unemployment tax return for reporting federal taxes is Form 940, shown in Exhibit 8.)

Once again, let us point out that these are two separate and distinct entries. One records the payroll and the other records the payroll tax expense. The only connection between the two entries is the FICA Tax Payable credit amount, which should be the same in both journal entries. Note the cost of employees to the

Exhibit 7 Form 941: Employer's Quarterly Federal Tax Return

Form **941** (Rev. October 2000) Department of the Treasury Internal Revenue Service	**Employer's Quarterly Federal Tax Return** ▶ See separate instructions for information on completing this return. Please type or print.		

Enter state code for state in which deposits were made ONLY if different from state in address to the right ▶ (see page 2 of instructions).

Name (as distinguished from trade name)	Date quarter ended
Trade name, if any	Employer identification number
Address (number and street)	City, state, and ZIP code

OMB No. 1545-0029

T	
FF	
FD	
FP	
I	
T	

If address is different from prior return, check here ▶

IRS Use

1 1 1 1 1 1 1 1 1   2   3 3 3 3 3 3 3 3   4 4 4   5 5 5

6   7   8 8 8 8 8 8 8 8   9 9 9 9 9   10 10 10 10 10 10 10 10 10 10

If you do not have to file returns in the future, check here ▶ ☐ and enter date final wages paid ▶

If you are a seasonal employer, see **Seasonal employers** on page 1 of the instructions and check here ▶ ☐

1	Number of employees in the pay period that includes March 12th . ▶	**1**		
2	Total wages and tips, plus other compensation		**2**	
3	Total income tax withheld from wages, tips, and sick pay		**3**	
4	Adjustment of withheld income tax for preceding quarters of calendar year		**4**	
5	Adjusted total of income tax withheld (line 3 as adjusted by line 4—see instructions) . .		**5**	
6	Taxable social security wages . . . . . **6a** × 12.4% (.124) =	**6b**		
	Taxable social security tips . . . . . . **6c** × 12.4% (.124) =	**6d**		
7	Taxable Medicare wages and tips . . . **7a** × 2.9% (.029) =	**7b**		
8	Total social security and Medicare taxes (add lines 6b, 6d, and 7b). Check here if wages are not subject to social security and/or Medicare tax . . . . ▶ ☐		**8**	
9	Adjustment of social security and Medicare taxes (see instructions for required explanation) Sick Pay $ _____ ± Fractions of Cents $ _____ ± Other $ _____ =		**9**	
10	Adjusted total of social security and Medicare taxes (line 8 as adjusted by line 9—see instructions)		**10**	
11	**Total taxes** (add lines 5 and 10)		**11**	
12	Advance earned income credit (EIC) payments made to employees		**12**	
13	Net taxes (subtract line 12 from line 11). **If $1,000 or more, this must equal line 17, column (d) below (or line D of Schedule B (Form 941))**		**13**	
14	Total deposits for quarter, including overpayment applied from a prior quarter		**14**	
15	**Balance due** (subtract line 14 from line 13). See instructions		**15**	
16	**Overpayment.** If line 14 is more than line 13, enter excess here ▶ $ _____ and check if to be: ☐ Applied to next return **OR** ☐ Refunded.			

• **All filers:** If line 13 is less than $1,000, you need not complete line 17 or Schedule B (Form 941).

• **Semiweekly schedule depositors:** Complete Schedule B (Form 941) and check here . . . . ▶ ☐

• **Monthly schedule depositors:** Complete line 17, columns (a) through (d), and check here. . . . . ▶ ☐

17	**Monthly Summary of Federal Tax Liability.** Do not complete if you were a semiweekly schedule depositor.			
	(a) First month liability	**(b)** Second month liability	**(c)** Third month liability	**(d)** Total liability for quarter

Sign Here | Under penalties of perjury, I declare that I have examined this return, including accompanying schedules and statements, and to the best of my knowledge and belief, it is true, correct, and complete.

Signature ▶   Print Your Name and Title ▶   Date ▶

For Privacy Act and Paperwork Reduction Act Notice, see back of Payment Voucher.   Cat. No. 17001Z   Form **941** (Rev. 10-2000)

Exhibit 8   Form 940: Employer's Annual Federal Unemployment Tax Return

Form **940**	**Employer's Annual Federal Unemployment (FUTA) Tax Return**	OMB No. 1545-0028
Department of the Treasury Internal Revenue Service (99)	► See separate Instructions for Form 940 for information on completing this form.	2000

		T	
⌐ Name (as distinguished from trade name)	Calendar year ⌐	FF	
		FD	
Trade name, if any		FP	
		I	
Address and ZIP code	Employer identification number	T	

A Are you required to pay unemployment contributions to only one state? (If "No," skip questions B and C.) ☐ Yes ☐ No

B Did you pay all state unemployment contributions by January 31, 2001? ((1) If you deposited your total FUTA tax when due, check "Yes" if you paid all state unemployment contributions by February 12, 2001. (2) If a 0% experience rate is granted, check "Yes." (3) If "No," skip question C.) . . . . ☐ Yes ☐ No

C Were all wages that were taxable for FUTA tax also taxable for your state's unemployment tax? . . . . . ☐ Yes ☐ No

If you answered "No" to any of these questions, you must file Form 940. If you answered "Yes" to all the questions, you may file Form 940-EZ, which is a simplified version of Form 940. (Successor employers see **Special credit for successor employers** on page 3 of the instructions.) You can get Form 940-EZ by calling 1-800-TAX-FORM (1-800-829-3676) or from the IRS Web Site at **www.irs.gov.**

If you will not have to file returns in the future, check here (see **Who Must File** in separate instructions), **and** complete and sign the return . . . . ► ☐

If this is an Amended Return, check here. . . . . ► ☐

Part I   Computation of Taxable Wages

1	Total payments (including payments shown on lines 2 and 3) during the calendar year for services of employees	**1**	
2	Exempt payments. (Explain all exempt payments, attaching additional sheets if necessary.) ►	**2**	
3	Payments of more than $7,000 for services. Enter only amounts over the first $7,000 paid to each employee. (See separate instructions.) Do not include any exempt payments from line 2. The $7,000 amount is the Federal wage base. Your state wage base may be different. **Do not use your state wage limitation.**	**3**	
4	Total exempt payments (add lines 2 and 3)	**4**	
5	**Total taxable wages** (subtract line 4 from line 1) . . . . ►	**5**	

Be sure to complete both sides of this form, and sign in the space provided on the back.

For Privacy Act and Paperwork Reduction Act Notice, see separate instructions.   Cat. No. 11234O   Form **940** (2000)

- DETACH HERE -

Form **940-V**	**Form 940 Payment Voucher**	OMB No. 1545-0028
Department of the Treasury Internal Revenue Service	Use this voucher only when making a payment with your return.	2000

Complete boxes 1, 2, 3, and 4. Do not send cash, and do not staple your payment to this voucher. Make your check or money order payable to the **"United States Treasury".** Be sure to enter your employer identification number, "Form 940", and "2000" on your payment.

1 Enter the first four letters of your last name (business name if partnership or corporation).	2 Enter your employer identification number.	3 Enter the amount of your payment.
		$.

Instructions for Box 1	4 Enter your business name (individual name for sole proprietors)
—Individuals (sole proprietors, trusts, and estates)— Enter the first four letters of your last name.	Enter your address
—Corporations and partnerships—Enter the first four characters of your business name (omit "The" if followed by more than one word).	Enter your city, state, and ZIP code

employer; that is, in this example, it costs the employer the gross wages of $5,000 plus the payroll taxes of $693. This represents a total cost to the employer of $5,693.

Employees often do not realize what the costs of their employment actually are to the employer. In this case, there is a 14 percent difference between the gross wages of the employees and the total payroll cost to the employer (and this does not include the cost of any additional benefits the employer provides to its employees). Since fringe benefits and payroll taxes can be costly, clubs may hire independent contractors rather than employees to perform certain services—such as accounting, data processing, computer networking—and save on payroll taxes. However, the IRS rules for determination of employee status versus independent contractor status are very strict and detailed, and they are beyond the scope of this chapter.

Reporting Tips

Certain employees of clubs, such as table servers, commonly receive tips from the customers. There are both federal and state regulations on tip reporting, and the calculation of tip reporting can be complex. For additional information, see IRS Publication 531, "Reporting Tip Income."

Certain provisions of state and federal laws allow employers to apply a tip credit against the minimum wage of tipped employees. In this way, the employer can reduce the amount of gross wages paid to those employees. Assume, for example, that the minimum wage is $5.15 per hour and that the state allows a 40 percent maximum tip credit. Under these conditions, the employer could apply a credit of $2.06 (40 percent of $5.15) toward the hourly wage of tipped employees as long as the actual tips received by the employees were not less than the maximum allowable tip credit. In this case, the employer would comply with the law by paying employees $3.09 per hour ($5.15 − $2.06).

The next illustration shows how the gross wages payable to an employee are calculated when the actual tips received by the employees are greater than the maximum tip credit. Assume that an employee who worked 40 hours reports tips of $90 and is paid a minimum wage of $5.15 per hour. Also, assume that the employer applies a maximum tip credit of $2.06. The gross wages payable to this employee would be calculated as follows:

Gross wages: 40 hours at $5.15/hour		$206.00
Less lower of:		
Maximum FLSA tip credit (40 hours at $2.06)	$82.40	
Actual tips received	90.00	
Allowable tip credit		− 82.40
Gross wages payable by employer		$123.60

If the actual tips received by the employee were less than the maximum allowed tip credit, the *tips received* would be subtracted from the gross wages of $206 to determine the actual gross wages payable by the employer. It is important to note that the gross taxable earnings of a tipped employee include both the gross wages payable to the employer and the actual tips received by the employee.

Questions occasionally arise regarding overtime pay for tipped employees. Tipped employees must earn time and one-half for overtime hours worked. Using the $5.15 minimum wage and 40 percent ($2.06) tip credit mentioned above, an employee earning minimum wage would have a cash wage of $3.09. The time and one-half cash wage rate would *not* be $3.09 × 1.5 ($4.63) for overtime hours. The overtime hourly rate would equal $5.15 × 1.5, or $7.73. The overtime cash wage would equal this amount less the tip credit, or $7.73 − $2.06, or $5.67.

The Tax Equity and Fiscal Responsibility Act of 1982 (TEFRA) established regulations that govern tip reporting requirements for food and beverage operations. The regulations state that the tips reported by hospitality establishments should be at least eight percent of the qualified gross receipts of the business. Receipts from banquets, for which gratuities and service charges are often charged automatically, do not qualify. If the tips reported do not meet this eight percent requirement, the deficiency is called a *tip shortfall*. When there is a shortfall, the employer must provide each directly tipped employee with an information sheet showing the tips reported by the employee and the tips that should have been reported.

More information on tip reporting can be obtained from the Internal Revenue Service. The most useful publication and forms are Publication 531: "Reporting Tip Income." Form 8027: "Employer's Annual Information Return of Tip Income and Allocated Tips," and Form 8846: "Credit for Employers Social Security and Medicare Taxes Paid on Certain Employee Tips." In addition, the National Restaurant Association has a useful publication called "Tips on Tips—A Guide for Employers of Tipped Workers." The IRS also has the helpful Publication 1872: "Tips on Tips— A Guide to Tip Income Reporting."

Finally, many clubs have instituted nontipping policies and automatically add a set percentage of food and beverage sales chits as a gratuity. These gratuities are considered wages and should be added to the payroll and taxed accordingly if paid out to the service employees.

Determining Employee Status

A common problem in payroll accounting is the determination as to whether a particular club worker is an employee or a self-employed individual for income tax reporting purposes.

The IRS and the courts have applied several tests to determine a particular worker's status. The two major tests are the "common law employee test" and the "20 factor test" that was adopted by the IRS in 1987.

The "common law employee test" employs U.S. Treasury Regulation 31.3401(c)-1(b)-(c) and states that, generally, the relationship of employer and employee exists when the person for whom services are performed has the right to control and direct the individual who performs the services, not only as to the result to be accomplished by the work but also as to the details and means by which that result is accomplished. That is, an employee is subject to the will and control of the employer not only as to *what* should be done but *how* it should be done. It is not necessary that employers actually direct or control the manner in which the services are performed; it is sufficient if they have the right to do so.

The right to discharge is also an important factor indicating that the person possessing that right is an employer. Other factors characteristic of an employer, but not necessarily present in every case, are the furnishing of tools and the furnishing of a place to work to the individual who performs the services. In general, if an individual is subject to the control or direction of another merely as to the result to be accomplished by the work and not as to the means and methods for accomplishing the result, he or she is not an employee. Generally, physicians, lawyers, dentists, veterinarians, contractors, subcontractors, public stenographers, auctioneers, consultants, and others who follow an independent trade, business, or profession in which they offer their services to the public are not employees.

Since the determination of a worker's correct reporting status under the "common law employee test" can be difficult, the IRS, in Revenue Ruling 87-41 (1987), developed a 20 factor list to help.

1. *Instructions.* A person who is required to comply with instructions about when, where, and how to work is ordinarily an employee.

2. *Training.* Training of a person by an experienced employee or by other means is a factor of control and indicates that the worker is an employee.

3. *Integration.* Integration of a person's services into the business operations generally shows that the person is subject to direction and control and accordingly is an employee.

4. *Services rendered personally.* If the services must be rendered personally by the individual employed, it suggests an employer-employee relationship. Self-employed status is indicated when an individual has the right to hire a substitute without the employer's knowledge.

5. *Hiring, supervising, and paying assistants.* Hiring, supervising, and payment of assistants by the employer generally indicates that all workers on the job are employees. Self-employed persons generally hire, supervise, and pay their own assistants.

6. *Continuing relationship.* The existence of a continuing relationship between an individual and the organization for whom the individual performs services is a factor tending to indicate the existence of an employer-employee relationship.

7. *Set hours of work.* The establishment of set hours of work by the employer is a factor indicating control and accordingly the existence of an employer-employee relationship. Self-employed persons are "masters of their own time."

8. *Full time required.* If the worker must devote full time to the business of the employer, he or she ordinarily will be an employee. A self-employed person on the other hand may choose for whom and when to work.

9. *Doing work on the employer's premises.* Doing the work on the employer's premises may indicate that the worker is an employee, especially if the work could be done elsewhere.

10. *Order or sequence of work.* If a worker must perform services in an order or sequence set by the organization for whom he or she performs services, this indicates that the worker is an employee.

11. *Oral or written reports.* A requirement that workers submit regular oral or written reports to the employer is indicative of an employer-employee relationship.

12. *Payment by hour, week, month.* An employee usually is paid by the hour, week, or month, whereas a self-employed person usually is paid by the job on a lump sum basis (although the lump sum may be paid in intervals in some cases).

13. *Payment of business expenses.* Payment by the employer of the worker's business or travel expenses suggests that the worker is an employee. Self-employed persons usually are paid on a job basis and take care of their own business and travel expenses.

14. *Furnishing of tools and materials.* The furnishing of tools and materials by the employer indicates an employer-employee relationship. Self-employed persons ordinarily provide their own tools and materials.

15. *Investment in facilities.* The furnishing of all necessary facilities (equipment and premises) by the employer suggests that the worker is an employee.

16. *Realization of profit or loss.* Workers who are in a position to realize a profit or suffer a loss as a result of their services generally are self-employed, while employees ordinarily are not in such a position.

17. *Exclusive work.* A person who works for a number of persons or organizations at the same time is usually self-employed.

18. *Offering services to the general public.* Workers who make their services available to the general public are usually self-employed. Individuals ordinarily hold their services out to the public by having their own offices and assistants, placing a sign in front of their office, holding a business license, and by advertising in newspapers and telephone directories.

19. *Right to discharge.* The right to discharge is an important factor in indicating that the person possessing the right is an employer. Self-employed persons ordinarily cannot be fired as long as they produce results that measure up to their contract specifications.

20. *Right to terminate.* An employee ordinarily has the right to end the relationship with the employer at any time he or she wishes without incurring liability. A self-employed person usually agrees to complete a specific job and is responsible for its satisfactory completion or is legally obligated to make good for failure to complete the job.

If a club is having difficulty determining employees' status for a given class of workers, management should complete and submit IRS Form SS-8, and the IRS will determine employees' work status.

Endnotes

1. All IRS forms and publications discussed in this chapter may be downloaded free of charge from the Internal Revenue Service's Web site at http://www.irs.gov/forms_pubs/index.html.

Key Terms

employee's earnings record—An individual record kept for each employee during the calendar year that shows gross wages earned and amounts withheld and deducted. Used at the end of the year to prepare IRS Form W-2.

Federal Insurance Contributions Act (FICA)—An act that levies employment taxes on employers and employees as part of the federal Social Security program. Employers must deduct FICA taxes from employees' wages.

Federal Unemployment Tax Act (FUTA)—A federal law imposing a payroll tax on employers for the purpose of funding national and state unemployment programs.

imprest payroll account—A payroll account for which a predetermined, fixed amount of funds are maintained or replenished as part of typical control procedures.

master payroll file—A payroll file containing employee information, including employee names, addresses, Social Security numbers, wage rates, and payroll deduction information.

payroll journal—A journal containing a record of each payroll check issued, along with the corresponding gross pay and various deductions for taxes, health care, and so on.

payroll taxes—Additional taxes paid by the employer, which are based on employee wages. The three major payroll taxes are a result of the Federal Insurance Contribution Act (FICA), the Federal Unemployment Tax Act (FUTA), and the State Unemployment Tax Act (SUTA).

State Unemployment Tax Act (SUTA)—An unemployment tax rate levied by individual states. The rate varies by state. However, employers may use the state tax rate as a credit against the federal rate.

Review Questions

1. What six major control features can a club use to safeguard payroll?
2. What basic items should be included in a payroll master file?
3. What information is provided in a payroll journal?

4. What information is provided by an employee earnings record?

5. What are the differences between the entry to record the payroll and the entry to record the payroll taxes?

6. What does the acronym *FICA* stand for?

7. Is a FICA tax an employer tax or an employee tax?

8. What do FUTA and SUTA represent?

9. Are FUTA and SUTA taxes paid by the employer, the employee, or both?

10. What is usually the most difficult timekeeping area for a club to control? What is the recommended way to deal with this area?

 **Problems** —————————————————————————————————

Problem 1

You have just assumed the position of general manager at the Lakeside Country Club. The club currently employs the following procedures to control payroll:

    a. At the end of each shift, the club's dining room employees write down their hours on a blank piece of paper and leave it on the desk of the food and beverage manager.

    b. All club employees are paid by checks drawn on the general bank account of the club.

    c. All individual paychecks are kept in the respective departments until they are claimed by employees.

    d. The current human resources manager of the club carefully reviews all prospective employees, authorizes their hiring, prepares the payroll, and distributes the checks.

    e. The golf course maintenance workers report for work at the maintenance building located apart from the clubhouse, where other employees report for work. Every Wednesday, they turn in their hours directly to the payroll clerk.

Required:

Draft a memo suggesting changes that the operation ought to make to better control payroll for the club.

Problem 2

The payroll journal for the Elite Athletic Club on the August 31 payday shows the following:

Employee	Gross Wages	Federal Income Tax	FICA	State Income Tax	Health Insurance	Union Dues	Net Pay
Shanahan	$800	$224	$50	$38	$18	$20	?
Koslov	750	210	46	36	16	20	?
Yzerman	720	200	44	34	0	0	?
Federov	820	232	52	40	24	24	?

Assume that Elite's FUTA rate is 6.2 percent and that its SUTA rate is 4.8 percent. Also, assume that all wages are subject to federal and state unemployment taxes and that all wages are subject to FICA taxes. Round to the nearest dollar.

Required:

Calculate the following for the August 31 payroll:

    a. The total gross payroll for this pay period.

    b. The total net payroll for this pay period.

    c. The club's total liability for FICA taxes for the pay period.

    d. The club's liability for FUTA taxes for the pay period.

    e. The club's liability for SUTA taxes for the pay period.

Problem 3

The board of the Waldorf Club has asked you, the general manager, to do an analysis of the cost of the assistant manager, Mr. Trump, to the club. The relevant costs for this analysis is listed below:

Trump's Gross Salary	$64,000
FICA Tax Rate	7.65% on earnings up to $72,600
SUTA	5.20% on earnings up to $7,000
FUTA	6.2% on earnings up to $7,000
Federal Income Tax Rate	28% on all earnings
State Income Tax Rate	5.4% on all earnings

Required:

    a. Calculate the club's total annual cost of employing Trump.

    b. Compare the above cost to the annual take-home pay of Trump.

Chapter 13 Outline

Competencies

1. Describe typical software applications used by clubs: word processing software, spreadsheet software, and database management software. (pp. 285–291)

2. Describe accounting applications currently used in clubs, and describe transaction technologies that may become commonplace in clubs in the near future. (pp. 291–295)

3. Describe the Internet and the World Wide Web, and explain how clubs are using the Web. (pp. 295–302)

13

Club Technology Applications

DURING THE PAST DECADE, nothing has enhanced the professionalism or increased the productivity of the club industry more than computer technology. Computer technology has changed the way club managers plan, coordinate, evaluate, and control operations. With improved operational efficiency, clubs are better able to meet their members' needs. Generic software, data mining, accounting applications, transaction processing, the Internet, and Web site applications are important components of a club's technology strategy that will be discussed in this chapter.

Generic Software Applications for Clubs

Word processing, electronic spreadsheets, database management, and Internet software are just some of the types of generic application software programs available to clubs today. These applications may be bundled and marketed together as an integrated software package (that is, an application suite). There are many application software products on the market, some more sophisticated than others. Software products often vary in relation to the specific commands that users must master in order to operate the software programs. Instead of discussing the details of particular products offered by specific manufacturers, in the following sections we will present a general explanation of the features of generic software programs.

Word Processing Software

Word processing software is a valuable office tool that can increase the productivity of club personnel engaged in business-writing tasks. Revisions to original documents can be made quickly and efficiently, and typographical and grammatical errors can be automatically corrected while the user inputs text. Advances in technology, such as scanners (also known as optical character recognition [OCR] devices), are also increasing the efficiency of word processing. OCR devices automate the time-consuming input stage of word processing. These devices are able to scan typed copy and convert it into an electronic form that can be entered into the word processing system.

Powerful, sophisticated word processing software packages give clubs great flexibility in the layout and design of letters, memos, reports, and business forms.

This chapter was written and contributed by Michael L. Kasavana, NAMA Professor in Hospitality Business, *The* School of Hospitality Business, Michigan State University, East Lansing, Michigan.

The options available through these software packages often eliminate the need for clubs to contract the services of local printing companies. Direct mail advertising, the club's newsletter, staff manuals, menus, and club letterhead are examples of the kind of work that can be produced in-house if a club has a good word processing program and a quality printer. This capability saves time and money and increases management's control over project scheduling and completion.

Many word processing software packages permit a user to view more than one document at a time on the computer's display screen. Special keystroke commands or menu bar options can split the screen into several sections. Each window can contain text or graphic material from a separate document. Space limitations on the user's screen determine the number of windows the user can effectively work with at any given time. However, just two or three windows can permit a user to efficiently perform a variety of editing tasks. For example, text or graphic material from one document on the screen can be copied and inserted into a second document that appears on the same screen. Having both documents on the screen at the same time enables the user to verify the success of the transfer immediately. This technique is often referred to as "copy and drag."

Sophisticated word processing software enables a user to search through an entire document and quickly find a word, phrase, or sentence. A few simple keystrokes or menu bar options automatically move the cursor through the document, stopping only at each occurrence of the sought-after word or phrase. When the search function is coupled with a "replace" function, the user can replace a word or phrase with another word or phrase. This can be an enormous time-saver. Changes that would once have entailed retyping the entire document can be made within seconds.

Spreadsheet Software

With an automated accounting system, figures are entered only once into an accounting record. Programs that prepare mathematically correct journals, ledgers, and financial statements can be constructed based upon these captured amounts. The speed with which electronic **spreadsheet software** can generate information can greatly help club managers make decisions. With electronic spreadsheet software, a manager can have a variety of information and reports in a short amount of time. Most electronic spreadsheet software packages have graphics capability and are able to generate graphs (bar charts, line graphs, pie charts, and so forth) from spreadsheets. This can be a valuable management tool for communicating information to the club's board and other club members. Once a spreadsheet has been saved, it can be retrieved and revised as necessary.

Since spreadsheet software packages normally provide many more columns than there are letters in the alphabet, the alphabet is repeated in a number of series (for example, from A through Z, then from AA through AZ, and so on) until all the columns are identified. Along the vertical border on the left side of the spreadsheet are numbers that are used to identify the rows within the spreadsheet. The rows and columns intersect to form cells. The coordinates of a cell—the particular column letter and row number—make up what is typically called the "cell address." Before the user inputs data, the cells of an electronic spreadsheet are empty.

Spreadsheet cells can hold alpha data, such as labels to identify the contents of columns and rows; numeric data, such as dollar amounts; and formulas that instruct the computer to carry out specific calculations, such as adding all the numbers in a certain range of cells. A "cell range" is a group of adjacent cells.

When textual information is entered into a cell, the text is referred to as a "label." Labels are used as column heads and row titles to organize and identify numeric values that are eventually entered into other cells. Since entered formulas become part of the spreadsheet, amounts within a cell or range of cells can be changed and the formulas will immediately recalculate a new total. This recalculation feature of electronic spreadsheet software enables users to update spreadsheet data and obtain the results almost instantly. It also offers club managers opportunities to explore various scenarios (that is, "what if" possibilities). For example, a club manager might analyze operational costs and revenues under different circumstances to project an appropriate club member assessment.

Advanced electronic spreadsheet programs enable the user to take advantage of online assistance, linked spreadsheets, macro commands, and the integration of spreadsheets with other software applications.

Database Management Software

There are numerous examples of database management software programs used within the club industry. These programs are used in relation to personnel file management, payroll processing, marketing research, general ledger accounting, tax reporting, direct mailings, sales reporting, and many other areas.

Simply stated, **database management software** allows club managers to catalog and store information about the club for future use. A "database" is a collection of related facts and figures designed to serve a specific purpose. There are many non-computerized forms and styles of databases in common use. For example, a personal checkbook is a database; it collects facts and figures that are designed to monitor personal finances. Other common databases include address books, telephone books, and dictionaries. The design and organization of these everyday databases are essential to users. The data within an address book, telephone book, and dictionary are sorted alphabetically so that users can quickly access the particular data they need. The checks in a personal checkbook are numbered sequentially. If an individual keeps to this numbered sequence when issuing checks, the returned canceled checks can be stored in the same numbered sequence, enabling the person to easily retrieve any particular check.

A database management system resembles a filing cabinet in function. File cabinets have separate file drawers. Each file drawer contains separate file folders. The folders within each drawer contain similar records of related information. Each record within a folder contains specific facts and/or figures. In the language of database management software, the file cabinet is called the database, the drawers of the cabinet are called database files, the folders within the drawers are called database records, and the detailed facts and/or figures in the records are stored in database fields.

For example, a club might set up an inventory database for inventory control. Assume that this database is made up of a single file. The file would contain one record for each inventory item, and each record would contain a number of fields, within which would be stored information such as the item's name, number, cost, quantity on hand, re-order point, and so on. Users of the computer system can access this database to perform any number of desired functions, such as:

- Generate inventory checklists to assist with taking physical inventory

- Perform variance analyses on the differences between the actual quantities of inventory items on hand versus the quantities listed in inventory

- Calculate the monetary value of items in inventory

Database management programs control the structure and organization of databases as well as the means by which data is handled within a computer system. These programs limit the number of times that data must be handled and ensure that all users accessing the database are working with the same information. In addition, these programs enable users to create, access, and merge data files; to add, select, and delete data; and to index, sort, and search data files for information that is eventually printed as reports for use by management.

Consider the organization of a master payroll file. The file would contain a record for each employee. Each record would be made up of fields identified by labels such as employee number, employee name, address, pay rate, withholdings, deductions, and so on. One of these fields would serve as the primary key field, which could be used to search the data file for a particular record. Since the primary key field must contain unique information, the employee-number field would function best as the key field of the master payroll file. Two employees may, by chance, have the same name, but when a club assigns employee numbers on a sequential basis, it guarantees that a particular number in the sequence identifies one particular employee.

The database of a club may be organized into many data files (such as personnel files, financial data files, member history files, and so forth). These files may contain dozens of records and hundreds of fields containing thousands of pieces of data. Database management programs structure the relationships among files, records, and fields in a way that ensures rapid access to information. However, not all database management programs structure a database in the same way.

An advantage of database management programs is their ability to support a query language. Inputting a query may necessitate the following keystrokes or tool bar selections:

- Entering a command, such as "Locate"

- Defining the scope of the command (for example, "Member Receivables")

- Specifying command conditions (for example, "Overdue 90 days")

Database management commands are usually entered as simple words, such as DISPLAY, SUM, COUNT, LOCATE, LIST, and so on. Defining the scope of the command identifies which areas of the database will be affected by the command. Specifying command conditions stipulates the circumstances under which the command will operate. In addition, output specifications control the generation and formatting of reports and additional database files. Since data stored in a database is independent of its application, database management programs are able to separate related information and generate a variety of reports.

The real strength of a database management software package may lie in its ability to perform multiple searches across a broad spectrum of field categories. For example, consider the advantages of a multiple-search routine for tracking member attendance at club social functions during the past three months. The first search procedure might index the database file in terms of a primary key field, which is the broadest field category involved in the search. In our example, the primary key would be the membership database. Subsequent searches focus on secondary keys, which order and limit the primary key field. In our example, the number of visits to the club in the past three months would be included. Using the multiple-search feature of a database management program can provide rapid results. Multiple-search routines can be extremely useful when users work with large and complex databases. Consider how a multiple-search routine can be used by a club's dining room manager to find a substitute server who is available on Tuesday evenings between 4 and 7 P.M. Initially, a personnel database file would be searched for all persons qualified as food servers. Subsequent search passes through the file would result in a selective deletion of names whose work-availability schedules fail to coincide with the day and time criteria. Remaining records would be of those employees who satisfy the multiple-search criteria.

Breakthroughs in Database Management. Historically, clubs have captured and stored member transactional and activity data in ways that made it difficult to access the data, evaluate it, and apply it to management decision-making. Recent innovative technology—involving centralized data storage (data warehousing) that assists effective data categorization (data marting) and analysis (data mining)—has become available to the club industry. Data mining software is critical to such technology. Data mining software is designed to identify relationships, patterns, and trends within a large data set. Due to the nature of its functionality, this software is often referred to as "siftware." Siftware is intended to turn data into information and information into insight. Together, data warehousing and data mining can re-energize a club's information system.

Data warehouses. A **data warehouse** is a large collection of data that can be used to support management decision-making. It is the combination of many different databases throughout a club. Development of a data warehouse includes the development of software to extract data from operating club systems plus the installation of a warehouse database system that provides club managers with flexible access to the data.

A data warehouse can serve as the central focal point of a club's information system and provide reports or answers unavailable through traditional database query methods. A data warehouse is created to serve as a facility for integrating data from a diverse set of internal (operational) and external (environmental) applications. A data warehouse also possesses a greater capacity to organize, store, and process large amounts of data than typical club computer systems. Internal data entering a data warehouse is transformed from raw application data (such as financial transactions) into meaningful characteristics that are subject-specific (for example, individual-member activity or buying patterns). External data is captured and classified so that meaningful comparisons to internal activities can be conducted.

Normally, four levels of data are maintained in a data warehouse: (a) historical data, (b) current data, (c) lightly summarized data, and (d) highly summarized data. Historical data tends to be accessed infrequently and therefore may even be placed on a different storage medium (disk or tape) than current data. Current data reflects the most recent occurrences of events, activities, and purchases at the club, and tends to be of greatest interest to managers. Lightly summarized data— for example, a weekly aggregation of food and beverage covers—is data, distilled from current data, that is likely to have a bearing on a forthcoming management decision. Highly summarized data is compact and easily accessible by subject area and is constructed from all other data forms (monthly food and beverage reports, for example). A data warehouse can be highly cost effective for a club, depending on the volume of stored data, frequency of access, and cost of storage media.

Data marts. A **data mart** is a database or collection of databases, smaller than a data warehouse, that is designed to help club managers make business decisions. Whereas a data warehouse combines databases from the entire club, a data mart is smaller and usually focuses on a single club area or department. Because a data mart contains data that is forwarded to the club's data warehouse, it is a natural extension and companion to the data warehouse. A department manager within a club may rely upon a data mart to provide relevant information for departmental decision-making.

In general, there are two types of data mart users: "farmers" and "explorers." A farmer is someone who knows what data he or she wants and regularly and predictably goes to the same place to find it. For example, the club's golf professional may review the history of golf lessons taken or rounds played by members. An explorer is an individual who does not know what data is desired and engages in a random, sporadic data hunt. Consider the golf professional seeking to identify clothing sales on Tuesdays and Wednesdays. The data mart structure tends to work best for farmers, not explorers.

When a club operating department has its own data mart, it can customize and capture data as it flows into or out of the club's data warehouse. A data mart does not need to service the entire club, only a single area or department, and therefore can be streamlined, summarized, and structured as appropriate. If a club department has its own data mart, it can select data mining software that is tailored to its specific needs.

Mining club data. Data mining can be defined as the extraction process used to derive information from a data warehouse or data mart. The key to successful data mining for club managers is to take disparate data sources and extract information for enhanced decision-making. Data mining involves the discovery of new information through identifying and understanding heretofore undiscovered trends, patterns, or variable correlations within the data. If a club could use data mining to sift through data and discover information that could improve member relations, then the club is more likely to gain a competitive advantage. Important considerations of data mining include reliability and ease of operation.

There are at least three factors influencing the potential adoption of data mining software within the club industry: (1) the decreasing cost of computing technology, (2) the availability of powerful data-mining techniques, and (3) the increased knowledge of end users.

Club Accounting Applications

Club management systems can vary in the number of back-office software applications (or modules) they contain. Modules that typically are included in back-office software packages include:

- Accounts receivable

- Accounts payable

- Payroll accounting

- Financial reporting

An accounts receivable module monitors outstanding balances of member accounts. Accounts receivable balances can be automatically transferred from point-of-sale applications or can be posted directly into an accounts receivable program. Once a transaction has been entered into the back-office system, account monitoring begins. Account billing and the aging of accounts receivable are also tracked by the club's back-office software.

An accounts payable module tracks club purchases, creditor positions, and the club's banking status. Accounts payable activities normally consist of posting vendor invoices, determining amounts due, and printing checks for payment. Generally, there are three major files maintained by a club's accounts payable module: a vendor master file, an invoice register file, and a check register file. The vendor master file contains an index of vendor names, addresses, telephone numbers, vendor code numbers, standard discount terms (time and percentage), and space for additional information. An invoice register file is a complete list of outstanding invoices cataloged by vendor, invoice date, invoice number, and/or invoice due date. This file becomes especially important when club managers wish to take advantage of vendor discount rates. The calculation and printing of bank checks for payment to vendors is monitored through the check register file. Check production and distribution is summarized into a payables report and reconciled with the club's bank statements.

A payroll accounting module is an important part of a club's back-office package, because of the complexities involved in properly processing employee time and attendance records, unique employee benefits, pay rates, withholdings, deductions, and required payroll reports. The payroll accounting module must be capable of handling job codes, employee meals, uniform credits, service charges (tips), taxes, and other data that affect the net pay of club employees. The unique nature of payroll data dictates that special care be taken to maintain an accurate payroll register, protect the confidentiality of payroll data, and closely control the issuing of payroll checks.

A financial reporting module involves the specification of a chart of accounts (a list of financial statement accounts and their account numbers) and a systematic approach to recording transactions. The design of the financial reporting module is often crucial to an effective back-office system. Adherence to a uniform system of accounts for clubs helps provide a logical approach to the design of back-office applications. A financial reporting module generally is capable of tracking accounts receivable, accounts payable, cash, and adjusting entries. It can also produce flash reports and periodic reports. Flash reports normally involve operational statistics (such as number of dinners sold, average check, member activity, and so forth) and general ledger highlights (such as accounts receivable summaries, cash balances, and so forth). A statement of financial position and a statement of activities are examples of periodic accounting reports. Many packages are also able to generate periodic reports on cash flow, fixed assets, and disbursements.

Transaction Technologies

Should clubs accept credit cards as a method of payment? Are there alternatives to credit cards that may be more appealing to club managers? Can clubs adapt to the prepaid card phenomenon? Will smart cards finally become a viable option for processing transactions in clubs? The answers to these and related questions may significantly influence a club's cash flow.

Credit Cards

Although nearly every type of business within the hospitality industry welcomes credit cards as an acceptable and often preferred form of settlement, most clubs have been reluctant to provide their members with this payment option. Club managers usually cite two key principles as justification for an anti-credit-card stance. First, since a club provides personalized member services, direct payment for services rendered helps differentiate clubs from commercial competitors. Second, the fees credit card companies charge for processing transactions are likely to distort the club's cost of goods sold to the point that it will place an unnecessary burden on operations. Such arguments ignore a growing interest among many club members to use credit cards at their clubs, an interest fanned by cardholder affinity programs (that is, programs in which cardholders accrue points or other incentives, based on the amount of their charges).

Clubs that accept credit cards for account reconciliation offer a compelling reason for doing so: credit cards promote increased levels of spending. Hotels, restaurants, and casinos have taken advantage of this fact for quite some time. Club members using credit cards buy more, knowing that credit card payments can be deferred and paid incrementally while valuable affinity points are collected.

In order to receive payment for transactions settled with a credit card, those clubs that allow credit card usage begin by submitting purchase invoices (or online transaction records) to credit card companies for reconciliation. In turn, these companies charge the clubs transaction fees (termed "discount fees") to cover the costs associated with transaction processing and account maintenance. Club managers should consider whether the increase in revenues will offset the cost of the fees associated with credit card transactions.

Credit Card Technology. In order to provide a level of security for credit card users, the magnetic stripe on the back of a credit card typically contains three data storage tracks. Usually track 1 contains up to 79 alphanumeric characters reserved for identifying the cardholder and the card's issuing agency (a bank or travel company, for example). Track 2 normally holds up to 40 numbers used to identify the account number, electronic banking or database reference, or similar descriptor. Track 3 can be used to store up to 215 numbers. The banking industry tends to use tracks 1 and 2 for storing a variety of credit card information, including the cardholder's name, account number, and the account date of expiration, while leaving track 3 empty.

The magnetic-stripe technology used by credit cards is reliable, difficult to counterfeit, and has a low cost per use. For clubs offering members the opportunity to make credit card purchases of club products and services via the club's Web site, there is a set of encryption techniques designed to protect proprietary cardholder information throughout the transaction. Secure Electronic Transaction (SET) technology is dedicated to ensuring account confidentiality and thereby reducing the potential for fraud.

Prepaid Cards

A **prepaid card** is a card in which value is stored, and for which the holder has paid the issuer in advance. To date, prepaid cards have seen limited use in clubs. Given the explosion of prepaid cards in telecommunications and many other industries, prepaid cards may become more appealing to clubs as more creative applications are developed. Unlike with credit cards, with prepaid cards payment is received in advance of the purchase of a good or service, thereby providing the club with an accelerated cash flow.

With prepaid card transactions, there is no need for receivables or invoices, and there are none of the internal control concerns associated with cash. As goods are purchased, the prepaid card's value declines. Once the card balance is zero, the card is no longer valid for transactions. Prepaid cards can be designed on a spend-down-only basis or with the capability to accept additional deposits. To answer security concerns, prepaid cards can be programmed to require users to enter a personal identification number (PIN) or personal access number (PAN) before they can use their card. Since prepaid cards have limited negotiability and acceptability, they may provide the clubs that issue them with a unique competitive advantage (members must go to their clubs to use the cards).

Prepaid cards can be used to replace coins, tokens, coupons, or other forms of discounts or payment plans traditionally offered by clubs. Members might prefer prepaid cards for security reasons (because they eliminate the need to carry cash) or control reasons (for example, to limit a child's spending—a parent could provide a card with a value of $25 to his or her child). Prepaid cards can be used by club members to pay for vending machine items and video games. Clubs may also consider prepaid cards for golf and other recreational fees, function room amenities, and business-center expenditures. The cards can also be used as club member rewards or purchase incentives.

Smart Cards

A **smart card** is a credit-card-sized plastic card that usually contains an embedded integrated circuit (a microprocessor and a memory chip). Smart cards (also referred to as "chip cards") hold information in electronic form and can control who has access to this information and how the information is used. Smart cards are termed "smart" since the card itself contains sufficient information to control access to its stored data. The type of data stored on a club member's smart card can include the type of club membership the cardholder has, demographic information about the member, emergency-contact telephone numbers, and other information. In addition, smart cards can be used for vending machines, parking lot gates, locker room facilities, and other club assets not overseen by employees. Given such enhanced capabilities, smart cards can be used in more sophisticated ways than magnetic-stripe cards.

Smart cards are not inherently linked to a bank and there is no need to involve any agency beyond the club. Although there is a comparatively high start-up cost, the volume of information contained in the cards and the way the information can be controlled (PIN or PAN access) provide strong reasons for club managers and boards to consider using smart cards at their clubs.

The face of a smart card can be quite attractive, featuring the club's logo and/or other graphic designs as well as text. External attractiveness provides a marketing benefit but has no effect on how the card works. The card's integrated circuit holds information in electronic form that can be easily accessed by a variety of electronic data-processing equipment. When a smart card is inserted into a specialized card reader, the information on the card can be read and updated, as needed. Since the card can be authenticated off-line, at the point-of-sale, the club's transaction processing is simplified. Smart cards are considered virtually impossible to copy or falsify, but there is a limited scope of protection in the case of loss or fraudulent data entry. Several types of smart cards possess the capacity for a single password to restrict usage. More sophisticated smart cards are capable of managing several applications and passwords and can use authentication and ciphering (encoding and decoding) techniques to provide an enhanced level of comfort and security for their users. Unlike a credit card, a smart card does not need to be involved with a financial institution for the card to have value. The card's value is maintained on-board and therefore can be limited to club operations. It is important to note that a smart card can perform as a prepaid card.

Smart Card Formats. One type of smart card is referred to as a "read-only" card. With a read-only card, the information stored on the card can be read but not altered, expanded, or modified.

A second type of smart card is the "read-and-add-only" card. The read-and-add-only card provides a means for information to be added to the card's memory, but previously stored data cannot be modified or deleted. In essence, once data is added and stored, the smart card functions as a read-only card. For example, a smart card authorized for a predetermined number of purchase units (for example, a new member's admission to various club activities) can be marked as used or spent. The marks indicating usage can be added to the card but cannot be erased, thereby controlling the number of times the card can be used for complimentary entry (the card can simultaneously capture usage data). A read-and-add-only format is not refillable; once its properties are exhausted, the card expires.

A "modify or erase" smart card enables data to be added or deleted so long as there is sufficient storage (memory) capacity. This smart card format has the most versatility and offers exceptional on-board security and password protection. As a protection against card loss and therefore potential content loss, some smart card processing devices are connected to a centralized network to track and record transactions throughout the smart card transaction base. This feature will significantly increase the cost of a smart card system to a club, however.

Electronic Wallets

Smart cards are expected to give rise eventually to the electronic wallet, also called the "e-wallet" or "virtual wallet." The term **"e-wallet"** is used to describe a smart card with sufficient on-board computer processing power and storage capacity to become a repository for complex personal, financial, and transactional data. The power of an advanced smart card is likely to lead to a reliance on "virtual cash." With a virtual cash system, money can be transferred to a smart card through an automated teller machine, PC keyboard, or special serial port connection, thereby refreshing or extending the card's value without an actual currency exchange. Similarly, "cybercash" may also have electronic wallet applications. With cybercash, the money for electronic transactions is stored on the purchaser's hard drive, not in a financial institution. With such transactional settlement techniques there is less dependence on actual cash and more on virtual cash. Additionally, with virtual cash there is an audit trail of all transactions, since they are conducted via electronic means.

While e-wallets and cybercash appear to be far outside the realm of current club applications, club managers should be aware of these transaction tools. They may become commonplace sooner than many managers think.

Internet Applications for Clubs

The **Internet** is a large and complex series of computer networks designed to provide universal access to information and communication services around the world. Often referred to as the "information superhighway," the Internet resembles the intricate traffic patterns of local and county roads with connections to state and interstate highways. In fact, the Internet was initially conceived at about the same time as the development of interstate highways. The design of the interstate highway system, linking major cities across the country, was based on the need to maintain a continuous flow of supplies throughout the country. The roadways were designed with sufficient alternate routing so that a steady flow of materials to all parts of the nation could be assured.

Similar ideas were important in the creation of the Internet. Using the interstate highway system as a model, the government turned its attention to similarly securing its intelligence system. The focus shifted from protecting vehicular traffic patterns to ensuring a continuous movement of data between mainframe computers at various strategic locations from coast to coast. Internet planners sought to create a myriad of alternate communication routes across a wide range of computer platforms. The Internet has created a communications and information explosion that has the potential to affect virtually every aspect of the club industry.

Most club networks connect individual personal computers to a separate computer, called a "server" or "file server." The file server controls the flow of information along the club's computer network. It can also be used to establish a gateway to other computer networks beyond the club's office environment. The Internet takes the concept of networks to its fullest application by connecting large numbers of very complex networks. The Internet is an affiliation of tens of thousands of private, commercial, educational, and government-supported networks around the world. When a user connects to the Internet, data and information can be shared with millions of other users.

The World Wide Web

The **World Wide Web (WWW)**, also known simply as the Web, is only one of the many different parts of the Internet. It is the best-known part because its user-friendly features have attracted millions of users. Unlike text-only sites found on much of the Internet, the Web offers an incredibly rich combination of text, images, sound, animation, and video. The visual options of the Web and the surging numbers of "surfers" have enticed millions of businesses, organizations, educational institutions, government agencies, and individuals to create their own Web pages and participate in the dissemination of information along the Web.

Much of the user-friendly nature of the Web stems from the hypertext transfer protocol (http) that structures information on the Web. This protocol is a set of file-download commands embedded within the hypertext markup language (html) used to place text, graphics, video, and other information displays on the Web. The "http" indicates that the Web page can handle non-sequential links to other hypertext pages—a trait characteristic of all Web pages.

A **uniform resource locator (URL)** designates the Internet address of a site, usually the site's homepage. A site's homepage is the first screen or Web page presented when a destination site is located. URLs are usually built into the hypertext of a Web document, enabling users to jump from site to site along the Web. The URL for a club, hotel, restaurant, or individual consists of a series of letters and punctuation marks that may seem confusing, even intimidating, to a novice user. Each grouping of letters represents a section of the path that leads to a desired site.

Clubs on the Web

A variety of software applications are available to help clubs use the Internet. The most popular Internet software applications are email, Web browsers, and search engines. **Email** (electronic mail) was one of the first Internet applications and remains its most popular. Email enables Internet users to communicate with people down the hall, across town, or on the other side of the world. The only requirement is that the sender know the intended receiver's email address. The alphanumeric format of an email address is generally based on the name of the intended receiver, coupled with the name of the email system and the host computer network. For example, the most commonly used format for an email address is *localname@domain.* "Localname" refers to the Internet name of the intended receiver (or sender). The domain portion of the address identifies the host computer system on which the intended receiver (or sender) has an email account. Either side of the @ symbol can be extended, allowing for a more precise identification of an individual or host computer system.

One of the greatest advantages of email over normal postal delivery, or what regular email users call "snail mail," is not just the speed of the communication, but the convenience of the communication. Email messages can be sent or received at any time, day or night. In addition, most email software packages allow the user to attach multimedia files to email messages.

Keeping track of Internet addresses is one of the functions performed by a Web browser. The term "Web browser" refers to software that coordinates and organizes information downloaded from the Internet. The most popular Web browsers are by Netscape (Navigator) and Microsoft (Internet Explorer). Web browsers tend to have similar designs and operating procedures. They generally feature a toolbar along the top of the computer screen with pull-down menus, icons for accessing utility programs, and a directory for saving (bookmarking) the Internet addresses of sites frequently visited by the user. Bookmarking a favorite site on the Web saves the path used to direct the browser to the site, enabling the user to go back to the site quickly, without having to remember and input a long Internet address. (Think of bookmarking as similar to the redial feature of a touch-tone phone.) It's not a good idea to randomly bookmark every site you like, because the individual addresses will get lost in a long miscellaneous list of favorites. To alleviate this problem, many browsers allow you to organize bookmarked sites into specific categories and store them in labeled folders.

When you don't know a particular Web site's address, the best way to find it is to use a **search engine.** Commonly used search engines include:

Yahoo	www.yahoo.com
Netscape	www.netscape.com
Web Crawler	www.webcrawler.com
Lycos	www.lycos.com
Excite	www.excite.com

A search engine is a software program that reads indexed Web sites and creates site lists and links that match a user's inquiry. Most search engines provide tips on how to efficiently search for information. Generally, the more specific your query, the more relevant will be the list of sites your query generates. However, even if the resulting list is long, you can usually scroll or page through the list and decide which sites are worth a look. Then it's simply a matter of clicking on the link or address to go directly to the Web site.

Club Web Sites. As clubs strive to solidify one-to-one relationships with their members through invigorated membership loyalty programs, Web sites can play a central role. For most clubs, the question is not whether to create and support a Web site, but how to create the most efficient site to accomplish the club's goals.

Club managers who are thinking of creating a club Web site for the first time should be aware that there are at least five possible fees associated with Web sites. Potential fees include: (a) a fee for the club's domain name (address), (b) a Web site development fee, (c) a Web site maintenance (content) fee, (d) a Web site hosting (server) fee, and (e) a Web site promotion fee.

In order to attract and retain online visitors, a club should focus on elements of design, quality, and content for its Web site. Club Web sites, which in the early days were composed of text and digitized photos in simple layouts that resembled printed brochures, have evolved into more interactive designs.

The initial development and continuing maintenance of a club's Web site content is often a collaborative effort by club managers, employees, and members. A club can derive many benefits from its Web site: the site is accessible seven days per week, 24 hours a day by authorized users anywhere in the world; posting club information on the site can reduce printing and distribution expenses; the site gives the club the capability to communicate with club members rapidly and inexpensively via email and online messaging; the site is a promotional outlet for club products and services; and the site is an additional retail outlet for the club (via e-commerce).

Web site features. In general, a club Web site is deemed more effective if it avoids clutter, restricts extraneous and irrelevant content, and minimizes download time. Exhibit 1 lists features that can be found on club Web sites. The following are several commonly accepted Web site design principles that clubs should consider following:

- *Remove dates from all Web pages, unless dates are to be routinely changed as content changes.* There is probably little else that informs a visitor of Web-site neglect more quickly than a "last updated" tag that is beyond one or two months old.

- *Remove all counters at the Web site.* A low number of visitors indicates a potential problem to those visiting a given site. Being the 106th visitor and returning several weeks later to discover that you are the 108th visitor does nothing to spur your interest in the site. Removing (or hiding) a counter responsible for tracking hits/visits has no obvious downside. Statistics for a variety of Web activities, including visits, can be obtained in a number of ways, none of which need to be visible to a site visitor.

- *Consider automatically filtering and feeding current items to the Web site.* Current information stimulates visitor interest in the Web site and communicates a sense of caring to visitors. Regularly posting current information informs users that the site will be worth a visit on a regular basis. Many clubs find that providing status reports on club activities (upcoming events, construction projects) and timely notices (listing daily or weekly dining room specials, for example) keep members interested in their clubs' Web sites.

Exhibit 1 Features Found on Club Web Sites

- Club welcome/history/mission
- Membership information
- Events calendar
- Food and beverage facilities
- Recreational facilities
- Sample menus/function-room offerings
- Club amenities
- Links to staff members
- Message from the club's president/board of directors/COO
- Links to the board of directors
- The club's newsletter
- Event registration information
- Real estate/community offerings
- Online guest registration book
- Club rules/dress codes
- Recent competitive results from golf leagues, tennis tournaments, and so on
- Reciprocal club listings/links
- Kids Club/Kids Corner/kids' area
- Gift shop/pro shop promotions
- Banquet/catering services
- Members-only access area
- Links to members/member businesses
- FAQ (frequently asked questions) section
- Visual/virtual tours of the club
- Merchandise advertising/sales
- Event ticket promotions/sales
- Club and club staff honors/awards
- Club Managers Association of America link
- Ladies' page/section
- Links to the chef's home page
- Downloadable membership application
- Online employment application
- Photo scrapbook/art gallery
- Online dinner, tee-time, and tennis court reservations
- Tech-talk section (encyclopedia of technology terms)
- "Live" kitchen cam

- *Do not think of the Web site as a hypertext table of contents.* This is perhaps the design mistake that makes club members and other Web surfers most frustrated. Too often club Web sites are poorly organized, cluttered, and illogical in content presentation due to a concentration on **hyperlinking** site pages or features. The best Web site design approach tends to be the simplest. Some clubs have home pages with just three entry points: Members Only, Prospective Members, and General Information. Having such simple access options helps club members and other site visitors navigate through the site.

- *Avoid hyperlinking to irrelevant or inactive Web sites.* Few things are more frustrating to Web site visitors than being presented with a long list of unexplained hyperlinks. While hyperlinks to reciprocal clubs are logical, there are numerous hyperlinks that will be less obvious to visitors (links to member-owned businesses, alternate recreational facilities, unrelated off-premises activities, and so on). In addition, nothing drives away return visitors faster than hyperlinks to invalid (dead) Web sites. The club's image is likely to be damaged if members and other Web surfers lose confidence in its site.

- *Avoid using technology tricks to attract visitors.* Current animation techniques, streaming audio, video players, and other popular technology features are likely to become outdated or superseded by enhanced applications. Relying on tricks or gimmicks to attract visitors will not prove as valuable as providing stimulating content, interactivities, or links to relevant sites. Care must be exercised to avoid relying on technological gadgets to attract visitors.

Web site IRS guidelines. The Internal Revenue Service has yet to publish a list of acceptable Web site content for exempt entities such as private clubs. For now, a basic guideline for clubs is to avoid posting any information on their Web sites that would not be generally accepted in print. For example, modeling a club Web site after a commercial business intent on selling logoed merchandise, food and beverage items, and golf or tennis lessons could bring unwanted governmental attention.

The following items may be considered in line with the 501(c)(7) exempt status of a club:

- Promoting club features, facilities, and staff members

- Emphasizing unique features of the club (signature golf course holes, health spa amenities, swimming facilities, architectural façades, and so forth)

- Discussing the club's history and mission

- Establishing a communication link between the club and its members

- Partitioning a secured portion of the site (members-only access) for protecting proprietary club information

- Providing useful and relevant hyperlinks to other Web sites

- Posting financial information such as the club's annual 990 tax return and the 501(c)(7) exempt status application

The following items may be inconsistent with the provisions of 501(c)(7):

- *Advertising commercial products or services.* Advertising commercial products or services should be avoided (for example, monogrammed merchandise, instructional lessons, and so forth). Income from nonmembers must be classified as nonmember income and may threaten the club's private status exemption.

- *Promoting nontraditional club activities.* Promoting nontraditional club activities such as catering to private residences, selling holiday turkeys and hams, and selling baked goods or wines as carry-out items may also prove problematic.

- *Soliciting club members in an uncommon manner not normally found throughout the club industry.*

- *Promoting reciprocal arrangements involving nonmember activities.* Promotion of reciprocal club arrangements involving nonmember activities is likely to raise issues concerning the club's relationship to the public.

Web site privatization. Currently, a significant percentage of clubs on the Internet have implemented a private, members-only partition. While the home page of the club's Web site is accessible to anyone with a Web browser, access to specific member-oriented information is password-protected. Public access typically is limited to general club information such as driving directions, an overview of club facilities, and staff contacts. Partitioning the site can offer authorized club members online access to the following types of club information and services:

- Club bylaws, rules, and regulations
- Club newsletter
- Club event calendar
- Member/staff directory
- Member email services
- Bulletin board system (BBS) for message exchange
- Member account review and payment system
- Event/function/activity registration
- E-commerce transactions (pro shop and catalog sales)
- Searchable member database
- Member profiles (including photos)
- Food and beverage menus and specials
- Recreational facility scheduling (tee and court times)
- Member feedback, polling, and survey pages
- Tournament competition support and results

When Internet technology is modified to include controlled site access (that is, members only), it is referred to as an **intranet.** The same technologies, architecture, and network protocols that underlie the Internet are applied to intranet applications. An intranet's Web sites look and act just like any other Web sites, but the firewall surrounding an intranet keeps unauthorized users from entering. A club's intranet site helps foster a sense of community among its members. However, care should be exercised to ensure that no unauthorized person will have the capability to communicate with the club's membership, for any purpose.

Some clubs have developed what are called "extranets." An **extranet** is a private intranet with a provision for limited outside-user entry—for example, a club might permit its purveyors to respond to purchase orders put up on the club's intranet.

Summary

Generic software, data mining, accounting applications, transaction processing, the Internet, and Web site applications are important components of a club's technology strategy. Word processing, electronic spreadsheets, database management, and Internet software are just some of the types of generic application software programs available to clubs today.

Word processing software is a valuable office tool that can increase the productivity of personnel engaged in business-writing tasks. With a word processing program, revisions to original documents can be made quickly and efficiently, and typographical and grammatical errors can be automatically corrected while the user inputs text.

With an automated accounting system, figures are entered only once into an accounting record. Programs that prepare mathematically correct journals, ledgers, and financial statements can be constructed based upon these captured amounts. The speed with which electronic spreadsheet software can generate information can greatly help club managers make decisions.

Database management software allows clubs to catalog and store information about their operations for future use. A database is a collection of related facts and figures designed to serve a specific purpose. Recent innovative technology—involving centralized data storage (data warehousing) that assists effective categorization (data marting) and analysis (data mining)—has become available to the club industry. A club's data warehouse contains integrated, historical data from the entire club. A data mart is a database or collection of databases, smaller than a data warehouse, that focuses on a single club area or department. Data mining can be defined as the extraction process used to derive information from a data warehouse or data mart. The key to successful data mining is to take disparate data sources and extract new information by identifying and understanding heretofore undiscovered trends, patterns, or variable correlations within the data.

Club management systems can vary in the number of back-office software applications (modules) they contain. Modules that are typically included in back-office software packages include: accounts receivable, accounts payable, payroll accounting, and financial reporting.

Traditionally, most clubs have been reluctant to accept credit cards. Clubs that do allow members to use their credit cards for account reconciliation point out that this practice promotes increased levels of spending among club members. For this reason, and because an increasing number of club members want to be able to use their credit cards at their clubs, more and more clubs are considering this payment option.

To date, prepaid cards have seen limited use in clubs. Given the explosion of prepaid cards in numerous other industries, prepaid cards may become more appealing to clubs as more creative applications are developed.

A smart card is a credit-card-sized plastic card that typically has a tiny computer chip embedded within it. It stores information in electronic form and can control who has access to the information and how it is used.

Smart cards are expected to give rise eventually to the electronic wallet, also called the "e-wallet" or "virtual wallet." An e-wallet is a smart card with sufficient on-board computer-processing and storage capacity to become a repository for complex personal, financial, and transactional data.

A variety of software applications are available to help clubs use the Internet. The most popular Internet software applications are email, Web browsers, and search engines.

Many clubs have created their own Web sites. A club can derive many benefits from its site: the site is accessible seven days per week, 24 hours a day by authorized users anywhere in the world; posting club information on the site can reduce printing and distribution expenses; the site gives the club the capability to communicate with club members rapidly and inexpensively via email and online messaging; the site is a promotional outlet for club products and services; and the site is an additional retail outlet for the club (via e-commerce). For most clubs, the question is not whether to create and support a Web site, but how to create the most efficient site to accomplish the club's goals.

Key Terms

data mart—A database or collection of databases designed to help club managers make business decisions. Whereas a data warehouse combines databases from the entire club, a data mart is smaller and focuses on a particular club area or department.

data mining—The extraction process used to derive information from a data warehouse or data mart.

data warehouse—A large collection of raw data, pulled from throughout a club, that is used to support management decision-making.

database management software—Software that stores related facts and figures for a specific purpose.

e-wallet (electronic wallet)—A device similar to a smart card that serves as a repository for complex personal, financial, and transactional data.

email (electronic mail)—Internet-based rapid delivery communications network.

extranet—Private intranet with provision for limited outside user interactivity.

hyperlink—An element in an electronic document that links to another place in the same document or to an entirely different document; hyperlinks allow non-linear progression within or between Web-based documents or Web site locations.

Internet—A large and complex series of computer networks providing universal access to information and communication services.

intranet—A private network based on Internet protocols that is accessible (typically via a password) only to people with authorization. An intranet's Web sites look and act just like any other Web sites, but the firewall surrounding an intranet fends off unauthorized access.

prepaid card—A card in which value is stored, and for which the holder has paid the issuer in advance.

search engine—Software that matches a user's inquiry to indexed Web site lists and linkages.

smart card—A credit-card-size plastic card that usually contains an embedded integrated circuit (a microprocessor and a memory chip). Smart cards hold information in electronic form and can control who has access to this information and how the information is used. Also referred to as "chip cards."

spreadsheet software—Software that is used to create mathematically based journals, ledgers, and financial reports.

uniform resource locator (URL)—A Web site address.

word processing software—Software for the creation, editing, and production of text and images.

World Wide Web (WWW)—A popular part of the larger Internet that is user-friendly and features text, image, sound, animation, and video.

Review Questions

1. What are some of the features of word processing software and spreadsheet software?

2. What are the benefits of a database management software program?

3. What is a data warehouse? a data mart?

4. How do accounts receivable, accounts payable, payroll accounting, and financial reporting modules help clubs perform accounting tasks?

5. How do prepaid cards and smart cards work, and how can they be used in clubs?

6. What is an electronic wallet?

7. What are some commonly accepted Web site design principles that clubs should follow?

8. Why should a club add a "members-only" partition to its Web site?

Case Studies

Mini-Case One

Chef Raymond is struggling to control food and beverage costs in his club's banquet operation. In an effort to contain expenditures, the chef purchases a spreadsheet software package. He then enters the ingredient data from each of the club's banquet-item recipes into a spreadsheet file. Since the club has a limited banquet menu, the chef completes the data entry in only a few hours. Now, as members sponsor functions and order menu items, the chef can run the program and calculate item costs. This method leads to more accurate costing and therefore more accurate banquet pricing. Feeling confident in this approach, Chef Raymond instructs the kitchen staff to enter all recipe data for all menu items appearing on the club's lunch and dinner menus.

Discussion Questions

1. Was the chef wise to purchase a spreadsheet program to perform recipe costing? What are the relative advantages and disadvantages of a recipe costing program over a spreadsheet program?

2. In order to maintain current menu item costs, the chef is required to input all ingredient cost data on a regular basis. Hence, if beef appears in two dozen recipes, then Chef Raymond would need to adjust the ingredient cost for beef in 24 different spreadsheet cells. How could this redundant data handling be avoided?

3. What should the chef do to develop a more comprehensive recipe costing procedure?

Mini-Case Two

As the Rose and Orange Club's general manager, Ms. Holly Lynn is very interested in improving member relations. It occurred to her that the club needed a feature-rich Web site. She surveyed the club's membership and was surprised to learn that only about 15 percent had access to the Internet. After reviewing the survey results, she wondered what should be done. With so few members online, it seemed illogical to spend several hundred dollars developing a Web site that so few members could enjoy. It was at that point that she realized the solution to the problem was to offer Internet access through a program sponsored by the club. She contacted a local Internet Service Provider (ISP) and negotiated a reduced rate for club members who subscribed to the ISP's services. In a relatively short time, the percent of members online swelled to 85 percent. It was now time to launch her club's Web site.

Discussion Questions

1. When Holly works with the club's Web site designers, what are the most important features and principles to keep in mind?

2. What Web address, or URL, might be reasonable for this club?

3. Do you feel the ISP's reduced access fee was a good idea? How can Holly ensure that club members perceive the ISP offering as a benefit of club membership?

Chapter 14 Outline

Leases and Their Uses
    Advantages and Disadvantages of
      Leases
    Provisions of Lease Contracts
Lease Accounting
    Classification of Leases
    Operating Leases
    Capital Leases
    Illustration of Accounting for Capital
      Leases
Leasehold Improvements
Leases and Their Effect on Financial Ratios
Choosing to Lease or Buy

Competencies

1. Define the basic terms of leasing, list the advantages and disadvantages of using lease agreements in clubs, and describe the common provisions of lease contracts. (pp. 307–309)

2. Describe the differences between operating leases and capital leases, and explain the accounting procedures involved in handling each type. (pp. 309–317)

3. Explain the role of leasehold improvements and the impact that leasing may have on financial ratios. (pp. 317–318)

4. Demonstrate the accounting steps involved in making the decision to lease or buy. (pp. 318–319)

14

Lease Accounting

LEASING ENTITLES A CLUB to use equipment, land, or buildings without buying them. Leasing often provides a way to use resources when purchasing them is not possible or desirable. For example, a club may lease land because that land is not for sale. A club may lease equipment for a single day for a special function. This chapter will address a number of issues regarding lease accounting, including:

- The advantages and disadvantages of leasing resources

- Executory costs in relation to leases

- How leases are classified for accounting purposes

- The criteria for capitalizing leases

- How to amortize leasehold improvements

- Incremental interest rates

- Common provisions of lease agreements

- How cash flows are discounted

In addition, we will focus on the differences between operating leases and capital leases, and present guidelines for accounting for the different types of leasing arrangements. We will investigate the effects that leases may have on a club's financial statements and ratios. Finally, we will consider the lease-versus-buy question and provide a model for making a reasonably objective decision.

Leases and Their Uses

A **lease** is an agreement conveying the right to use resources (equipment, buildings, and/or land) for specified purposes and a limited time. From an operational perspective, the resource is available for use; operating personnel generally have little concern whether the club owns or leases it. Lease agreements govern the parties to the lease, usually the lessor and the lessee. The **lessor** owns the property and conveys the right of its use to the **lessee** in exchange for periodic cash payments called **rent**.

Leasing is popular in the United States with businesses in general and with the hospitality industry in particular. For example, restaurants may lease space in shopping malls, lodging companies may lease hotels, and many clubs choose to lease golf carts.

Advantages and Disadvantages of Leases

The following list presents some of the advantages of leasing.

- Leasing conserves working capital because it requires little or no cash deposit; cash equal to 20 to 40 percent of the purchase price is required when purchasing property and equipment. For the cash-strapped club, leasing may be the only way to obtain the desired property or equipment.

- Leasing often involves less red tape than buying with external financing. Although a lease agreement must be prepared, it usually is less complicated than the many documents required to make a purchase, especially when long-term financing is involved.

- Leasing allows more frequent equipment changes, especially when equipment becomes functionally obsolete. However, the lessee cannot expect this flexibility to be cost-free. The greater the probability of technological obsolescence, the greater the lease payment (all other things being the same).

- Leasing generally places less restrictive contracts on a lessee than financial institutions often place on long-term borrowers.

- Leasing has less negative impact on financial ratios, especially when the leases are not capitalized. Equipment acquired for use through an operational lease is not shown on the balance sheet. Future rent obligations also do not appear on the balance sheet, although some footnote disclosure may be required. For this reason, leases are often referred to as **off-balance-sheet financing**.

- Operating leases may allow an operation to obtain resources without following a capital budget.

Therefore, in many cases, leasing may be a lower overall cost alternative for many clubs. However, there are also disadvantages of leasing, including:

- Any residual value of the lease equipment benefits the lessor unless the lessee has the opportunity to acquire the leased property at the end of the lease.

- The cost of leasing in some situations is ultimately higher than purchasing. This is especially true when there are only a limited number of less-than-competitive lessors.

- Disposal of a financial lease before the end of the lease period often results in additional costs.

Provisions of Lease Contracts

Each lease is a unique product of negotiations between the lessor and lessee that meets the specific needs of each party. However, all lease contracts normally contain certain provisions. The following list presents some of these common provisions.

1. Term of lease. The term of a lease may be as short as a few hours (usually for a piece of equipment) or as long as several decades (as is common with real

estate). Leases should be long enough to ensure a proper return on the investment for leasehold improvements and other costs.

2. Purpose of lease. This provision generally limits the lessee to using the property for certain purposes. For example, a lease may state, "The lessee shall use the leased premises as a private club and for no other purpose without first obtaining the written consent of the lessor."

3. Rental payments. The lease specifies the amount of rental payment and when it is due. It also indicates any adjustments; for example, adjustments for inflation are often based on the consumer price index for a given city. **Contingent rent** is also specified. For example, a lease may stipulate that contingent rent equal to three percent of all annual food and beverage sales in excess of $700,000 is due the fifteenth day of the first month after the end of the fiscal year.

4. Renewal options. Many leases contain a clause giving the lessee the option to renew the lease. For example, a lease may provide "an option to renew this lease for an additional five-year period on the expiration of the leasing term upon giving lessor written notice 90 days before the expiration of the lease."

5. Obligations for property taxes, insurance, and maintenance. Leases, especially long-term leases, specify who shall pay the **executory costs**—property taxes, insurance, and maintenance costs—on the leased property. A lease in which the lessee is obligated to pay these costs in addition to the direct lease payments is commonly called a **triple-net lease**.

6. Other common lease provisions include:

   - The lessor's right to inspect the lessee's books, especially when part of the lease payment is tied to sales or some other operational figure.

   - The lessor's obligations to restore facilities damaged by fire, tornadoes, and similar natural phenomena.

   - The lessee's opportunity to sublease the property.

   - The lessee's opportunity to make payments for which the lessor is responsible, such as loan payments to preclude default on the lessor's financing of the leased property.

   - Security deposits, if any, required of the lessee.

   - Indemnity clauses protecting the lessor.

Lease Accounting

Historically, leases were accounted for simply as executory contracts; the rental expense was generally recognized with the passage of time. Leases were not capitalized as assets, nor were liabilities recognized for the lessee's obligations under lease contracts. However, as leases have become more sophisticated and economically similar to sale/purchase transactions, many accountants have argued for a change in lease accounting.

The Accounting Principles Board, the past accounting rule-making body, issued four opinions regarding lease accounting. The Financial Accounting Standards Board (FASB), the present rule-making body, has issued more than ten statements relating to lease accounting. A major result of these rules is that many long-term leases are now capitalized (recorded as fixed assets with recognition of a liability).

Most of the remainder of this chapter presents lease accounting guidelines for lessees. Lease accounting for lessors is beyond the scope of this chapter. Our discussion is meant to cover the major elements of lease accounting and is certainly not exhaustive. The reader interested in further study of lease accounting should consult an intermediate accounting text and/or FASB statements.

Classification of Leases

In general, lessees classify leases for accounting purposes as either *operating leases* or *capital leases*. At the extremes of what is essentially a continuum, operating leases differ substantially from capital leases. Depending on their specific provisions, however, they can also be hard to distinguish. **Operating leases** (also called *service leases*) are normally (but not always) of relatively short duration, and the lessor retains the responsibility for executory costs. They can usually be canceled easily. **Capital leases** (also called *financing leases*) are of relatively long duration, and the lessee often assumes responsibility for executory costs. In addition, they are generally noncancelable or at least costly to cancel. Capital leases are capitalized; operating leases are not.

The FASB has established four capitalization criteria for determining the status of noncancelable leases. If a noncancelable lease meets *any* of the four criteria, the lessee *must* classify and account for the lease as a capital lease. Noncancelable leases not meeting any of the four criteria are accounted for as operating leases. The FASB criteria are as follows:

1. The property is transferred to the lessee by the end of the lease term, referred to as the **title transfer provision**.

2. The lease contains a bargain purchase option, referred to as the **bargain purchase provision**.

3. The lease term is equal to 75 percent or more of the estimated economic life of the leased property, referred to as the **economic life provision**.

4. The present value of minimum lease payments (excluding executory costs) equals or exceeds 90 percent of the excess of fair market value of the leased property over any investment tax credit retained by the lessor, referred to as the **value recovery provision**.

The bargain purchase option (criterion #2) means that the purchase price at the end of the lease period is substantially less than the leased property's expected market value at the date the option is to be exercised. The bargain price is generally considered substantially less than the market value only if the difference, for all practical purposes, ensures that the bargain purchase option will be exercised. The "economic life" (criterion #3) refers to the useful life of the leased property. The following list explains several terms in the value recovery provision (criterion #4):

- *Minimum lease payments* consist of minimum rental payments during the lease term and any bargain purchase option. If no bargain purchase option exists, the minimum lease payments include any guaranteed residual value by the lessee or any amount payable by the lessee for failure to renew the lease. Minimum lease payments do not include contingent rent (such as a percentage of sales). Executory costs are also excluded in determining minimum rental payments when the lease specifies that lease payments include these costs.

- *Fair market value* represents the amount the leased item would cost if it were purchased rather than leased.

- *Investment tax credit* is a credit that the federal government used to allow against the federal income tax liability of the hospitality operation. When it was allowed, up to 10 percent of the cost of qualifying equipment could typically be taken as a credit. The credit generally applied to personal property (such as equipment), but not to real property (such as land and buildings). Investment tax credits are no longer allowed by current tax laws; however, if they are reinstated, they would be treated as indicated by criterion #4. Note that, when there is no investment tax credit, criterion #4 in effect states that if the present value of minimum lease payments (excluding executory costs) equals or exceeds 90 percent of the fair market value of the leased property, the lease must be capitalized.

- *Residual value* refers to the estimated market value of the leased item at the end of the lease term. When the residual value is guaranteed by the lessee, then the lessee is ultimately liable to the lessor for the residual value.

Operating Leases

Operating leases are accounted for as simple rental agreements, and the expense is generally recognized when the rent is paid. For example, if a club leases storage space for $200 per month and pays rent on the first day of each month, the monthly rental payment would be recorded as follows:

Rent Expense	$200	
Cash		$200

When rent is paid in advance, it should be recorded in a prepaid rent account. For example, if the club had paid three months' rent in advance, the proper entry would be:

Rent Expense	$200	
Prepaid Rent	400	
Cash		$600

This accounting entry recognizes rent expense for the current month and delays recognition of rent for the following two months (based on the matching principle).

In the event rent is paid for a period beyond 12 months from the statement of financial position date, the rental payment should be recorded as "deferred rent" and shown as a deferred charge on the statement. Any rent paid for future periods is recognized during the period to which it relates by an adjusting entry. In the example above, the adjusting entry to recognize the second month's rent would be:

Rent Expense	$200
Prepaid Rent	$200

Capital Leases

A capital lease is similar to the purchase of a fixed asset. Therefore, the accounting for capital leases recognizes an asset and applicable liabilities. The amount to be recorded as an asset and a liability is the present value of minimum lease payments, as defined earlier in relation to the fourth capitalization criterion. The lease payments are discounted using the lessee's incremental borrowing rate, or, if known, the lessor's implicit rate of interest in the lease if it is lower than the lessee's incremental borrowing rate. The former is used more often because the lessee does not usually know the lessor's implicit interest rate in the lease. The lessee's **incremental borrowing rate** is the rate of interest the lessee would have to pay if financing the purchase of the leased item.

Executory costs included with the lease payments must be excluded in determining the present value of minimum lease payments. However, a bargain purchase option or a lessee's guaranteed residual value must be included. For example, a lease agreement may require a monthly payment of $1,000, of which $200 is for maintenance. This $200 cost is excluded in determining the present value of minimum lease payments. On the other hand, if the lessee guarantees a residual value of $2,000 for the leased item, the present value of $2,000 should be included in determining the present value of minimum lease payments.

When the lessee makes subsequent lease payments, the lease obligation (the liability account) is reduced by the difference between the lease payment (excluding executory costs) and the interest on the lease obligation. The interest is calculated by using the effective interest method, which results in a constant rate of interest throughout the lease term. This is accomplished by multiplying the interest rate used in discounting the minimum lease payments by the lease obligation for the lease period. For example, assume that a lease payment is $5,000 for the month, including $500 for property taxes, and the lease obligation for the period is $480,000. Further assume that the lessee's incremental borrowing rate is 10 percent. The entry to record the lease payment is as follows:

Property Tax Expense	$ 500	
Interest Expense	4,000	
Lease Obligations	500	
Cash		$5,000

The interest expense of $4,000 is determined as follows:

$$\text{Interest} = \text{Lease Obligation} \times \text{Incremental Borrowing Rate} \times \text{Time (in Years)}$$

$$= \$480,000 \times .10 \times {}^{1}/_{12}$$

$$= \underline{\underline{\$4,000}}$$

Therefore, the lease obligation is debited by $500, determined as follows:

$$\text{Reduction in Lease Obligation} = \text{Lease Payment} - \text{Executory Costs} - \text{Interest Expense}$$

$$= \$5,000 - \$500 - \$4,000$$

$$= \underline{\underline{\$500}}$$

Illustration of Accounting for Capital Leases

Assume the Chambers Club signs a lease agreement with a major computer manufacturer for the use of a back-office computer system. Provisions of the lease agreement and other relevant facts for classifying the lease are as follows:

1. The term of a lease is three years, commencing on January 1, 20X1. The lease is noncancelable.

2. Annual payments of $55,000 are due at the beginning of each year.

3. The leased computer has a fair market value of $130,000 at January 1, 20X1.

4. The estimated economic life of the computer is five years, and there is no expected residual value.

5. The Chambers Club is to pay all executory costs directly except for annual maintenance costs of $10,000, which are included in the annual lease payments.

6. The lease contains no renewal or bargain purchase options, and the equipment reverts to the lessor at the end of the lease period.

7. The Chambers Club's incremental borrowing rate is 12 percent.

8. The Chambers Club depreciates its own computer equipment on a straight-line basis.

9. The lessor's implicit rate of return on leasing the computer to the Chambers Club is unknown.

10. There are no tax credits applicable to this situation.

The Chambers Club must determine whether the lease should be capitalized by comparing the lease provisions to the FASB lease capitalization criteria. Exhibit 1 illustrates this comparison. As the exhibit indicates, the lease should be capitalized, based on criterion #4, because the present value of lease payments, excluding

Exhibit 1   FASB Lease Capitalization Criteria

**FASB Lease Capitalization Criteria
and the lease of computer equipment
by the Chambers Club**

Lease Capitalization Criteria	Computer Lease Provisions	Capitalize Yes/No
1. Title transfer provision	Item 6 states the "equipment reverts to the lessor at the end of the lease."	No
2. Bargain purchase provision	Item 6 states the lease contains no bargain purchase options.	No
3. Economic life provision	$\dfrac{\text{Life of lease}}{\text{Useful life of equipment}} = {}^3/_5 = 60\%$ $60\% < 75\%$	No
4. Value recovery provision	$45,000 (2.6901)* = $ $130,000 (.9) = $ excess of PV of lease payments over 90% of FMV is $121,055** (117,000) $ 4,055	Yes

* For the derivation of this factor, see Exhibit 2.
** This amount is actually $121,054.50; however, the detail of cents is dropped here and throughout the rest of this illustration.

Exhibit 2   Present Value of Five Lease Payments—Chambers Club

Annual lease payments	$ 55,000
Less: Amount for executory costs	10,000
Net lease payment	45,000
Present value of an annuity for 2 payments at 12% (1.6901) Plus present value factor for the initial (undiscounted) payment (1.0000) = 2.6901	× 2.6901
	$ 121,055

executory costs, exceeds 90 percent of the fair market value of the leased equipment. The calculations are as follows:

Fair market value of leased equipment	$130,000
90 percent factor	× .90
	$117,000
Present value of lease payments (see Exhibit 2)	$121,055
Excess of lease payments	$ 4,055

The journal entry to record the capitalization of the leased equipment accompanied by the first payment of $55,000 is as follows:

Leased Equipment Under Capital Leases	$121,055	
Prepaid Maintenance	10,000	
Cash		$ 55,000
Obligations Under Capital Leases		$ 76,055

This single entry consists of the capitalization of the lease at $121,055 (the present value of the three lease payments of $55,000 less $10,000 related to maintenance), the recognition of the related liability at $76,055, the initial payment of $55,000, and $10,000 related to maintenance.

The single entry could have also been recognized in two parts.

(1) Capitalization of lease

| Leased Equipment Under Capital Leases | $121,055 | |
| Obligations Under Capital Leases | | $121,055 |

This entry simply records the present value of the three lease payments.

(2) Lease payment

Obligations Under Capital Leases	$45,000	
Prepaid Maintenance	$10,000	
Cash		$55,000

This entry records the initial cash payment, the $10,000 executory payment, and the reduction in the "obligation" account.

The prepaid maintenance would be written off throughout the year by a monthly entry of $833 ($1/12$ of the annual payment):

| Maintenance Expense | $833 | |
| Prepaid Maintenance | | $833 |

Future payments will result in the recognition of interest expense, the reduction of the obligation under capital leases, and prepayment of maintenance for the next year. In practice, at year-end (December 31, 20X1), interest expense would be accrued by debiting interest expense by $9,127 and crediting accrued interest by $9,127 because of the matching principle.

The Chambers Club would record its second lease payment on January 1, 20X2, as follows:

Interest Expense	$ 9,127	
Obligations Under Capital Leases	35,873	
Prepaid Maintenance	10,000	
Cash		$55,000

Exhibit 3   Lessee's Amortization of Obligation under Capital Leases—Chambers Club

Date of Payment	(1) Annual Lease Payment	(2) Interest Expense[1]	(3) Reduction in Liability[2]	(4) Balance of Liability Account[3]
1/1/X1				$ 76,055
1/1/X2	$ 45,000	$ 9,127	$ 35,873	49,182
1/1/X3	45,000	4,818	49,182	–0–

*Rounding error of less than $5.

Note: The total annual lease payments ($135,000) less the balance of the obligation at January 1, 20X1 ($121,055), equals the interest expense of $13,945.

[1]Interest expense is calculated by multiplying the annual interest rate (12%) by the prior balance of the liability account.

[2]The reduction in the liability is computed by subtracting the interest expense (column 2) from the annual lease payment (column 1).

[3]The balance of liability account (column 4) is reduced each year by the amount in column 3.

The interest expense of $9,127 results from multiplying the $76,055, recorded as "obligations under capital leases" through the year, by the Chambers Club's incremental borrowing rate of 12 percent. The reduction in the liability "obligations under capital leases" of $35,873 is the difference between the net lease payment of $45,000 and the interest expense of $9,127. Exhibit 3 shows the amortization of the $76,055 lease obligation over the term of the lease.

The leased equipment should be depreciated over its lease term of three years. The annual entry for depreciation expense (based on straight-line) would be as follows:

Depreciation Expense	$40,352	
Accumulated Depreciation—Capital Leases		$40,352

This entry assumes a zero salvage value because the equipment reverts to the lessor at the end of the lease term. At the end of the three-year term, the leased equipment is returned to the lessor and the two accounts, "leased equipment under capital leases" and "accumulated depreciation — capital leases," each at $121,055, are reduced to zero:

Accumulated Depreciation—Capital Leases	$121,055	
Leased Equipment Under Capital Leases		$121,055

Throughout the three-year period, the following expenses related to the leased item were incurred:

Maintenance—$10,000/year	$ 30,000
Depreciation—the capitalized cost of the lease	121,055
Interest Expense—the sum of the three net lease payments less the capitalized cost of the lease ($135,000 − $121,055)	13,945
Total Expense	$165,000

Notice that the total expense equals the three annual payments of $55,000.

Leasehold Improvements

Buildings that are leased for several years often require extensive improvements before the commencement of operations. Often, the space leased is not capitalized since none of the capitalization criteria is met. However, any improvements to the space must be capitalized as **leasehold improvements**. For example, the cost of walls, ceilings, carpeting, and lighting installed in leased space is capitalized. The leasehold improvement is recognized as an intangible asset, and the cost must be amortized against revenue over the life of the lease or the life of the leasehold improvement, whichever is shorter. For example, assume that the Chambers Club leased three acres of adjoining land for parking facilities and the land was improved by adding storm sewers, sidewalks, lighting, and pavement at a cost of $200,000. Further assume that the life of the improvement is 10 years, while the land was leased for 30 years. The annual amortization of the leasehold improvement would be $1/10$ of the cost—$20,000 per year for ten years. This expense is generally recognized monthly ($1/12$ of annual amortization) as follows:

Amortization of Leasehold Improvement	$1,667	
Leasehold Improvement		$1,667

Leases and Their Effect on Financial Ratios

Whether a leased item is accounted for as a capital lease or an operating lease can have a major impact on the financial statements, especially the statement of financial position. Therefore, several financial ratios are also affected. Property leased under an operating lease is not shown on the statement of financial position, while property leased under a capital lease is shown. The statement's disclosure of capital leases includes both assets and liabilities. Therefore, most financial ratios involving noncurrent assets and long-term liabilities are affected by how leases are accounted for. Four financial ratios affected by capitalizing leases are shown in Exhibit 4.

In general, capitalizing leases negatively affects these ratios; the ratios suggest a less desirable financial situation than they would if the leases had been

Exhibit 4   Financial Ratios Most Affected by Lease Accounting

Ratio	Ratio Formula	How capital lease affects ratio
1. Asset turnover	revenue ÷ average total assets	Capitalizing leases results in increasing the average total assets, therefore reducing the asset turnover ratio.
2. Return on assets	net income (increase in net assets) ÷ average total assets	Increased average total assets will also reduce the return on assets.
3. Debt-equity ratio	total debt ÷ total equity	Capitalizing leases results in increasing the total debt, therefore increasing the debt-equity ratio.
4. Number of times interest earned ratio	earnings before interest and taxes ÷ interest expense	Capitalizing leases results in increased interest expenses, therefore reducing this ratio.

accounted for as operating leases. For example, if a lease is capitalized, assets and liabilities increase. This means the net income for profit-oriented clubs must also increase in order to maintain a constant return on assets. Thus, many clubs prefer not to capitalize leases. They often negotiate lease provisions so that the lease does not qualify as a capital lease under any of the FASB's four capitalization criteria.

Choosing to Lease or Buy

Should a club lease or buy property? The elements to consider when answering this question include the effect of the decision on taxes (for clubs subject to income taxes), whether funds to finance the purchase must be borrowed, and the time value of money.

Suppose the management of the Skelton Club is deciding whether to buy or lease a truck for use on its golf course. Assume that the purchase cost of the truck is $20,000, while the annual lease payments would be $5,000 for the first year and $4,565 for the next four years (paid at the end of years 1–4). Because the lease payments total $23,260, the apparent advantage to the Skelton Club of buying over leasing is $3,260.

However, we must not forget to consider the time value of money. Assume that the Skelton Club would have to borrow funds at 12 percent if it were to finance the purchase of the truck. This is the lessee's incremental borrowing rate. As stated earlier, lease payments must be discounted by this rate (or, less commonly, by the lessor's implicit rate of interest in the lease) for financial accounting purposes. Therefore, the future cash flows covering the lease payments for years 1–4 should be discounted as follows:

Present value of first payment	$5,000
Present value of next four (annuity) payments:	
$4,565 $(PVA_{n=4,k=12})$ = $4,565 (3.0373)	13,865
Total:	$18,865

This result suggests that leasing the truck would cost $1,135 less ($20,000 − $18,865) than buying it.

However, there are yet other considerations—in particular, taxes and the salvage value of the truck at the end of the five years. Tax considerations for the purchase option involve depreciation expense each year; those for the lease option involve treating the lease payment as an expense each year. Salvage value also must be considered since, under the buy alternative, the salvage value provides cash.

Assume that, based on discussions with the truck retailer, the Skelton Club's general manager estimates that the salvage value of the truck will be $2,000—that is, the truck can be sold for $2,000 at the end of year five. Further assume that the discount rate is still 12 percent, that the Skelton Club's marginal tax rate is 34 percent, and that the club uses straight-line depreciation. Exhibit 5 presents the effects of considering taxes and salvage value. Leasing again appears to be less costly than buying, this time by $1,315. Note, however, that a higher estimated salvage value would at some amount lead us to prefer buying to leasing. In addition, the use of accelerated depreciation rather than straight-line depreciation would reduce the cost of buying because depreciation and thus cash flows would be speeded up (and therefore discounted less).

Still, our analysis is incomplete. Consider that the Skelton Club might have chosen to finance the purchase. For this case, assume that $5,000 would be paid down and $15,000 would be borrowed. Further assume that the $15,000 would be borrowed at 12 percent for four years with equal annual payments. The annual payment would be $4,939, based on $15,000 divided by 3.0373 (from the table of present value factors for an annuity for four annual payments at 12 percent).

Exhibit 6 reflects the discounted cash flows from buying and financing the truck, including the effects of tax shields related to interest expense and depreciation. The net purchase cost is $13,201, which is essentially the same as the net cost of leasing of $13,138. Thus, from a financial point of view there appears to be little difference between leasing and buying when all relevant factors of borrowing, taxes, and the time value of money are considered in this particular example.

In a truly competitive environment, there should be little difference in the cost of leasing versus the cost of buying. However, this truly competitive environment most likely exists only in major metropolitan areas. In noncompetitive markets, a smaller number of lessors will have greater economic power.

Summary

Leasing is a special type of financing used by many clubs. By entering into a lease agreement, the lessee acquires the right to use specific resources for a limited time and a specific purpose. The advantages for the lessee include the conservation of working capital, the benefits of tax deductions that might not otherwise be available, and, in some cases (when the lease is accounted for as an operating lease), a favorable effect on the statement of financial position ratios. In exchange for these advantages, the lessee must make some sacrifices. In many instances, the residual value of the property remains with the lessor, there may be substantial penalties for termination of the lease contract, and the cost of leasing may be higher than

Exhibit 5   Discounted Cash Flow Payments Considering Tax Effects and Salvage Value

Assumptions

Marginal tax rate = 34%

Discount Rate = 12 %

Method of depreciation= straight-line

	0	1	2	3	4	5
			Cash Flows			
			Years			
Purchase Option:						
Cost	$20,000					
Salvage Value						($2,000)
Tax Shield-Dpr.	———	($1,224)[1]	($1,224)	($1,224)	($1,224)	($1,224)
Net Cash Flow	$20,000	($1,224)	1,224	1,1224	1,224	($3,224)
PV Factors	1	.8929	.7972	.7118	.6355	.5674
PV of Cash Trends	$20,000	(1,093)	($976)	($871)	($778)	($1,829)
PV of Purchase Option	$14,453					
Lease Option:						
Lease Payouts	$5,000	$ 4,565	$ 4,565	$ 4,565	$ 4,565	———
Tax Shield:						
Lease Payments	———	(1,700)	(1,552)	(1,552)	(1,552)	(1,552)
Net Cash Flow	$5,000	2,865	3,013	3,013	3,013	(1,552)
PV Factors	1	.8929	.7972	.7118	.6355	.5674
PV of Cash Flows	$5,000	$ 2,558	$ 2,402	$ 2,145	$ 1,915	($881)
PV of Lease Option	$13,139					

Apparent advantage to lease option: $14,453 − $13,139 = $1,314

(1) Depreciation expense × marginal tax rate: tax shield − depreciation

Depreciation expense: $\dfrac{cost - salvage\ value}{life\ in\ years} = \dfrac{\$20,000 - \$2,000}{5} = \$3,600$

$\$3,600 \times .34 = \$1,224$

purchasing the leased item. The operator contemplating a lease arrangement must weigh the advantages and disadvantages before entering into the contract. In many cases in the club industry, the lease contract proves advantageous.

There are many aspects common to most leases. Provisions contained in most lease contracts include the length and purpose of the contract, the specific rent payments, any lessee obligations, and renewal options.

When deciding between leasing and purchasing an asset, many businesses consider how the agreement will affect the financial statements. Depending upon

Exhibit 6   Discounted Cash Flow Payments for Financing the Truck Purchase

			Years			
	0	1	2	3	4	5
Purchase Option:						
Down Payment	$ 5,000					
Loan Payments		$ 4,939	$ 4,939	$ 4,939	$ 4,939	—0—
Tax Shield:						
Depreciation[1]		(1,224)	(1,224)	(1,224)	(1,224)	($1,224)
Interest		(612)	(439)	(340)	(180)	—0—
Salvage Value	——	——	——	——	——	(2,000)
Net Cash Flow	5,000	3,103	3,276	3,375	3,535	($3,224)
PV Factors	1	.8929	.7972	.7118	. 6355	.5674
PV of Net Cash Flows	$ 5,000	$ 2,771	$ 2,611	$ 2,402	$ 2,246	($1,829)
PV of Purchase Option	$ 13,201					

[1] See Exhibit #5 for detail

[2] Interest tax shield:

Year	Interest		Marginal Tax Rate		Interest Tax Shield
1	$ 1,800	×	.34	=	$ 612
2	1,423		.34		439
3	1,001		.34		340
4	529		.34		180

its terms, a lease will either be capitalized (recorded on the statement of financial position as an asset and liability) or treated as an operational lease (expensed as the payments are made). If capitalized, certain financial ratios can be negatively affected. Some managers avoid capital leases because of this effect.

In addition to accounting for the initial lease, leasehold improvements must be recorded and subsequently amortized over either the life of the lease or the life of the improvement, whichever is shorter.

Management should study all the variations of the lease agreement before signing any contract. Establishments judged solely on their financial ratios will probably be more interested in whether a lease is capitalized. Other establishments may value the difference between the total lease payments and the benefits of having a present cash flow.

To determine whether it is better to lease or buy a certain resource, calculate the total cost of each option. Consider the time value of money with regard to both lease payments and, if appropriate, loan payments. Also consider the tax effects of both options (including the effect of using straight-line or accelerated depreciation) and the fact that the purchase option might provide salvage value. In competitive markets, there should be little difference between the final costs of leasing and buying.

🔑 Key Terms ─────────────────────────────────────

bargain purchase provision—One of four Financial Accounting Standards Board capitalization criteria for determining the status of noncancelable leases. If a lease has a bargain purchase option, the lessee must classify and account for the lease as a capital lease. A bargain purchase option gives the lessee the option to purchase the leased property at the end of the lease at a price substantially lower than the leased property's expected market value at the date the option is to be exercised.

capital leases—Lease agreements that are of relatively long duration, generally noncancelable, and in which the lessee assumes responsibility for executory costs. For accounting purposes, capital leases are capitalized in a way similar to the purchase of a fixed asset (that is, recorded as an asset with recognition of a liability).

contingent rent—Rent based on specified variables, such as a percentage of revenues above a given amount.

economic life provision—One of four Financial Accounting Standards Board capitalization criteria for determining the status of noncancelable leases. If the lease term is equal to 75 percent or more of the estimated economic life of the leased property, the lessee must classify and account for the lease as a capital lease.

executory costs—Obligations for property taxes, insurance, and maintenance of leased property.

incremental borrowing rate—The rate of interest a lessee would have to pay if financing the purchase of the item to be leased.

lease—An agreement conveying the right to use resources (equipment, buildings, and/or land) for specified purposes for limited periods of time. The lessor owns the property and conveys the right of its use to the lessee in exchange for periodic cash payments called rent.

leasehold improvements—Renovations or remodeling performed on leased buildings or space prior to the commencement of operations. For accounting purposes, all leasehold improvements are capitalized (that is, recorded as an asset with recognition of a liability).

lessee—Party that makes periodic cash payments called rent to a lessor in exchange for the right to use property.

lessor—Party that owns property and conveys the right of its use to the lessee in exchange for periodic cash payments called rent.

off-balance-sheet financing—Term sometimes applied to operating leases, because property acquired for use through such leases is not shown on the statement of financial position. Future rent obligations also do not appear on the statement of financial position, although some footnote disclosure may be required.

operating leases—Lease agreements that are usually of relatively short duration, easily canceled, and in which the lessor retains responsibility for executory costs.

For accounting purposes, operating leases are not capitalized, but simply recognized as an expense when rent is paid.

rent—Cash payments made by a lessee to a lessor.

residual value—With regard to leasing, the estimated market value of a leased item at the end of the lease term.

title transfer provision—One of four Financial Accounting Standards Board capitalization criteria for determining the status of noncancelable leases. If the property is transferred to the lessee by the end of the lease term, the lessee must classify and account for the lease as a capital lease.

triple-net lease—A form of lease agreement in which the lessee is obligated to pay property taxes, insurance, and maintenance on the leased property.

value recovery provision—One of four Financial Accounting Standards Board capitalization criteria for determining the status of noncancelable leases. If the present value of minimum lease payments (excluding executory costs) equals or exceeds 90 percent of the excess of fair market value of the leased property over any applicable investment tax credit retained by the lessor, the lessee must classify and account for the lease as a capital lease.

Review Questions

1. What are three major advantages to the lessee of lease financing?
2. What are some provisions common to most leases?
3. What are the FASB's four criteria for determining if a lease is a capital or an operating lease?
4. What major effects do capital leases (compared to operating leases) have on an operation's balance sheet?
5. What are leasehold improvements?
6. What are lease executory costs and how do they influence the determination of whether a lessee should capitalize a lease?
7. What is meant by guaranteed residual value? How does it affect the present value of lease payments?
8. At what value is a capitalized lease recorded?

Problems

Problem 1

Jimmy's Club has recently leased a computer that does not meet any of the FASB's accounting requirements for capitalizing the lease. The three-year lease contract requires the club to make an original payment of $4,000 on July 1, 20X1, for the first and last month's rent expense of $2,000 each. On August 1, 20X1, the club is required to make the next month's payment of $2,000. Jimmy's Club maintains its books on a strict accrual accounting basis.

Required:

1. Prepare the journal entry to record the original payment for July 1, 20X1.

2. Prepare the adjusting journal entry for July 31, 20X1.

3. Prepare the journal entry for the August 1, 20X1, payment.

Problem 2

The Forest Run Club has just signed a lease contract for several major machines (ovens and so forth). The lease requires an initial payment of $10,000 when the lease was signed and five future payments of $10,000 each, at one-year intervals. The restaurant's incremental interest rate is 12 percent. The club's accountant has determined that the lease must be capitalized.

Required:

1. Determine the amount of the capitalized lease.

2. Prepare an amortization table for the liability related to the capitalized lease. (Use the format provided in Exhibit 3 of this chapter.)

Problem 3

Cody Murphy, golf course superintendent, desires to obtain a fairway mower for the Mason Country Club. His options are as follows:

Purchase

1.	Cost	$25,000 (payable at time 0)
2.	Salvage Value	$5,000
3.	Life of mower	5 years
4.	Method of depreciation	straight-line
5.	Marginal tax rate	24%
6.	Cost of capital	12%

Lease

1. Annual lease payments commencing at time 0 = $5,000
2. Assume the lease is an operating lease.
3. Assume there is no option to purchase the mower.
4. Tax rates and cost of capital are the same as shown under purchase option.

5. Lease term = 5 years.

6. All maintenance is the responsibility of the lessee.

Required:

Prepare a comparative analysis of the options. Which option do you recommend? Why?

Chapter Appendix:
Sample Lease

A B C University
123 College St.
School City, MI 45678

ATTN: Students

RE: **A B C University**

Dear Customer:

In executing the enclosed documents, it is essential that you carefully observe the following points:

IMPORTANT!

1. All copies of each document must be signed and dated by an **authorized** party (Corporate Officer, Partner or Owner), where indicated. The name and title of signer must be typed or legibly printed beneath the signature.

2. **The documents must NOT be altered without first consulting this office.** Any authorized changes (erasures, deletions, additions, etc.) must be initialed by both parties to the contract.

3. **PAYMENTS: It is extremely important to review the payment schedule on the enclosed Contract to understand the due date of your Scheduled Payments. If you have any questions pertaining to this matter, please feel free to call for a clarification.**

4. The Contract **STIPULATES THAT INSURANCE COVERAGE IS REQUIRED.** Please contact your insurance agent as soon as the equipment is delivered requesting that a Certificate of Insurance be prepared according to the enclosed Insurance Letter. The insurance agent should forward the Certificate of Insurance to us **immediately** after it is prepared.

5. If you are claiming a sales tax exemption, a valid certificate must be completed, signed and returned with the above documents.

6.   If a documentation fee and use tax (if applicable) have been invoiced, the amounts are due no later than upon delivery of the equipment.

The signed documents should be returned to us via an overnight service in order to track the documents and to speed delivery of the equipment. Please Note: Final acceptance of this transaction cannot take place until we have received all of the documents properly signed and dated and the Certificate of Insurance has been received.

Please forward the fully executed documents to the following address:

Associates Leasing, Inc.
8001 Ridgepoint Drive,
Irving, Texas 75063-3117

Attn: Golf & Turf
Fax # 1-888-810-4102
Phone #1-800-421-0606

Thank you,

The Associates
Enclosures

701020
Execution Letter 1.02

8001 Ridgepoint Drive, Irving, Texas 75063-3117

ASSOCIATES LEASING, INC.

Name and Address of Lessee (" Lessee")
A B C University

Name and Address of Lessor ("Lessor")
Associates Leasing, Inc.

1 2 3 College St.
School   MI   45678

8001 Ridgepoint Drive
Irving   TX   75063

DESCRIBE EQUIPMENT FULLY

Sixty (60) Club Car DS Gasoline Golf Cars complete with all attachments and accessories

Equipment Location
1 2 3 College St.
School   Graduate   School   MI   45678

A. TERM: **60**   Months following the first day of the month when the first payment is due after delivery of the Equipment.

B. PAYMENT SCHEDULE: THE ADVANCE RENTAL PAYMENT, IF ANY, IS PAYABLE AT THE ELECTION OF LESSOR, UPON THE EARLIER OF DELIVERY OF THE LEASE APPLICATION TO LESSOR OR THE EQUIPMENT TO LESSEE. THE REMAINING RENTAL PAYMENTS ARE PAYABLE MONTHLY ON THE FIRST DAY OF EACH MONTH BEGINNING ON THE FIRST

OF _____ (MO./YR.).

C. RENTAL PAYMENT: (i) **60** Payments of $ **4,766.00**, or (ii) for other than equal successive monthly installments:

   The Rental payment shall commence one month after delivery of the Equipment to the Lessee if delivery occurs on the first through the fifteenth of the month, or commence two months after delivery of the Equipment if the delivery occurs on the sixteenth through the last day of the month.

D. ADVANCE RENTALS: FIRST RENTAL PAYMENT(S) PLUS APPLICABLE TAXES

DELIVERY AND ACCEPTANCE OF EQUIPMENT (Check Appropriate Box)

Lessee's obligations and liabilities under this Lease are absolute and unconditional under all circumstances and regardless of any failure of operation or loss of possession of any item of Equipment or the cessation or interruption of Lessee's business for any reason whatsoever.

☐ On _____, the Equipment leased under this Lease was delivered to Lessee with all installation necessary for the proper use of the Equipment completed at a location agreed to by Lessee and the Equipment was inspected by Lessee and found to be in satisfactory condition in all respects and delivery thereof was unconditionally accepted by Lessee.

☒ The Equipment leased under this Lease has not yet been delivered to or accepted by Lessee and, upon delivery, Lessee agrees to execute such delivery and acceptance certificate as Lessor or Lessor's assignee requires.

THE UNDERSIGNED HEREBY AGREE TO ALL THE TERMS AND PROVISIONS SET FORTH ON ALL FOUR PAGES OF THIS LEASE AND ALL RIDERS EXECUTED IN CONNECTION HEREWITH. LESSEE ACKNOWLEDGES RECEIPT OF A COMPLETE COPY OF THIS LEASE TOGETHER WITH ALL RIDERS AND OF LESSOR'S STANDARD RETURN CONDITIONS.

LESSEE:
A B C University

By _____

Title _____

Date: _____ Federal Tax ID #: _____

LESSOR:
Associates Leasing, Inc.

By _____

Title _____

Date: _____ Federal Tax ID #: _____

TERMS AND PROVISIONS OF LEASE

1. **EFFECTIVE DATE:** The terms and provisions of this Lease Agreement ("**this Lease**") and the obligations and liabilities of Lessee under this Lease are effective on the date of Lessor's acceptance of this Lease ("**Effective Date**"), even though the Term and Lessee's obligation to pay the remaining Rental Payments may begin on a later date. This Lease shall mean and include all Riders executed in connection with the Lease.

2. **LEASE:** Lessor hereby leases to Lessee, and Lessee hereby hires and takes from Lessor, under and subject to the terms and provisions hereof until the end of the Term specified above ("**Term**"), the personal property described above and on any supplemental schedule(s) identified as constituting a part of this lease (herein, with all present and future attachments, accessories, replacement parts, repairs, and additions, and all proceeds thereof, referred to as "**Equipment**"). This Lease is for the Term commencing on the date the Equipment is delivered to Lessee. For the Term or any portion thereof, Lessee agrees to pay to Lessor aggregate rentals equal to the sum of all Rental Payments (including advance rentals) in accordance with the Payment Schedule.

3. **PLACE OF PAYMENT AND OBLIGATION TO PAY:** All Rental Payments are payable without notice or demand. All amounts payable under this Lease to Lessor are payable at Lessor's address set forth herein or at such other address as Lessor may specify from time to time in writing. Except as otherwise specifically provided herein, Lessee's obligation to pay the Rental Payments and all other amounts due or to become due under this Lease shall be absolute and unconditional under all circumstances, regardless of any set-off, counterclaim, recoupment, defense or other claim whatsoever. "**Interim Rental**" shall mean the per day rental for the period from the date of delivery of the Equipment ("**Delivery Date**") to the first Rental Payment date calculated as monthly Rental Payment divided by 30 times the number of days from the Delivery Date through the end of the month prior to which first Rental Payment for the Equipment is due. Interim Rental is payable upon delivery of the Equipment to the Lessee unless deferred by Lessor to the first monthly Rental Payment date.

Page 1 of 4 of Lease Agreement dated _____ between _____ **A B C University** _____ (Lessee)

and _____ **Associates Leasing, Inc.** _____ (Lessor) .

Original

4602001
1.01

Lessee's Initials [   ]

4.   DELINQUENCY CHARGES: For each Rental Payment or other sum due under this Lease which is not paid when due, Lessee agrees to pay Lessor a delinquency charge calculated thereon at the rate of 1 1/2% per month for the period of delinquency or, at Lessor's option, 5% of such Rental Payment or other sum due under this Lease, provided that such a delinquency charge is not prohibited by law, otherwise at the highest rate Lessee can legally obligate itself to pay and/or Lessor can legally collect. **Lessee agrees to reimburse Lessor immediately upon demand for any amount charged to Lessor by any depositary institution because a check, draft or other order made or drawn by or for the benefit of Lessee is returned unpaid for any reason and, if allowed by law, to pay Lessor an additional handling charge in the amount of $25.00 or in the event applicable law limits or restricts the amount of such reimbursement and/or handling charge, the amounts chargeable under this provision will be limited and/or restricted in accordance with applicable law.**

5.   NO WARRANTIES BY LESSOR, MAINTENANCE, AND COMPLIANCE WITH LAWS: Lessor makes no representations or warranties as to the character of this transaction for tax or other purposes. Lessee acknowledges and agrees that: the Equipment is of a size, design, capacity and manufacture selected by Lessee; Lessor is not the manufacturer of the Equipment or the manufacturer's agent; LESSEE LEASES THE EQUIPMENT "AS IS" AND LESSOR HAS NOT MADE, AND DOES NOT MAKE, ANY REPRESENTATION OR WARRANTY, EXPRESS OR IMPLIED, AS TO THE VALUE, CONDITION, QUALITY, MATERIAL, WORKMANSHIP, DESIGN, CAPACITY, MERCHANTABILITY, DURABILITY, FITNESS OR SUITABILITY OF THE EQUIPMENT FOR ANY USE OR PURPOSE, OR ANY OTHER REPRESENTATION OR WARRANTY WHATSOEVER, EXPRESS OR IMPLIED. Lessee will not assert any claim whatsoever, regardless of cause, against Lessor. Lessee will not bring any suit or claim against or make any settlement with the manufacturer or seller to Lessor of the Equipment (both herein called "Seller") without Lessor's prior written consent; and the selection, servicing and maintaining of the Equipment shall be entirely at Lessee's risk and expense. Lessee agrees, at its own cost and expense: (a) to cause the Equipment to be operated with care and only by qualified personnel (or Lessee's customers) in the regular course of Lessee's business; (b) to comply with all applicable laws, rules and regulations relating to the Equipment, with any published instructions or specifications of the Seller and with all of the terms of any insurance policy covering the Equipment; (c) to obtain, or sign any documents Lessor deems necessary and any certificates of title required or permitted by law with respect to the Equipment; (d) to maintain the Equipment in good operating condition, repair and appearance; and (e) to furnish Lessor promptly with such financial statements and other information as Lessor may reasonably request from time to time.

6.   STIPULATED VALUE: "Stipulated Value" as of any date shall mean an amount equal to all accrued and unpaid Rental Payments and all other amounts then due and remaining unpaid plus all unaccrued Rental Payments plus the Fair Market Value (as determined in accordance with Paragraph 15 of this Lease) of the Equipment in the same condition as when received by Lessee, reasonable wear and tear from the normal use thereof alone excepted, as well as in the condition required upon its return determined in accordance with Paragraph 17 of this Lease.

7.   INSURANCE: Lessee shall bear all risk of loss of, damage to, or destruction of the Equipment from the date of its delivery until its return. If, for any reason, any of the Equipment is lost, stolen, destroyed or damaged beyond repair, Lessee shall (a) immediately and fully inform Lessor with regard thereto, and (b) promptly, at the option of Lessor, either (i) replace the lost, stolen, destroyed or damaged beyond repair Equipment with Equipment satisfactory to Lessor, or (ii) pay to Lessor the Stipulated Value calculated as of the date of payment thereof. Any amounts actually received by Lessor from insurance or otherwise on Lessee's behalf for such loss or damage shall be applied to reduce Lessee's obligation under this paragraph. Except as expressly provided herein, the total or partial destruction of the Equipment or the total or partial loss of use or possession thereof to Lessee, shall not release or relieve Lessee from its obligations and liabilities under this Lease. Lessee agrees to procure and maintain at all times on and after the Effective Date such liability, physical damage and other insurance as Lessor may require from time to time. Lessee agrees that all such insurance shall be in form and amount and with insurers satisfactory to Lessor, and that Lessee will deliver promptly to Lessor certificates or, upon request, policies satisfactory to Lessor evidencing such insurance. All liability policies shall name Lessor as an additional insured, and all physical damage policies shall provide that payment thereof shall be made to Lessor and Lessee as their interests may appear. Each policy shall provide that Lessor's interest therein shall not be invalidated by any acts, omissions or neglect of anyone other than Lessor, and shall contain the insurer's agreement to give Lessor at least 30 days prior written notice before cancellation or any material change in the policy shall be effective as to Lessor, whether such cancellation or change is at the direction of Lessee or the insurer.

8.   TAXES: Lessee shall be liable for all taxes, levies, duties, assessments, and other governmental charges (including any penalties and interest, and any fees for titles or registration) levied or assessed against Lessee, Lessor or the Equipment, upon or with respect to the lease or the purchase, use, operation, leasing, ownership, value, return or other disposition of the Equipment, or the rent, earnings or receipts arising therefrom, exclusive, however, of any taxes based on Lessor's net income. **Unless Lessor notifies Lessee in writing otherwise, Lessor will file all returns and remit all personal property taxes applicable to the Equipment. Lessee agrees to reimburse Lessor for all such personal property taxes immediately upon receipt of Lessor's invoice including without limitation such taxes assessed or arising during the term of this Lease but remitted by Lessor after the termination of this Lease.** At Lessor's option, Lessee agrees to remit, along with Lessee's rental payments under this Lease, an amount equal to a percentage of Lessor's reasonable estimate of the personal property taxes that will be assessable against the Equipment during the succeeding tax year. Any such amounts remitted to Lessor will be credited by Lessor against Lessee's obligations under this paragraph. Lessee will remain obligated in the event that such amounts are insufficient to fully reimburse Lessor for the actual amount of such taxes and any surplus will be either credited to Lessee's other obligations to Lessor or returned to Lessee. If requested, Lessee agrees to file promptly on behalf of Lessor all requested tax returns and reports concerning the Equipment in form satisfactory to Lessor, with all appropriate governmental agencies and to mail a copy thereof to Lessor concurrently with the filing thereof. Lessee further agrees to keep or cause to be kept and made available to Lessor any and all necessary records relevant to the use of the Equipment and pertaining to the aforesaid taxes, assessments and other governmental charges. **The obligations arising under this paragraph shall survive payment of all other obligations under this Lease and the termination of this Lease.**

9.   LESSOR'S TITLE, STORAGE AND IDENTIFICATION OF EQUIPMENT: Title to the Equipment will at all times remain in Lessor and Lessee will at all times, at its own cost and expense, protect and defend the title of Lessor from and against all claims, liens and legal processes of creditors of Lessee and keep the Equipment free and clear from all such claims, liens and processes. Lessee agrees not to alter or modify the Equipment without first obtaining in each instance the prior written approval of Lessor. Upon the expiration or termination of this Lease, Lessee, at Lessee's sole expense, shall return the Equipment unencumbered to Lessor at a place to be designated by Lessor, and in the same condition as when received by Lessee, reasonable wear and tear resulting from normal use thereof alone excepted. If Lessee fails to perform duly and promptly any of its obligations under this Lease (including, without limitation, insuring the Equipment), Lessor may perform the same, but shall not be obligated to do so, for the account of Lessee to protect the interest of Lessor or Lessee or both, at Lessor's option. Any amount paid or expense (including reasonable attorney's fees), penalty or other liability incurred by Lessor in such performance shall be payable by Lessee upon demand as additional rent for the Equipment.

10.   POSSESSION, LOCATION OF EQUIPMENT, RIGHT OF INSPECTION AND ASSIGNMENT: The Equipment will be kept by Lessee at the location indicated herein, and will not be removed from said location without the prior written consent of Lessor. Lessor shall have the right to inspect the Equipment at all reasonable times and from time to time as Lessee may require. Lessee will not sell, assign, transfer, pledge, encumber, secrete, sublet or otherwise dispose of any of the Equipment or any interest of Lessee in or under this Lease without Lessor's prior written consent. This Lease and all rights of Lessor under this Lease will be assignable by Lessor without Lessee's consent. LESSEE HEREBY WAIVES, RELINQUISHES AND DISCLAIMS AS TO ANY ASSIGNEE OF LESSOR ALL CLAIMS, RIGHTS OF SET-OFF AND DEFENSES LESSEE MAY HAVE AGAINST LESSOR, INCLUDING THE RIGHT TO WITHHOLD PAYMENT OF ANY MONIES WHICH MAY BECOME DUE UNDER THIS LEASE. After receiving notice of any assignment by Lessor, Lessee agrees that it will not, without the prior written consent of the assignee, purchaser or secured party, (i) prepay any amounts owing under this Lease; (ii) modify or amend this Lease; or (iii) exercise any rights which are exercisable only with the consent of the Lessor.

Page 2 of 4 of Lease Agreement dated _____ between _____ A B C University _____

and _____ Associates Leasing, Inc. _____ (Lessor).

4602001
1.01

Original

Lessee's Initials

(Lessee)

11. **DEFAULT AND REMEDIES:** An event of default shall occur if: (a) any Rental Payment or any other amount owed by Lessee to Lessor or to any affiliate of Lessor, whether under this Lease or under any other instrument or agreement, is not paid promptly when due; (b) Lessee breaches any warranty or provision hereof or of any other instrument or agreement delivered by Lessee to Lessor or to any affiliate of Lessor; (c) Lessee ceases to do business as a going concern, becomes insolvent, makes an assignment for the benefit of creditors, admits in writing its inability to pay its debts as they become due, or takes advantage of any law for the relief of debtors; (d) any property of Lessee is attached; (e) a petition in bankruptcy or for an arrangement, reorganization, composition, liquidation, dissolution or similar relief is filed by or against Lessee under any present or future statute, law or regulation; (f) Lessee or its shareholders take any action looking to its dissolution or liquidation or if there is any material change in the ownership, management or control of Lessee; or (g) a trustee or receiver is appointed for Lessee or for any substantial part of its property. Upon the occurrence of an event of default Lessee shall be in default under this Lease and Lessor may, at its option, with or without notice to Lessee (a) declare all sums due and to become due under this Lease and all other sums then owing by Lessee to Lessor to be immediately due and payable; (b) proceed by appropriate court action or actions or other proceedings either at law or in equity to enforce performance by Lessee of any and all provisions of this Lease and to recover the damages for the breach thereof; (c) require Lessee to assemble the Equipment and deliver same forthwith to Lessor at Lessee's expense at such place as Lessor may designate which is reasonably convenient to both parties; (d) exercise one or more of the rights and remedies available to a secured party under the Uniform Commercial Code, whether or not this transaction is subject thereto; (e) enter, or its agents may enter, without notice or liability or legal process, into any premises where the Equipment may be, or is believed by Lessor to be, and repossess all or any part thereof, disconnecting and separating the same from any other property and using all force necessary and permitted by applicable law, Lessee hereby expressly waiving all further rights to possession of the Equipment after default and all claims for injuries suffered through or loss caused by such repossession; and/or (f) apply any security deposit or other amounts held by Lessor to any indebtedness of Lessee to Lessor. In addition, Lessee agrees to pay, to Lessor, as liquidated damages for loss of the bargain and not as a penalty, (1) the Stipulated Value plus (2) all expenses of retaking, holding, preparing for sale, selling and the like, including reasonable attorneys' fees and other legal expenses, less (3) any amount actually received by Lessor from the re-lease, sale or other disposition of the Equipment. **Lessee hereby waives any right to trial by jury in any proceeding arising out of this Lease.** Nothing herein contained will require Lessor to re-lease, sell or otherwise dispose of the Equipment. No remedy of Lessor under this Lease shall be exclusive of any other remedy herein or provide by law, but each shall be cumulative and in addition to every other remedy. A waiver of a default shall not be a waiver of any other or a subsequent default. If allowed by law, **the reasonable fees of attorneys** retained by Lessor shall include the amount of any flat fee, retainer, contingent fee or the hourly charges of any attorney retained by Lessor in enforcing any of Seller's rights under this Lease or in the prosecution or defense of any litigation related to this Lease or the transactions contemplated by this Lease. All notices to Lessee relating hereto will be considered received when delivered in person or mailed to Lessee at the address set forth in this Lease, or at any later address designated in writing by Lessee.

12. **INDEMNITY:** Lessor (which term as used herein includes Lessor's successors, assigns, agents, and servants) shall have no responsibility or liability to Lessee, its successors or assigns or any other person with respect to any Liabilities (as "Liabilities" is herein defined), and Lessee hereby assumes liability for, and hereby agrees, at its sole cost and expense, to indemnify, defend, protect and save Lessor and keep it harmless from and against, any and all Liabilities. The term **"Liabilities"** as used herein shall include any and all liabilities, obligations, losses, damages, penalties, claims, actions, suits, costs, expenses and disbursements of whatsoever kind and nature, including legal fees and expenses, (whether or not any transaction contemplated hereby is consummated) imposed on, incurred by or asserted against Lessor or the Equipment (whether by way of strict or absolute liability or otherwise) and in any way relating to or arising out of this Lease or the selection, manufacture, purchase, acceptance, ownership, delivery, non-delivery, lease, possession, use, operation, condition, servicing, maintenance, repair, improvement, alteration, replacement, storage, return or other disposition of the Equipment (including without limitation, (i) claims as a result of latent or patent defects, whether or not discoverable by Lessor or Lessee, (ii) claims for trademark, patent or copyright infringement, and (iii) tort claims of any kind (whether based on Lessor's alleged negligence or otherwise), including claims for injury or damage to property, or injury or death to any person (including Lessee's employees) or, for any interruption of service, loss of business, anticipatory profits, or consequential damages. Provided, however, that Lessee shall not indemnify Lessor from any liabilities based exclusively on either: (i) the gross negligence, or (ii) willful misconduct of Lessor or its agents or employees. Lessee agrees to give Lessor prompt written notice of any claim or liability hereby indemnified against. **The indemnities arising under this paragraph shall survive payment of all other obligations under this Lease and the termination of this Lease.**

13. POWER OF ATTORNEY AND FINANCING STATEMENT: LESSEE HEREBY APPOINTS LESSOR OR ANY OFFICER, EMPLOYEE OR DESIGNEE OF LESSOR OR ANY ASSIGNEE OF LESSOR (OR ANY DESIGNEE OF SUCH ASSIGNEE) AS LESSEE'S ATTORNEY-IN-FACT, IN LESSEE'S OR LESSOR'S NAME, TO: (a) PREPARE, EXECUTE AND SUBMIT ANY NOTICE OR PROOF OF LOSS IN ORDER TO REALIZE THE BENEFITS OF ANY INSURANCE POLICY INSURING THE EQUIPMENT; (b) PREPARE, EXECUTE AND FILE ANY INSTRUMENT WHICH, IN LESSOR'S OPINION, IS NECESSARY TO PERFECT AND/OR GIVE PUBLIC NOTICE OF THE INTERESTS OF LESSOR IN THE EQUIPMENT; AND (c) ENDORSE LESSEE'S NAME ON ANY REMITTANCE REPRESENTING PROCEEDS OF ANY INSURANCE RELATING TO THE EQUIPMENT OR THE PROCEEDS OF THE SALE, LEASE OR OTHER DISPOSITION OF THE EQUIPMENT (WHETHER OR NOT THE SAME IS A DEFAULT HEREUNDER). This power is coupled with an interest and is irrevocable so long as any indebtedness hereunder remains unpaid. Lessee agrees to execute and deliver to Lessor, upon Lessor's request such documents and assurances as Lessor deems necessary or advisable for the confirmation or perfection of this Lease and Lessor's rights hereunder, including such documents as Lessor may require for filing or recording. LESSEE FURTHER AGREES TO PAY A ONE-TIME UCC FILING FEE TO COVER LESSOR'S COST FOR SUCH FILING(S) AND OTHER DOCUMENTATION COST, IF PERMITTED BY LAW. LESSEE AGREES THAT A CARBON, PHOTOGRAPHIC OR OTHER REPRODUCTION OF THIS LEASE OR OF A FINANCING STATEMENT MAY BE FILED AS A FINANCING STATEMENT.

14. GENERAL PROVISIONS: To the extent that any court of law at any time deems Lessee to have an interest in any of the Equipment during the Term, Lessee hereby grants Lessor and its affiliates a first perfected security interest in the Equipment and all proceeds thereof including, accounts, chattel paper, documents, general intangibles and instruments arising from the sale, lease, rent or other disposition of the Equipment. The grant of the security interest in this Lease does not grant Lessee the right to sell, lease, rent or otherwise dispose of the Equipment which rights are, except upon the prior written consent of Lessor, denied to Lessee. The security interest granted by Lessee to Lessor herein shall secure all of Lessee's existing or hereafter arising liabilities and obligations of Lessee to Lessor or any affiliate of Lessor whether such liabilities and obligations arise under or apart from this Lease and whether they arise during the Term thereafter. Lessor shall not be required to segregate any Security Deposits, Advance Rentals, and other amounts from time to time held by Lessor under this Lease ("**Advance Payments**") in a separate account and no such amount will bear interest or otherwise accrue profits. In the event Lessor ever receives any income, increases or profits from or related to such Advance Payments, such amounts, if any, shall be the property of Lessor. Any provisions hereof contrary to, prohibited by or invalid under applicable laws or regulations shall be inapplicable and deemed omitted from this Lease, but shall not invalidate the remaining provisions hereof. No provision of this Lease shall require the payment or the collection of any amount that would be considered interest in excess of the maximum permitted by applicable law. If any such excess is hereby provided for, or shall be adjudicated to be so provided, in this Lease or otherwise in connection with this Lease, the provisions of this paragraph shall govern and prevail and neither Lessee nor the guarantors, successors, or assigns of Lessee shall be obligated to pay the excess amount or any other excess sum paid for the use, forbearance, or detention of credit pursuant hereto or advanced in connection herewith. In the event Lessor ever receives, collects, or applies any such amount of rent or other charges, such amount which would be in excess of the maximum amount permitted by applicable law shall be applied as a payment and reduction of the amounts due under the Lease; and, if the payments under the Lease have been paid in full, any remaining excess shall forthwith be paid to Lessee. In determining whether or not the amounts paid or payable exceeds the Maximum Rate, Lessee and Lessor shall, to the extent permitted by applicable law, (i) characterize any non-rental payment as an expense, fee, or premium rather than as interest, (ii) exclude voluntary prepayments and the effects thereof, and (iii) amortize, prorate, allocate, and spread in equal or unequal parts the total amount of any payments determined throughout the entire contemplated term of the Lease so that interest for the entire term does not exceed the Maximum Rate. The term "Maximum Rate" shall mean the greater of: (A) the highest rate which Lessor agree to the Maximum Rate as the rate of interest agreed to between Lessor and Lessee. This Lease and any addenda referred to herein constitute the entire agreement of the parties hereto. No oral agreement, guaranty, promise, condition, representation or warranty shall be binding. All prior conversations, agreements or representations related hereto and/or to the Equipment are superseded hereby, and no modification hereof shall be binding unless in writing and signed by an officer of the party to be bound. The only copy of this Lease that will be constitute "chattel paper" for purposes of the Uniform Commercial Code is the original of this Lease marked "Original For Associates". This Lease will be governed by and construed in accordance with the laws of the state of Texas.

Page 3 of 4 of Lease Agreement dated _____ between _____ **A B C University**

and _____ **Associates Leasing, Inc.** _____ (Lessor).

4602001
1.01

Original

15. FAIR MARKET VALUE: The term **"Fair Market Value"** of the Equipment in the return condition required as used herein shall be determined on the basis of, and shall be equal in amount to, the value which would obtain in an arms-length transaction between an informed and willing buyer-user (other than a buyer currently in possession) and an informed and willing seller under no compulsion to sell. If Lessor and Lessee are unable to agree upon a determination of the Fair Market Value of such Equipment, such value shall be determined in accordance with the foregoing definition by a qualified independent appraiser selected by Lessor. The appraiser shall be instructed to make such determination within a period of 45 days following appointment, and shall promptly communicate such determination in writing to Lessor and Lessee. The expenses and fees of the appraiser's determination of such Fair Market value shall be conclusively binding upon both Lessor and Lessee. The expenses and fees of the appraiser shall be borne by Lessee.

16. HOLDOVER: In the event that Lessee retains possession of the Equipment after the end of the Term of this Lease, all terms, provisions and conditions of this Lease shall continue in full force and effect until Lessor recovers the physical possession of the Equipment and Lessee shall be obligated to pay to Lessor Rental Payments during each month (or any part thereof) when Lessor is not in possession of the Equipment after the end of the Term of the Lease in an amount equal to one and one half times the monthly Rental Payments required during the Term of the Lease.

17. RETURN OF EQUIPMENT: Lessee shall, at Lessee's sole cost and expense, return all, but not less than all, of the Equipment to Lessor immediately upon the expiration of the Term or any Renewal Term of this Lease, at Lessee's sole expense, Lessee shall return the Equipment unencumbered to Lessor at a place to be designated by Lessor, and in the same condition as when received by Lessee, reasonable wear and tear resulting from normal use thereof alone allowed and pursuant to the terms and conditions contained in Lessor's **Standard Return Conditions** for equipment similar to the Equipment subject to this Lease (a copy of which has been delivered to Lessee in conjunction with this Lease).

LESSOR'S ASSIGNMENT

For value received, Lessor sells and assigns to Associates Leasing, Inc. (**"ALI"**), free and clear of all liens and encumbrances, all right, title and interest in and to this Lease and the Equipment. Lessor warrants to ALI that at the time of the execution of this Assignment, Lessor was the owner of the Equipment and Documents ("Documents") will mean and refer to the Lease and any schedules, guaranties, security agreements or other documents, instruments or certificates executed or delivered in connection with the Lease) subject only to the interests of the Lessee in the Equipment under the terms of the Lease; no party, other than ALI and Lessee, will have any interest in the Equipment and this Assignment conveys the Equipment and Documents to ALI free and clear of all liens, encumbrances or other interests of whatever kind in favor of any third party whatsoever; Lessor will forever defend ALI's title in and to the Equipment and Documents against any and all persons whatsoever; the Documents are genuine, enforceable and in all respects what they purport to be; all signatures, names, addresses, amounts and other statements and facts contained in the Documents and herein are true and correct; all parties to the Documents have the capacity to contract and none of such parties is a minor; Lessor is the lessor under the Lease, the Lease is the only lease covering the Equipment and is the entire agreement between Lessor and Lessee; all originals of the Documents other than Lessee's copy have been or will be delivered to ALI; Lessor will comply with all its warranties and other obligations under the Lease; the Documents are and will continue to be free from defenses, counter-claims, cross-claims and set-offs, and are in compliance with all applicable laws and regulations; the Equipment has retained and will retain its character as personal property; there are no termination, purchase or renewal options or rights of third parties in or to the Documents or Equipment except as stated therein; there has been no prepayment of rental or other monies owing under the Documents except as stated in the Lease and no down payment, security deposit or advance rental required to be paid by Lessee was loaned directly or indirectly by Lessor and such amount has been paid by Lessee in cash or as otherwise set forth in the Lease, and no part thereof was properly installed if required, Lessor; the Equipment was delivered in satisfactory condition to Lessee on the date, if any, set forth above, was properly installed if required, and was unconditionally accepted by Lessee; neither Lessor nor Lessee is in default under the Lease and Lessor has no knowledge of the occurrence of any event which, with the passage of time or the giving of notice, would constitute a default under the Lease; the security interest or reservation of title evidenced by the Lease is and, after assignment, will continue to be valid, first, prior to all others and effective against all persons; Lessor has caused or will promptly cause such actions or procedures to be taken as are required or permitted by statute or regulation to perfect such security interest or reservation of title in ALI's favor, including, without limitation, filing financing statements, recording documents and obtaining Certificates of Title disclosing ALI's interest; Lessor has taken all necessary corporate action which may be required to authorize the acts called for herein; and this Assignment is not in violation of any indenture, loan agreement or other agreement to which Lessor is a party or by which it may be bound. **Lessor acknowledges that ALI will be relying upon the foregoing warranties and that the knowledge of ALI of any breach of any such warranty will not impair or constitute any waiver of any such warranty or of any of Lessor's obligations with respect thereto.** ALI will have no obligation to notify Lessor of any breach of any such warranty which may come to its attention or to undertake or continue to undertake any cure or remedy of any defect in the Documents. Lessor will continue liable hereunder notwithstanding ALI's waiver of or failure to enforce any of the terms, covenants or conditions contained in the Documents or any release of, or failure on the part of ALI to realize upon or protect the Equipment or any interest therein. If any of the foregoing are untrue or breached by Lessor, Lessor shall, without requiring ALI to tender this Lease or the Equipment or to proceed against Lessee or any other party of any security, repurchase this Lease and the Equipment on demand and pay ALI in cash, an amount equal to the Stipulated Value as of the date of payment plus all costs and expenses paid or incurred by ALI with respect to this Lease and/or the Equipment.

LESSOR:

By: _____

Name: _____   Title: _____

Page 4 of 4 of Lease Agreement dated _____ between _____ A B C University

and _____ Associates Leasing, Inc.   (Lessor).

Original

(Lessee)

Lessee's Initials

4602001
1.01

STANDARD RETURN CONDITIONS AND
PURCHASE OPTION RIDER
(Club Car)

This Standard Return Conditions and Purchase Option Rider (this "Rider") is attached to and incorporated into the terms of that certain Associates Leasing, Inc. Lease Agreement (the "Lease") between Associates Leasing, Inc. and _____ A B C University _____, as Lessee, dated _____ xx-xx-xx _____.

1. **RETURN OF EQUIPMENT.** Notwithstanding anything to the contrary contained in the Lease, and in addition to the terms and conditions contained therein and herein, if Lessee does not exercise, or is precluded from exercising, Lessee's option to purchase the Equipment set forth below at the expiration of the term of the Lease, Lessee shall, at Lessee's sole cost and expense, return all, but not less than all, of such equipment to Lessor immediately upon the expiration of the Term of the Lease pursuant to the terms and conditions contained in the Lease and, with respect to each item of Equipment, as applicable, the following must be true:

(A) All Safety Equipment must be in place and meet applicable federal, state and other governmental standards.

(B) All covers and guards must be in place with no sheet metal, plastic, or cowling damage.

(C) All parts, pieces, components and optional equipment must be present, installed and operational. All accessories that accompany units shall be returned in proper order.

(D) All motors shall operate smoothly without overheating and shall have good bearings and bushings.

(E) All electronic controls shall operate per manufacturer's specifications. Controls which bypass normal operations shall be repaired at Lessee's expense.

(F) All electrical systems shall be able to provide electrical output as specified by the manufacturer.

(G) All batteries shall be in good, safe operating condition with no dead cells or cracked cases. Batteries shall hold a charge and provide adequate power to operate the equipment.

(H) All Equipment shall have serviceable tires, retaining proper air pressure, and without repair patches.

(I) All oil and grease seals must contain lubrication in the manufacturers designed reservoir.

(J) All Equipment must have a relatively clean appearance.

(K) All Equipment shall be free from excessive wear necessitating major component repair or replacement caused by lack of recommended maintenance as detailed in customer operation/maintenance manual furnished with each item of Equipment.

(L) All Equipment shall be free from structural damage or bent frames.

(M) All Equipment attachments, if any, must be in good operating condition.

2. **RETURN PERFORMANCE.** Each item of Equipment must be able to complete the following tests:

(i)   Operate normally in forward and reverse directions through all its speed ranges or gears.
(ii)   Steer normally right and left in both forward and reverse.
(iii) Have all functions and controls work in normal manner.
(iv) Be able to stop with its service brakes in a safe distance in both forward and reverse.
(v)   Operate without leaking any fluids.
(vi) Perform its designed functions in a satisfactory manner.

Notwithstanding the above, repairs under $100.00 will not be billed to the Lessee.

3.   **REQUIRED PURCHASE.** If any item of Equipment is damaged or does not meet the standards set forth above for the return condition of such Equipment, or if the Lessee fails to discharge Lessee's obligations set forth above with regard to any item of Equipment, Lessee shall pay to Lessor, immediately upon demand, the Stipulated Value applicable to such item of Equipment.

4.   **LESSEE'S OPTION TO PURCHASE.** Lessor hereby grants to Lessee the option to purchase all, but not less than all, of the Equipment at the expiration of the Term of the Lease. Lessee agrees to give Lessor at least 60, but not more than 120 days, prior written notice of its intent to exercise the option to purchase. The purchase price (the **"Purchase Option Price"**) to be paid to Lessor for the Equipment will be $ _____**(AMOUNT)**_____ (insert a dollar amount or **"FMV"**) plus an amount equal to all accrued but unpaid rentals under the terms of the Lease, plus applicable taxes, if any, on the above sum, all payable in cash on the expiration date of the Lease. Lessor is authorized to apply the amount of any security deposit to the Purchase Option Price and the balance, if any, of the Purchase Option Price must be received by Lessor no later than ten (10) days prior to the last day of the Lease Term. Upon receipt of the total Purchase Option Price and all other amounts payable under this Lease, Lessor shall convey the Equipment to Lessee "AS-IS, WHERE-IS, WITHOUT ANY WARRANTIES OF ANY TYPE, KIND, CHARACTER OR NATURE, EXPRESS OR IMPLIED, INCLUDING WITHOUT LIMITATION, WARRANTIES OF MERCHANTABILITY OR FITNESS FOR ANY PARTICULAR PURPOSE."

Page 1 of 2 of Standard Return Conditions and Purchase Option Rider dated **xx-xx-xx** between __A B C University__
(Lessee) and __Associates Leasing, Inc.__ (Lessor).

400001
1.01
RTRNCOND.CC

Lessee's
Initials

5. **DEFINED TERMS.** All capitalized terms used herein but not otherwise defined herein shall have the definitions prescribed for such terms in the Lease.

6. **DEFAULT BY LESSEE.** If Lessee at any time defaults in any of its obligations to Lessor, such default will be considered an abandonment of the purchase option contained in this Rider and the option herein will immediately expire and become null and void.

7. **OPTION NOT ASSIGNABLE.** It is agreed that Lessee's rights under this Rider are not assignable and that no modification of the provisions hereof will be binding unless in writing and signed by an officer of the party to be charged.

8. **FAIR MARKET VALUE.** The term "FMV" as used herein means Fair Market Value and shall be determined on the basis of, and shall be equal in amount to, the value of the Equipment in the return condition specified in this Rider, which would be obtained in an arms-length transaction between an informed and willing buyer-user (other than a buyer currently in possession) and an informed and willing seller under no compulsion to sell. If on or before 60 days prior to the expiration of the Term of the Lease, Lessor and Lessee are unable to agree upon a determination of the Fair Market Value of such Equipment, such value shall be determined in accordance with the foregoing definition by qualified independent appraiser selected by Lessor. The appraiser shall be instructed to make such determination within a period of 45 days following appointment, but in no event later than 10 days prior to the expiration of the Term of the Lease, and shall promptly communicate such determination in writing to Lessor and Lessee. The appraiser's determination of such Fair Market value shall be conclusively binding upon both Lessor and Lessee. The expenses and fees of the appraiser shall be borne by Lessee.

LESSOR : Associates Leasing, Inc.

By _____

Name _____

Title _____

LESSEE: A B C University

By _____

Name _____

Title _____

Page 2 of 2 of Standard Return Conditions and Purchase Option Rider dated **xx-xx-xx** between A B C University (Lessee) and **Associates Leasing, Inc.** (Lessor).

ASSOCIATES LEASING, INC.
A SUBSIDIARY OF ASSOCIATES CORPORATION OF NORTH AMERICA

Date _06/22/2000_

To: _____
    (Insurance Agent)

    _____
    (Address)

    _____
    (City, State, Zip)

    _____
    (Telephone)

    _____
    (Fax)

Gentlemen:

We have entered into a Lease with ASSOCIATES LEASING INC., **8001 Ridgepoint Drive Irving, TX 75063** , whereby they have an insurable interest in the following described property:

Sixty (60) Club Car DS Gasoline Golf Cars complete with all attachments and accessories

1 2 3 College St.
School   MI   45678
_____
              (Location of Property)

                                    $ _240,000.00_
                                        (Value)

Under the terms of the Lease we are required to insure the property against all risks and obtain Public Liability and Property Damage in minimum amounts of: PL **750,000.00** , PD **750,000.00** Please place the necessary coverage and provide them with a copy of the complete Policy or a Certificate of Insurance showing the following information:

Name of Insured
Name of Insurance Agent
Name of Insurance Company
Effective Date of Coverage
Expiration Date of Coverage

Policy Number
Description of Property Insured
Description of Limits of Coverage
Any Exclusions and Special Conditions of Coverage

In addition to the above Policy or Certificate, please execute and send to them the attached Loss Payable Endorsement and a copy of an Endorsement naming them as Additional Insured as regards to the PL and PD Coverage.

Sincerely,

Lessee: **A B C University**

By: _____

Title: _____

Address: **1 2 3 College St.**

School _____ **MI** _____ **45678**
(City, State, Zip)

ORIGINAL

CERTIFIED COPY OF RESOLUTIONS

The undersigned certifies that undersigned is the _____ Secretary of
                                                    (Insert "Assistant" if Assistant Secretary or title if other officer)

A B C University _____ , a _____ MI _____ corporation ("this Corporation"),
        (Name of Corporation)

and that as such, undersigned is authorized to execute this Certification on behalf of this Corporation, and further certifies that the following is a

true and correct copy of resolutions adopted at a meeting of the Board of Directors of this Corporation, duly called and held on _____
                                                                                                                                      (Date)

at which meeting a quorum was present and acting throughout, and the proceedings of said meeting were in accordance with the charter and by-laws of this Corporation, and that said resolutions have not been in any way amended, annulled, rescinded or revoked and are in full force and effect:

"RESOLVED, that the President, Secretary, Treasurer or any Vice President, Assistant Vice President, Assistant Secretary or Assistant Treasurer of this Corporation, or their duly elected or appointed successor in office, be and each hereby is authorized and empowered (either alone or in conjunction with any one or more of such officers of this Corporation) in the name and on behalf of this Corporation to take from time to time all or any of the following actions: (1) to, on a with or without recourse basis, sell, assign, pledge, transfer, negotiate and grant a security interest, or any thereof, to Associates Commercial Corporation, Associates Leasing, Inc., Associates Rental Systems, Inc., their affiliates, their predecessors-in-interest, and/or any party that has assigned or intends to assign any receivables (as defined herein) to them (all of which are herein singularly and collectively called "Associates," as appropriate) in or with respect to all or any of this Corporation's inventory, machinery, equipment and receivables (the term "receivables" as used herein being defined to include the accounts, contract rights, general intangibles, instruments and chattel paper now or hereafter owned or entered into by this Corporation, including without limitation conditional sales contracts, chattel mortgages, security agreements, leases, drafts, notes, accounts receivable and other forms of obligation owing to or owned by this Corporation, together with all things, rights and powers pertaining thereto); (2) to borrow from Associates or agree to repay Associates such sum or sums of money as in the exclusive judgment of such officer or officers this Corporation may require, either secured or unsecured; (3) to execute (by means of rubber or other stamp or legend, without designation of the individual affixing such stamp or legend being required or by other means) and deliver any and all schedules, assignments, transfers, endorsements, repurchase agreements, bills of sale, agreements or other instruments, in the form and containing such representations and warranties required by Associates, in connection with the sale, assignment, pledge, transfer, negotiation and/or grant of security interest to Associates of or with respect to the inventory, machinery, equipment and receivables of this Corporation, and to delegate to one or more employees of this Corporation the authority and power to do all or any actions authorized in this clause (3); (4) to execute on behalf of this Corporation and deliver to Associates, in the form required by Associates, any and all promissory notes, security agreements, conditional sale contracts, mortgages, other agreements, instruments and documents of any nature, including without limitation master loan agreements providing for borrowings on a revolving basis, ("Agreements") of this Corporation evidencing the indebtedness thereunder, the obligations guarantied and/or the amount or amounts borrowed or any renewals or extensions thereof, plus charges, if any, such Agreements to bear such rate of interest, provide for the payment of such late charges and expenses, be payable at such times and in such manner, with or without fixed installments, and contain such terms and conditions as such officer may agree to (the signature of such officer thereon to be conclusive proof of such officer's agreement thereto); (5) to enter into with Associates leasing agreements of equipment, vehicles and other chattels; (6) purchase equipment, vehicles and other chattels from Associates and execute retail installment contracts, conditional sale contracts, security agreements, promissory notes and other agreements with Associates evidencing the purchase of the chattels by this Corporation from Associates and the resulting indebtedness due to Associates from this Corporation; (7) to execute and deliver receivables to Associates; (8) to execute and deliver to Associates Lessee's Agreements and Sublessee's Agreements acknowledging and granting certain rights of and obligations to Associates that relate to the receivables; (9) to unconditionally and absolutely, jointly and severally guarantee to Associates the full, faithful and prompt performance, payment and discharge by any party of all such party's present and future obligations to Associates, absolute or contingent, secured or unsecured, matured or unmatured, by executing and delivering to Associates any guaranty or similar agreement; (10) to carry out, or if agreeable to Associates to modify, amend or terminate any instruments or agreements at any time existing between this Corporation and Associates; and (11) to do any acts, including but not limited to the mortgage, pledge, creation of security interest or hypothecation from time to time in favor of Associates of any or all present and future assets (real and personal) of this Corporation ("Collateral") to secure any and all present and future obligations of this Corporation to Associates, absolute or contingent, including but not limited to any obligations arising out of the transactions referred to herein and any renewals or extensions thereof, and to execute all instruments and agreements deemed necessary or proper by Associates in respect of the Collateral securing any of such obligations of this Corporation, and to affix the seal of this Corporation to any instruments or agreements if so required or requested by Associates.

RESOLVED, that any schedules, assignments, bills of sale, promissory notes, security agreements, conditional sale contracts, mortgages, guaranties, Lessee's Agreements, Sublessee's Agreements or other instruments, agreements or documents executed pursuant to these resolutions by an officer of this Corporation, or by an employee of this Corporation acting pursuant to delegation of authority, may be in such form and contain such terms, provisions, representations and warranties (including, without limiting the generality of the foregoing, waiver of all rights to notice and hearing prior to the exercise by Associates of its right to repossess Collateral without judicial process or to replevy, attach or levy upon Collateral without prior notice or hearing and warrants of attorney to confess judgment against this Corporation and to proceed against the assets of this Corporation) as they shall in their sole discretion determine.

RESOLVED, that all acts and deeds heretofore done by any of such officers of this Corporation for and on behalf of this Corporation in entering into, executing, acknowledging or attesting any schedules, assignments, bills of sale, promissory notes, security agreements, conditional sale contracts, mortgages, guaranties, Lessee's Agreements, Sublessee's Agreements or other instruments, agreements or documents, or in carrying out the terms and intentions of these resolutions are hereby ratified, approved and confirmed.

RESOLVED, that the Secretary or any other officer of this Corporation shall file with Associates a certified copy of these resolutions and a list of the names of the officers of this Corporation, and shall from time to time advise Associates in writing of the names of the employees of this Corporation to whom any power or authority provided in these resolutions has been delegated and of any changes in such officers or employees, and Associates shall be entitled to conclusively assume that these resolutions remain in full forces and effect, that all persons so named as officers of this Corporation are and continue to be such officers, and that all powers and authorities permitted by these resolutions to be delegated to an employee of this Corporation have been and continue to be properly delegated to all persons so named as employees, except in each case as, and until, Associates shall be otherwise notified in writing by the Secretary or any other officer of this Corporation."

I do further certify that this Corporation is in good standing in all jurisdictions in which it is required to be qualified to do business and that the execution of the schedules, assignments, bills of sale, promissory notes, security agreements, conditional sale contracts, mortgages, guaranties, Lessee's Agreements, Sublessee's Agreements or other instruments, agreements or documents authorized hereunder is not a violation of the charter, by-laws or agreements of this Corporation.

Page 1 of 2 of Certified Copy of Resolutions dated _____ between __A B C University_____ (Debtor)

and __Associates Leasing, Inc._____ (Secured Party) .

621674
Cert. Copy of Res.
(Broad)
1.00

Debtor's Initials

I do further certify that the following are officers of this Corporation:

President _____ Secretary _____

Vice President _____ Treasurer _____

As an officer of this Corporation and pursuant to the foregoing Resolutions, I do hereby delegate to each of the following employees of this Corporation:

_____ _____ _____
Name (Type or Print)   (Signature)   (Title or position)

_____ _____ _____
Name (Type or Print)   (Signature)   (Title or position)

_____ _____ _____
Name (Type or Print)   (Signature)   (Title or position)

the authority and power to transact on behalf of this Corporation any and all business which is permitted under such Resolutions.

IN WITNESS WHEREOF, I have hereunto set my hand and affixed the seal of this Corporation this date, _____ .

(Corporate   Seal)

_____
Secretary

Page 2 of 2 of Certified Copy of Resolutions dated _____ between **A B C University** _____ (Debtor)

and **Associates Leasing, Inc.** _____ (Secured Party) .

621674
Cert. Copy of Res.
(Broad)
1.00

SCHEDULE A

This SCHEDULE A is attached and made a part of that certain Lease dated _____ between _____

A B C University
_____

_____ ("Lessee") and Associates Leasing, Inc.

_____ ("Lessor")

covering the Equipment described below. This SCHEDULE A may also be attached to and made a part of any documents, including but not limited to the CERTIFICATE OF DELIVERY ("Documents") prepared in connection with the Lease.

Sixty (60) Club Car DS Gasoline Golf Cars complete with all

attachments and accessories

Serial Numbers:

Lessee hereby authorizes the attachment of a photocopy of this SCHEDULE A bearing a copy of the Lessee's signature to any Document, and such photocopy shall constitute an original of this SCHEDULE A for the intent and purpose of the Document to which it is attached.

LESSEE: A B C University

By: _____

Title: _____

Associates Commercial Corporation
Associates Leasing, Inc.

CERTIFICATE OF DELIVERY

Customer Certification

Please provide the information requested, sign and return promptly to the selling dealer.

I hereby certify that I, on behalf of the customer, personally inspected the equipment described below and that said equipment was delivered in proper working order on this _____ day of _____ , _____ ; and that I, on behalf of the customer, accept delivery of said equipment.

DESCRIPTION OF EQUIPMENT:

Sixty (60) Club Car DS Gasoline Golf Cars complete with all

attachments and accessories

A B C University

By: _____

Title: _____

8001 Ridgepoint Drive, Irving, TX 75063-3117

701015
Cert of Delivery
1.01

Competencies

1. Explain the tax classifications of clubs, including tax basics and tax avoidance. (pp. 353–355)

2. Explain how federal income tax affects clubs in relation to exemptions, IRS guidelines, unrelated business income, nonmember income, and tax forms, and identify provisions of state and local taxes, including the application of sales taxes and federal income tax rates. (pp. 355–370)

3. Catalog retention of business records according to prescribed guidelines. (pp. 370–373)

15

Taxes

IN 1789, BENJAMIN FRANKLIN wrote, "But in the world nothing can be said to be certain, except death and taxes."[1] Most hospitality businesses including clubs and individuals view taxes similarly—as a necessary evil. Most also try to pay as little tax as legally possible. Club financial managers try to minimize their club's income taxes in order to increase the owners' financial return (profit-oriented clubs) or to reduce a club's expenses (not-for-profit clubs). Questions regarding taxes addressed in this chapter include the following:

- What are the criteria for tax exemption for a social club?
- What is unrelated business income?
- What is nonmember income?
- What is the purpose of a member function questionnaire?
- Which tax forms must be filed with the federal government regarding federal income taxes?
- What are the tax rates for income subject to federal income taxation?
- What levels of government receive sales taxes?

This chapter covers the tax classification of clubs, tax concepts in general, tax avoidance, the federal income tax exemption requirements of clubs, other federal taxes, tax forms, state and local taxes, income tax rates, and retention of business records.

Tax Classifications of Clubs

Private social clubs are either member-owned or investor-owned. Member-owned clubs are generally organized under the non-profit corporate statutes of particular states and are eligible for federal and state income tax exemption. Some clubs may fail to qualify for the exemption or may choose to forego the exemption in the interest of greater operational flexibility.

Investor-owned clubs are almost always taxable, profit-oriented organizations. Many newer clubs have been organized to provide amenities to adjacent residential or resort developments. Many of these clubs are owned by the developer first, but are then acquired by members as the associated development matures.

This chapter was co-authored by Kevin Reilly, U.S. National Director of Taxation and Managing Director of the Washington, DC, office of PKF Worldwide.

The two major tax classifications of member-owned social clubs are tax-exempt clubs, often referred to in this chapter as **Section 501(c)(7) clubs**, and taxable clubs, which are governed according to Section 277 of the Internal Revenue Code (IRC). Since the majority of private member-owned clubs are tax-exempt, most of the tax issues in this chapter are directed at these clubs.

According to Section 501(c)(7) of the IRC, clubs organized for pleasure, recreation, and other nonprofitable purposes are exempt from federal income taxes if substantially all of their activities are for such purposes and no part of their net earnings are for the benefit of their members. This statement will be discussed in detail later in this chapter. **Unrelated business income**, income not related to their purpose, is subject to federal income taxes. This income, to a large extent, relates to nonmember income. If the unrelated business income is too large, the 501(c)(7) may lose its tax exempt status!

Section 277 clubs are subject to taxes on their income. Of course, the taxability of their income is not simple. The taxable clubs must track both member and nonmember income and associated expenses.

Tax Basics

Taxes are a major source of revenues for government entities at the federal, state, and local levels. Though the popular press has carried many articles over the past decade about smaller and more efficient government operations, the total tax revenues and expenditures continue to rise annually.

Taxes may be imposed on any of four primary tax bases including income, wealth, transactions, and people. Taxes on income are paid primarily by individuals and corporations. Federal, state, and local income taxes withheld and remitted to the various governmental entities by social clubs are a major source of income to governments. As discussed in the next section, tax-exempt clubs pay taxes on unrelated business income, while profit-oriented clubs pay income taxes on their taxable incomes.

Taxes on wealth refer to taxes on assets both real (such as buildings and land) and intangible (such as bonds). The wealth taxes include property taxes, estate and inheritance taxes, gift taxes, and net wealth tax. Of these, clubs pay property taxes, on their property.

Transactions refer to the sale of goods and services in the marketplace. Common taxes on transactions include sales taxes, value-added taxes, turnover taxes, excise taxes, and severance taxes. Many clubs pay state and local sales taxes, which are discussed in a general sense later in this chapter. In addition, clubs pay excise taxes on a number of purchases including gasoline, diesel fuel, and alcoholic beverages.

Finally, taxes imposed on people are referred to as lump-sum taxes and are based on the amount per person. This type of tax is not common in the United States.

Clearly, social clubs remit a large amount of taxes in various forms to the various governmental entities. The major focus is on federal income tax in this chapter.

Tax Avoidance

Tax avoidance—that is, planning a transaction to mitigate the tax impact or to avoid the application of taxes completely—is entirely legal and should be aggressively pursued. Judge Learned Hand stated it well:

> Over and over again courts have said there is nothing sinister in so arranging one's affairs as to keep taxes as low as possible. Everybody does so, rich or poor; and all do right, for nobody owes any public duty to pay more than the law demands: taxes are enforced extractions, not voluntary contributions. To demand more in the name of morals is mere cant.[2]

Club executives can and should conduct their club's business so as to achieve the lowest possible tax cost within the constraints of other business considerations and the prevailing tax laws and regulations. Good tax planning is simply good business management.

For example, the management of a tax-exempt club may choose not to provide services to nonmembers when the provision would possibly jeopardize the club's tax-exempt status. An example for a profit-oriented club is the acquisition of another club. An incorporated seller must decide whether to sell stock of the club or its assets. Assuming a gain on the transaction, the after-tax differences between these two alternatives can be dramatic. Even in a situation generating an overall loss, tax recognition of gain may be required on certain elements of the transaction if the decision was to sell assets rather than stock.

The point of all this is that, with proper tax planning, tax laws frequently allow both buyer and seller to realize most of their opposing goals. This fairly complex example also illustrates the need for most managers to consult tax experts in order to minimize their taxes. Recognizing these opportunities for tax planning and avoiding excessive or burdensome taxes is perfectly legal and represents a key management responsibility.

In contrast to avoidance, **tax evasion** is the fraudulent denial or concealment of a current or future tax liability, such as under-reporting income or claiming unsubstantiated or excessive deductions. A club that intentionally fails to report or under-reports revenues, interest, fees, or profits from business transactions is guilty of tax evasion. Similarly, tax evasion occurs when non-deductible expenses (such as personal expenses or costs related to personal use of business property) are intentionally deducted on tax returns as business expenses. Activities of this nature are illegal and untenable for the management of any club.

Federal Income Tax Exemption

Clubs have been exempt from federal income tax since 1916, although recent attempts have been made to limit this exclusion. The tax-exempt status of clubs is determined by laws passed by Congress, regulations and rulings of the Treasury Department and the Internal Revenue Service, and decisions handed down by various courts. Obviously, loss of federal income tax exemption is costly to a club; a manager must ensure that the club meets all legal requirements to maintain the exemption.

Financing of Clubhouse Renovations

The gathering place for many member activities is the clubhouse. Besides containing the food and beverage facilities, the clubhouse houses lockers, meeting rooms, and offices just to mention a few areas. The clubhouse is normally depreciated over a long period of time, but nonetheless it must periodically undergo major renovations. Just how have these renovations been financed? How much have dues been increased to cover renovation costs? What interest rates have clubs paid on loans for renovations? Answers to these questions and many others are provided by a recent study of 125 clubs conducted at Michigan State University.

Clubs of respondents differed in membership size from less than 250 members to over 2000. The largest respondent group (32 percent) was clubs with between 501–750 members. The median respondent's club also had between 501–750 members.

The age of the club's clubhouse that was recently renovated varied from less than five years (six percent) to over 50 years (34 percent). The mode response was over 50 years, while the median response was 36–50 years. As expected, the renovations were conducted in a majority of clubs with older facilities.

The cost of these recent clubhouse renovations varied from less than $250,000 (21 percent) to over $5,000,000 (11 percent). The mode response was less than $250,000, while the mean response was $500,000 to $1,000,000. The major methods of financing clubhouse facility renovations included dues (11 percent), capital assessments (30 percent), loans (23 percent), capital reserves (21 percent), and some combination of these methods (15 percent).

Thirty-one clubs responding to the survey indicated dues were used to finance clubhouse facility renovations. Twenty-five of the 31 clubs increased their dues to raise the required capital. Their dues increases varied from one percent to 25 percent with a median increase of five percent.

Just over 50 clubs raised cash for their clubhouse renovation by using capital assessments. The total raised ranged from $45,000 to $7,000,000 and the median amount raised was $450,000. On a per-member basis, the amounts varied from $20 to $20,500 and the median was $1,800.

Forty-seven clubs used debt financing to fund their clubhouse renovations. The loan amounts ranged from a low of $125,000 to a high of $6,000,000. The median loan amount was $1,381,500. The loans varied in length from two years to 30 years. The median length was 10 years while the mode (10 clubs) was 15 years. The annual interest rates on these loans ranged from 5.96 percent to 10.25 percent and the median was 7.97 percent. Thirty-eight club executives reported the percentage of the cost of the renovation financed with loans which ranged from 28 percent to 100 percent. Fourteen clubs used loans to finance 100 percent of the renovation costs.

Finally, 35 clubs used capital reserves to cover the cost of their clubhouse financing. The amounts ranged from $30,000 to $3,000,000 with a median response of $350,000.

IRS Guidelines

Internal Revenue Code section 501(c)(7) sets five general criteria for tax exemption; a club must meet all five:

1. The organization must be a club.

2. The club must be organized for pleasure, recreation, or other nonprofitable purposes.

3. Substantially all club activities must be for pleasurable, recreational, or nonprofitable purposes.

4. No part of the net earning of a club may inure to the benefit of any private shareholder.

5. At no time during the tax year can the charter, bylaws, or other governing instrument of the club contain a provision that discriminates against any person on the basis of race, color, or religion. (Note that sex discrimination is not prohibited.)

Club financial executives must understand the five guidelines to understand why certain questions appear on the IRS annual information return Form 990, why certain questions are on the club's application for exemption (Form 1024), and why an IRS examiner probes certain documents during an audit.

Must Be a Club. The Internal Revenue Service has said that, to be a club, an organization must have the following:

- membership of individuals

- personal contacts

- fellowship

- commingling of members

The requirement for individual membership derives from the requirement of personal contacts and fellowship between members. The IRS contends that although fellowship need not be present between each and every member of a club, it must constitute a material part of the organization's activities. Fellowship cannot play a material part where the club is composed of artificial entities. As a result, the IRS ruled that gross receipts from corporate members will be a factor in determining whether a club qualifies as a social club. It is advisable, as a general rule, not to allow corporations as members. Note that under this rule a federation of clubs will not qualify for exemption.

 The IRS has ruled that a social club does not jeopardize its exempt status by admitting corporation-sponsored individuals, if they have the same rights and privileges as regular individual members and are approved by the club's membership committee on the same basis as all other members. Caution should be used in accepting checks from members' employers. The IRS has treated as unrelated business income amounts paid to a social club by a corporation wholly-owned by members of the club for meals and other services provided to clients of the corporation. Clubs should attempt to obtain payment for large events directly from the individual member rather than his or her employer.

Personal contacts and fellowship must play a material part in the life of an organization for it to come within the meaning of the term "club." If an organization's only activity is to operate and maintain a television cable system providing services to members in their homes, the group does not qualify as a "club" because those services do not afford an opportunity for personal contacts and fellowship among the members. National or statewide organizations made up of individuals, but broken down into local groups, satisfy the requirements for fellowship if fellowship constitutes a material part of the activities of each group.

A commingling of members must also play a material part in the activities of the organization for it to be a "club." An automobile club with the principal activity of rendering automobile services to its members, but with no significant social activities, does not qualify for exemption as a social club. An organization that conducts regular bowling tournaments for its members could qualify for exemption if its overall program is designed to promote a commingling of members for their pleasure and recreation.

Examples of the requirements for commingling are found in two IRS rulings involving flying clubs. The first ruling involved a club that was open to everyone interested in flying. The members did not join to participate in flying for recreation but rather to obtain economical flying facilities, suitable for their individual business or personal use. No expectation that members would form personal relationships with other members existed. Little commingling among members for social or recreational purposes occurred. The IRS said the club did not qualify for social club exemption. Another flying club, however, did qualify for exemption. This group limited its members to those interested in flying as a hobby and members had to be approved by a two-thirds vote of the club members. The members of this club were in constant personal contact with each other at formal board and general membership meetings and at informal meetings to schedule the use of aircraft. There was a constant commingling to maintain and repair club-owned aircraft. In addition, the members flew together in the club's aircraft. The IRS ruled that this club met the commingling requirement.

Organized as a Club. To be exempt from federal income tax, a club must be organized for the purposes set forth in the statute. The purposes of an organization are generally listed in its articles of incorporation, corporate charter, or other instrument creating the group. Thus, the IRS requires that a club send a copy of such a document along with its application for federal tax exemption. Any changes in the instrument must be filed along with the organization's annual information tax return. Some court cases suggest that extrinsic evidence may be provided to show the real purpose of a club, but every effort should be made to properly set forth the purposes of a club in its organizing instruments.

Activities having a pleasure and recreation purpose are, in some instances, broader and more varied in concept than may be expected. For instance, a non-profit organization formed to bring family members into closer association through social activities revolving around matters of common historical and gene-alogical interest to the members as a group was ruled by the IRS to be exempt. The IRS said that promoting closer ties among family members and providing social commingling among them were similar to providing pleasure and recreation for the members of a social club and that the organization therefore qualified for exemption under section 501(c)(7).

If a club is organized for business purposes rather than for pleasure, recre-ation, or other nonprofit reasons, it is clear that the club is not exempt. Therefore, an investment club would not be considered a social club. The IRS looks at the facts and circumstances to see if profit making is a major purpose and to determine exemption.

Substantial Rule. Prior to 1976, statutes and regulations required exempt clubs to be organized and operated "exclusively" for pleasure, recreation, and other non-profitable purposes. Thus, a club could not run an untaxed, profitable business on the side to offset expenditures or help members avoid paying dues. Courts were reluctant to apply a literal meaning to "exclusively," and case law suggested that clubs could engage in some nonexempt activity and still retain their exemption. The proper mix was generally a matter of "facts and circumstances," which had to be individually decided by courts. Unfortunately, courts frequently used conflict-ing sets of standards. Clubs with incidental profits that were either negligible or nonrecurring were generally able to maintain their exempt status. The 1976 modifi-cations to the Code changed "exclusively" to "substantially," thus ending many of the interpretative problems. As a result, a club may now earn income from non-member sources to a limited extent and may have a limited amount of investment income without losing its exempt status.

In 1976, Congress concluded that a strict line of demarcation between the exempt and nonexempt activities of social clubs was no longer necessary. It then required a tax-exempt social club to be substantially devoted to pleasure, recre-ation, and other nonprofitable purposes, but liberalized the extent to which an exempt club could obtain income from nonmembers and investment income. With the 1976 Act, Congress intended to make clear that a tax-exempt club may receive some outside income without losing its exemption.

Whether substantially all of an organization's activities are related to its exempt purposes must be decided on the basis of all the facts and circumstances. However, the facts-and-circumstances approach applies only if the club earns more outside income than is permitted under the 1976 guidelines. If the outside income is less than the guidelines permit, the club's exempt status should not be challenged on this basis.

Under the 1976 guidelines, a tax-exempt club may receive up to 35 percent of its gross receipts, including investment income, from sources outside of its mem-bership. Within this 35 percent limit, no more than 15 percent of the gross receipts may come from use of a social club's facilities or services by the general public. If a social club permits nonmembers to use its club facilities and receives 15 percent of its gross receipts from these nonmember sources, the club then may receive no more than 20 percent of its gross receipts from investment income. If a club has outside income in excess of the 35 percent limit (or the 15 percent limit in the case of gross receipts derived from nonmember use of the club's facilities), all the facts and circumstances are taken into account to determine whether the club qualifies for exemption.

If a club loses its exempt status for that year, all of its income, even that received from its membership, is subject to tax for that year. In such a case, under the provisions of Section 277 of the IRC, the income received from the club's members, but only this income, could be offset by the cost of services and goods furnished the members. A member loss cannot be offset against the club's other sources of income.

Social clubs are required to carry on activities traditionally carried on by exempt clubs. Even the changes made in 1976 allowing additional unrelated business income do not permit clubs to actively conduct a nontraditional business.

The IRS has taken the position that the provision of personal services to members may constitute the active conduct of a business not traditionally carried on by exempt social clubs. A nontraditional business has been defined as any business which, if conducted on a membership basis, would not further the club's exempt purpose. In some cases, the IRS has proposed that receipt of any gross receipts from a nontraditional activity might require revocation of the club's exempt status retroactively.

The line between acceptable and unacceptable activities is a fine one. Providing hotel-type sleeping rooms on an occasional basis to members and the rental of mini-office space by half day or a day was permitted; however, when these activities become long-term arrangements, a questionable activity arises. The operation of a full-service barbershop was questionable. A parking garage used in connection with activities other than those at the club, the operation of a service station, a takeout food service, and the operation of flower and gift shop or retail liquor store were deemed nontraditional.

Clubs cannot lease to others and simply use intermediaries to conduct clearly nontraditional activities according to the IRS. A rental of space must be at arms length and be for a fair value.

The IRS has indicated that it will not challenge a club's tax exemption if the income from nontraditional activities is less than five percent. This five percent is included in the 15 percent limit and includes all income from nontraditional activities, even income from members. Unfortunately, this is an unofficial position of the IRS.

Inurement. Section 501(c)(7) says, "... no part of the earnings of which inures to the benefit of any private shareholder." The statute is generally interpreted to refer to members as well. Inurement—direct financial benefit to members—endangers a club's exempt status. The IRS has held that a social club with active members who pay substantially lower dues and initiation fees than do associate members does not qualify for exemption under section 501(c)(7) of the Code, even though both classes of members may enjoy the same club rights and privileges. The IRS ruled, in effect, that the active members are being subsidized by the associate members and that this subsidy constitutes inurement.

A provision in a club's charter that its assets will, upon dissolution, be paid to the members or shareholders is not, in itself, sufficient to cause a club to lose its tax-exempt status. Every club could, eventually, disband or dissolve; the potential distribution of club assets is not sufficient for the club to lose its tax-exempt status.

As another example, a club purchased an office building and used part of it as a clubhouse. The part not used as a clubhouse was leased to commercial tenants. The club's gross rental income from the tenants amounted to approximately 75 percent of the club's total gross income. The club used the rental income to defray operating expenses of the building and to expand its facilities. The IRS ruled that the club was not exempt; one reason was that net income from the lease inured to club members in the form of improved and expanded facilities.

A "horse-and-trailer" riding club sponsored a rodeo for the pleasure and recreation of its members and the community; it charged outsiders for the cost of the rodeo. The U.S. Tax Court held that the enhancement of the club's facilities and retirement of its debt from the receipt did not constitute inurement.

A social club that regularly opens its golf course to the general public in exchange for payment of established green fees also runs into the problem of inurement. Such income from the public is considered inurement to the benefit of the club's members because it is used to maintain and improve club facilities.

Another example of inurement is the payment of sick, disability, and death benefits by a club to its members or their families. The Tax Court has said that, when a club makes such payments, part of the club's net earnings inures to the benefit of members, thus jeopardizing the club's exempt status.

If the cost of a benefit is not significant, inurement may not be a factor. For instance, one court has said that sport coats, bearing the emblem of the club and worn only at club functions, for which the total cost was $1,365.50, did not constitute inurement. The same court also held that sending flowers to sick members was not a financial benefit to the ailing person.

Clubs sometimes have tournaments in which their members compete for prizes. Awarding cash prizes to tournament winners from tournament entry fees also does not raise the question of inurement.

An incidental sale of property will not deprive the club of its exemption even if a substantial gain realized on the sale of club property exceeds the 35 percent threshold. A relief provision permits a club that receives significant income such as from the sale of its clubhouse or similar facility to exclude the amount from the 35 percent calculation.

The IRS has ruled that even though a profit is realized, the sale will not cause a club to lose its exemption if the sale is incidental; it is not a departure from the club's exempt purpose. If profit is the primary motivation, the sale will not be considered incidental. All the facts and circumstances of a sale will be considered in determining the club's primary purpose in making the sale, including: (1) the purpose of the club in purchasing the property; (2) the use the club makes of the property; (3) the reasons for the sale; and (4) the method used for making the sale.

When a club sold 10 acres of land that was originally acquired only because the original sellers refused to sell less than the entire tract to the club initially, the IRS ruled the sale was incidental and would not adversely affect the tax exemption. The IRS did note that the tract, used as a practice range and turf-grass nursery, had not been improved since its acquisition. Furthermore, the club had not intended to improve the land to enhance its value or prepare it for sale. The club was also allowed to sell the property in small parcels since an appraiser stated it was doubtful the property could be sold as a single tract within a reasonable time period. The IRS reached a similar conclusion where a club had planned to use a parcel of land as the site of a new clubhouse. After learning that the cost of the new facility would be prohibitive, and the intended use was in violation of local zoning ordinances, the club decided to sell the unimproved parcel and use the proceeds to make improvements to its existing facilities.

In contrast, however, where a club subdivided the land into building lots, made improvements, and marketed the properties over a period of years at substantial profits, the IRS ruled that the sales were not incidental. The IRS concluded that the primary motivation for the subdivision and sales technique was to increase profits. Therefore, the club was not operated substantially for exempt purposes.

Although an incidental sale of club property will not be included in the 35 percent test when considering a club's exempt status, the gain is still taxable. Taxable unrelated business income includes gross income (excluding any exempt function income) less allowable deductions directly connected with the production of the gross income. Capital gains and losses are not excluded from the computation of unrelated business income unless they qualify for nonrecognition under special reinvestment provisions.

If property used directly in the club's exempt function is sold and other property is purchased and so used, gain will only be recognized to the extent that the sale price of the old property exceeds the cost of the new property. Tax is not imposed because the organization is merely reinvesting the funds formerly used for the benefit of its members in other types of assets to be used for the same period. The qualified reinvestment must be made during a four year period beginning one year before the date of sale and ending three years after.

When a club sold its facilities located on the front eight acres of a 16-acre tract and used the proceeds to construct new facilities on the back eight acres, no gain was recognized to the extent the proceeds were reinvested within the allotted three-year period.

Where a question exists whether the club used the property in its nonprofit activities, the IRS has ruled that even if the organization had made no use of the land, the sale would qualify for nonrecognition treatment. The club had shown that the property was purchased as part of a single transaction, the property was to be used in the performance of exempt functions, and no evidence existed that the property was purchased for investment purposes.

A club that sells property used for club purposes and distributes the net sales proceeds to its members in dissolution of the club must recognize gain. Since the club did not purchase replacement property, the gain does not qualify for this relief.

This nonrecognition provision only applies to the gain from a club's sale of property, not on income from an option on the sale of property. Any option premium is unrelated business taxable income to the club.

Discrimination. Until 1976, the tax law did not deal explicitly with the question of whether an income tax exemption for social clubs was incompatible with discrimination on account of race, color, or religion. In 1972, in *McGlotten v. Connolly,* the U.S. District Court of the District of Columbia held that discrimination on account of race was not prohibited under the U.S. Constitution in the case of a club merely because of the club's exemption from federal income tax under section 501(c)(7).

In 1976, Congress took the view that it is inappropriate for a social club to be exempt from income taxation if its written policy is to discriminate on account of race, color, or religion. Now, a club may lose its federal tax-exempt status for any tax year if, at any time during that year, the organization's charter, bylaws, or other governing instrument or any other written policy statement contains a provision that provides for discrimination against any person on the basis of race, color, or religion. Although compelling constitutional arguments can be raised against this 1976 provision because it makes tax exemptions contingent on the forfeiture by club members of their rights of association and privacy, this requirement has not been challenged in court and remains part of the federal tax law.

A club may still be selective on a basis other than race, color, or religion and maintain its exempt status under section 501(c)(7). For instance, a club may restrict its membership to the members of a particular political party or to homeowners in a particular housing development; such a restriction will not by itself cause a loss of exemption.

Exempt or Taxable?

Some exempt clubs may be considering a switch to a taxable status (Section 277) because of the many qualifications and limitations associated with maintaining their tax exemptions. Clubs should be aware of a whole set of limitations that apply when clubs relinquish their exempt status.

Any membership organization—and specifically a social club operated primarily to furnish goods or services to its members—must still maintain a separate accounting of member and nonmember activities. All deductions attributable to member activities are allowed only against member income; any excess member deductions must be carried forward to offset member income in succeeding years. Taxable clubs still are denied a dividends-received deduction and are subject to the profit-motive requirement to deduct expenses against nonmember and investment income. Only expenses incurred in the conduct of a trade or business or for the production of income are allowable.

A club that is otherwise entitled to exemption will not lose its exempt status because it raises revenues from its members other than by dues and assessments. The principal income of a club may be derived from a bar or restaurant that only members and guests are permitted to use; the club's exemption will not be affected.

The fact that a club derived a principal part of its revenues from its recreational facilities does not affect its exempt status as long as the facilities are used only by the members and their guests. For instance, revenue from gaming devices does not affect a club's exempt status, although the gaming devices may be illegal under local law and raise other legal questions.

Unrelated Business Income

As stated earlier, income not related to the purpose constituting the basis for the club's federal income tax exemption is unrelated business income (UBI). It is taxable at regular corporate business rates; payment of this tax bears no relationship to a club's income tax exemption.

The UBI of an exempt social club includes all gross income, less all allowable deductions directly connected to producing that income. Gross income, for this purpose, does not include exempt function income. **Exempt function income** is the club's gross income from dues, fees, charges, or similar amounts paid by members as consideration for providing goods, facilities, or services to the members, their dependents, or guests in the course of serving the exempt purposes of the club.

Thus, a country club's gross income for unrelated business taxes does not include gross income from members for their use of the club's golf course. It does include such income from nonmembers.

Passive income, such as interest and dividends set aside for religious, charitable, scientific, literary, or educational purposes or for the prevention of cruelty to children or animals, will generally not be subject to UBI tax. Income set aside for these purposes is also exempt function income.

If club facilities or personnel serve to produce both exempt and gross income, expenses, depreciation, and similar items must be reasonably allocated between the two uses.

The allocation of costs to reduce UBI presents complex problems for clubs. The IRS has in several, but not all, cases been unwilling to accept use of the simplest allocation method—the "gross to gross" approach. However, in a 1985 Circuit Court case, a "gross to gross" allocation formula based on the ratio of nonmember sales to total sales was used and the IRS conceded that these indirect expenses were reasonably allocated.

Nonmember Income

From a tax perspective, *nonmember* means persons other than members and their dependents or guests. A member's spouse and dependent children are treated as members of a social club. An individual who is a guest of a member and who does not reimburse the member for his or her expenses is a member for tax purposes. Persons who are invited guests and pay for their own activities are identified as nonmembers. This also includes members of a social club who are visiting another club under a reciprocal arrangement. These visiting members are effectively paying the club they are visiting and are considered to be nonmembers. The IRS adopted guidelines in 1971 describing circumstances under which nonmembers who use a social club's facilities are assumed to be guests of members. The guidelines describe the records required when nonmembers use a club's facilities and the circumstances under which a host-guest relationship is assumed for purposes of complying with the exemption requirements and for computing exempt function income.

The guidelines provide that when a group of eight or fewer individuals, at least one of whom is a member, uses club facilities, it is assumed for audit purposes that the nonmembers are the guests of the member. This rule applies only if the member or the member's employer pays the club directly for such use. If 75 percent or more of a group using club facilities are members, provided it is likewise assumed for audit purposes that the nonmembers in the group are guests of members, the same guidelines apply when one or more of the members or the member's employer pays the club directly for such use. Payment by a member's employer is assumed to be for a use that serves a direct business objective of the employee-member. In all other situations, a host-guest relationship is not assumed; it must be substantiated.

The club must maintain adequate records to substantiate that a group consisted of eight or fewer individuals, that at least one of them was a member, and that payment was received by the club directly from members or their employers. If a member pays a club directly, the club is under no obligation to inquire about reimbursement the member might later receive.

The club must likewise maintain adequate records to substantiate that 75 percent or more of the persons in the groups larger than eight were, in fact, members of the club at the time of such use and that payment was received by the club directly from members or their employers. When a member pays a club directly, the club is under no obligation to inquire about reimbursement.

With respect to all other occasions involving nonmember use, the club must maintain books and records of the payment received. The record, known as the **member function questionnaire**, must contain the following information:

1. Date

2. Total number in party

3. Number of nonmembers in the party

4. Total charges

5. Charges attributable to nonmembers

6. Charges paid by nonmembers

7. When a member pays all or part of the charges attributable to nonmembers, the member must sign a statement indicating whether he has been or will be reimbursed for such nonmember use and, if so, the amount of the reimbursement.

8. If the member's employer reimburses the member or directly pays the club for charges attributable to nonmembers, the member must sign a statement indicating: the name of the employer; the amount of payment attributable to nonmember use; the nonmember's name and business or other relationship to the member; and the business, personal, or social purpose of the member served by the nonmember use.

Exhibit 1   Sample Questionnaire for Group Party

MEMBER FUNCTION QUESTIONNAIRE

(Host Member's Name)   (Acct. No.)   (Date of Function)

Total Number in Group _____   Total Charges $_____

Number of Nonmembers in Group _____   Nonmember Charges $_____

The Following Questions Must be Answered by the Host Member

                                                                   Yes   No

1. I have been or will be reimbursed for nonmember charges, or others
   will pay club directly.

2. I will be reimbursed by nonmembers, other than my employer, or they
   will pay the club directly.

   a. If yes, indicate amount paid by nonmembers: $_____

   b. If you claim a *gratuitous* payment for your benefit, indicate Donor's

      Name _____and your relationship to Donor

      _____

3. I will be reimbursed by my employer, or he will pay the club directly.
   If yes, complete the following:

   a. Employer's name and address: _____

   b. Indicate the amount of the payment attributable to nonmember use: $_____

   c. If a large number of nonmembers is involved and they are readily identifiable as a par-
      ticular class of individuals, please indicate such class and business or other relationship
      to the member.

      Class of individuals: _____

      Relationship to member: _____

      (OR Use other side of this form to indicate each nonmember's name and business or
         other relationship to the member.)

   d. Indicate your business, personal, or social purpose served by this nonmember use.

      Member's position in company: _____

      Purpose served: _____

   Signature of member _____   Date _____

**Under the Tax Reform Act of 1969, the above information must be obained for all func-
tions of more than eight people.** (Prepared by Pannell Kerr Forster.)

9. When a nonmember pays the club or reimburses a member and claims that the
   amount was paid gratuitously for the benefit of a member, the member must
   sign a statement that indicates the donor's name and relationship to the member and contains information to substantiate the gratuitous nature of the payment or reimbursement.

Under the 1971 guidelines, failure to maintain records or make them available to
the IRS for examination precludes use of the audit assumptions set forth in the
guidelines. See Exhibit 1 for a sample form which may be used as a record of a
social function that may include nonmembers.

According to Mitchell Stump,[3] nonmember income will be generated in most areas of a club. From a club's pro shop to its lounge, there is a likelihood of receiving nonmember income. Most clubs generally recognize the obvious sources and do a good job of accounting for nonmember income. Some not-so-obvious sources of nonmember income are overlooked. Below is Stump's list of nonmember income sources. This is not meant to be a comprehensive list but a very useful list for each club financial executive of a 501(c)(7) tax exempt club to consider.

1. Pro shop sales to guests of members paid directly by the guest where the club owns the pro shop is considered to be nonmember income.

2. Catering food and beverage to members' residences or to their businesses is nonmember income. This also includes food gift packages, wine, holiday turkeys, ham, and baked goods.

3. Where the pro shop activities belong to golf and/or tennis professionals, a percentage of the rent income paid to the club for usage of club space is nonmember income. The percentage should be based on the ratio of sales to nonmembers and total sales.

4. All income from corporate members is nonmember income. This income should not be confused with income from corporate-*sponsored* individual members of a social club.

5. Nonmember income includes the sale of club assets not qualifying for income exclusion as a like kind exchange or where there is not a timely and proper investment of sales proceeds.

6. Reciprocal club income of all types must be classified as nonmember income.

7. Club Web pages and Web sites are providing sources of nonmember income. Stump's example is "clubs may be generating bartering income to be classified as nonmember income if Web pages are developed and maintained at no charge to the club in exchange for the Web page developer opportunity to create and keep advertising or referral income."

8. Sales of merchandise via Web sites should be classified as nonmember income depending on who makes the purchase and what the usage of the products is.

9. Selling Web page links is another source of nonmember income.

Tax Forms

Applications for Exempt Status. A social club seeking exemption must file an application on forms specifically prescribed by the Internal Revenue Service. Social clubs use Form 1024, Application for Recognition of Exemption Under Section 501(a) or for Determination Under Section 120. The application for tax-exempt status should be filed with the District Director of the IRS district in which the club is located.

Annual Information Return. Even though social clubs are exempt from federal income tax, they must file an annual information return, Form 990, Return of Organization Exempt from Income Tax. Clubs with gross receipts of less than $10,000 in each tax year do not have to file. The return is due on or before the 15th day of the fifth month after the end of the club's accounting period. If a club fails to file the form by the due date, or if it files an incomplete return, it can be required to pay $10 for each day after the due date until the return is filed (not exceeding $5,000), unless it can show reasonable cause for its failure to file. If the IRS demands that a delinquent return be filed, a similar $10 penalty for each day may be imposed on the person who fails to file the return for the club.

Tax on Unrelated Business Income. Clubs exempt from federal income taxation are subject to a tax on unrelated business income and must file Form 990-T, Exempt Organization Business Income Tax Return. Clubs with such income of $1,000 or more must file the return on or before the 15th day of the fifth month after the close of the club's tax year, the same as for Form 990, the annual information return. Exempt clubs are required to make quarterly payments of estimated tax on unrelated business income. Estimated tax payments must be made currently if a club reasonably expects its estimated tax for the year to equal $40 or more. Payments are to be made in the same manner as regular corporate estimated taxes, with underpayment penalties applicable.

State and Local Taxes

State and local taxes vary from state to state; only general highlights can be noted here. Club financial executives should check with their state and local taxing authorities to verify that their club complies with all applicable regulations.

In some instances, clubs may collect the tax and act as an agent of the state or local taxing authority to remit the fees. In other instances, the tax is imposed on the club and the club itself owes the tax.

Clubs should use extreme care when the law provides for them to act as an agent of the state or local government; under some statutes, failure to remit the tax amounts to embezzlement.

A club's exemption from federal income tax does not necessarily exempt that club from state or local taxes. Nor does the fact that the club is organized under state law as a nonprofit corporation automatically exempt it from taxation.

Some states have adopted the provisions of the federal income tax so that clubs exempt from federal income tax are also exempt from state income taxes. Such clubs exempt from state income taxation, however, may still be subject to tax on unrelated business income. Such states may also require clubs to file annual information returns.

Sales Taxes

Sales taxes are not applied uniformly from state to state, and local statutes, rules, and regulations must be consulted. The financial executive of a social club should determine, with the club's attorney or independent accountant, whether the club is required under state and local law to pay the tax and whether it is required to collect the tax. Most states require a club both to collect **sales taxes** on sales of tangible personal property and to pay sales taxes on its purchases. States frequently exempt charitable organizations, but a social club is not generally considered under most state laws to be a charitable organization, even though it may be organized as a nonprofit corporation.

Clubs will probably have to collect sales taxes on meals and beverages sold to members. Some states require sales taxes to be paid on service charges. Tax laws of some jurisdictions also require sales taxes to be collected on rentals, including the rental of rooms and equipment. Country clubs, for instance, may have to collect sales tax on the rental of golf carts, clubs, and other such equipment and also on rooms and other accommodations rented to members and their guests.

Some states require sales tax to be collected on dues paid to organizations. In addition, where dues are not really dues but rather a fee that entitles a member to attend events sponsored by the organization, states often require payment of the tax.

If a club makes its facilities available to the public, there is an even greater probability that state or local jurisdictions impose a tax on sales to the public.

Most states with sales taxes require clubs to pay the tax on purchases of tangible personal property for use in the club. Moreover, if property is purchased out of state, the club may be required to pay a "use" tax to the state which, typically, is at the same rate as the sales tax. However, if clubs buy items for resale, the clubs do not generally pay taxes on purchases. Clubs are required to collect the tax when the items subsequently are sold. Some jurisdictions require clubs buying for resale to provide exemption certificates to those from whom they purchase the resale items.

Club executives should determine whether the laws of their jurisdiction specify how the tax must be stated on bills to members. Some state laws require sales tax to be stated separately.

As with all taxes collected by a club, proper records must be maintained and the tax fully remitted when due. Some state laws provide that sales taxes collected by retailers are held in trust until remitted to the state; failure to properly remit taxes constitutes embezzlement.

State and local sales tax laws can be very complex. Clubs should periodically inventory their sales and purchases and confirm, with their legal counsel, whether they are subject to sales taxation. A club should not rely on individuals or companies from whom purchases are made to advise the club of its tax liability.

Federal Income Tax Rates

The corporation federal income tax rates for 2000 can be seen in Exhibit 2. The corporate rates, like personal federal income rates, are graduated rates—that is, the higher the taxable income, the higher the rate. For example, a club with taxable income of $150,000 will pay $22,250 plus $.39 of every dollar of taxable income over $100,000 to the federal government. For this club, the **marginal tax rate**—the tax rate applicable to the next dollar of income—is 39 percent. The **average tax rate** is determined by dividing the income tax expense by taxable income. For a club with $150,000 of taxable income, it is determined as follows:

Exhibit 2   Corporation Federal Income Tax Rates (2000)

Taxable Income						
Over		But Not Over	Pay		+ % on Excess	of the amount over –
0	–	50,000	$	0	15%	$ 0
50,000	–	75,000		7,500	25	50,000
75,000	–	100,000		13,750	34	75,000
100,000	–	335,000		22,250	39	100,000
335,000	–	10,000,000		113,900	34	335,000
10,000,000	–	15,000,000		3,400,000	35	10,000,000
15,000,000	–	18,333,333		5,150,000	38	15,000,000
18,333,333		....		6,415,667	35	18,333,333

$$\text{Average Tax Rate} = \frac{\text{Taxes on } \$150{,}000}{\text{Taxable Income}}$$

$$= \frac{\$22{,}250 + .39\,(\$50{,}000)}{\$150{,}000}$$

$$= \underline{\underline{27.83\%}}$$

As the taxable income beyond $150,000 increases for this club, the average tax rate increases as well. When taxable income reaches $18,333,333, both the average and marginal tax rates equal 35 percent.

For a club's financial manager concerned with federal income taxes, which rate should be used in decision making? Since virtually all decisions are mar-ginal—that is, they deal with issues affecting *additional* income—the marginal rate should be used.

Of interest to club financial executives are differences of taxable and tax-exempt clubs with regard to selected tax issues. Exhibit 3 lists a few major issues and the requirements of both Section 227 and Section 501(c)(7) clubs.

Retention of Business Records

Club financial executives need to understand what records must be kept and for what length of time. Condon O'Meara McGinty & Donnelly, LLP, a CPA firm spe-cializing in the club industry, has issued some recommended guidelines (see Exhibit 4). These guidelines have been developed based on the Uniform Commer-cial Code, the Internal Revenue Code, and the Employee Retirement Income Secu-rity Act. Other governmental agencies may have special requirements that club

Exhibit 3   Comparison of Taxable and Tax-Exempt Clubs Regarding Selected Tax Issues

Issue	Taxable (Section 227)	For Exempt (Section 501(c)(7))
Federal Tax Form	1120	990,990T
Net income from member activities	taxable	non taxable
Net income from nonmember activities	taxable	taxable
Net investment income	taxable	taxable
Amount of nonmember income	unlimited	limited to 15% of its qualified income
Reciprocal arrangements with other clubs	yes—classified as nonmember income	yes—classified as nonmember income
Allowability of payment of dividends to members	yes	no
Maximum amount of unrelated business income	none	limited to 35% of its qualified income

executives must consider. The schedule provided in Exhibit 4 should be considered only a guide.

Summary

Governmental rules and regulations affect nearly every aspect of the private club, including financial management, personnel supervision, and membership policies. Today's professional club managers and financial executives must be constantly aware of what can and cannot be done under the plethora of laws. Both club members and club employees look to the club executive for guidance. These executives in turn should fully utilize the advice and counsel of the club's attorney and accountant. Other sources of information and training on these matters are provided by the education programs and publications of the National Club Association and the Club Managers Association of America.

Endnotes

1. Letter to Jean Baptiste Le Roy, 13 Nov. 1789.

2. Commissioner v. Newman (CA-2), 47-1 USTV 99175, 159 Fed.(2d)848.

3. Mitchel Stump, "Identifying and Rewarding Nonmembers Income," *Club Management*, March-April 2000, pp. 44, 46, 48.

Exhibit 4   Recommended Guidelines for Retention of Business Records

Permanent Records

- Canceled checks for taxes, purchases of property, special contracts, etc. (checks should be filed with the papers pertaining to the underlying transaction).
- Capital stock (membership certificates) and bond records: ledger, transfer registers, stubs showing issues, record of interest coupons, options, etc.
- Cash books
- Chart of accounts
- Correspondence (legal and important matters)
- Deeds, mortgages, and bills of sale, as well as contracts and leases
- Financial statements—end of year (other months optional) including audit reports of Certified Public Accountants General ledgers
- Insurance records, current accident reports, claims policies
- Journals
- Minute books of directors and stockholders, including by-laws and charter
- Property records—including appraisals, costs, depreciation reserves, and end-of-year trial balances, depreciation schedules, blueprints and plans, and computational records related to the above areas
- Tax exemption determinations from federal, state, and local agencies
- Tax returns and worksheets, revenue agents' report and other documents relating to determination of income tax liability

Six to Seven Years

- Accident reports and claims (settled cases)
- Accounts payable/voucher register
- Accounts receivable ledgers and trial balances
- Bank statements, including bank reconciliations
- Canceled checks (see exception under Permanent Records)
- Cash receipts and disbursement records
- Contracts and leases (expired)
- Employee personnel records after termination (if a retirement plan was in effect, regardless if employee was a plan participant); if employee was a participant in a pension plan, consult your plan advisor.
- Expense analyses and expense distribution schedules
- Inventory records
- Invoices from vendors
- Notes receivable ledgers and trial balances
- Payroll records and summaries, including payments to pensioners
- Pension and/or welfare plan returns and reports (from filing date of such returns and reports)
- Pension and/or welfare plan accounting records
- Purchase orders (purchasing department copy)
- Scrap and salvage records--inventories, sales, etc.
- Employee time records
- Voucher register and trial balances
- Vouchers for payments to vendors, employees, etc. (includes allowances and reimbursement of employees, officers, etc., for travel and entertainment expenses)

Exhibit 4   *(continued)*

Three to Four Years

- Duplicate deposit tickets
- Employee personnel records after termination (see exception under Six to Seven Years)
- Employment applications
- General correspondence
- Expired insurance policies
- Internal audit reports, including working papers (in some situations, longer retention periods may be desirable)
- Members' house account transactions (charges and credits)
- Miscellaneous internal reports
- Petty cash vouchers
- Sales records and summaries

One Year or Less

- Chits
- Correspondence of unimportant nature with customers or vendors
- Receiving sheets
- Requisitions
- Stockroom withdrawal forms

Source: Condon O'Meara McGinty & Donnelly, LLP.

Key Terms

average tax rate—The average rate in a graduated tax rate system that is paid by the tax payer. It is determined by dividing income tax expense by taxable income.

exempt function income—The club's gross income from dues, fees, charges, or similar amounts paid by members as consideration for providing goods, facilities, or services to the members, their dependents, or guests in the course of serving the exempt purposes of the club.

marginal tax rate—The tax rate applicable to the next dollar of taxable income.

member function questionnaire—Form for capturing information from all functions of more than eight persons.

nonmember income—Club income from persons other than members, their dependents, and guests.

sales taxes—Taxes levied on the sales of a club. This tax is generally levied at the state level.

section 277 clubs—Clubs subject to federal income taxes.

section 501(c)(7) clubs—Clubs exempt from federal income taxes.

tax avoidance—Legally avoiding the payment of taxes.

tax evasion—The illegal and fraudulent denial or concealment of a current or future tax liability.

unrelated business income—Income not related to the stated purpose of the club and subject to federal income taxes.

Review Questions

1. What are the criteria for tax exemption for a social club?
2. What is unrelated business income?
3. What is nonmember income?
4. What is the difference between tax avoidance and tax evasion?
5. How is the average tax rate computed?
6. What is meant by marginal tax rate?
7. What is the purpose of a member function questionnaire?
8. What levels of government receive sales tax?
9. What are five examples of nonmember income?
10. What are some examples of business records that should be retained on a permanent basis?

Problems

Problem 1

Social clubs have many sources of income. You are requested to indicate whether the income is member or nonmember income of the Big Business Club (a tax-exempt social club) for each source listed below:

		Member	Nonmember
1.	XYZ Corporation paid its monthly dues to the Big Business Club.		
2.	Susan Smith, a member of the Big Business Club, purchased her dinner on Wednesday evening at the club.		
3.	Jerry Williams, a member of the Armington Country Club, playsgolf at the Big Business Club under a reciprocal arrangement. The Green Fees are $100.		
4.	M. Kase, president of the club, has the club send fruit baskets as holiday gifts to three associates.		

5.	Ray Smith pays his monthly dues for November.		
6.	General Works, Inc., pays the dues of Sharon Ride (chairperson of General Works, Inc.) for November.		
7.	The Big Business Club is paid $3,000 of dividends from its stock investments during November.		

Problem 2

The Capital Club, a section 277 social club, has taxable income of $500,000. Based on the graduated tax rate in Exhibit 2, determine the following:

1. Its federal taxes.

2. Its average tax rate.

3. Its marginal tax rate.

Index